ECONOMIC ANALYSIS
Theory and application

———————•·❮∞❯·•———————

C. E. Ferguson
Late Professor of Economics
Texas A&M University

S. Charles Maurice
Professor of Economics
Texas A&M University

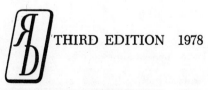

THIRD EDITION   1978

RICHARD D. IRWIN, INC.   Homewood, Illinois   60430
Irwin-Dorsey Limited   Georgetown, Ontario   L7G 4B3

ISBN 0-256-02027-2
Library of Congress Catalog Card No. 77–088289

Printed in the United States of America

1 2 3 4 5 6 7 8 9 0 A 5 4 3 2 1 0 9 8

LEARNING SYSTEMS COMPANY—
a division of Richard D. Irwin, Inc.—has developed a
PROGRAMMED LEARNING AID
to accompany texts in this subject area.
Copies can be purchased through your bookstore
or by writing PLAIDS,
1818 Ridge Road, Homewood, Illinois   60430.

ECONOMIC ANALYSIS
Theory and application

ECONOMIC ANALYSIS
Theory and application

C. E. Ferguson
Late Professor of Economics
Texas A&M University

S. Charles Maurice
Professor of Economics
Texas A&M University

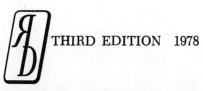

THIRD EDITION   1978

RICHARD D. IRWIN, INC.   Homewood, Illinois   60430
Irwin-Dorsey Limited   Georgetown, Ontario   L7G 4B3

ISBN 0-256-02027-2
Library of Congress Catalog Card No. 77–088289

Printed in the United States of America

1 2 3 4 5 6 7 8 9 0 A 5 4 3 2 1 0 9 8

Learning Systems Company—
a division of Richard D. Irwin, Inc.—has developed a
Programmed Learning Aid
to accompany texts in this subject area.
Copies can be purchased through your bookstore
or by writing PLAIDS,
1818 Ridge Road, Homewood, Illinois   60430.

To
Ann, Charles, and Mike

Preface

————◦⟨∞⟩◦————

The textbook is designed for undergraduate courses in basic micro-economics—the theory of value and distribution. This third edition has two major objectives. The primary purpose is to present the basic funda-mentals of price theory. The secondary, but quite important, purpose is to illustrate how the fundamentals of price theory can be applied to the solution of real-world, decision-making problems and to give students experience in solving these problems.

Many users of the first two editions of *Economic Analysis* have pointed out that students are becoming increasingly interested in applying the tools of microeconomic theory to business and personal decision making. Moreover, many teachers of microeconomics have noted an increasing number of noneconomics majors taking this course. Since this may be the last economics course these nonmajors will take, they are most interested in applying the theory. Also, economics majors and agricultural economics majors are becoming more "application oriented"—more interested in using microeconomic theory to solve problems.

Therefore, as the makeup and orientation of these classes have changed, the teachers have changed their preferences as to the type of text demanded. Or, perhaps the preferences changed some time ago, and I have just noted the fact. In any case, the changes in this edition are in response to what I feel has been a change in demand.

The fundamental theory sections—the presentation of the basic tools of economics—have been changed very little. Some of the more esoteric graphical proofs have been eliminated, as have some rather tedious discussions of several relatively obscure points of theoretical analysis. The introductory chapter has been replaced with an entirely new introduction, which is much more oriented to undergraduate students. Where possible, I have tried to make the theoretical material easier to understand.

Some new theoretical material has been added. For example, in the final chapter there is a discussion of property rights and externalities. A section on the production possibilities frontier is included in this edition, and the section on market failure has been expanded. An important addition is the incorporation of time and the cost of time into the basic economic theory. Several applications use the theory of the cost of time to analyze the problems of conservation and use of natural resources and to discuss some portions of the theory of capital investment. Many minor changes have been made to improve the readability of the book.

While *Economic Analysis* remains primarily a theory text, the fundamental changes are in the analysis of real-world problems and the application of the theory. The number of pages dealing with applications has been doubled. Furthermore, there has been an extensive change in the types of applications included. I have removed many of the illustrations taken from journal articles that were basically extensions of theory rather than applications and have added many more applications designed to apply theory already learned. In addition, I have eliminated several statistical estimations of cost curves, production functions, and elasticities, and have added applications and exercises that show students how to use the tools themselves. In most cases, I have tried to explain how to analyze contemporary, real-world or business-type problems.

To make it easier to separate the pure theory from the applications and exercises, these applications, exercises, and "asides" have been set apart in this new edition. An "application" generally shows how economists have solved or analyzed real-world decision-making problems. These include analyses of topics of current interest—conservation of resources, energy crises, pollution, shortages of medical care, and other such problems. Frequently an application will be an analysis of how an individual would use a portion of economic theory to solve a business or household problem—in short, how a knowledge of economic theory aids in decision making.

The "exercises" are designed to afford students the opportunity of using the theory they have learned to analyze current problems or make decisions. Generally, the "answers," if there are any, are given at the end of the exercise. Sometimes an "application" and an "exercise" are presented together. An "aside" may contain a geometric proof; it may extend the theory further; it may be a brief extension of an application or exercise; or it may present some relevant statistical results.

Finally, the number of problems at the end of each chapter is also more than doubled. These problems are separated into two sections: (1) technical problems, the solution of which is somewhat mechanical, and (2) analytical problems, which involve the application of theory to analyze problems in a "thought provoking" manner. The increased number of questions and analytical problems is in response to suggestions from many users of the earlier editions.

The text effectively lends itself to several teaching approaches. Chapter 2 is a review of supply and demand, subjects generally covered in principles courses. Some instructors may wish to omit this chapter, or cover only the applications. For some classes the interest may be only in theory and not in applications. Since all applications are set apart, they can be omitted without loss of continuity.

Some instructors may wish to cover production and cost theory as well as the theory of the firm before developing the theory of consumer behavior. Chapters 3 and 4, consumer theory, can be left until later, allowing the students to skip from Chapter 2 to Chapter 5, the theory of production. Nothing in Chapters 3 and 4 is necessary for understanding the material in these later chapters. Finally, individual instructors may wish to cover the material in the final chapter, particularly the material on market failure and property rights, immediately after the theory of perfect competition, Chapter 7.

I would like to thank several people who helped me with the revision of this text. My colleagues at Texas A&M, Wendy Gramm, Ray Battalio, John Kagel, Arthur DeVany, Sam Gillespie, Steve Pejovich, and especially Charles Smithson made valuable suggestions and provided me with a great many good questions and exercises. My graduate assistant, Phil Porter, was of great help in the final stages of preparation, as were Ann Rusleen, and Charles Maurice. Alan A. Fisher, at that time at the University of California at Berkeley, made available many questions several years ago. I used some of these in this edition. Robert P. Schultz of Wittenberg University and Harvey J. Reed of the University of Miami made useful suggestions concerning changes from the second edition.

I particularly wish to thank John Moore of the University of Virginia and J. Peter Mattila of Iowa State University for their extremely valuable help. If it were not for the fact that the term "invaluable" has no meaning in economics, I would say that the help I received from Rodney Mabry of Clemson University, during the early stages of revision, and Bruce T. Allen of Michigan State, during the latter stages, has been "invaluable." Thus, I must simply say that I appreciate their tremendous help very, very much. I also wish to thank Billie Ribbe for her secretarial and editorial efforts on the revision. Finally, I wish to express my great appreciation to Jim Sitlington for his great help and patience during this revision.

January 1978   S. CHARLES MAURICE

Contents

(APPLICATION: Analysis of ceiling price on crude petroleum.) Further effects of ceiling prices. Summary. (APPLICATION: Some extensions of the theory.)

Introduction: *Monopoly and profit maximization. Important points developed.* Demand and marginal revenue under monopoly. (EXERCISE: A computation.) Short-run equilibrium under monopoly: *Cost under monopoly. Short-run equilibrium. Numerical illustration.* (ASIDE: Some evidence concerning changes in monopoly power in the United States.) Long-run equilibrium under monopoly. (APPLICATION: Analysis of effects of disvestiture.) Cost of monopoly to society: *Comparison with perfect competition. Consumer surplus and the welfare loss from monopoly.* (APPLICATION: Welfare loss from monopoly in the United States.) (EXERCISE: Optimal antitrust activity.) Price discrimination under monopoly: *Price discrimination in theory.* (ASIDE: An algebraic proof.) (APPLICATION: Some examples and analyses of price discrimination.) Multi-plant monopoly. (APPLICATION: Use of the theory in decision making.) Monopoly regulation: *Price regulation. Taxation.* (APPLICATION: Taxation of natural resources.) Monopoly price cutting. (EXERCISES: The value of a monopoly and price cutting as a barrier to entry.) Summary. (APPLICATION: A study of the effect of environmental regulations.)

Introduction. Fundamentals of monopolistic competition: *Two demand curves. Short-run equilibrium. Long-run equilibrium.* (APPLICATION: Zero profit without price competition.) (EXERCISES: Application to the petroleum situation.) *Comparison of long-run equilibria.* Oligopoly. (ASIDE: Suppression of inventions and forcing of undesired "extras" by oligopolists.) (EXERCISE: Regulated oil prices and the effect on drilling.) Oligopoly and collusion: *Cartels and profit maximization. Cartel and market sharing.* (APPLICATION: Price competition and advertising in the legal profession.) *Short and turbulent life of cartels. Price leadership in oligopoly.* (APPLICATIONS: Some problems concerning cartels.) Competition in oligopoly markets: *Oligopoly and price rigidity.* (ASIDE: Some evidence about oligopolist price rigidity.) *Non-price competition.* (APPLICATION: An effect of the ban on broadcast advertising on cigarette consumption.) *Government and oligopolistic nonprice competition.* Summary. (APPLICATIONS: Some market incentives for oligopolists to reduce pollution and install safety devices.)

Introduction: *Fundamentals of the theory. Basic points developed.* Demand for a productive service: Perfect competition in input markets, one

1

Scope of economics

1.1 INTRODUCTION

You are beginning a course in economic theory and economic analysis. Some of you have had a beginning Principles course; for others, this is your first course. In the Principles course you were concerned with some economic theory, but you were also probably taught a great deal about economic institutions, such as how government operates, characteristics of businesses, and so forth.

In this course you will be concerned with learning the basics of economic theory—the fundamental tools used by economists—and with using the theory to analyze real economic problems. The theories you will learn in this course are relatively simple but very relevant and applicable to the solution of many important economic problems. Let us emphasize at the very beginning that simple as the theories may be, they are very similar to those theoretical methods used by highly paid professional economists in government, business, and universities to analyze important real-world problems. The mathematical and statistical techniques used by these economists are more advanced, but the fundamentals of the theoretical structure are frequently quite similar.

You will apply the theories you learn to analyzing such problems as the impact of OPEC (Organization of Petroleum Exporting Countries),

1

the reasons for shortages of natural gas, the effect of divestiture of integrated oil companies. These are the same types of questions now being analyzed by recent winners of Nobel Prizes in economics, such as Paul Samuelson and Milton Friedman. You will analyze problems quite similar to those that now concern economists who at this time are high-ranking government officials. You will be concerned with problems of decision making similar to those that are now being considered by top financial analysts employed by the nation's largest banks and industrial firms. Most important, the basic theories used by you and other students are the same as those used by these highly trained professional economists. The only difference lies in the level of sophistication of the tools.

This is a different situation from that encountered by undergraduate students in other fields. Students in undergraduate chemistry and physics courses do not work on the same types of problems being addressed by Nobel Prize winners in chemistry and physics. Beginning mathematics students are many years from using the techniques employed by their professors to solve problems. This, however, is not the case with beginning or intermediate economics students.

Let us reemphasize: *the basic theoretical tools, the fundamental methods of analysis, and the overall approaches to the solution of economic problems for the professional economist are those that you will learn and use in this course.* Economic theory is essentially a way of thinking about problems. The economic way of thinking does not change fundamentally as one acquires more sophisticated tools.

1.2 THE SCIENCE OF ECONOMICS

Thomas Carlyle, a Scottish historian of some repute, was fond of criticizing economists. It was he who referred to Malthus and Ricardo as "the respectable professors of the dismal science," thereby giving economics a name it has never quite overcome—possibly, as John Kenneth Galbraith has said, because it has never quite deserved to. In one sense economics remains a dismal science, in that economists all note that there is no such thing as a "free lunch," even though economists no longer make the dire predictions about the inevitable poverty of society that were being made at the time Carlyle coined his phrase.

The dismal nature of economics stems from the definition of economics. As most beginning texts avow, economics is a study of the method of allocating scarce physical and human means (resources) among unlimited wants or competing ends. In other words, economics is the study of scarcity, which results when people want more than can be produced. Since wants are unlimited for society and the resources used to produce things to satisfy the wants are finite or limited, all wants cannot be satisfied. Some things are, therefore, scarce. To satisfy some wants, the satisfaction of other wants must be sacrificed.

Those who know economics tend to be a somewhat cynical lot. They have a habit of asking what something will cost—cost in the sense of what will have to be sacrificed. People with some economic expertise tend to scoff a bit when politicians promise more schools, more police, more buildings, more of everything, at no additional cost to society. They frequently respond to the promise that society can have many more military goods along with more consumption goods with "nonsense." To have more of some goods society must give up other goods.

Thus economics has become fundamentally the science of decision making. Most basic theory, if not all, is designed to aid in making decisions and in understanding the consequences of economic decisions made by others. These economic decisions are necessary because of scarcity. Societies and individuals must make choices between desirable goals. All goals cannot be met.

How nice it would be if society and individuals could have more and more of the good things without having to give up anything. To the extent that economists continually point out the costs of these "good things," then economics still merits the title "dismal science" in some respects.

From another point of view, however, those who know some economics have a rather cheerful or optimistic outlook. Economists have recently begun to present arguments counter to the current fad of "doomsday" philosophies. Those who espouse the "doomsday" approach are fond of pointing out that some natural resource or group of natural resources will be totally depleted in a specific number of years, if society continues to use the resources at the current rate. Or they prophesy shortages of many resources in the future. That is, they say that in a few years society will need a certain amount of the resource, but this amount will not be available.

Economists are quick to point out flaws in such doomsday arguments. The major flaw, they say, is ignoring the functioning of the market. As society uses up some resource the amount of that resource decreases, causing the resource to become more and more scarce. This increasing scarcity, as we all know, drives up the price of the resource. The increased price causes consumers to economize on their consumption of the resource. The increased price also induces increased exploration for additional deposits. It causes deposits that were unprofitable to exploit under the lower prices to become profitable, thus adding to the amount available. Finally, the higher price brings about research and development in other areas in search of a substitute commodity. Much of our theoretical analysis in the text analyzes the fundamentals behind such processes.

In any case, those who understand the operation of economic markets argue that when something becomes scarcer the most benefit to society may well occur without immediate strict rationing or price controls; that market forces may to some extent alleviate the problem. This is certainly not to deny the functioning of government in the process. But, when a "crisis" occurs, economists often point out that the crisis is not without precedent; there are economic forces that may offer a solution.

1.3 USES OF ECONOMICS

Of course the major reason for studying economic theory is that it is useful. Very few students who take this course go on to become Ph.D.'s in economics. Everyone, however, must make economic decisions every day. We all will continue to face the problems of scarcities and, consequently, must continue to make choices.

All students will, therefore, find economics useful in their private and professional lives. Students who choose business as a career will find economics particularly useful (students who become doctors or lawyers or who enter other professions are in business also). A knowledge of economics is extremely important in business decision making if profit is a motivation. For example, one way economics is useful in business is in predicting what the effect will be of an external change that affects the business. What would be the effect of gasoline rationing? A change in the tax laws? Stricter antitrust laws? An increase in the minimum wage? Further, economics is useful in predicting whether or not to expand a business and whether to sell an asset or hold it in anticipation of a future price increase. Decisions concerning whether or not to stay open extra hours or produce additional output are basically economic decisions. The decision whether or not to change jobs is based on economics.

More and more, students are going to work in government—federal, state, or local. A knowledge of economics is of great use in many of these occupations. A frequent duty of people who work for all branches of government is to forecast the effect of some action to be taken by the branch of government for which they work. At the local level, for example, what will be the effect of a change in zoning regulations? Stricter pollution standards? Changes in tax rates? Increased urban renewal? At the state level decisions on allocation of funds between education and highways is of great importance. And, what would be the effect of a state minimum wage higher than the federal minimum? At the federal level economic decisions are made when considering the effect of changes in income tax and welfare laws. And, for another example, what would be the effect of stricter enforcement of laws concerning illegal drugs? Economic theory is probably the most important tool used by policy makers in making predictions. Throughout this text we will develop and apply many of the tools needed to analyze questions relevant to government policy makers.

Many students take positions in nonprofit institutions other than government—in hospitals, universities, and foundations. Since these institutions are greatly affected by economic forces, the decision makers must have a good deal of economic understanding. Because these institutions are not basically motivated by profit does not mean that they must not make decisions based on economic variables. Hospital planners must adapt to changes in the minimum wage, to extensions of government intervention in health insurance, and so on. University administrators must predict future enrollment, which is affected by such economic forces as the interest rate, inflation, and the business cycle. Foundations must anticipate changes in the tax laws. Certainly we could go on and on in this area.

Finally, a good understanding of economics is important in a person's private life also. Obviously, to be a well-informed citizen and voter one needs to know economics. But, a knowledge of economics is useful also in the private decision-making process. After all, we stressed that economics is the science of decision making; people make decisions in their private lives based on economic factors as well as in their business lives. The type of home appliance to install, as we shall see below, is in large part based upon economic variables, such as the interest rate. Economic factors, such as predicted employment opportunities for women, influence the decision of families to have children. This does not, of course, mean that other, non-economic variables do not affect such decisions, but economic forces play an important part. The decision concerning leaving a job and returning to school in order to train for a different job requires economic analysis, as does the decision to go on to graduate school.

We have barely skimmed the surface, mentioning only a few types of decisions for which economic reasoning is extremely useful in making the correct decision. We will bring up many more examples and actually analyze these problems throughout the entire text. As you increase your expertise in applying economics, in using the tools to make an analysis, you will have the satisfaction of actually solving the problems yourself. It is through practice that you increase your ability to solve problems.

1.4 PURPOSE OF THEORY

Since this course is basically concerned with economic theory, we might take time to explain how and why theory is used. No doubt you have heard statements such as, "That's OK in theory, but how about the real world?" The fact is that theory is designed to apply to the real world; it allows us to gain insights into the economy that would be impossible without a theoretical structure. We can make predictions from theory that hold in the real world even though the theoretical structure abstracts from most actual characteristics of the world.

To summarize, the purpose of theory is to make sense out of confusion. The real world is a very complicated place. There are an infinite number of variables that are in continual change. Theory is concerned with knowing which variables are important to the issue at hand and which are not. The theoretical structure allows us to concentrate on a few important forces and ignore the many, many variables that are not important. In other words, when using theory we abstract away from the irrelevant.

It is this ability to abstract—to cast aside all factors insignificant to the problem—that allows us to come to grips with the issue at hand without becoming bogged down in unimportant issues. This is not to say that economists do not use a considerable amount of statistical data; they certainly do. But the data required and the statistical method of approach are generally based upon sound economic theory. Let us consider some simple examples of the use of theoretical analysis, the types of situations that may be relevant to you in a few years.

APPLICATION

How to use economic theory: A preview

Suppose you are employed in the office of a U.S. congressman, whose committee is preparing to debate an increase in the federal excise tax on gasoline. You are told to do some research in order to determine what effect this increase in taxation will have. You have three days to prepare your report.

Clearly, going to every individual gasoline consumer personally or perhaps by mail survey is out of the question. Even a very large sample would not be particularly meaningful, because people who would be affected by the change in taxes would have the incentive to distort their answers somewhat. In any case what people say they will do and what they do often differ.

Therefore, you must ignore all nonessential features and concentrate only upon the important aspects of the problem. You would first point out that an increase in the excise tax is an increase in the cost of gasoline. Using standard economic theory based on past experience you would predict that the increase in the price of gasoline would cause people to consume less gasoline. You would ignore possibilities such as a huge oil discovery in Antarctica, or a dramatic cost-reducing discovery in refining technology. In short, you concentrate on the basics.

Thus the simple theory of demand (which we will explore in depth below) allows you to make a broad general prediction about the direction of the effect. That is, you can predict that gasoline consumption will probably fall after the increase in tax. But the theory alone will not allow you to estimate the magnitude of the impact. The theoretical structure will not describe accurately how any one individual will react. It is not meant to. It is designed to help you make general statements without worrying about how any one individual will react. The features used will be only the important ones.

After predicting the direction of the effect of the proposed changes, you would probably gather some statistical data about the effect of price changes on gasoline consumption in order to help in estimating the magnitude of the effect. But only with the use of the theory would you know what type of data to gather. We will consider the problem more fully in Chapter 2.

You might also be required to predict the effect of the gasoline tax on automobile sales, on the production mix of small cars and large cars, on the demand for mass transit in large cities, on the rate of unemployment. How would you go about providing the best infortion?

Let us take another example of the use of economic theory, this time in a business application. You know enough theory right now to handle this one. Suppose Florida is in the grip of a most severe cold spell. The severe freeze causes forecasts of vast losses in the orange crop.

You manage a large grocery store. What would you do about your

orders of frozen orange juice? Would you consider raising the price
of the orange juice you now have on hand?

You know that the price of oranges is going to increase no matter
what you do yourself, so you might as well benefit by the increase.
How do you know the price of oranges will rise? The supply of
oranges will be drastically reduced from the freeze. When the supply
of something falls, you can predict that the price will increase (other
things remaining relatively unchanged). You made your prediction
about orange prices based upon a theoretical concept about supply.
Certainly your prediction could prove invalid if something else
changed dramatically—perhaps some scientist discovers that orange
juice causes heart attacks. But in making predictions you are generally wise to ignore remote possibilties that might affect your forecast. For example, the price of canned orange juice also is affected
to some extent by the price of the metal used in making cans and
the wages of orange pickers. But the California and Texas orange
harvests may be above normal, and you may well be wise to analyze
and estimate these factors as they could be significant even when
compared with a dramatic reduction in the Florida orange crop.
Therefore, you probably answered the question the way a professional economist would. We could show many other examples, but
we will postpone them until you have the theory in hand to allow you
to solve the problems yourself.

The above example concerning the orange freeze and the price of
orange juice is an extremely simple, but quite illustrative, example of the
process of theoretical reasoning. We deduce conclusions using very
simple assumptions, while ignoring forces that *could* affect the consequences but in all likelihood will not. Not only economists but people in
business, government, and everyday life make predictions using similar
principles. With the use of economic theory we have a more formalized
structure or method of analysis for handling economic questions.

Using this formal but simple theoretical structure we can answer thou-
sands of questions such as those about the effect of the freeze in Florida
or the increase in gasoline taxes. These questions are important both to
individuals and to governments; and they can be given answers that are
approximately correct. In carrying out our analysis we must remember
that while everything depends on everything else, most things depend in
an essential way upon only a *few other things*. We usually ignore the

general interdependence of everything and concentrate only upon the *close interdependence* of a few variables. If pressed far enough, the price of beef depends not only on the prices of pork and other meats and fowls, but also on the prices of butane, color televisions, and airline tickets. But as a first approximation we ignore the prices of butane, TVs, and so on. We temporarily hold *other things constant*, and concentrate our attention on a few closely related variables.

In this text we adopt that basic approach. We assume that *most*, but not all, of the economic interrelations can be ignored. We analyze our problems and realize that our answers are first approximations. We carry out our analysis on the basis of real-world conditions, and then we go through purely logical analysis. Before we make any definite statements or predictions about the real world, we must go through the interpretation stage. Here it is necessary to realize that we have held many "other things" constant. Thus we must conclude that a freeze in Florida will *tend* to cause an increase in the price of oranges. If our theory is sound, the answers, even though first approximations, will be qualitatively correct. This is about all one can demand of economic theory. Quantitative results are up to the econometricians; that is, those interested in testing economic theories. This text consists mostly of the theory and applications, but the testing aspect will not be totally ignored.

1.5 STRUCTURE OF THE COURSE

We might briefly examine what types of material will and will not be covered in this text. Economic theory is generally divided into two major branches—macroeconomics and microeconomics. Microeconomics, the subject of this book, is concerned with organizing individual behavior, or the behavior of small groups of individuals. Some examples are analyses of the forces that determine the price and the amount of beef consumed by a group of customers, the reasons for a natural gas shortage, why the price of hand calculators has fallen as most other prices have been rising, and why price must increase for firms to be induced to supply more output. Macroeconomics, on the other hand, is concerned with aggregates over the economy as a whole; for example, the total level of unemployment in a society, the rate of inflation, the effect of changing the supply of money in a society, the forces affecting the level of interest rates, per capita rates of consumption, and so on.

By way of contrast, in microeconomics we study the forces that affect relative prices—why the price of oil rises relative to the price of coal, even though both are increasing. Macroeconomics courses analyze why the entire price level, the "cost of living," rises or falls. In this course we will study reasons why wage rates in a particular industry change relative to rates in other industries. This contrasts with the macro approach, which analyzes reasons for changes in the wage level for the whole economy. To summarize, we will be concerned with analyzing behavior of individuals and groups of individuals but not the behavior of aggregates in the economy as a whole, such as all households or all businesses.

Typically, a course in microeconomics is divided into three major sectors. This text follows that approach. The first area concerns the behavior of individual consumers and groups of consumers. Such behavior determines the demand for goods and services. The second major area covers the theories of firms and industries. Among these theories are the theories of production and cost. The behavior of firms and industries determines the supplies of goods and services. The third major area covers the theories of distribution. In this area we study the forces that affect the payment to the owners of resources—labor, capital, land, management. The owners of these resources receive wages, salaries, rents, profits, and interest from those firms that purchase the resources.

Sometimes economists simplify the economy by thinking of it as being divided into two sectors: (1) households, composed of individuals who purchase and consume commodities, produced by the other sector (2) firms. But the households must have income to purchase the goods and services produced and sold by the firms, which must in turn hire the resources owned by the households, if they are to produce the goods. Thus, we can think of the economy as consisting of resource owners who sell their resources to firms in order to attain income with which they buy their consumption goods. This is a rather simplistic view, of course, but one does get from such a view a beginning idea of how the economy functions.

The major thing limiting the amount of goods and services that such a society produces and consumes is the amount of resources in the society available to produce goods and services. Clearly, as either the technology improves or as the resources owned by the society increase, the society can have more of some goods without giving up some other goods. But during any one period of time the total supply of resources limits the total amount of goods possible; and if the society wishes more of certain things, it must give up some other things that are also desired. Thus, the society experiences scarcity, and scarcity is the subject of study for economists. We shall analyze this concept more completely in Chapter 6 with an analysis of this limit to the amount of goods and services a society can have at any one time, that is, with the production possibilities of the society as a whole.

1.6 SUMMARY

We emphasized at the beginning of this introductory chapter that economics is the science of decision making. These decisions arise because of this important concept of scarcity. If it were not for scarcity, there would be no problems of economic decision making. No decision about what to produce and what to consume would be necessary. Everyone could have everything desired. But because scarcity does exist, economic decisions are necessary; people make such decisions about production and consumption every day. The study of economics enables us to understand how and why individuals make these decisions. It allows us to predict the consequences of such decisions, and it helps us all in actually making better decisions.

We have thus far discussed only the scope and structure of economics. We have mentioned what economics is and what it can do. Now we will begin developing the basic theory and applying that theory to problems. We will show how economists have used theories as simple as those to be developed here to solve interesting, sophisticated, and highly relevant business and social problems. We will be dealing with problems as vast as the pollution question, the conservation of natural resources, and the consequences of an oil embargo. We will analyze less important—but still relevant—problems such as the effect of the ban on television advertising of cigarettes. We will also discuss how economics is used in business decision making; how it is applicable to the decisions of households. There will be many examples of both types.

We should stress that the purely theoretical sections make up a large part of the text and form a self-contained unit. Very little, if any, new theoretical material is introduced in the applications. Thus the applications can even be omitted—they are easily spotted because they are marked off—if one is interested only in theory. But the applications are designed to show how theory is used. They are primarily to give you practice in using the theory. After all, in economics, as in mathematics, riding a bike, playing baseball, dancing, speaking a foreign language, and so on, one learns how to do something by actually doing it. If practice doesn't make perfect, it will at least make you better. Finally, the applications are designed to give you some fun, as you become better and better at doing the analysis yourself. At the end of each chapter you will find some problems that will allow you plenty of practice.

2

Demand and supply

2.1 INTRODUCTION

In Chapter 1 we emphasized that economics is concerned with the problem of scarcity. Because goods are scarce, they have a price. Markets evolve to enable exchange to take place. In these markets goods sell for a price. Therefore, a fundamental task of economics is to analyze the factors that determine the price and purchases of commodities. The more important determinants of price and quantities sold are usually separated into two categories: those affecting the demand for a good and those affecting supply. The purpose of this chapter is to explain what demand and supply are and to show how they determine price and quantity in markets. We shall also show how the concepts of demand and supply can be used to solve problems.

Thomas Carlyle, mentioned in Chapter 1 as the man who gave economics the name "the Dismal Science," said about economists also, "It is easy to train an economist: teach a parrot to say Demand and Supply." This is another epigram that has survived because it is humorous and contains a certain amount of truth.

In fact, demand and supply are such important tools of analysis that we will devote several chapters to investigating the underlying forces behind these two concepts. In this chapter, however, we take many of the underlying forces as given in order to discuss rather generally what demand and supply are and more specifically how demand and supply determine prices in markets. We first examine demand, supply, and their determinants; then we put the two together to investigate how they determine price and quantity sold in markets. These simple concepts are used to analyze some rather complex real-world problems.

The basic concepts to be developed in Chapter 2 are:

1. The determinants of demand and demand elasticity.
2. The determinants of supply and supply elasticity.
3. How price and quantity are determined in the market.
4. The effect of floor and ceiling prices.
5. The effect of changes in supply and demand.

2.2 INDIVIDUAL AND MARKET DEMAND SCHEDULES

An individual's or a household's demand schedule for a specific commodity is the quantity of that commodity that either is willing and able to purchase at each price in a list of prices during a particular time period. For example, if someone (or a household) would buy during some time period, say a week, 6 units of a particular item at $6 each, 10 units at $5 each, and 15 units at $4 each, that would be the demand schedule for that commodity. Of course, we could extend the list of prices to $3 and $2 and determine how many units would be purchased at these prices also. That list is also a demand schedule.

As you would expect, consumers are willing and able to buy more at lower prices. This result follows from the *law of demand*. If you doubt the law of demand, try to think of a specific item you would buy in larger amount if its price were higher. A major reason for the law of demand is that consumers tend to substitute relatively cheaper goods when the price of other goods rises. Since a considerable portion of Chapters 3 and 4 are devoted to analyzing the law of demand and this "substitution effect," we now simply assume that the following is correct: people are willing and able to buy more at lower than at higher prices.

Principles. An individual's demand schedule is a list of prices and of the corresponding quantities that an individual is willing and able to buy in some time period. Consumers generally are willing and able to buy more of an item the lower its price; that is, quantity demanded per time period varies inversely with price.

2.2.a Aggregating and graphing demand schedules

Suppose a very large group of people gather together to buy their weekly supply of some commodity. Suppose also that an auctioneer in the market has everyone turn in a list indicating the amount of the good he is willing and able to purchase that day at each price, $1, $2, $3, $4, $5, $6, and so forth. When the auctioneer adds up the amounts that each person is willing and able to buy at each of the prices, the figures are those shown in Table 2.2.1. The table shows a list of prices and of quantities that consumers demand per period of time at each price in the list. This list of prices and quantities is called a *market demand schedule.* It is the *sum* of the demand schedules of all the individuals in the market. Again, since people are willing to buy more at lower prices than at higher prices, quantity demanded and price vary inversely in the market.

Principles. The market demand schedule is the sum of the quanties that all individual consumers in the market demand at each price. In the market, quantity demanded varies inversely with price.

Quite often it is more convenient to work with the graph of a demand schedule, called a *demand curve*, rather than with the schedule itself. Figure 2.2.1 is the graph of the schedule in Table 2.2.1. Each price-quantity combination ($6–2,000, $5–3,000, and so on) is plotted; then the six points are connected by the curve labeled *DD'*. This curve indicates the quantity of the good consumers are willing and able to buy per unit of time at *every* price from $6 to $1. Since consumers demand more at lower prices, the curve slopes downward.

Note that when deriving a demand curve from a set of price-quantity data given by a demand schedule, one assumes that price and quantity are infinitely divisible. Price can be *any* number between $6 and $1;

TABLE 2.2.1

MARKET DEMAND SCHEDULE

Quantity demanded	Price per unit (dollars)
2,000............................	6
3,000............................	5
4,000............................	4
5,000............................	3
5,500............................	2
6,000............................	1

FIGURE 2.2.1

MARKET DEMAND CURVE

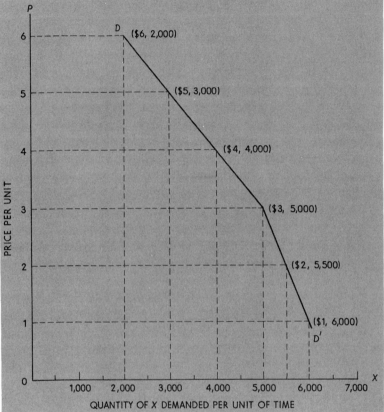

quantity demanded can also be any number. This assumption is not too unrealistic when we consider that the quantity is *per unit of time*. In any case the sacrifice in realism is more than counterbalanced by the gain in analytical convenience.

We must emphasize that when drawing market demand curves, we draw them sloping downward to conform with the law of demand. Since individuals are assumed to demand less as price increases, less is demanded in the entire market as price rises. Furthermore, as price increases, some individual may purchase nothing at all, again causing the quantity demanded to decrease.

good is going to rise, they have an incentive to increase their
urchase before the price rises. On the other hand, expecting
ll causes some purchases to be postponed.

ore, when economists draw up a demand curve such as the
igure 2.2.1, they do so under the assumption that *other things
he same.* The other things are (1) consumers' incomes (and
me distribution among consumers), (2) tastes, (3) the prices
goods, and (4) expectations. It is not that economists think price
ole determinant of the quantity that people purchase, but they
rested in *isolating* the effect of price changes.

Changes in demand

en price falls (rises) and consumers purchase more (less) of a
other things remaining the same, we say that *quantity demanded*
ses (decreases). We do not say that demand increases or decreases
price changes. Recall that demand is a *list* of prices and quantity
nded at each price on the list.

emand increases or decreases only if one or more of the factors held
tant when deriving demand changes. For example, if incomes of
sumers change, causing them to demand more of a good at each

FIGURE 2.2.2

SHIFTS IN DEMAND

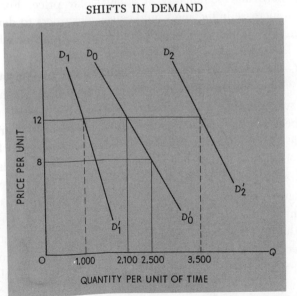

2.2.b Factors influencing demand

Some people who are not particularly \
ing accuse economists of saying that pric
the purchases of consumers. They say tha
the many other influences, style, taste, an
consumers. This accusation is not really va
that there are many forces other than pric
demanded.

But recall from Chapter 1 that a fundamer
in economics is to hold all other influences co
on one important variable. Economists do no
fluence upon purchases; they do say that price
portant effect upon quantity purchased. Therel
the effect of price, economists hold constant th
concentrate upon the relation between quantity
relation shown by demand curves. In this way at
strictly upon the effect of price. But, when usin
should be aware of the other things that influenc
but are held constant when deriving demand.

First, a consumer's income affects the amount den
For some consumers an increase in income would cau
more of a particular commodity at a particular pric
modities an increase in income would cause consumers
some given price. Thus we generally hold income const
demand.

Second, the prices of *other* goods must be held c
they affect how much of a good is purchased at a g
example, suppose both beef and pork sell for $1 a poun
price of beef fall to $.50 per pound. Consumers would
less pork at $1 a pound when beef is $.50 than when beef

Third, changes in consumers' tastes can affect how much
of a good at a given price. If some influential movie or tel
are photographed wearing a certain style of clothing, cons
wish to imitate would probably be willing to buy more of t
the prevailing price. Since changes in tastes affect the deman
modities, economists hold tastes constant when deriving demand

Finally, people's expectations affect demand. When people

price of a
rates of I
price to f
There
one in F
remain
the inc
of other
is the
are inte

2.2.c

Wl
good,
incre
wher
dem

D
cons
con

price than they did previously, the demand for that good increases. If the change in income causes consumers to demand less of a good than before at each price, then demand decreases.

Figure 2.2.2 illustrates changes in demand. Assume that the demand curve for a good is at first $D_0 D'_0$; at a price of $12 per unit, consumers purchase 2,100 units per period of time. If price falls to $8 *quantity demanded* increases to 2,500 units. Now begin with demand at $D_0 D'_0$ and a price of $12. Assume that tastes change and demand decreases (shifts to the left) to $D_1 D'_1$. Now consumers demand only 1,000 units per period of time at the price $12. In fact, it is easy to see that at every price consumers are willing and able to buy less of the good after the shift than before. This shows a *decrease in demand.* Now let something, previously held constant, change, causing demand to increase (shift to the right) to $D_2 D'_2$. At $12 consumers now purchase 3500 units per period; and at every other relevant price they buy more than before. This shows an *increase in demand.* But, to repeat, if demand is $D_0 D'_0$ and price falls from $12 to $8, other things remaining the same, we say that *quantity demanded* changes from 2,100 to 2,500. These relations may be summarized as follows:

Relation. When price falls (rises), other things remaining the same, quantity demanded rises (falls). When something held constant in deriving the demand curve changes, demand increases or decreases. An increase in demand indicates consumers are willing and able to buy more at each price in the list. A decrease in demand indicates they are willing and able to buy less at each price. Changes in demand are represented by shifts in the demand curve; changes in quantity demanded are shown by movements along the original demand curve. Do not confuse changes in quantity demanded with increases or decreases in demand.

APPLICATIONS

Changes in demand and changes in quantity demanded

It is often crucial for decision makers in government or business to know the difference between changes in quantity demanded because of price changes, and changes in demand because something held constant changes. The distinction between the two is important because of the different effects of each.

At this time there is a considerable amount of pressure in the

United States for the federal government to subsidize all medical care or at least to cover a large portion of such care. Other countries have already gone to such subsidies. Many proponents of such plans seem to argue that the only effect would be that people would go on consuming the same amount of medical care as before but the government would pay the medical bill, or at least a large part of the bill. If you were an aide to a U.S. representative what advice would you give to the congressman?

In the first place the government subsidy represents a decrease in the price of medical care. (We ignore the increase in taxes to pay for the subsidy.) One would certainly assume that the demand for medical care is down-sloping (statistical studies have shown that this is in fact the case). At lower prices people would seek medical attention for problems that they would possibly treat at home if prices were higher. Thus a distinct decrease in price would create a significant burden on already overloaded medical facilities and personnel. This would create the serious problem of increasing medical care in response to the increase in quantity demanded.

Suppose you are asked to predict the effect on the demand for medical care as the per capita income of the economy rises—that is, society grows wealthier. You are correct if you responded that this would probably lead to an increase in demand. As people grow wealthier they would demand more medical care at all prices. As we shall show below, and as you would probably expect now, this increase in demand will have the effect of increasing the price of medical care.

What effect on the demand for medical care do you think would result from an increase in the average age of a society? What would happen to the demand for medical doctors if government allowed less well-trained paramedics to treat reasonably minor injuries and illnesses?

2.3 DEMAND ELASTICITY

We have emphasized, without a full explanation, that quantity demanded falls when price rises and vise versa. Economists, and those who use economics in decision making, are frequently interested in the effect that changes in price and quantity have on total expenditure, which is simply price times quantity demanded. Note, however, that the changes in price and quantity tend to have offsetting effects. For example, an increase in price alone would tend to increase expenditure, whereas the resulting decrease in quantity would tend to decrease expenditure. Thus we would assume that the effect on total expenditure depends upon which force dominates, the increase in price or the decrease in quantity demanded.

You have probably guessed that if the percentage increase in price exceeds the percentage decrease in quantity demanded, total expenditure rises; but, total expenditure falls if the percentage increase in price is less than the percentage decrease in quantity. Similarly, if the percentage decrease in price exceeds (is less than) the percentage increase in quantity demanded, total expenditure falls (rises). We see then that the effect of a price change depends upon the relative responsiveness of quantity demanded to price along a demand curve. The measure of this relative responsiveness along a given demand curve is called the *elasticity of demand*. This is a concept of great interest to both economists and business decision makers. Obviously, in business one would like to know the effect of a change in price on sales and what determines such an effect.

2.3.a Responsiveness of quantity demanded to price

For some products, a small change in price over a certain range of the demand curve results in a significant change in quantity demanded. In this case, quantity demanded is very responsive to changes in price. For other products, or perhaps for the same product over a different range of the demand curve, a relatively large change in price leads to a correspondingly smaller change in quantity demanded. That is, quantity demanded is not particularly responsive to price changes. As we noted above, the change in total expenditure, or what is sometimes called total revenue, depends upon how responsive quantity demanded is to changes in price.

Economists have a precise way of classifying demand according to the responsiveness of quantity demanded to price and the effect of changes in price on total expenditure. Economists classify demand as elastic or inelastic according to the degree of responsiveness. More specifically, demand is said to be elastic if a proportional change in quantity demanded exceeds the proportional change in price, whereas it is inelastic if the proportional change in quantity demanded is less than the proportional change in price.

Thus we can relate changes in total revenue or total expenditure to changes in price through the concepts of demand elasticity or inelasticity.

TABLE 2.3.1

RELATIONS BETWEEN DEMAND ELASTICITY
AND TOTAL EXPENDITURE (TE)

	Elastic demand $|\%\Delta P| < |\%\Delta Q|$	Unitary elasticity $|\%\Delta P| = |\%\Delta Q|$	Inelastic demand $|\%\Delta P| > |\%\Delta Q|$
Price rises........	TE falls	No change in TE	TE rises
Price falls........	TE rises	No change in TE	TE falls

First suppose the price change "outweighs" the quantity change in terms of percent, that is, quantity demanded is not particularly responsive to price and hence demand is said to be inelastic. In this case when price rises and quantity falls, total expenditure increases. If price decreases and quantity demanded increases under the inelastic demand, total expenditure falls. On the other hand if demand is elastic, the percentage change in quantity demanded exceeds the percentage change in price. In this case, when price rises and quantity falls, total revenue falls because of the greater quantity effect. Clearly a price decrease leads to an increase in quantity demanded, and with an elastic demand total revenue rises.

Finally, we classify a demand as having unitary elasticity when the percentage change in price is exactly offset by the percentage change in quantity demanded. In this case a change in price results in no change in total expenditure. All of these relations are summarized in Table 2.3.1. In the table the terms $|\%\Delta P|$ and $|\%\Delta Q|$ are the absolute values of the pertage changes in price and quantity. Algebraically they will always be of opposite sign.

We should now emphasize that it is not accurate to say that a given demand curve is elastic or inelastic. In many cases, demand curves have both an inelastic and an elastic range, along with a point or range of unitary elasticity. We can only speak of demand as being elastic or inelastic over a particular range of price or quantity magnitudes.

2.3.b Computation of elasticity

We have thus far talked of elasticity and inelasticity only in very general terms. It is useful at times to have a specific measure of relative responsiveness rather than merely speaking of demand as being elastic or inelastic. For example, we might wish to determine, over a certain range of prices, which of two demand curves is more elastic. For this we need a measuring device. That device is the coefficient of price elasticity (E):

$$E = -\%\triangle Q/\%\triangle P = -\frac{\triangle Q/Q}{\triangle P/P} = -\frac{\triangle Q}{\triangle P} \cdot \frac{P}{Q},$$

where $\triangle$ is "the change in," and P and Q denote price and quantity demanded.

Since price and quantity vary inversely, a minus sign is used in the formula to make the coefficient positive. From the formula we see that the relative responsiveness of quantity demanded to changes in price measures the ratio of the proportional change in quantity demanded relative to that of price. If E is less than one, demand is inelastic, $|\%\triangle Q| < |\%\triangle P|$. If E is greater than one, demand is elastic, $|\%\triangle Q| > |\%\triangle P|$. If $E = 1$, demand has unitary elasticity, $|\%\triangle Q| = |\%\triangle P|$.

TABLE 2.3.2

DEMAND AND ELASTICITY

Price	Quantity demanded	Total expenditure	Elasticity
$1.00	100,000	$100,000	ELASTIC
.50	300,000	150,000	UNITARY
.25	600,000	150,000	INELASTIC
.10	1,000,000	100,000	

The process of deriving the coefficient of elasticity between two price-quantity relations involves a simple computation; certain problems, however, are involved in selecting the proper base. As an example, let us consider the demand schedule given in Table 2.3.2. Suppose price falls from $1 to $0.50; quantity demanded rises from 100,000 to 300,000 and $P \times Q$ or TE rises to $150,000. By the analysis of subsection 2.3.a, demand is elastic since total expenditure increases.

Let us now compute E:

$$E = -\frac{\triangle Q/Q}{\triangle P/P} = -\frac{(100,000 - 300,000) \div 100,000}{(\$1 - \$0.50) \div \$1} = -\frac{-2}{1/2} = 4.$$

As expected, the coefficient is greater than one. But some caution must be exercised. $\triangle Q$ and $\triangle P$ are definitely known from Table 2.3.2; but we really do not know whether to use the value $Q = 100,000$ or $Q = 300,000$ and the value $P = \$1$ or $P = \$0.50$. Try the computation with the "other" values of P and Q:

$$E = -\frac{(300{,}000 - 100{,}000) \div 300{,}000}{(\$0.50 - \$1) \div \$0.50} = \frac{2}{3}.$$

It actually looks as though demand is inelastic, despite the fact that we know it is elastic from the total expenditure calculation.

The difficulty lies in the fact that elasticity has been computed over a wide arc of the demand curve but evaluated at a specific point. We can get a much better approximation by using the *average* values of P and Q over the arc. That is, for large changes such as this, we should compute E as

$$E = -\frac{Q_1 - Q_0}{Q_1 + Q_0} \div \frac{P_1 - P_0}{P_1 + P_0},$$

where subscripts 0 and 1 refer to the initial and the new prices and quantities demanded. Using this formula, we obtain

$$E = -\frac{(100{,}000 - 300{,}000) \div (100{,}000 + 300{,}000)}{(\$1 - \$0.50) \div (\$1 + \$0.50)} = \frac{3}{2}.$$

Demand is indeed elastic when allowance is made for the very discrete or finite change in price and quantity demanded.

Exercise. Compute E for a change in price from \$0.25 to \$0.10 and from \$0.50 to \$0.25. Use the averaging method.

Summary. Demand is said to be elastic, of unitary elasticity, or inelastic according to the value of E. If $E > 1$, demand is elastic; a given percentage change in price results in a greater percentage change in quantity demanded. Thus small price changes result in more significant changes in quantity demanded. When $E = 1$ demand has unit elasticity, meaning that the percentage changes in price and quantity demanded are precisely the same. Finally, if $E < 1$, demand is inelastic. A given percentage change in price results in a smaller percentage change in quantity demanded.

2.3.c Graphical computation of elasticity

The formulas developed in Section 2.3.b are relevant for arc elasticity, the price elasticity for movements between two discrete points on a demand curve. At times, however, we are interested in elasticity at a specific point or the elasticity for very small changes in price and quantity. Understanding the method of graphical computation of point elasticity permits one to estimate price elasticity by a visual inspection of the demand curve. We first present the results without proof.

FIGURE 2.3.1

ESTIMATION OF POINT ELASTICITY

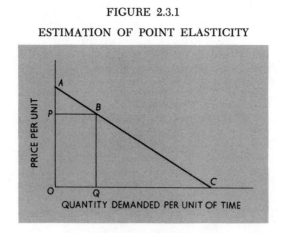

First consider the case of a linear demand such as that shown in Figure 2.3.1. The point elasticity of demand at any price and quantity, such as OP and OQ at point B, can be computed as the ratio of $\dfrac{BC}{AB}$. This ratio is equal to the ratios $\dfrac{QC}{OQ}$ and $\dfrac{OP}{AP}$. These ratios are estimates of the elasticity at a point for very small changes in price and quantity.

Thus we can locate a point on DD', the linear demand curve in Figure 2.3.2, such that $DP = PD'$; at this point, demand has unitary price elasticity, or $E = 1$. Next consider *any* point to the left of P, such as P_1. At P_1, $E = (P_1D'/DP_1) > 1$. Thus for a linear demand curve the coefficient of price elasticity is greater than unity at any point to the left of the midpoint on the demand curve. Demand is elastic in this region. Finally, at any point to the right of P, say P_2, the coefficient of price elasticity is $E = (P_2D'/DP_2) < 1$. Over this range, demand is inelastic.

When demand is not linear, such as DD' in Figure 2.3.3, one can easily approximate point elasticity in the following manner. Suppose we want to compute the elasticity of DD' at point R. First draw the straight line AB tangent to DD' at R. Note that if AB were actually the demand curve, RB/AR would be its elasticity at point R. Note also that for very small movements away from R along DD', the slope of AB is a relatively good estimate of the slope of DD'. Now the elasticity formula may also be written as

$$E = \frac{-1}{\Delta P/\Delta Q} \cdot \frac{P}{Q}.$$

FIGURE 2.3.2

RANGES OF DEMAND ELASTICITY
FOR LINEAR DEMAND CURVE

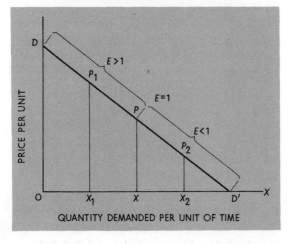

FIGURE 2.3.3

COMPUTATION OF POINT ELASTICITY
FOR NONLINEAR DEMAND CURVE

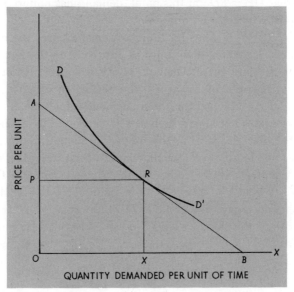

Since the slopes of DD' and AB (which are tangent at R) are approximately equal in the neighborhood of R, $\triangle P/\triangle Q$ is the same for each curve. Therefore, the elasticity of AB at R is approximately equal to the elasticity of DD' at R. The point elasticity of DD' at R is approximately RB/AR.

These results may be summarized as follows:

Relation. Given any point R on a demand curve, construct the straight line from the vertical to the horizontal axis tangent to the curve at R. Call this line ARB. The coefficient of price elasticity is approximately RB/AR. If the demand curve is linear this measure is precise. Furthermore, for a linear demand curve: (a) demand is elastic at higher prices, (b) has unit elasticity at the midpoint of the demand curve, and (c) is inelastic at lower prices. Thus, in case of linear demand, elasticity declines as one moves downward along the curve.

ASIDE

Statistical estimation

We do not stress the concept of point elasticity purely for the logical beauty of the geometry. Point elasticity is not all geometry. Business and economic decision makers are frequently interested in the coefficient of elasticity for very small movements along a demand for a product. Furthermore, demand functions are frequently represented by (or are assumed to be closely related to) the equation

$$Q_D = AP^b,$$

where Q_D and P are obviously quantity demanded and price, while A and b are parameters to be estimated. It turns out that this demand has constant elasticity and the coefficient of elasticity is precisely the parameter b. Thus over a short range the term b gives some notion of elasticity. Statisticians can be easily (though expensively) employed to estimate elasticity.

For those of you who understand the concept of natural logarithms and a little elementary statistics the computational process is very simple. Those of you who do not or are not interested can skip the remainder of this application with zero loss of economic understanding. We only wish to show that the concept of point elasticity is an actual analytical tool and not just a geometrical exercise.

One can estimate the coefficient of elasticity in the following way. Use logarithms to write the demand equation as

$$\log_e Q_D = \log_e A + b \log_e P.$$

This is now a linear equation in logs. One can use simple regression techniques (generally learned in the introductory statistics class) to estimate the coefficient b, which is the elasticity. As will be shown below, economists and statisticians generally include a few addiditional variables.

Economists sometimes use geometry to prove theorems such as those formulas used above for estimating elasticity from a graph. We present such a proof here only for those interested in such things. Those interested only in economics and its applications, and not geometry, may omit the following proof with absolutely no loss of economic understanding.

ASIDE

A geometric proof

In Figure 2.3.4 the line *CF* is a linear demand curve for commodity *X*. The problem is to measure price elasticity at point *R*,

FIGURE 2.3.4

COMPUTATION OF POINT ELASTICITY

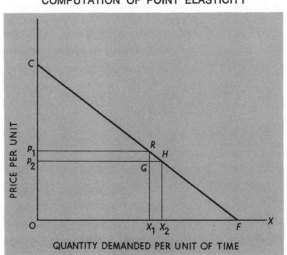

where price is Op_1 and quantity demanded is Ox_1. First let price fall very, very slightly from Op_1 to Op_2, so quantity demanded increases from Ox_1 to Ox_2; that is, p_2 and x_2 are very near p_1 and x_1.

Next, consider the formula for point elasticity:

$$E = - \Delta Q/Q \div \Delta P/P.$$

From the figure, $\Delta Q = x_1 x_2$ and $Q = Ox_1$ at R. Similarly $\Delta P = p_1 p_2$ and $P = Op_1$ at R. Thus,

$$E = - \frac{x_1 x_2 / Ox_1}{p_1 p_2 / Op_1} = \frac{x_1 x_2}{p_1 p_2} \cdot \frac{Op_1}{Ox_1}.$$

Since $x_1 x_2 = GH$ and $p_1 p_2 = RG$,

$$\frac{x_1 x_2}{p_1 p_2} = \frac{GH}{RG}.$$

Furthermore RGH and $Rx_1 F$ are similar right triangles inasmuch as each corresponding angle is equal. Thus

$$\frac{GH}{RG} = \frac{x_1 F}{Rx_1} = \frac{x_1 F}{Op_1},$$

since $Rx_1 = Op_1$. Hence

$$E = \frac{GH}{RG} \cdot \frac{Op_1}{Ox_1} = \frac{x_1 F}{Op_1} \cdot \frac{Op_1}{Ox_1} = \frac{x_1 F}{Ox_1}.$$

But $x_1 F/Ox_1 = Op_1/p_1 C = RF/RC$. Thus graphically the coefficient of price elasticity at the point R is

$$E = \frac{RF}{RC}$$

Utilizing this formula, it is easy to determine the ranges of demand elasticity for a linear demand curve. First note the following relations in Figure 2.3.4. When $RF = RC$, $RF/RC = 1$; hence, at that point the demand curve has unit elasticity. Second, when $RF > RC$, $RF/RC > 1$ and demand is elastic. Finally, when $RF < RC$, $RF/RC < 1$ and demand is inelastic.

2.3.d Factors affecting demand elasticity

Whether demand is elastic or inelastic is an important consideration especially for government policy in individual commodity markets. For example, suppose the demand for wheat is elastic. An increase in the price of wheat would accordingly result in a proportionately greater reduction in quantity demanded. Farmers would thus obtain a smaller total revenue from the sale of wheat. Now suppose the government establishes a minimum wheat price above the market equilibrium price. Wheat sales would be reduced, and so too would farmers' incomes, unless the price support were accompanied by a minimum sales guarantee. On the other hand, if the demand for wheat is inelastic, as it probably is over the relevant range, a minimum price above the equilibrium price would increase farmers' total revenue.

Price elasticities range quite widely. For any given demand, two basic factors determine elasticity: availability of substitute goods and the number of uses to which a good may be put. These factors go a long way toward explaining variations in elasticities.

The more and better the substitutes for a specific good, the greater its price elasticity will be at a given set of prices. Goods with few and poor substitutes—wheat and salt, for example—will always tend to have low price elasticities. Goods with many substitutes—wool, for which cotton and manmade fibers may be substituted, for instance—will have higher elasticities.

Of course, the definition of a good affects greatly the number of substitutes and thus its elasticity of demand. For example, if all of the gasoline stations in a city raised the price of gasoline five cents a gallon, the total sales would undoubtedly fall off some but in the absence of close substitutes, probably not much. If all of the Gulf stations—but no others—raised price a nickel, the sales of Gulf gasoline would probably fall substantially. There are many good substitutes for Gulf gasoline at the lower price. If one service station alone raised price, its sales in the long run would probably fall almost to zero. Some might continue buying there, perhaps the owner's wife and mother, but the availability of so many easily accessible substitutes would encourage most customers to trade elsewhere, since the cost of finding a substitute service station is so small. Thus, the way in which a good is defined means a great deal.

Similarly, the greater the number of uses a commodity has, the greater its price elasticity will be. Thus a commodity such as wool—which can be used in producing clothing, carpeting, upholstery, draperies, and tapestries, and so on—will tend to have a higher price elasticity than a commodity with only one or a very few uses—butter, for example.

Finally, we should discuss to some extent the effect of time upon the demand for a commodity. To illustrate, let us consider the following application.

APPLICATION

Regulation of natural gas

Let us now look at the example of natural gas. At the time of writing there is considerable pressure to take off the regulation on gas prices and let prices increase. What predictions would you make, using your knowledge of demand theory and information about the real world, about the effect of such a change upon quantity demanded of natural gas in the very near future, in a few years, and in a rather long period of time, say a decade or two.

We examine first the very near future, say within the year. Our theory says that when the price of something increases, people demand less. But, in most cases people already have their gas-using appliances installed. Manufacturing plants that use gas are already built. But some can still change rapidly. I have been told that in the last ten years, many industrial and utility boilers have in fact been designed so as to be able to use two fuels interchangeably. One of the two is always gas; the other is either coal or oil. These could change from gas to coal rapidly. Furthermore, even during a very short period of adjustment people will respond to some extent by decreasing the temperature setting in their homes. This decreases the gas usage to some extent. Possibly, those who use gas to heat water can decrease to some extent the use of hot water. But the point is that over a fairly short period the use of natural gas will not be particularly responsive to the increase in price even though the use will be somewhat responsive. For the most part, however, people do not suddenly change from gas to electricity in response to a reasonably small increase in prices. Consumers are rather limited in their form of adaptation. While people do respond to some extent, demand is rather inelastic when the time period of adjustment is short.

Given a longer period of adjustment, users of natural gas can decrease consumption even more. Builders of new homes can insulate better. People can increase the insulation in older homes; they can install storm windows. Businesses can find alternative fuels. An even longer period of time results in gas appliances wearing out and substitution being made where it is economically feasible. In summary, if people think the price increase is permanent, the longer the time period in which consumers have to adapt to a price change, the more elastic is the demand for the product. This adaptation can be in response to a price increase or a price decrease.

EXERCISE

Trace out the effects of a significant increase in the price of gasoline over time. Use a short time period, an intermediate time period, and a very long time period. This is also an important policy question.

Thus we can see from the application above that the longer the time period of adjustment, the more elastic is demand. Of course, we can treat the effect of time within the framework of the effect of available substitutes on elasticity. The greater the time period of adjustment, the more substitutes become available and economically feasible. As we stressed above, the more available are substitutes, the more elastic is demand.

EXERCISES

Use of elasticities

Businesses generally like to be able to predict the effect of certain activities on the price that they must pay for inputs that they use in producing goods and services. Frequently, they have available information concerning changes in output; they also have available through business publications broad general estimates of the demand elasticity for key products.

In 1973 there was a boycott on imported oil. Government agencies predicted that the decrease in imported crude would cause a 20 percent decrease in the amount of petroleum available. Estimates of demand elasticity at the time for petroleum were between 0.8 and 1.4. What would persons in business predict about the price of petroleum based upon these estimates?

Elasticity is defined as

$$\frac{\%\,\Delta Q}{\%\,\Delta P}.$$

For the two estimates

$$\frac{20\%}{\%\,\Delta P} = 0.8 \text{ and } \frac{20\%}{\%\,\Delta P} = 1.4.$$

Thus one would predict that the price of petroleum would rise between 14.3 percent and 25 percent, depending upon which elasticity is chosen.

If government sales of wheat to foreign sources reduce the available wheat by 10 percent, what will happen to the price of wheat if demand elasticity is 1.2? If someone in business has reason to believe that the demand elasticity for a product is between 1.5 and 2, by what percent will sales rise if the price is reduced 10 percent?

$$1.5 = \frac{\% \Delta Q}{10\%} \text{ and } 2 = \frac{\% \Delta Q}{10\%}$$

Thus the percent increase in quantity sold will be between 15 percent and 20 percent.

APPLICATION

Demand elasticities and energy saving plans

In the Spring of 1977 President Carter in a speech to the nation released his plan to conserve energy. There were several points, but one of the more important was a large tax on the purchase of "gas guzzlers," automobiles that had a rather low miles-per-gallon rating, this to be combined with a subsidy on the purchase of new automobiles that had miles-per-gallon ratings higher than a particular level. The plan was designed to raise the price of gas guzzlers and lower the price of small cars that were gas efficient. This would in the long run effectively increase the average gasoline mileage of automobiles being driven in the United States. This increase in average mileage would, it was alleged, decrease gasoline consumption in the country over the long run.

No one questioned this postulated effect for some time. The major argument was about the effect on the automobile industry. But most analysts had neglected the effect of demand elasticity on automobile sales.

In an article appearing in the May 23, 1977, issue of *National Observer,* it was pointed out that when relative demand elasticities are taken account of, the heavy tax on large cars combined with the subsidy on small cars may cause *more rather than less* gasoline to be consumed even though the tax-subsidy scheme would increase the average gasoline mileage of cars on the road.

This article pointed out several problems with the program, most of which we shall neglect here. The principal argument was based upon the difference in demand elasticities for small cars and large cars. First, it was pointed out that most studies indicated that the demand for large, gas-inefficient cars was relatively inelastic. But studies showed also that the demand for small, gas-efficient cars was relatively elastic.

If this is the case people would, in response to the higher price, decrease their purchases of larger cars as is predicted by demand theory. But potential Cadillac or Lincoln purchasers would not move all the way to Toyotas or Pintos. They may step down a little in response to higher prices caused by taxes. But, if the demand for the large cars is not very elastic, even inelastic, the purchase of the larger cars would not fall much.

On the other hand, the subsidy on smaller cars would tend to lower their prices. If the demand for small cars is rather elastic this lower price would cause a rather substantial increase in the purchase of small cars. People would perhaps be induced by the lower price to buy a second car. Some who previously used public transportation would be marginally induced to buy a car.

Thus if the sales of the "gas guzzlers" did not fall much while the sales of small cars increased significantly, the *number* of cars on the road may well increase even though the average gas mileage increased. Thus more cars being driven, even with higher gas mileages, might well, it was predicted, *increase rather than decrease the total gasoline consumption.*

The question is of course an empirical one. The point we want to make here, however, is that the difference in relative demand elasticities should have at least been considered. That difference could make a policy designed to have one effect, conserve gasoline, have an entirely different effect, increase the use of gasoline. By the time you are reading this the effect may already be evident. As of now, the result is certainly not self-evident as was thought at the time of the proposal. Those who thought so neglected elasticity, a most important concept for government officials. If in a few years you are a young assistant to a congressman or high government official, remember this little problem of relative elasticities when a similar situation arises. It might get you a raise. Just in passing, it might also get you fired if this kind of proposal is the Congressman's pet project, and you have shown that it won't work. Don't worry, there are a lot of good jobs available for people with a good knowledge of economics.

2.3.e Other elasticities

At times, economists are concerned with the relative responsiveness of quantity demanded to changes in either income or the price of some related good. To measure this responsiveness, we use the coefficients of income elasticity and cross elasticity.

As you will recall, when deriving a demand curve for a good, we hold constant such things as income and the prices of related goods. The price of the good determines the *point* on the demand curve the consumer selects; income and the prices of related goods, among other things, determine the *position* of the demand curve; that is, how far from or close to the axes the curve stands.

The responsiveness of quantity demanded to income changes, other things remaining the same (including the price of the commodity in question), is measured by the coefficient of income elasticity (E_M). Specifically, the income elasticity of demand is the ratio of the percentage change in quantity demanded to the percentage change in money income. Symbolically

$$E_M = \frac{\Delta Q/Q}{\Delta M/M} = \frac{\Delta Q}{\Delta M} \cdot \frac{M}{Q}.$$

Note that we do not put a minus sign in the equation. As we shall show in Chapter 4, quantity demanded can vary either directly or inversely with income; that is, $\Delta Q/\Delta M$ can be either positive or negative. Therefore, E_M can be either positive or negative.

Similarly, it is possible to measure the responsiveness of quantity demanded to changes in the price of some related good. This is called cross price elasticity of demand. Hold everything constant except the price of some related good Y. The cross elasticity is the ratio of the percentage change in the quantity demanded of good X to the percentage change in the price of Y. More specifically,

$$E_{xy} = \frac{\Delta x/x}{\Delta p_y/p_y} = \frac{\Delta x}{\Delta p_y} \cdot \frac{p_y}{x}.$$

As in the case of income elasticity, one can make no general statement about the sign of E_{xy}. At a given price of X, quantity demanded may vary directly with the price of some related good; that is, $\Delta x/\Delta p_y$ is positive. For example, the quantity of Fords demanded at a particular price will increase if the price of Chevrolets rises and will decrease if the price of Chevrolets falls. Goods such as these are sometimes called substitutes; E_{xy} is positive. On the other hand, if the price of gasoline rises and the quantity of Fords demanded decreases at a particular price, E_{xy} would be negative. Fords and gasoline, and similarly related pairs of goods, are sometimes called complements. It should be emphasized that in these examples, *demand* shifts; we are not considering changes in quantity demanded along a stationary demand curve.

APPLICATION

Income elasticities of housing

Branches of the federal and state governments have recently become quite interested in the availability of private housing. In making their development plans governmental officials are naturally interested in the income elasticity of demand for housing. A study published in 1971 estimated the elasticity of rental expenditure with respect to income as between 0.8 and 1.0. The estimated elasticity for owner-occupants was estimated to lie between 0.7 and 1.5.*

In making plans over the next 10 years people who work for government might wish to predict the increase in the demand for housing (rental and owner-occupied) due to increases in yearly real per capita income, which is expected to increase between 2 and 3 percent a year. Those making predictions generally realize that they cannot come up with a precise single estimate. They, therefore, will frequently make their estimate over a range. Using your knowledge of elasticities, and the figures given above, how would you estimate the increase in housing demand due to increases in real income?

First, we must estimate the expected increase in real per capita income ten years hence. If income increases 2 percent per year, then income at the end of the first year will be 1.02 times that at the first of the year; at the end of the second year it will be (1.02) times (1.02) times income at the beginning of year one. To generalize, at the end of the tenth year, income will be $(1.02)^{10}$ times income at the beginning of the period. Since $(1.02)^{10}$ equals 1.218, real per capita income will increase by 21.8 percent, if income increases 2 percent a year. (Note, that for simplicity we have not resorted to averaging.)

If income increases 3 percent a year, income in 10 years will be 34.3 percent higher, since $(1.03)^{10}$ equals 1.343. Using estimates for the elasticity, we can solve for the percent increase in the demand for rental housing because of income increases over the ten-year period with the formula

$$E_M = \frac{\% \Delta Q}{\% \Delta I}.$$

---

* See Frank de Leeuw, "The Demand For Housing: A Review of Cross Section Evidence," *The Review of Economics and Statistics,* vol. 53, February 1971, pp. 1–10.

We can summarize the results for rental housing in a table showing the percent change in quantity under each possible combination.

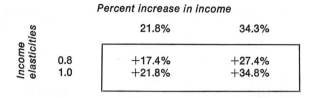

Percent increase in income

		21.8%	34.3%
Income elasticities	0.8	+17.4%	+27.4%
	1.0	+21.8%	+34.8%

Thus the range of increase lies between 17.4 percent and 34.3 percent.

The estimates of the percent increase in the demand for owner-occupied housing due to increases in income are summarized in the following table.

Percent increase in income

		21.8%	34.3%
Income elasticities	0.7	+15.3%	+24.0%
	1.5	+32.7%	+51.5%

Note that the range of estimation is far greater in the case of owner-occupied housing because the range of elasticities was greater.

We must emphasize that these estimates are estimates of the increase in the amount that would be demanded at a given real price. A person trained in economics would hedge by pointing out that increases in price would curtail to some extent the increase in quantity demanded.

2.3.f Summary

Demand is price inelastic, elastic, or unitary as $- \%\triangle Q / \%\triangle P$ is less than, greater than, or equal to one. A decrease in price occasions a decrease, an increase, or no change in total expenditure, respectively. The elasticity of a good is influenced primarily by the availability of substitute goods and by the number of uses to which a good may be put. Economists also use income elasticity to measure the effect of income changes upon quantity demanded and cross elasticity to measure the effect of changes in the prices of related goods upon quantity demanded of the good in question.

APPLICATION

Demand for legal services

A recent article by Rodney M. Mabry points out the importance of accurately estimating demand elasticities and some problems involved in making such estimates.* Mabry points out that many legal associations use "suggested, advisory, or minimum" fee schedules that should be collected by lawyers. He then notes that even though the intent is to raise the incomes of lawyers, these tactics may not be successful for the industry. The basic point involves the elasticity of demand for legal services. Why?

Consider Figure 2.3.5. The fee for legal services in a particular area is plotted on the vertical axis; the quantity demanded at each fee is plotted on the horizontal. Suppose the prevailing fee is OF_1; at this fee OQ_1 is demanded per period of time. (We ignore differences in types of legal services for analytical simplicity.) Now let the legal association set the new fee at OF_2. Clearly the quantity demanded will fall, in this case to OQ_2. The reason for the decline is that there are substitutes for many forms of legal services. Some of these are doing one's own legal work, asking the advice of friends, making out one's own will, or simply not using legal services.

Even though the fee has risen, an important consideration is

FIGURE 2.3.5

DEMAND FOR LEGAL SERVICES

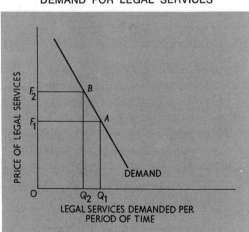

---

* See Rodney H. Mabry, "A Note on the Elasticity of Demand for Legal Services," *Southern Business Review,* Spring 1975, pp. 8–11. This application section is based upon that article.

what happens to the total revenue. If the area OF_1AQ_1, which represents the total revenue before the fee increase, exceeds the area OF_2BQ_2, the total revenue after the fee increase, the total revenue received declines, even though fees are up. Clearly the results depend upon whether demand is elastic or inelastic. The more inelastic is demand, the more total revenue rises as fees are increased. But if demand is elastic, total receipts fall.

In the above-cited paper it is suggested that because of certain peculiarities associated with the legal profession, the demand for legal services is more elastic than is supposed. It is suggested that there is a bandwagon effect involved in the demand for lawyers. That is, if fees decline, people hire more lawyers. But additional offensive or defensive lawyers create an additional demand for defensive and offensive lawyers, respectively. If one party adds a second lawyer in a case, the opposing party might well add an addition lawyer to counteract.

How important this added effect may be would have to be an empirical question. But, this analysis shows that in some instances the total effect of changing price might not be apparent at first.

2.4 SUPPLY SCHEDULES

To get at an understanding of supply, suppose that a large number of farmers sell cabbage in the same market. One particular farmer is willing to grow and sell 1,000 cabbages per season if the price per unit of cabbage is $0.25. If the price of cabbage were $0.35, he would be willing to grow more, say 2,000. The higher price induces the farmer to take land out of cultivation of other crops and put it into the cultivation of the now relatively more lucrative cabbage. A still higher price, $0.50 perhaps, would be required to induce him to market 3,000 cabbages, and so on. That is, the farmer allocates time and land so as to make as much money as possible. Higher and higher prices are required to induce him to reallocate more and more time and land to cabbage production.

A portion of the farmer's cabbage supply schedule might, therefore, be as follows:

Price	Quantity supplied
$0.25	1,000
.35	2,000
.50	3,000
.75	4,000
1.25	5,000

This schedule shows the *minimum price* that induces the farmer to supply each amount in the list. Note that in contrast to demand analysis, price and quantity supplied are directly related. We must postpone the explanation of why price and quantity vary directly until Chapter 7, after we have analyzed cost and production. For the present we assume that the supply schedule shows the minimum price necessary to induce producers voluntarily to offer each possible quantity for sale. We also assume that an increase in price is required to induce an increase in quantity supplied.

Just as the market demand schedule is the sum of the quantities demanded by all consumers, the market supply schedule shows the sum of the quantities that suppliers (firms) would supply at each price. If all cabbage farmers had the same supply schedule as that shown in the above table and there were 10,000 cabbage farmers, then 10,000,000 would be supplied at $0.25, 20,000,000, at $0.35, and so on. Thus our definition of supply is analogous to that of demand.

Definition. Supply is a list of prices and the quantities that a supplier or group of suppliers (firms) would be willing and able to offer for sale at each price in the list per period of time.

2.4.a Graphing supply schedules

First, consider the supply schedule in Table 2.4.1. This table shows the minimum price necessary to induce firms to supply, per unit of time, each of the six quantities listed. In order to induce greater quantities, price must rise; or, in other words, if price increases from $4 to $5, firms will increase quantity supplied from 6,000 units to 6,500 units. Remember that we are assuming a large number of non-colluding firms; in case of a single firm supplying the entire market, a different principle applies (as shown in Chapter 8). Figure 2.4.1 shows a graph of the schedule in Table 2.4.1.

TABLE 2.4.1

MARKET SUPPLY SCHEDULE

Quantity supplied (units)	Prices (dollars)
7,000	6
6,500	5
6,000	4
5,000	3
4,000	2
3,000	1

FIGURE 2.4.1

MARKET SUPPLY CURVE

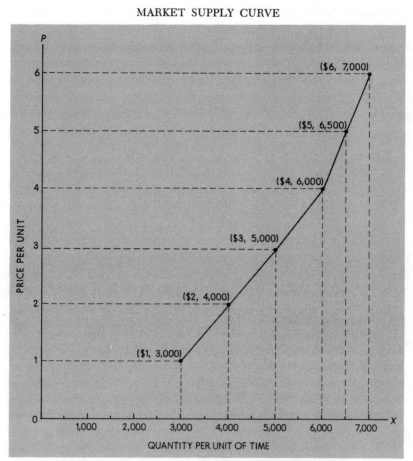

This supply curve is drawn under the assumption that price and quantity are directly related, so the curve is positively sloped.

2.4.b Factors influencing supply

As in the case of demand, we might ask why the supply schedule in Table 2.4.1 is what it is. Why, for example, does a price of $5 rather than a price of $4 induce a quantity supplied of 6,500? Or why is not a lower quantity supplied at each price in the list? A much more thorough discussion of supply is undertaken in Chapter 7. For now, we will only mention briefly four factors that affect supply. These are the factors generally held constant when drawing a supply curve.

First, technology is assumed to be constant. If a more efficient method of production is discovered, firms generally change the amounts they are willing to supply at each price. Second, the prices of factors of production are usually held constant. For example, a change in wage rates or in the prices of raw materials will change the supply curve. Third, the prices of related goods (in production) are held constant. If the price of corn rises while the price of wheat remains the same, some farmers will switch from growing wheat to growing corn, and less wheat will be supplied. Fourth, the expectations of producers are assumed not to change.

2.4.c Changes in supply

When price rises and firms are induced to offer a greater quantity of a good for sale, we say *quantity supplied* increases. When one or more of the factors mentioned in Section 2.4.b change, firms are induced to offer more or less at each price in the schedule; in this case we say supply changes. Consider Figure 2.4.2 in which $S_0S'_0$ is the initial supply curve. If price falls from $O\bar{p}$ to Op', the quantity of X supplied decreases from Ox_0 to Ox'_0, other things remaining the same. If technology changes and supply consequently changes from $S_0S'_0$ to $S_2S'_2$, we say supply increases. Firms now wish to offer Ox_2 at price $O\bar{p}$, and they wish to offer more

FIGURE 2.4.2

SHIFTS IN SUPPLY

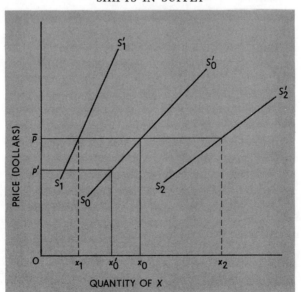

units for sale at each price in the entire range of prices. A movement from $S_0S'_0$ to $S_1S'_1$ is a decrease in supply. Firms then wish to offer less for sale at each price in the range.

These relations may be summarized as follows:

Relations. When price rises (falls), other things remaining the same, quantity supplied rises (falls). When something held constant in deriving supply changes, for example, technology, supply increases or decreases. If firms are induced to offer more (less) at each price, supply has increased (decreased).

2.5 SUPPLY ELASTICITY

As is the case for demand, the coefficient of supply elasticity measures the relative responsiveness of quantity supplied to changes in price *along a given supply schedule*. The computation technique is essentially the same as that used for demand elasticity.

2.5.a Computation

The coefficient of supply elasticity is defined as

$$E_s = \frac{\Delta Q/Q}{\Delta P/P} = \frac{\Delta Q}{\Delta P} \cdot \frac{P}{Q},$$

where ΔQ is the change in quantity supplied, ΔP is the change in price, and P and Q are price and quantity supplied. Since Q and P are assumed to change in the same direction, the coefficient is positive. One can use an averaging technique like that discussed for demand when the changes are discrete; that is, when differences in the bases used affect E_s.

If the percentage change in quantity supplied exceeds the percentage change in price, supply is elastic and $E_s > 1$. If the two percentages are equal, supply has unitary elasticity and $E_s = 1$. If the percentage change in price exceeds the percentage change in quantity, supply is inelastic and $E_s < 1$. Therefore, the more elastic is supply, the more responsive is quantity supplied to price changes.[1] Note, however, that in contrast to

---

[1] Estimating supply elasticity at a point on a supply curve is quite simple. First, draw a tangent to the curve at the point where elasticity is to be calculated. Extend the tangent toward the left until it reaches the origin, the vertical axis, or the horizontal axis. If the tangent crosses the vertical axis, supply is elastic at the point; if it crosses the horizontal axis it is inelastic; if it passes through the origin, supply has unitary elasticity. For a straight line supply, merely check which axis supply crosses and make the same estimation as described for a tangent line.

demand we cannot relate supply elasticity to positive or negative changes in total dollar value supplied; that is, changes in price times quantity supplied at that price. Since price and quantity vary directly, an increase in price increases quantity supplied and hence increases the dollar value of quantity supplied whether supply is elastic or inelastic. A fall in price likewise decreases the dollar value of quantity supplied.

2.5.b Determinants of supply elasticity

The responsiveness of quantity supplied to changes in price depends in very large measure upon the ease with which resources can be drawn into the production of the good in question, in case of a price increase, or withdrawn from production of that good and attracted into production of another good, in case of a price decrease. If additional quantities can be produced only at much higher costs, then a very large increase in price is needed to induce more quantity supplied. In these cases supply is rather inelastic. On the other hand, if more can be produced at a very small increase in cost, quantity supplied is quite responsive to price changes, and supply is rather elastic. To summarize, suppose the price of a particular good increases. If the resources used to produce that good are readily accessible without increasing their prices much and if production can physically be increased easily, supply is more elastic than if the opposite is the case; that is, supply would be less elastic if the additional resources are obtainable only at rapidly increasing prices. For a price decrease, elasticity depends upon how rapidly resources can be released from production of the good in question and moved into the production of other goods.

One can think also of the elasticity of the supply of persons to an occupation. For some occupations a small increase in the average wage or salary induces rapid entry into that occupation. Thus supply is elastic if entry is easy. For other occupations the supply is more inelastic because entry is induced only at a much higher wage. Possibly, it is difficult to train for the occupation. In any case the elasticity of persons to an occupation depends upon how easily people can enter the occupation after a wage increase and how willing they are to enter. In the case of wage decreases, elasticity depends upon how rapidly people leave the occupation.

As you have probably deduced by now the length of the time period of adjustment is a crucial determinant of supply elasticity, either in the case of goods and services or entrants into an occupation. Clearly the more time permitted suppliers to adapt to a change in price, the more responsive is quantity supplied and hence the more elastic is supply. Obviously, over a very short period of time supply would generally be quite inelastic.

Economists frequently distinguish between momentary, short-run, and long-run supply and supply elasticity. As an example, let us consider the supply of people in a particular profession, say lawyers. Three supply curves for lawyers are shown in Figure 2.5.1. $L_M L'_M$ is the momentary supply of lawyers. At a moment of time there are OL_M lawyers, and this number cannot be instantaneously changed. Suppose the average income of lawyers rises from Op_0 to Op_1; at that moment or over a very short period of time, the number of lawyers cannot be increased. Since quantity does not respond at all, the vertical supply curve $L_M L'_M$ is infinitely inelastic.

Within a reasonably short period of time, however, the increase in the average income of lawyers will induce an increase in the number of lawyers, perhaps from OL_M to OL_{SR}. The increase in income will induce some retired lawyers to begin practice again; some businesspeople with law degrees will be induced to leave their companies and enter practice. The resulting short-run supply curve is $S_{SR}S'_{SR}$, the supply curve when a reasonably short period of adjustment is permitted. This curve is more

FIGURE 2.5.1

EFFECT OF TIME OF ADJUSTMENT
ON SUPPLY ELASTICITY

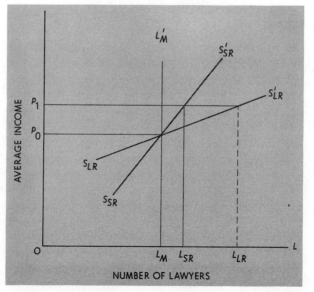

elastic than $L_M L'_M$ because when some adjustment time is permitted, quantity supplied is more responsive to price changes.

The long-run supply curve is $S_{LR} S'_{LR}$, which allows sufficient time for *all* adjustments to be made (we shall define short run and long run more precisely in Chapters 5 and 6). In our example, higher average incomes will induce more college graduates to enter law school, and the period of adjustment is long enough to permit them to begin practicing law. Alternatively, if average income declines relative to other professions requiring similar periods of training, the number of lawyers will decline appreciably. Thus, the long-run supply curve $S_{LR} S'_{LR}$ is more elastic than $S_{SR} S'_{SR}$ because quantity is more responsive to price when sufficient adjustment time is permitted.

2.6 MARKET DETERMINATION OF PRICE AND QUANTITY

The purpose of studying supply and demand is to prepare us to analyze their interaction, which determines market price and quantity. A primary reason for separating them is to isolate the factors that determine each so that we can analyze the market effects of changing these factors. Before further analyzing the underlying forces behind the two schedules (in later chapters), we will first examine the interaction of supply and demand in the market.

2.6.a Equilibrium

Suppose that in the market for a good, demanders and suppliers have the particular schedules set forth in Tables 2.2.1 and 2.4.1 respectively. These schedules are combined in Table 2.6.1. Suppose also that an auctioneer, who does not know the schedules, is assigned the task of finding a price that clears the market; that is, a price at which quantity demanded equals quantity supplied. The auctioneer does not know the market-clearing price, since the schedules change from time to time. Therefore, he begins by picking some price at random and announcing this price to the demanders and suppliers, who then tell him the amounts they wish to purchase or sell at that price. The first price chosen may or may not clear the market. If it does, exchange takes place; if not, the auctioneer must choose another price, but this time he need not proceed purely at random.

The auctioneer knows from long experience that if quantity demanded exceeds quantity supplied (we call this situation excess demand), an in-

TABLE 2.6.1

MARKET DEMAND AND SUPPLY

Price (dollars)	Quantity supplied	Quantity demanded	Excess supply (+) or demand (−)
6......	7,000	2,000	+5,000
5......	6,500	3,000	+3,500
4......	6,000	4,000	+2,000
3......	5,000	5,000	0
2......	4,000	5,500	−1,500
1......	3,000	6,000	−3,000

crease in price will cause quantity demanded to decrease and quantity supplied to increase; that is, excess demand will decrease when price rises. He knows also that if quantity supplied exceeds quantity demanded (called excess supply), a reduction in price causes a reduction in quantity supplied and an increase in quantity demanded; that is, a price reduction reduces excess supply.

Suppose the first price chosen is $5; 3,000 units are demanded but 6,500 units are offered for sale. There is an excess supply of 3,500 units at that price. To reduce excess supply the auctioneer reduces price, say to $1. Now, since consumers demand 6,000 but producers are willing to supply only 3,000, excess demand is 3,000. The auctioneer raises price to $4 and quantity supplied exceeds quantity demanded by 2,000. He therefore reduces price to $3. Quantity demanded equals quantity supplied and the market is cleared. The equilibrium price and quantity are $3 and 5,000 units.

We can also express the equilibrium solution graphically. In Figure 2.6.1, DD' and SS' are the market demand and supply curves (these are not graphs of the schedules in Table 2.6.1). It is clear that Op_e and Ox_e are the market-clearing or equilibrium price and quantity. Only at Op_e does quantity demanded equal quantity supplied. In this model we need not make our assumption about the auctioneer. Consumers and producers themselves bid the price up or down if the market is not in equilibrium.

Suppose price happens to be $O\bar{p}$, greater than Op_e. At $O\bar{p}$ producers supply $O\bar{x}_s$ but only $O\bar{x}_d$ is demanded. An excess supply of $\bar{x}_d\bar{x}_s$ develops. This surplus accumulates for the producers. When this happens producers are induced to lower price in order to keep from accumulating unwanted surpluses. (This is the same thing our auctioneer would have done.) Note that at any price above Op_e there is an excess supply, and producers will lower price. On the other hand, suppose price is $O\hat{p}$. Demanders are willing and able to purchase $O\hat{x}_d$, while suppliers are only willing to offer

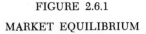

FIGURE 2.6.1

MARKET EQUILIBRIUM

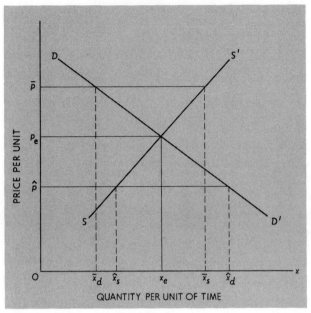

$O\hat{x}_s$ units for sale. Some consumers are not satisfied; there is an excess demand of $\hat{x}_s\hat{x}_d$ in the market. Since their demands are not satisfied, consumers bid the price up. Again, this is what our auctioneer would have done if a shortage existed. As consumers continue to bid up the the price, quantity demanded decreases and quantity supplied increases until price reaches Op_e and quantity is Ox_e. Any price below Op_e causes a shortage, and the shortage causes consumers to bid up the price. Given no outside influences that prevent price from being bid up or down, an equilibrium price and quantity is attained. This equilibrium price is the price that clears the market; both excess demand and excess supply are zero in equilibrium. Equilibrium is attained in the market because of the following:

Principles. When price is above the equilibrium price, quantity supplied exceeds quantity demanded. The resulting excess supply induces sellers to reduce price in order to sell the surplus. If price is below equilibrium, quantity demanded exceeds quantity supplied. The resulting excess demand causes the unsatisfied consumers to bid up price. Since prices below equilibrium are bid up by consumers and prices above equilibrium are lowered by producers, the market will converge to the equilibrium price-quantity combination.

2.6.b Demand and supply shifts

So long as the determinants of demand and supply do not change, the price-quantity equilibrium described above will not change. Before finishing our study of the market we must see how this equilibrium is disturbed when there are changes in one or more of the factors held constant in deriving demand and supply.

A bit of intuitive reasoning may ease the transition to the somewhat complicated graphical analysis that follows. Consider the career that you plan after graduation. Suppose you plan to become an economist. Suppose also that prior to your graduation Congress passes a law requiring that everyone who buys a share of stock or a bond must, for his own protection, consult with an economist. Would this law please you? Why, or why not? Does it not seem logical that economists' salaries would rise after this law is passed? People now must consult economists where previously they did not. How could they bid away the necessary economists from jobs in academics or government? They would do so simply by offering higher salaries. Before long economists' salaries would have generally risen since universities, government, and so on must meet the increasing bids of potential investors. Or, in terms developed in this chapter, the demand for economists rises. With a given supply of economists, salaries must rise. Of course, after a while the higher salaries may lure others into the profession and drive salaries back down again.

Consider another example. Does a cotton farmer bringing his crop to market want a large or small amount of cotton marketed at the same time? Obviously, a small amount because the larger the amount of cotton available, the lower the price of cotton will be. It should thus be intuitively clear that with a given demand the greater the supply, the greater will be the quantity sold but the lower the price will be. In like manner, the greater the demand—for economists, cotton, or anything else —the greater both *quantity* and *price* will be. These relations are intuitively clear; but they can be refined by graphical analysis, to which we now turn.

In panel A, Figure 2.6.2, Op_0 and Ox_0 are the equilibrium price and quantity when demand and supply are $D_0D'_0$ and SS'. Suppose income falls and demand decreases to $D_1D'_1$. At Op_0 quantity supplied exceeds the new quantity demanded by AB; that is, excess supply at Op_0 is AB.

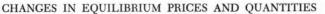

FIGURE 2.6.2

CHANGES IN EQUILIBRIUM PRICES AND QUANTITIES

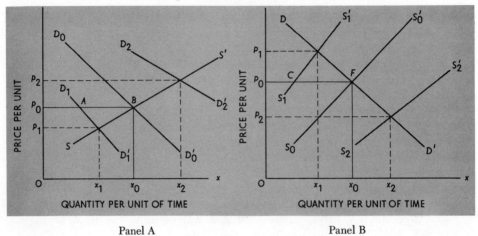

Panel A   Panel B

Faced with this surplus, sellers reduce price until the new equilibrium is reached at Op_1 and Ox_1. Now suppose the price of some substitute good increases so that demand increases to $D_2D'_2$. At price Op_1 quantity demanded far exceeds quantity supplied, and hence a shortage occurs. The excess demand causes consumers to bid the price up until the new equilibrium at Op_2 and Ox_2 is reached. We can see that if supply remains fixed and demand decreases, quantity and price both fall; if demand increases, price and quantity both rise. This direct relation between price and quantity would be expected when we consider that the movements take place *along* the supply curve, which is positively sloped.

Panel B, Figure 2.6.2, shows what happens to price and quantity when demand remains constant and supply shifts. Let demand be DD' and supply $S_0S'_0$. The original equilibrium thus occurs at price Op_0 and quantity Ox_0. Now let input prices rise so that supply decreases to $S_1S'_1$. The shortage of CF at Op_0 causes consumers to bid up price until equilibrium is reached at Op_1 and Ox_1. Now let technology improve so that supply increases to $S_2S'_2$. The surplus at Op_1 causes producers to lower price. Equilibrium occurs at Op_2 and Ox_2. Thus we see that if demand remains constant and supply decreases, price rises and quantity falls; if supply increases, price falls and quantity increases. This inverse relation is expected since the movement is *along* a negatively sloped demand curve.

The direction of change is not always immediately apparent when

FIGURE 2.6.3

EFFECTS OF SUPPLY AND DEMAND SHIFTS

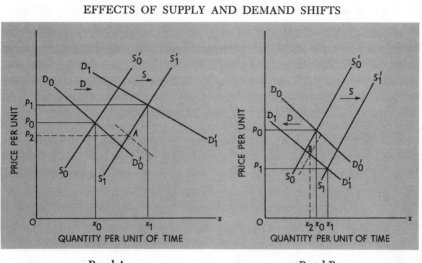

Panel A   Panel B

both supply and demand change simultaneously. In panel A, Figure 2.6.3, $D_0D'_0$ and $S_0S'_0$ are the initial demand and supply curves. Their intersection determines the equilibrium price and quantity, Op_0 and Ox_0. Now suppose supply increases to $S_1S'_1$ and demand increases to $D_1D'_1$; price rises to Op_1 and quantity rises to Ox_1. While quantity always increases when both demand and supply increase, price may either increase, decrease, or even remain the same. Suppose supply shifts to $S_1S'_1$ but demand shifts only to the position indicated by the dashed demand curve crossing $S_1S'_1$ at A. With this shift quantity still rises (although by a lesser amount), but price falls to Op_2. Furthermore, by constructing the change in supply or demand still differently, we can cause price to remain at Op_0 while quantity increases.

To see the effect of a decrease in both supply and demand, consider $D_1D'_1$ and $S_1S'_1$ in panel A as the original schedules. Next, let them both decrease to $D_0D'_0$ and $S_0S'_0$. Quantity and price decrease from Ox_1 and Op_1 to Ox_0 and Op_0. While quantity always decreases when both curves decrease, price need not fall.

Exercise. In order to see the point just made, manipulate supply or demand so that price rises above Op_1 as both curves decrease.

Panel B, Figure 2.6.3, shows the effect of an increase in one curve accompanied by a decrease in the other. Let supply *increase* from $S_0S'_0$ to

$S_1S'_1$ and let demand *decrease* from $D_0D'_0$ to $D_1D'_1$. Price falls from Op_0 to Op_1 and quantity rises from Ox_0 to Ox_1. While price *must* fall when supply increases and demand decreases, quantity need not increase. Suppose that while demand went to $D_1D'_1$ supply increased only to the position indicated by the dashed line crossing $D_1D'_1$ at B. The new equilibrium entails a price reduction (although not so large as before), but now quantity decreases to Ox_2 rather than rising to Ox_1. To see the effect of a decrease in supply accompanied by an increase in demand, simply assume that demand shifts from $D_1D'_1$ to $D_0D'_0$ and supply from $S_1S'_1$ to $S_0S'_0$. Price must rise. In this illustration quantity decreases; but quantity may change in either direction.

Exercise. Prove this last point for yourself.

Principles. (1) When demand increases (decreases), supply remaining constant, both price and quantity increase (decrease). (2) When supply increases (decreases), demand remaining constant, price falls (rises) and quantity rises (falls). (3) When both demand and supply increase (decrease) quantity increases (decreases), but price can either increase or decrease, depending upon the relative magnitude of the shifts. (4) When supply and demand shift in opposite directions the change in quantity is indeterminant, but price always changes in the same direction as demand.

ANALYTICAL EXERCISE

To show how a misunderstanding of the simplest economic theories—shifts in supply curves and elasticity of demand—can cause erroneous or perhaps unwise policy recommendations, let us consider a policy of the mayor of a very large city several years ago. At that time the rate of theft, mugging, and armed robbery by persons addicted to drugs was rising rapidly. Since those who needed drugs were unable to earn enough to purchase sufficient amounts, they were turning to crime.

The mayor was well aware of the problem. He said that he strongly intended to drastically reduce drug-related crime—mugging, theft, etc. His policy to reduce this type of crime was to crack down strongly on the drug traffic; he would arrest drug dealers and reduce the amount of drugs on the street. What advice would you give the mayor if he really wanted to reduce drug-related crime?

You probably recognize that the increased crackdown on drug

traffic would reduce the supply of drugs—the amount of reduction depending upon the severity of the policy. The supply reduction would, as you know, drive up the price of drugs. Will more or less money be spent on drugs after the price increase? We have seen that this effect depends upon the elasticity of the demand for a product.

It appears quite likely that the demand for drugs, particularly by addicts, would be quite inelastic. Thus, less drugs would be purchased at the higher price, but more would be spent on drugs. Where would this increase in expenditure come from? To a large extent from *increases* in mugging, burglary, armed robbery, and so on. Thus this policy to decrease crime could have the effect of increasing crime.

2.6.c Functions of prices

It should be becoming apparent that prices have two social functions. Prices are a rationing device for users of the product, and they serve as an inducement for producers to produce more or less of a product.

Prices perform a rationing service in the sense that society uses the product in the highest valued uses. Take water, for example. In the sense that some water is necessary for the continuation of life, water is a necessity; in the sense that it is used to wash cars and fill swimming pools, it is not. Suppose the price of water in a community is extremely low; perhaps the community gives people water free. How would you expect water to be used?

Certainly people would drink all the water they wanted. They would satisfy their desire for luxuriant lawns because they could water generously. They would install more swimming pools and wash cars more frequently. Car wash firms would spring up. People would not be particularly careful about fixing leaky faucets or turning off drips.

Suppose now that the society finds itself running short of water from time to time. Government asks people to refrain voluntarily from using so much water. But this does not, as usual, work very well. Each consumer knows that his or her actions alone have only an infinitesimal effect on total consumption. This is why voluntary restraints do not work very well unless there are serious social sanctions. (We shall return to this point below.) The community government now begins to increase the price of water to consumers. How would you expect consumers to react?

Not all, but some, would do with a less luxuriant lawn. This is not to say that everyone would stop watering. But some people would water less.

Some people would wash their cars less frequently. A few swimming pools might not be built that otherwise would be. Some people would be more careful about water leaks. As price increased consumers would eliminate the less valued uses of water. In this sense the higher price of water rations the supply of water to the more highly valued uses. Clearly the effect takes some time; but it does take place.

APPLICATION

What is wasteful usage?

In the first fireside chat of his presidency, President Carter stressed that the American people have been extremely wasteful of oil. Have the American people been extremely wasteful of oil?

The truth is that people have "wasted" oil—and the products produced from oil—only in the sense of reacting to prices. Until recently the price of oil and its products was very low. Even now the price of gasoline is low compared to prices in many other countries. Because of this low price, people used products such as gasoline in uses of lower value than would have been the case at much higher prices. People bought cars with bigger engines; they drove faster; tune-ups were less frequent. In the case of natural gas the price was so low that people used more gas to heat rather than insulating more thoroughly.

In any case it was not so much that people deliberately set out to waste gas and oil. At the lower prices they put gas and oil to lower-valued uses. Higher prices would have rationed these commodities to higher-valued uses—and they have. As gas prices rise people insulate better; they keep houses cooler in the winter; they substitute other sources of heat. In this sense they become less "wasteful," but only in response to a price increase.

In fact, we can go even further and say that, assuming energy prices were market-determined, people who restricted their consumption voluntarily below what they would otherwise have consumed at the market price may well have saved energy but in doing so probably wasted other resources. These were the resources they purchased with the income they saved on energy consumption. This point is difficult, if not impossible, to show without tools developed later in the text.*

---

* I am indebted to Professor Bruce Allen of Michigan State University for pointing out this last extension.

The other function of prices is the inducement to produce. Since supply is upward sloping, a higher price causes more to be produced; a lower price causes less to be produced. An increase in the price of a commodity signals producers to produce more. For example, if the price of wheat increases, land that was hitherto unprofitable in wheat production at the lower price now becomes profitable.

Alternatively, if price falls, this decrease is a signal to produce less. Society wants less of the product. Suppose the commodity experiencing a decrease in price is wheat; land that was previously profitable in wheat production is no longer profitable and is taken out of wheat production. In this way quantity supplied is reduced. Thus we can see that price rations a given quantity to higher-valued uses, and changes in price induce changes in output, the direction of change depending upon the way in which the price changes.

APPLICATION

Economic impact of consumer boycotts

At the time of writing this chapter there is an extensive campaign by some consumers to boycott coffee. There was recently some rather severe damage to the coffee crops in Brazil. As one would expect, this crop damage caused the price of coffee in the United States to increase dramatically. Again as would be expected, coffee drinkers were quite upset with the price increase. Many blamed it on a conspiracy of the coffee growers; others blamed it on the retailers; some even blamed communists or the CIA.

In any case, consumer groups are presently being formed to boycott coffee. This boycott is supposed to decrease the demand for coffee, thereby causing the price of coffee to be driven downward. Use the theory you have just learned to predict the consequences of the boycott.

Analysis: In the first place, if the boycott does in fact decrease the demand for coffee significantly, price will be driven down. The more effective the boycott, the further price will fall.

But, who benefits from the boycott? Not those doing the boycotting. Price will remain lower but not if the boycotters want to benefit from the decrease by consuming coffee at the lower price. If they begin to consume more coffee, price will be driven back up. Thus the boycott works as long as nothing is consumed. The primary beneficiaries are those coffee drinkers who do not participate in the boycott. They can buy coffee at reduced prices. There have been other recent boycotts to drive down retail prices. Meat is one example that comes to mind. But if the purpose is to drive down prices, boycotting is *most* successful when no one benefits.

Turn now to the incentive effect. If a boycott reduces prices, there is less incentive for the producers to expand production. In fact, if the price decreases sufficiently, there is the incentive to contract production. In this way a boycott counteracts to some extent the effect the boycotters desire. Boycotters want lower prices, but supply does not change; only quantity supplied changes.

A boycott can be successful if the objective is to drive firms out of the market or to alter the behavior of producing firms. Boycotts of the product of firms that pollute have altered the behavior of those firms. Nonunion firms have been forced to unionize or have been driven out of business by union boycotts. But if the purpose is to be able to consume a product at a lower price, boycotts do not work in that way.

2.7 SUPPLY AND DEMAND IN REAL MARKETS: ANALYSIS AND APPLICATION

By this time some students may question the relevance of demand and supply analysis to real-world problems. What if sellers do not know the demand or the supply schedules? In fact, do they even know what demand and supply are? It may therefore be profitable to show how demand and supply determine price and allocate output in the absence of perfect knowledge about the schedules. Some examples should help clear up this point.

2.7.a Theoretical example

Suppose one day the newspapers all print a scientific report stating that eating rhubarb makes people more healthy. Now we know, having gone through the first part of this chapter, that the demand for rhubarb probably increases. But perhaps the grocers, some of whom have not read this chapter, do not know this. How can the market allocate under these conditions?

First, consider what happens to the rhubarb on the grocers' shelves. Assuming that demand in fact increases, grocers find that what had previously been a week's supply of rhubarb at the established price now lasts only until Thursday morning. Customers complain that they cannot get rhubarb. We can use demand analysis to examine the situation *even though buyers and sellers are completely unaware of demand and supply analysis.*

Panel A, Figure 2.7.1, shows what happens in the retail market. Price is Op_r, and Ox_r per week is the rate of sales when demand is $D_r{}^0D^{0'}{}_r$. Demand increases to $D_r{}^1D^{1'}{}_r$. At Op_r consumers now want Ox'_r units per week. Grocery stores consequently run out of rhubarb before the week is over. The profitable thing for grocers is to order more rhubarb from wholesalers. When they do, the wholesalers sell more rhubarb and their stocks begin to run low. This is shown in panel B. The original demand is $D_w{}^0D^{0'}{}_w$; this is the demand by grocers for wholesale rhubarb. When demand at retail increases, demand at wholesale increases also. Before the shift in demand, retail grocers wanted Ox_w at a wholesale price of Op_w; they now want Ox'_w.

As their inventories run low, wholesalers instruct their buyers in the commodity market to buy more rhubarb. At any one time, however, there is a limit to the amount of rhubarb available. Therefore, as the buyers try to increase their purchases, they bid against one another and force price up. Panel C indicates what happens in the commodity market. The old demand of wholesalers for rhubarb was $D_c{}^0D^{0'}{}_c$ and price was Op_c. Suppose the quantity available is Ox_c (the supply at the moment). When wholesalers' demand rises to $D_c{}^1D^{1'}{}_c$, a shortage of $x_cx'_c$ develops at price Op_c. Price rises to Op'_c to ration the available rhubarb among the competing buyers. (It might be well to note that the scales of the graphs in Figure 2.7.1 are different.)

Wholesalers now pay a higher price in the commodity market and

FIGURE 2.7.1

SUPPLY AND DEMAND ANALYSIS OF REAL MARKETS

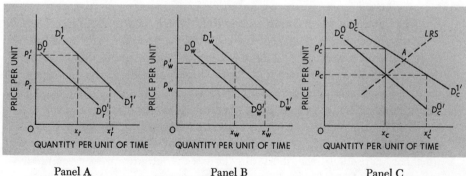

| Panel A | Panel B | Panel C |
| Retail market | Wholesale market | Commodity market |

consequently raise their price to grocers, to Op'_w perhaps. As they tell the grocers, their costs have risen and they are forced to raise prices. The grocers now pay the wholesale price of Op'_w, so they raise the retail price to Op'_r. As they tell their complaining customers, costs have risen so they are forced to raise prices. Costs to the grocers and to the wholesalers have, of course, risen, but ultimately it was the increased demand that caused the price rise. And this price must rise until it rations the available rhubarb to those prospective buyers who are both willing and able to pay the price.

Everything that occurs in the transition period occurs not because we draw some curves but because of individual action in the market. We use demand and supply curves only to analyze more clearly what takes place in the market.

We can take the analysis a few steps further. Suppose the higher price in the commodity market induces farmers to increase their rhubarb crop or induces farmers growing other crops to switch to rhubarb. Remember Ox_c and Op_c make up only one point on the long-run supply curve. Assume that there is an upward sloping long-run supply (LRS) passing through point A in panel C. In the commodity market price falls and quantity increases after all adjustments are made (point A, panel C). The increased quantity supplied causes price to fall and quantity sold to rise in the wholesale and in the retail market.

2.7.b Effect of time on adjustment

Recall from our discussion of the effect of time on supply that supply elasticity depends to some extent on the time period of adjustment. Supply curves are classified as momentary, short run, and long run. Thus the effect of a shift in demand on price and quantity sold depends upon the time period allowed for suppliers to adjust.

To examine this effect let us assume that the demand for beer increases substantially. Suppose that this increase in the demand for beer is thought to be permanent. Assume that the beer market has been in equilibrium. In Figure 2.7.2 the price of beer is OP_0; at this price, OQ_0 is consumed per time period. The original demand is DD.

Let demand increase to $D'D'$. At first the only effect is a price increase to OP_1. The momentary supply is the vertical line at Q_0. This higher price cannot elicit an increase in quantity supplied until a certain amount of time has elapsed. In the short run, however, output can be expanded. Breweries can work longer hours; they can be used more intensively by

FIGURE 2.7.2

EFFECT OF TIME ON PRICE
AND QUANTITY AFTER A DEMAND
INCREASE

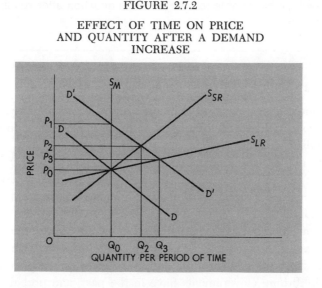

hiring additional workers. Unused capacity can be utilized. If S_{SR} is the short-run supply, the price falls to OP_2; output and sales increase to OQ_2.

In the long run new breweries can be opened by established firms, and new firms can enter the brewing business. Suppose the more elastic long-run supply (after all adjustments have been made) is S_{LR}. In the long run price falls to OP_3 and output and sales increase to OQ_3. This situation prevails until another change disturbs equilibrium.

EXERCISE

Effect of different time periods of adjustment

In Figure 2.7.2 let demand decrease. Trace through the effect upon price and sales in the momentary situation, in the short run and in the long run.

Go back to Figure 2.5.1. Draw a demand through point A, the original equilibrium point with price OP_1 and the amount of lawyers' services OL_M. Make demand increase. Draw in and discuss the effects in the momentary situation, the short run, and the long run.

As the controls on natural gas prices are released and as the price of natural gas rises, what will be the long-run economic impact?

You will be better able to deal with this question after reading the
next section.

2.8 FLOOR AND CEILING PRICES

As we noted, excess demand or excess supply can occur after a demand
or a supply shift. But market forces over time eliminate these. In fact, it is
the very existence of these excess demands and supplies, reflecting
changes in market conditions that allows the market to work. But, there
are also certain shortages (excess demands) and surpluses (excess supplies) that market forces do not tend to eliminate. These are much more
permanent in nature.

If there are two things that economists know how to do, these are (1)
how to create a shortage and (2) how to create a surplus. Governments
can create shortages and surpluses simply by legislating a price below or
above equilibrium. Governments have in the past, and probably will in
the future, decide that the price of a particular commodity is or will be
either "too high" or "too low." Without evaluating the desirability of such
interferences we can use demand and supply curves to analyze the
economic effects of the two types of interferences, the setting of minimum
and maximum prices, and the way in which these interferences cause
either a shortage or a surplus of the good.

2.8.a Theory

If the government imposes a maximum, or ceiling, price on a good, the
effect is to cause a shortage of that good (and frequently to create a black
market that rations the quantity available). In Figure 2.8.1 a ceiling price
Op_c is set on good X. No one can legally sell X for more than Op_c per unit,
which is below the equilibrium price, Op_e. At the ceiling price only Ox_e
is offered for sale; that is, the *momentary* supply is the vertical line at x_e.
Over a period of time the shortage grows worse. After a suitable time
period of adjustment, suppliers decrease the quantity supplied still more,
to Ox_s. Excess demand is now $x_s x_d$. Since quantity supplied is less than
quantity demanded at the ceiling price, there must be some method of
allocating the limited quantity among all those who are willing and able
to buy a larger amount. The sellers may devise the method; perhaps consumers have to stand in line, with suppliers deciding who comes first in
the line on the basis of under-the-counter offers. On the other hand, the

FIGURE 2.8.1

EFFECT OF CEILING PRICE

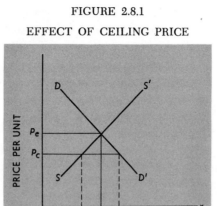

government may devise some system of rationing. But in this case, black markets will develop. In any case the market does the allocating. But when restricted by outside requirements, the allocation is either based upon nonmarket considerations or the market mechanism functions less effectively outside the law.

In contrast, the government may feel that the suppliers of the good are not earning as much income as they "deserve" and, therefore, set a minimum, or floor, price. We can see the results of such actions in Figure 2.8.2. Being dissatisfied with the equilibrium price and quantity,

FIGURE 2.8.2

EFFECT OF FLOOR PRICE

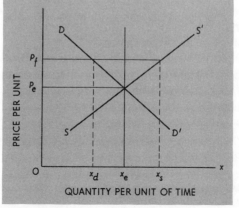

Op_e and Ox_e, the government sets a minimum price of Op_f. Since the law of demand could not concurrently be repealed, consumers demand less (Ox_d) and immediately a surplus of x_dx_e develops. In order to maintain the price Op_f, the government must find some way to limit supply, or it must agree to purchase the surplus. As firms are induced to supply more and as new firms are enticed into the industry by the higher price, the quantity supplied at Op_f increases. If SS' is the long-run supply curve, the increased quantity supplied causes a greater surplus, x_dx_s, which the government must now buy or allocate among producers; that is, the government could simply restrict production to Ox_d. The vertical slotted line at that point then becomes the new supply. A price of Op_f now clears the market.

2.8.b   The effect of specific floor and ceiling prices

Our theory leads us to expect that in the case of a governmentally imposed ceiling price, a shortage or excess demand will develop. Over time the supply will decrease and the excess demand will increase. We would expect also that in the case of durables the *quality* will also deteriorate through lack of maintenance. Several well-known, frequently cited examples tend to confirm this hypothesis.

APPLICATION

Effect of rent controls

A classical example of the effect of a ceiling price is the case of rent controls in large cities, for example, New York. A study by John C. Moorhouse showed that under rent controls landlords would curtail the maintenance of their housing.*

It was posited that since landlords could not raise rents after an increase in demand there was no reason to improve the quality of existing facilities. With a fixed quantity and an increased demand the excess demand is manifested by waiting lists for housing. Since the landlords cannot ration the space by increased prices, they lower cost by reducing the maintenance and hence by reducing the quality of existing housing space.

---

* John C. Moorhouse, "Optimal Housing under Rent Controls," *Southern Economic Journal*, July 1972, pp. 93–106.

After testing, it was found that the *gross* income of landlords showed no relation to maintenance, if rent controls are in effect. One can rent out an apartment at the fixed amount whether one continues to maintain it or not within the relevant range. This is expected because of the excess demand. The study found that net income is negatively related to maintenance. Landlords under rent control can increase *profit* by reducing upkeep. Therefore, when supply cannot be reduced quickly it seems probable that the quality of the existing supply will deteriorate in response to the ceiling. This is one way for suppliers to adjust.

There are many other cases in which governmental price ceilings caused a shortage of something and methods other than price were used to allocate the existing supply. During World War II price ceilings were imposed upon many consumer goods. Government rationed the supply, but the pressure of excess demand increased the expected profits of law violation, and extensive black market operations resulted. The usury laws place a ceiling price on the interest rates that can be charged on a loan. An excess demand for loans results. Who gets the loans? The least risky of course. Who are the least risky? Those with higher incomes. What happens to those who wish to borrow at the prevailing interest rate? They must go to illegal "loan sharks." Because of the extra costs of breaking the law and because government will not enforce the illegal contract, it is probable that these low-income borrowers pay more than they would in the absence of any regulation. Many other examples of the effects of ceiling prices can be observed.

EXERCISE

Causes of shortages

During the winter of 1977 the Eastern and Midwestern part of the nation experienced a brutal cold wave. Texas experienced no gas shortage during its abnormally cold spell. Pennsylvania was being faced with an extreme natural gas shortage. Firms were forced to close because of the gas shortage. Citizens were urged to keep their home temperatures low. Why did Pennsylvania experience such a gas shortage while Texas did not? Do not answer simply that Texas produces gas whereas Pennsylvania does not. Pennsylvania produces much coal while Texas produces little; neither state experienced a severe coal shortage. The only information you need is that at that time the price of gas shipped interstate was regulated below equilibrium price. Gas shipped intrastate was not regulated. Thus the price of gas in Texas was far above the price in Pennsylvania. But there was no shortage in Texas. Pennsylvanians benefited from regulated low prices but suffered from lack of gas. A regulated ceiling price benefits you *if you can get the good that is regulated.*

APPLICATIONS

More ceiling prices

A few years ago the price of beef in grocery stores rose substantially. There was considerable consumer protest at the time. Much of the consumer pressure was in the form of requesting the federal government to put a ceiling price on beef. One member of the Council of Economic Advisers noted the extreme difficulty of policing a ceiling price at the retail level. Because of the vast number of stores selling beef at retail, it would be very hard and very costly to keep black markets from arising. Therefore, the council member said that the ceiling price should be enforced at the stockyards. Because there are so few stockyards, the ceiling price should be much easier to enforce. Then the lower price at the stockyards could be passed along to the consumers in the form of lower beef prices at retail.

This suggestion was not enforced, for good reason. What is wrong with the suggestion? Would the retail price really be driven down by a ceiling price at the stockyards?

Let us analyze the situation with the aid of Figure 2.8.3. Assume that before the imposition of a ceiling price D_s in panel B is the demand curve of retailers for beef at the stockyards. It is derived holding the demand for retail beef constant. The supply curve at the stockyards is S_s. Equilibrium price at the stockyards is OP_s, and equilibrium quantity is OQ_s.

FIGURE 2.8.3

EFFECT OF CEILING PRICE
AT STOCKYARD

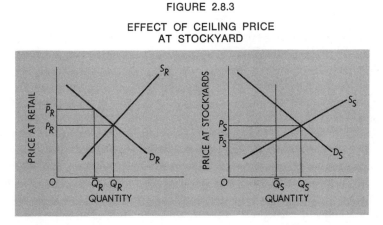

Panel A   Panel B

Panel A shows demand and supply conditions at retail. D_R is the consumers' demand for beef, and S_R, based upon a given wholesale price of beef at the stockyards, is the retailers' supply curve. The equilibrium price and quantity at retail are, respectively, OP_R and OQ_R.

Now let a ceiling price of $O\overline{P}_s$ be imposed at the stockyard. Retailers demand more at the lower prices, knowing that their consumers would buy more at lower prices. But now suppliers are only willing to supply $O\overline{Q}_s$ at this lower price. Thus although retailers wish to supply more beef to consumers at this lower stockyard price of beef, less is available for the retailers to supply. In panel A only $O\overline{Q}_R$ is available because only $O\overline{Q}_s$ is available at the stockyards. Thus, as we know, the price is driven up at retail by the reduced supply. In panel A price increases to $O\overline{P}_R$. Thus we can see that a ceiling price at the stockyards would have increased rather than decreased the retail price of beef. Furthermore, the lower price at the stockyards does not provide the incentive for beef producers to supply more beef.

We might look at one more example in which a ceiling price has an effect different from that desired or postulated. Several years ago the commander of a U.S. military base overseas became worried that his troops were drinking bootleg whiskey and many soldiers were consequently too ill to perform their duties. The bars around the base were licensed and inspected by the military. The whiskey sold in these bars was inspected and would not cause illness—if not drunk in too large quantities.

The base commander reasoned that if he forced the licensed bars to lower their prices, most soldiers would stop buying bootleg whiskey and would patronize the bars instead. The opposite happened. More soldiers than ever were becoming ill from bootleg whiskey after the price control went into effect at the bars. Why?

As you probably deduced, the lower bar price induced the bars to supply less legal liquor than before or some of them to close. There arose a large excess demand (shortage) of legal whiskey near the base. Because of the shortage of legal liquor, more, rather than less, bootleg liquor was sold than under the old price structure. Clearly the results were not the desired results.

Let us turn now to the effect of some floor prices. The typical example of the effect of a price floor, almost a cliché because of its inclusion in almost every elementary economics text, is the support price on many agricultural products. Demand for many of these products is supposedly inelastic. Higher prices would mean higher incomes for farmers (recall the relation between elasticity and revenue). Because of their large numbers it was almost impossible for farmers to get together and fix prices. Government then set a floor price for many agricultural products and, as our theory would predict, excess supply developed. Government had to purchase the resulting surplus from the farmers. In an attempt to lower the surplus, government put acreage controls on many products. Since farmers were certainly not stupid, they obviously put their worst land, not their best, into retirement. Furthermore, they substituted other imputs, like fertilizer, for land and thus increased the productivity of the land being used. For these reasons the excess supply has not been particularly reduced and the problem of persistent surpluses, which our theory predicts, continued. Also the prices to consumers remain higher than they would be in the absence of price controls.

While the farmer is generally cited when economists mention an example of misallocation from a minimum price set above equilibrium, many other cases of governmentally imposed price floors can be mentioned.

One case, not generally noted as such, is the price set by the Civil Aeronautics Board on the passenger fare that can be charged by airlines. A former senior staff economist for the Department of Transportation has said that he believed the regulated fares are on average above equilibrium. Certainly the evidence and theory would lead us to believe that this is in fact the case. First we observe that government regulates the routes that a particular airline can use. As in the case of acreage controls on farmers, this regulation is an attempt to limit the potential excess supply. Second, we see airlines discriminating by reducing fares for certain groups, such as wives or students, in an attempt to get around the regulations. Third, we see a good deal of non-price competition. Flights with movies, alcohol, meals, and beautiful stewardesses were all attempts to induce the limited demand at the regulated fare into particular airlines. We also observe a large amount of excess capacity on airplanes. This may indicate a price above equilibrium. We shall return to this point in Chapter 9.

Another example of a regulated floor price is the price of checking accounts or demand deposits at banks. Banks sell demand deposits to depositors. The depositors get a good (a checking account) and the banks gain reserves, through which they can make loans at interest. Since the government does not allow banks to pay interest to depositors on demand deposits, in effect, a floor price of zero is imposed upon checking accounts. Banks, unable to compete for deposits through lowering price (that is, paying interest), must compete in other ways. They give away premiums or gifts when one opens an account. They compete in luxurious surroundings, in courteous tellers and officers, and by giving other services to the consumers. If price were fixed below equilibrium we would observe a shortage and would see customers competing to get banks to take their deposits. Many other examples of floor prices could be analyzed.

Exercise. Think of some other examples of floor and ceiling prices. What does our theory predict? What do we observe? Think of some instances in which government sells an item below or above the market clearing price. What do we observe? Begin with camping privileges in popular national parks, water in large cities, government-owned housing, admission to state universities.

2.9 SUMMARY

In this chapter we have analyzed the following principles:

Principle. Demand is a list of prices and of the corresponding quantities that consumers are willing and able to buy at each price in the list per unit of time. Quantity demanded varies inversely with price. Demand (that is, the entire schedule) changes when something held constant in deriving demand changes. Among these are income, tastes, the prices of other goods, and expectations.

Principle. Demand elasticity measures the responsiveness of quantity demanded to price changes. The more (less) responsive quantity demanded is to price, the more elastic (inelastic) is demand. An increase in price causes total revenue to increase if demand is inelastic and to decrease if demand is elastic. The effects are opposite for a price decrease. In case of unitary elasticity there is no change in total revenue for a change in price. Elasticity is affected by the availability of substitutes, the number of uses, and adjustment time.

Principle. Supply is the list of prices and the corresponding quantity that will be supplied at each price in the list. Changes in technology, the price of inputs, and the prices of related (in production) goods will shift the entire schedule. Supply elasticity measures the responsiveness of quantity supplied to changes in price. The time period of adjustment is one of the principal determinants of elasticity.

Principle. When price in a market is such that quantity demanded equals quantity supplied the market is in equilibrium. Prices below equilibrium cause excess demand (or shortages). If prices are not artificially fixed, they will be bid up. Prices above equilibrium cause excess supply (or surpluses). If prices are not fixed they will be bid down. When supply and demand change, equilibrium price and quantity will change.

Every day economists use simple demand and supply analysis to solve complex problems and to answer questions dealing with the real world. In fact, demand and supply are probably the most frequently used tools in the economist's bag.

Therefore, much of the remainder of this book is devoted to demand and supply and to the factors that influence demand and supply. As we shall see, however, one must be able to decide *which* demand and *which* supply are relevant for the solution of a particular problem before being able to use these tools fruitfully.

In all cases a fundamental concept to remember is that when the price of something falls, more is taken; when the price of something rises, less is taken. In the next two chapters we turn to the theory of consumer behavior to see why this is so.

APPLICATION

Effect of excise taxes

Recall that in Chapter 1 we gave as an example of the way in which economics is used in decision making the problem of the assistant to a congressman having to predict the effect of an excise tax on gasoline. About all we could say then was that the tax would increase cost and therefore the price of gasoline. Thus less gasoline would be consumed. We then noted that the assistant would have to find statistical information to obtain an actual measure of the full effect. We now have sufficient theory to deal with the problem.

Let us turn first to the theoretical analysis of the problem. Suppose that DD' in Figure 2.9.1 is the economy's demand for gasoline. SS' is the original supply of gasoline prior to the imposition of the excise tax. Thus OQ_0 and Op_0 are respectively the equilibrium quantity and price.

Now an excise tax simply means that for every gallon of gasoline

FIGURE 2.9.1

EFFECT OF AN EXCISE TAX

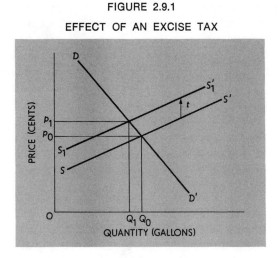

sold the seller must pay a stipulated amount to the federal government. This payment shifts supply upward (decreases supply). Demand does not shift. The consumer who pays 60¢ for a gallon of gasoline presumably does not care what portion of the price goes to the
seller and what portion to government. Consumers demand so much
at 60¢ and at every other price no matter what part goes to government.

Suppliers presumably do care what portion of the 60¢, if that is the
market price, goes to government and what portion they can keep.
For example, suppose at a price of 60¢ a gallon a group of suppliers
are induced to supply a million gallons per week to the market. This
means that they themselves must receive 60¢ a gallon to supply this
amount. Let a tax of 10¢ a gallon be imposed. Now, in order to induce
suppliers to supply 1 million gallons a week the price must be 70¢ a
gallon because only in this way can the suppliers keep 60¢ for themselves. Moreover, at every other quantity suppliers must receive 10¢
a gallon more to induce them to supply that same amount.

In terms of Figure 2.9.1, suppose the excise tax being debated
is t cents per gallon. By the arguments presented above, the
original supply SS' shifts upward by t cents to $S_1S'_1$. Thus at the old
price of Op_0 there is excess demand; consequently price is bid up to
Op_1 and quantity sold declines to OQ_1. Note that the extent of the
price rise and quantity decrease depends upon the slopes of supply
and demand. Note also that price does not rise by the full amount
of t cents. Price rises by the amount p_0p_1, which you can see upon

inspection is less than the distance t. Thus consumers absorb some of the tax in the form of higher prices and producers absorb the remainder of the tax.

We mentioned in the example in Chapter 1 that an actual prediction of the extent of the price increase depends upon statistical data. Suppose you, as the legislator's assistant, obtained statistical data that allowed you to estimate the demand and supply for gasoline in the congressman's district. You estimate from the data that demand per period is.

$$Q_D = 1,000,000 - 8,953P$$

and supply is

$$Q_s = 6,431P$$

where quantity is measured in gallons and price in cents. Setting $Q_D = Q_s$, the equilibrium price is approximately 65¢ and the equilibrium quantity is approximately 418,015 gallons.

Next estimate the impact of a 10¢ excise tax on price and quantity. As noted, demand remains constant. But suppliers can now receive only price less 10¢, so supply becomes, if other conditions have not changed,

$$Q_s = 6,431(P - 10).$$

Now set $Q_s = Q_D$ and solve

$$1,000,000 - 8,953P = 6,431(P - 10)$$

for the new price P. The new price is approximately 69.2 cents. Thus a tax of 10¢ a gallon would raise gasoline prices in the district by about 4.2 cents. In this way we used theory along with (hypothetical) data to make actual predictions about the impact of legislative changes.

PROBLEMS

At the end of this and all of the following chapters there will be two sections of problems. The first section will consist solely of technical problems. These problems are to test your understanding of the pure theory set forth in the chapter. The second section will consist of analytical problems. Some of these will be decision-making problems; others will call for analysis of economic problems; still others may be purely thought-provoking questions. In any case they will be problems concerned with analysis rather than pure technique.

TECHNICAL PROBLEMS

1. Consider the following table showing income, the quantity of the good demanded, and the price of the good.

Quantity	Income	Price
100......	$5,000	$16
120......	6,000	16

Compute the income elasticity of the good, using the averaging method. Next suppose the price of the good changes so that the schedule is now as follows:

Quantity	Income	Price
150......	$5,000	$10
130......	6,000	10

Compute again the income elasticity of demand. Note that the sign differs from the first example. Economists call goods whose income elasticity is negative (that is, whose quantity demanded varies inversely with income) "inferior." Note that the income elasticity can change when prices change. We will discuss inferiority much more fully in Chapter 4. Note for now that there is nothing inherent in the good itself that makes it inferior; it is inferior at one price, not inferior at another.

2. Consider the following table showing the quantity of some good X, the price of some other good Y, and income.

Quantity of X	Price of Y	Income
100......	$2	$5,000
120......	3	5,000

Compute the cross elasticity of demand, E_{XY}, using the averaging method. Suppose income changes to $10,000, so that the schedule is now

Quantity of X	Price of Y	Income
150......	$2	$10,000
130......	3	10,000

Compute again the cross elasticity of demand. Note that the sign changes. Economists frequently, though not always, classify two goods as substitutes when the quantity of one varies directly with the price of the second, and as complements when the price of the first varies inversely with the price of the second. Note that the cross elasticity can vary with income, so there is nothing inherent in the good itself that makes it a substitute or complement.

3. Begin by graphing straight line demand and supply curves determining equilibrium. Next let demand remain constant and shift supply. Show that the more elastic is demand the greater the change in equilibrium quantity and the less the change in equilibrium price for a given shift in supply. Let supply remain constant while demand changes. Analyze the effect of supply elasticity upon the changes in price and quantity.

4. The lower the price of a good, the greater the demand for the good, other things equal. Analyze.

5. "I earn $20 a week and spend it all on beer no matter what the price of beer is." Exactly what is this person's elasticity of demand for beer?

6. What factors affect the elasticity of demand for a commodity? Indicate the effect they have.

7. Other things equal, what happens to an individual's demand curve for a specific product under the following conditions: Explain your answer (for some changes the answer may be uncertain; explain).

   a. The person's income rises.
   b. The price of a substitute good rises.
   c. The price of a complement good rises.
   d. Money prices of all other goods and the total income of the individual double.
   e. Money prices of all other goods fall but income remains constant.

8. With market-determined prices housing units are scarce. With price ceilings shortages are a constant problem. Evaluate.

9. Assume the following demand and supply functions:

$$Q_D = 100 - 2P$$
$$Q_s = 10 + 4P$$

   a. What are equilibrium price and quantity?
   b. Supply shifts to

$$Q_s = 28 + 4P$$

   What are the new equilibrium price and quantity?

   c. Suppose you were appointed the chief of the government agency that regulates this industry; you wished to create a shortage of 13 units. What ceiling price would you set? Recall that a shortage is an excess demand equaling $Q_D - Q_s$. Use the first supply equation.

10. *a.* Consider an increase in the demand for petroleum engineers in the United States. Describe exactly what would happen in the momentary situation, the short run, and the long run?

    b. Consider a decrease in the demand for elementary school teachers. What would happen in the momentary situation, the short run, and the long run?

11. Derive a demand schedule (four price-quantity relations should be sufficient) that is elastic at the higher prices and inelastic at the lower. Compute the coefficient of elasticity between two of the points on the elastic portion and two in the inelastic. Graph the demand curve.

12. A subsidy is clearly the opposite of a tax; that is, the government gives a certain payment to each purchaser of a good, which the government for some reason or another thinks people should consume more of. Begin with an original set of supply and demand curves. Show equilibrium. Next show graphically the effect of the subsidy on market price and on equilibrium quantity. Discuss the way that the slopes of demand and supply affect the change in equilibrium price and quantity.

ANALYTICAL PROBLEMS

1. Prostitution is illegal. But in most cities there is a black marget for prostitution. Is the *black market* price for prostitutes higher, lower, or the same as it would be if prostitution were legal? Explain your answer.

2. A particular brand of coffee advertises that it sells coffee only in the West because there are only enough really good coffee beans for the West.

    a. What evidence would make you believe or disbelieve that this coffee is the "best" coffee? Be careful to say what "best" means to an economist.

    b. Accept the claim that this firm makes the "best" coffee. Is there something that the company can do to insure that there is "enough" of their coffee? Be sure to define "enough" in a way meaningful to an economist. Define "enough" in two ways—one to make the answer to this question "yes" and another to make the answer "no."

    c. "There are only so many really good coffee beans." What is implied by the ad in terms of supply and demand curves, and the pricing policy— i.e., draw the S and D curves, and the current price, implied by the ad quoted in part in the various parts of this question.

3. Some people say that without government price support programs farmers could not afford to grow some crops, like cotton; therefore the country would have no cotton without the support program. Analyze.

4. *a.* The recent destruction of much of Brazil's coffee crop has increased the price of tea. Why?

b. The coffee minister of Colombia (a country that also grows coffee) was recently quoted as saying that he hopes the U.S. coffee boycott over the next couple of years (during which time the Brazilian trees will be back to normal) will be a success in keeping down coffee prices during the period. Why would the minister of a coffee-producing country want a boycott to keep coffee prices down over the next two years? (This is a tough one; do not neglect the effect of price on quantity supplied.)

5. Some legislators want to put higher taxes on liquor and cigarettes because they assert that people, particularly poor people, spend too much of their income on liquor and cigarettes and not enough on other goods such as food. Thus if extra taxes are levied on liquor and cigarettes, people would spend less on these "bad" things and more on other "good" things. Evaluate.

6. Assume first an effective government-imposed maximum price is placed on a particular good. The price is set below equilibrium. Let the price ceiling be removed. Consumer spending on the good will incease only if demand is inelastic. Evaluate. (This is another tricky one.)

7. Much higher tuition was recently imposed in state universities in Texas. High school counselors are advising high school seniors to expect lower admission standards in state universities and higher standards and tuition in private universities in the state. Do you agree? Why or why not?

8. Several members of the economics faculty were standing in a rather long line at the Student Union cafeteria during one lunch hour. Some were heard to remark that they wished that the cafeteria would increase prices. Why?

9. Suppose that you were president of the United States during the 1870s. The price of whale oil (used at the time for lubrication and lighting) had more than quadrupled during the past decade. Whales were being practically exterminated (for reasons we will not explore until the last chapter). Could you make a case that Americans had clearly been wasting whale oil? Could you make a case that they were not? (We shall return to the whale oil situation in a later chapter.)

3

Theory of consumer
behavior: Tools of
analysis

3.1 INTRODUCTION

In the discussion of demand and supply in Chapter 2 we postulated certain characteristics of demand curves without analyzing the specific behavioral patterns upon which they are based. Since demand itself is directly related to the way in which consumers are willing and able to act, it is necessary to understand consumer behavior in order to understand the determinants of demand. This chapter and the following describe the modern theory of consumer behavior and the relations between that theory and the theory of demand. First, the tools of analysis are developed; then these tools are used to analyze the way in which consumer behavior affects demand, with particular emphasis upon explaining why market demand curves are negatively sloped.

3.1.a Principles of maximization

The basic point of this chapter is to analyze the determinants of consumer behavior. We will explain why a consumer chooses a particular group of goods and services and not some other group. Why does one person consume none of some good, like a motorcycle, while someone else with about the same income may own two or three motorcycles?

The method of analysis is really quite simple. You, as a consumer, have a given income and you desire goods. Most likely your income prohibits your purchasing everything you desire. Therefore, you must make a decision about which goods you purchase during a given week or any other period of time. You have an allocation problem. The problem of course is scarcity.

If you wish to consume more of some good in some future period than you are consuming now, you must give up some other goods. A new car this semester will cost you your trip to Europe this summer. Two additional hamburgers per week costs you a six-pack of beer a week. Say you are now eating about ten hamburgers a week. Why do you not eat two more? The obvious answer is that you value the two additional hamburgers less than you value what you would give up to purchase the hamburgers. Similarly, you do not choose to consume only eight hamburgers a week because you value in your mind the ninth and tenth hamburgers more than you value what you would purchase from the money you saved by giving up the two hamburgers.

If your two alternatives are the new car or the trip to Europe the decision is the same. If you value the new car more than you value the trip, then you give up the trip; if not, you give up the car.

Or suppose you would like a motorcycle. Why would you not choose to purchase one? Don't say you can't afford one. Clearly you could if you give up enough. The reason you do not purchase a motorcycle is simply that the added value or satisfaction you think you would receive from owning one is not sufficient to compensate you for what you would be forced to give up. I would like a deep-sea fishing boat very much. I do not own one because I value what I would have to give up even more.

The fundamental analytical tool is the concept of *marginal analysis.* Marginal means "a small change in." For someone to choose more of one good and less of some others, the marginal gain must outweigh the marginal loss from giving up the other goods. In economics we are concerned with small changes rather than all-or-nothing decisions. Consumers start at a particular plan of consumption then make changes in order to reach more preferred levels.

This is our basic theory. Consumers are constrained or restricted by limited incomes and the prices that must be paid for the goods. They attempt to reach the most preferred level of consumption possible, given these constraints. Once they attain this level they cannot become better off by giving up some goods in order to get others.

EXERCISE

Studying for examinations

Let us examine a problem that you probably have faced and solved, in order to show how marginal analysis is used. Imagine a college student cramming for final examinations. Only six hours of study time remain and the goal is to get as high an average grade as possible in three subjects: economics, mathematics, and statistics (that is, the goal is to maximize the sum of the test scores in the three subjects). The fixed constraint is the remaining time; the goal is to maximize the scores. The student must decide how to allocate the limited time among the subjects.

According to the best estimates he can make, his grade in each subject will depend upon the time allocated to it according to the following schedule:

Economics		Mathematics		Statistics	
Hours of study	Grade	Hours of study	Grade	Hours of study	Grade
0........	20	0........	40	0........	80
1........	45	1........	52	1........	90
2........	65	2........	62	2........	95
3........	75	3........	71	3........	97
4........	83	4........	78	4........	98
5........	90	5........	83	5........	99
6........	92	6........	86	6........	99

What should be his allocation? One method of solving the problem is to add the estimated grades from all possible combinations of study time. We see for example, that if the student allocates three hours to economics, two to mathematics, and one to statistics, his expected total grade is 227 or an average of 75⅔. By experiment we see also that this grade is higher than any other grade that can be obtained from six hours of study.

Sampling every possible combination of study times can be very complicated. There is a simpler method. First note that the student can obtain grades of 20, 40, and 80 in the three subjects without any study time. Let us now prepare a table showing the *additional* grade points per additional hour spent on each subject. Recall that this is called the *marginal* return or *marginal* increase.

Now the student can allocate by maximizing the marginal increase from each successive hour of studying up to six. He will allocate the first and the second hours to economics; the return there is highest,

25 and 20 points respectively. The highest return for the third hour is the 12 points he can add by studying mathematics. Each of the remaining three hours are worth 10 points in each of the three areas. As before, we obtain the same allocation, three hours in economics, two in mathematics, and one in statistics.

The third method is to allocate time until the ratio of the marginal increases in grade for each pair of subjects equals the ratio of the prices. The price of studying one subject an additional hour is *one hour;* the price ratio is accordingly unity between any two subjects. The allocation of time at which the ratios of all marginal increases are unity is where each marginal increase is ten, the same solution as above. This last method of allocation is probably not at all intuitively obvious to you now. The formal theory must be developed before this approach becomes clear.

3.1.b Important points developed

The basic concepts developed in Chapter 3 are:

1. What determines the amount of any good a consumer chooses to consume.
2. The fundamentals of indifference curves, indifference maps, and budget lines.
3. Why a consumer may choose to purchase none of some good.
4. The consequences of a change in the constraints.

3.2 BASIC ASSUMPTIONS

As is the case for any theory, the theory of consumer behavior makes some simplifying assumptions in order to go directly to the fundamental determinants of behavior. These assumptions allow us to abstract away from less important aspects of the decision process.

First, we assume that each consumer has complete information on all matters pertaining to consumption decisions. A consumer knows both the full range of goods available in the market and the technical capacity of each good to satisfy a want. Furthermore, the exact price of each good is known, and the consumer knows these prices will not be changed by his or her actions in the market. Finally, the consumer knows what his or her income will be during the planning period. Given all this information, we also assume that each consumer tries to maximize satisfaction from consumption *given* the limited income.

Admittedly these assumptions are abstractions from reality. Consumers have only a fairly accurate notion of what income will be for a reasonable planning period, not perfect knowledge. They only have a notion of the capacity of a good to satisfy a want, not precise knowledge of its capacity to satisfy. No consumer actually succeeds in the task of spending the limited income so as to maximize satisfaction. This failure is attributable to the lack of accurate information. Yet the more or less conscious effort to attain maximum satisfaction from a limited income determines an individual's demand for goods and services. The assumption of complete information does not distort the relevant aspects of the economic world.

Second, we assume that each consumer is able to rank all conceivable bundles of commodities. That is, when confronted with two or more bundles of goods, a consumer is able to determine the order of preference among them. For example, assume that a person is confronted with two choices: (a) five candy bars, six pints of ice cream, and one soft drink; or (b) four candy bars, five pints of ice cream, and three soft drinks. The person can say one of three things; (a) I prefer the first bundle to the second; (b) I prefer the second to the first; or (c) I would be equally satisfied with either.

Therefore, when evaluating two bundles of goods, an individual either prefers one bundle of goods to the other or is indifferent between the two. Since we will use the concept of preference and indifference frequently, it is essential to understand this concept thoroughly now. If a consumer prefers one group of goods to another group, he or she obviously believes a higher level of satisfaction will be gained from the preferred group. The less preferred bundle would, in the opinion of the consumer, give less utility than the other. If a person is indifferent between two bundles, he or she would be perfectly willing to let someone else (or perhaps the flip of a coin) determine the choice. An economist would say that in the consumer's mind either bundle would yield the same level of utility.

Much of what follows is based upon the consumer's ability to rank groups of commodities; it is important, however, to note what we *did not say* about consumer preference and indifference.

First, we did not say that the consumer estimates *how much* utility or *what level* of satisfaction will be attained from consuming a given bundle of goods. Only the ability to *rank* is fundamental; the ability to measure utility is not necessary.

Second, we did not imply that an individual can say by *how much* one bundle of goods is preferred to another. Admittedly, a consumer might be able to say one group of goods is desired a great deal more than another group, and perhaps just a little more than still another group. But "great deal" and "just a little" are imprecise; their meanings differ from one person to another. Therefore, at this level of abstraction the theory of consumer behavior is not based upon the assumption that the consumer is able to state the amount by which one bundle is preferred to another.[1]

Third, we did not say *we think the consumer should* choose one bundle over the other, or that we believe he will be better off if he did so. It is only necessary that the consumer be able to rank bundles according to the order of expected satisfaction.

Furthermore, we assume that the consumer's preference pattern possesses the following characteristics:

a. Given three bundles of goods (*A, B,* and *C*), if an individual prefers *A* to *B* and *B* to *C,* he must prefer *A* to *C.* Similarly, if an individual is indifferent between *A* and *B* and between *B* and *C,* he must be indifferent between *A* and *C.* Finally, if he is indifferent between *A* and *B* and prefers *B* to *C,* he must prefer *A* to *C.* This assumption obviously can be carried over to four or more different bundles.

b. It therefore follows that if an individual can rank *any pair* of bundles chosen at random from all conceivable bundles, he can rank *all conceivable bundles.*

c. If bundle *A* contains at least as many units of *each commodity* as bundle *B,* and more units of at least one commodity, *A* must be preferred to *B.*

Note, we did not say that if a real-world consumer *purchases* one good rather than another he prefers the chosen good. If you drive a Ford rather than a Rolls Royce, we cannot infer that you prefer a Ford to a Rolls. If the Rolls cost less than the Ford at the time of purchase, and you were aware of this, then we could make this inference. If, as was probably the case, the Rolls costs more, we can say nothing. If the two goods are presented at equal cost, and you choose one over the other we could say that you prefer that good. Or if two goods are priced differently and you choose the higher priced good, we could again deduce that you prefer that good. But if you choose the lower priced good, we could say nothing.

---

[1] It is not quite correct to say that it is impossible to measure the degree of preference. Advanced studies in price theory frequently deal to a greater or lesser extent with the application of probability theory to the problem of ranking bundles. Considerable controversy exists concerning the usefulness of that approach.

Summarizing, the assumptions necessary to analyze consumer behavior can be set out in the following condensed form:

Assumptions. (*a*) Each consumer has exact and full knowledge of all information relevant to consumption decisions—knowledge of the goods and services available and of their technical capacity to satisfy his wants, of market prices, and of his money income.

(*b*) Each consumer has a preference pattern that (*i*) establishes a rank ordering among all bundles of goods; (*ii*) in comparison of pairs of bundles either indicates that A is preferred to *B,* or *B* preferred to *A,* or they are indifferent; (*iii*) in three- (or more) way comparisons, if *A* is preferred (indifferent) to *B* and *B* is preferred (indifferent) to *C,* *A* must be preferred (indifferent) to *C;* (*iv*) a greater bundle (in the sense of having at least as much of each good and more of at least one) is always preferred to a smaller one.

ASIDE

Historical development of the theory

To put things into perspective we should note that the modern theory of consumer behavior went through a very long and changing period of development. While the process of development was a very long and involved one, our discussion of it will be quite brief; only the most important steps are mentioned.

The earliest psychological approaches to the theory of demand were based upon the notion of subjective utility, as found in the works of Herman Gossen (1854), William S. Jevons (1871), and Leon Walras (1874). Just as modern theorists do, they assumed that any good or service consumed by a household provides utility. In contrast to most modern theorists, however, they also assumed that utility is cardinally measurable and additive and that the utility derived from one good is independent of the rate of consumption of any other good. We must digress briefly for a definition:

Definition. Cardinal measurability implies that the *difference* between two numbers is itself numerically significant. For example, apples are cardinally measurable; and one may say that four apples are exactly twice as many as two apples. A measurement system is said to be *ordinal* if items can only be ranked as 1st, 2nd, 3rd, and so on. Note: Numerical significance cannot be attached to the difference between 1st and 2nd, 2nd and 3rd, and so on. Each measurement system ranks items. The difference is that in an ordinal system, one can say (for example) that x is greater than y; in a cardinal system, one can say by how much x exceeds y.

Now to return to our historical train of thought. The more of one good consumed, the greater the total utility associated with it. Each *additional* unit of the good consumed per unit of time adds to total utility, but each adds less than the previous unit. For example, one piece of candy per day might yield a measurable five units of utility. Two pieces per day might yield 9 units of utility; 3 pieces, 11 units; and so on. That is, the second piece of candy adds four units of utility, one less than the first. The third adds two units to the total, two less than the second. Since utility was assumed to be cardinally measurable and additive by these theorists, and since the consumption of one good was assumed to have no effect upon the utility derived from another, a person's total utility is simply the sum of the utilities provided by all the goods consumed.

Later economists, such as F. Y. Edgeworth (1881), G. B. Antonelli (1886), and Irving Fisher (1892), objected to the additivity assumption. Instead, they assumed that while utility is cardinally measurable, it is not simply the sum of the independent utilities obtained from the consumption of each good. These theorists related the level of total utility to the rates of consumption of all goods simultaneously. In terms of the previous example, the extra or *marginal utility* added by each additional piece of candy depends, among other things, upon the amount of ice cream consumed. Likewise, the extra or marginal utility added by each additional serving of ice cream depends, among other things, upon the amount of pie consumed. Nonetheless, this newer form of the theory rests upon the assumption of *cardinally* measurable utility.

Implicit in the paragraph above is an important definition:

Definition. Marginal utility is the addition to total utility attributable to the addition of one unit of a good to the current rate of its consumption. According to the paragraph above, the marginal utility of good X depends not only upon its rate of consumption but upon the rates of consumption of other goods as well.

The last major step in the development of modern utility theory enabled economists to use the concept of utility without resorting to the assumption of cardinal measurability. This final step, which is essentially attributable to Vilfredo Pareto (1906), led to the use of *in-*

difference curves in analyzing consumer behavior. Since we have covered the basic assumptions behind indifference curves, we can now turn to this crucial concept.

3.3 INDIFFERENCE CURVES

Using the assumptions set forth above, we can now analyze two concepts that are fundamental to the theory of consumer behavior: indifference curves and indifference maps.

Definition. An indifference curve is a locus of points—or particular bundles or combinations of goods—each of which yields the same level of total utility or satisfaction.

Definition. An indifference map is a graph that shows a set of indifference curves.

For analytical purposes let us consider a consumer who can use only two different goods, X and Y, each of which is continuously divisible or infinitesimally variable in quantity.[2] Figure 3.3.1 shows a portion of this consumer's indifference map consisting of four indifference curves labeled I–IV. Our consumer considers all combinations of X and Y on indifference curve I to be equivalent (for example, 20 X and 42 Y, and 60 X and 10 Y); that is, he believes these combinations will yield the same satisfaction and thus is indifferent among them. Since he is indifferent between the two specified combinations, he is obviously willing to substitute X for Y in order to move from point a to point b. In other words, he is willing to give up 32 units of Y to obtain 40 additional units of X. Conversely, if he is presently situated at b he is willing to forego 40 units of X to obtain an additional 32 units of Y. Thus he is willing to substitute at the *average* rate of ⅘ units of Y per unit of X.

All combinations of goods on indifference curve II (say 30 Y and

---

[2] Admittedly, the possibility of continuous variation in quantity *is* perhaps less frequently encountered than "lumpiness," but this assumption permits a great gain in analytical precision at the sacrifice of very little realism. The assumption that bundles consist of no more than two separate goods enables us to analyze the problem of consumer behavior with two-dimensonal graphs. This assumption is made, therefore, purely for simplicity of exposition. With the use of the differential calculus, bundles of any number of different goods can be handled. But the analytical results based on two goods are exactly the same as those based upon more than two. Here again, the gain in simplicity outweighs the loss of realism.

FIGURE 3.3.1

INDIFFERENCE CURVES

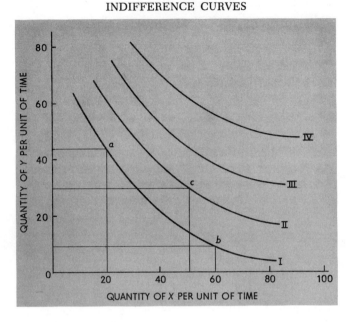

QUANTITY OF X PER UNIT OF TIME

50 X) are superior to *any* combinations of goods on I. Likewise, all combinations on III are superior to any combination on II. Each indifference curve that lies above a given indifference curve represents combinations of X and Y that are considered superior to, or capable of yielding more utility than, every combination on the lower curve. At every utility level designated by a particular indifference curve, the consumer is willing to substitute X for Y or Y for X at some rate so as to be on the same curve (that is, with the same satisfaction or utility level) but consuming different combinations of goods.

Since X and Y are assumed to be continuously divisible, each indifference curve specifies an infinite number of combinations that yield the same amount of satisfaction. Further, it is important to note that the specific utility numbers attached to I, II, III, and IV are immaterial. The numbers might be 5, 7, 12, 32 or 96, 327, 450, 624 or any other set of numbers that *increase*. For the theory of consumer behavior, only the shape of the indifference curves matters. That is to say, only the ordinal ranking of commodity bundles is important. Since a precise measurement of utility is unnecessary, the theory of consumer behavior does not have to be based on the questionable concept of measurable utility. The indifference curves and the concept of preference are all that are required

—all bundles of goods situated on the same indifference curve are equivalent; all combinations lying on a higher curve are preferred.

Relations. A consumer regards all bundles yielding the same level of utility as equivalent. The locus of such bundles is called an indifference curve because the consumer is indifferent as to the particular bundle consumed. The higher, or further to the right, an indifference curve, the greater is the underlying level of utility. Therefore, the higher the indifference curve, the more preferred is each bundle situated on the curve.

3.4 CHARACTERISTICS OF INDIFFERENCE CURVES

Indifference curves have four characteristics that are important in our discussion of consumer behavior. The first and fourth properties are assumed ones; the second is based upon our assumptions about consumer behavior; the third is a logical necessity.

For simplicity, assume once more that there are only two continuously divisible goods, X and Y. The X–Y plane is called *commodity space*. The first property is that each point in commodity space lies on one, and only one, indifference curve. This assumption is, of course, derived from the prior assumption that X and Y are continuously divisible. Each point in commodity space represents some specific combination of the two goods and hence some level of utility. As mentioned above, it is possible to take away Y and add X or take away X and add Y in an infinite number of ways and leave the consumer with the same level of satisfaction. Thus each point in commodity space lies on an indifference curve (and from the third property, each lies on only one indifference curve). However, for obvious reasons, when graphing an indifference map, only a relatively few curves are used to represent the entire map. But remember, an infinite number of indifference curves lie between any two indifference curves that are drawn.

Second, indifference curves are negatively sloped. This property is based on the assumption that a consumer prefers a greater bundle of goods to a smaller one. An upward sloping indifference curve would indicate that a consumer is indifferent between two combinations of goods, one of which contains more of *both* goods. The fact that a positive amount of one good must be added to the bundle to offset the loss of another good (if the consumer is to remain at the same level of satisfaction) implies negatively sloped indifference curves.

FIGURE 3.4.1

INDIFFERENCE CURVES CANNOT INTERSECT

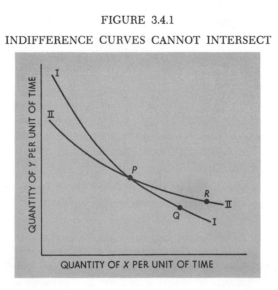

Third, indifference curves cannot intersect. This property is a logical necessity, as illustrated in Figure 3.4.1. In this graph I and II are indifference curves, and the points P, Q, and R represent three different bundles (or combinations of X and Y). R must clearly be preferred to Q because it contains more of both goods. R and P are equivalent because they are situated on the same indifference curve. In like manner, the consumer is indifferent between P and Q. Indifference is a "transitive" relation—that is, if a consumer is indifferent between A and B and between B and C, he must be indifferent between A and C. In our case, R and P are equivalent, as are P and Q. Hence R must be equivalent to Q. But as previously mentioned, R is preferred to Q because it contains more of both goods. Hence intersecting indifference curves, such as those shown in Figure 3.4.1, are logically impossible.

The fourth property is that indifference curves are *concave from above* —that is, an indifference curve must lie above its tangent at each point, as illustrated in Figure 3.4.2. The consequences of this property are discussed in the next section dealing with the marginal rate of substitution.

The results of this section may be summarized in the following:

Relations. Indifference curves have the following properties: (*a*) some indifference curve passes through each point in commodity space; (*b*) indifference curves slope downward to the right; (*c*) indif-

FIGURE 3.4.2

INDIFFERENCE CURVES ARE CONCAVE FROM ABOVE

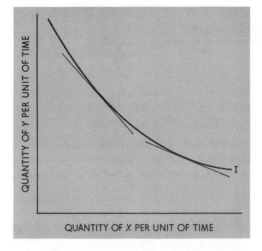

QUANTITY OF X PER UNIT OF TIME

ference curves cannot intersect; and (d) indifference curves are concave from above.

3.5 MARGINAL RATE OF SUBSTITUTION

As previously emphasized, one essential feature of subjective value
theory is that different combinations of commodities can give rise to
the same level of utility. In other words, the consumer is indifferent as
to the particular combination obtained. Therefore, as market prices might
dictate, one commodity can be substituted for another in the right amount
so that the consumer remains just as well off as before. He or she will, in
other words, remain on the same indifference curve. It is of considerable
interest to know the rate at which a consumer is willing to substitute one
commodity for another in consumption.

The reason for analyzing this rate of substitution so carefully lies in
the concept of utility maximization. As we shall see later in this chapter,
a consumer attains maximum satisfaction from a limited money income
when choosing a combination of goods such that the rate at which he
or she is *willing* to substitute goods is the same as the rate at which
market prices *permit* substitution. Therefore, to understand utility maximization one must understand the rate of substitution in consumption.

3.5.a Substitution in consumption

Consider Figure 3.5.1. An indifference curve is represented by I. The consumer is indifferent between bundle R, containing 4 units of X and 18 of Y, and bundle P, containing 11 units of X and 8 of Y. The consumer is willing to substitute 7 units of X for 10 of Y. The *rate* at which the consumer is willing, on average, to substitute X for Y is therefore

$$\frac{\triangle Y}{\triangle X} = \frac{RS}{SP} = \frac{18-8}{4-11} = -\frac{10}{7},$$

where $\triangle$ means "the change in." This ratio measures the average number of units of Y the consumer is willing to forego in order to obtain one additional unit of X (over the range of consumption pairs under consideration).[3] Thus the consumer is willing to give up 1⅗ units of Y in order to gain one more unit of X. Stated alternatively, the ratio measures the amount of Y that must be sacrificed (1⅗ units) per unit of X gained if the consumer is to remain at precisely the same level of satisfaction.

In our subsequent use, we would find it very cumbersome to have the

FIGURE 3.5.1

THE MARGINAL RATE OF SUBSTITUTION

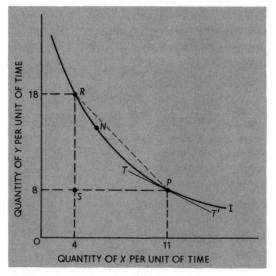

QUANTITY OF X PER UNIT OF TIME

------

[3] The ratio is, of course, negative since the change in Y associated with an increase in X is negative. This type of relation results directly from the postulate of negatively sloped indifference curves.

minus sign on the right-hand side of the equation above. Thus we define the rate of substitution as

$$-\frac{\Delta Y}{\Delta X} = \frac{10}{7}.$$

The rate of substitution given by the ratio above is obviously the negative of the slope of the broken straight line joining points R and P. The ratio could be quite different between two alternative points, say N and P. But as the point R moves along I toward P, the ratio RS/SP approaches closer and closer to the slope of the tangent TT' at P. In the limit, for extremely small movements in the neighborhood of P, the negative of the slope of I, which is the negative of the slope of its tangent at P, is called the *marginal rate of substitution of X for Y*.

> **Definition.** The marginal rate of substitution of X for Y measures the number of units of Y that must be sacrificed per unit of X gained so as to maintain a constant level of satisfaction. The marginal rate of substitution is given by the negative of the slope of an indifference curve at a point. It is defined only for movements along an indifference curve, never for movements among curves.

> **Note:** Since we wish the marginal rate of substitution to be positive, and since $\Delta Y/\Delta X$ is necessarily negative, the *minus* sign must be attached.

As should be obvious, the term *marginal* is again used (as it always is) to denote *the change in* when the change in question is very small.

> **Note.** We shall hereafter use the letters *MRS* to denote the marginal rate of substitution of X for Y in consumption or, more generally, the marginal rate of substitution of the variable plotted on the horizontal axis for the variable plotted on the vertical axis.

3.5.b Diminishing *MRS*

The requirement that indifference curves be concave from above implies that the *MRS* of X for Y diminishes as X is substituted for Y along an indifference curve. This is illustrated in Figure 3.5.2.

I is an indifference curve; R, N, Q, and P are four bundles situated on this curve. Consider a movement from R to N. In order to maintain the same level of utility, the consumer is willing to sacrifice slightly more

FIGURE 3.5.2

DIMINISHING MARGINAL RATE OF SUBSTITUTION

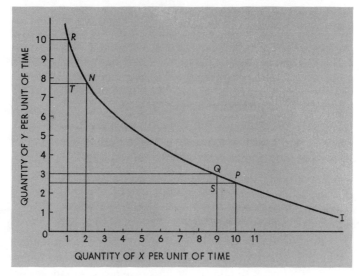

QUANTITY OF X PER UNIT OF TIME

than two units of Y to gain one unit of X. Now consider the consumer situated at Q. To move to P and gain one unit of X, the consumer now is willing to give up approximately ½ unit of Y.

This result follows logically from our assumptions that the more of a good one consumes, the more of that good he would probably be willing to trade for some other good. For example, if a person at a football game has ten hot dogs and one soft drink, he might be willing to trade three hot dogs for a soft drink. On the other hand, if the same person had only five hot dogs, but three soft drinks, he would perhaps be willing to trade only one hot dog for an additional soft drink.

Diminishing MRS is further illustrated in Figure 3.5.3. I is an indifference curve and P, Q, and R are three bundles situated on this curve. The horizontal axis is measured so that $OX_1 = X_1X_2 = X_2X_3$. Consider first the movement from P to Q. If P is very close to Q, or the amount X_1X_2 is very small, the MRS at Q is

$$\frac{OY_1 - OY_2}{OX_2 - OX_1} = \frac{Y_1Y_2}{X_1X_2}.$$

Similarly, for a movement from Q to R, the MRS at R is

$$\frac{OY_2 - OY_3}{OX_3 - OX_2} = \frac{Y_2Y_3}{X_2X_3}.$$

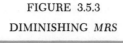

FIGURE 3.5.3

DIMINISHING *MRS*

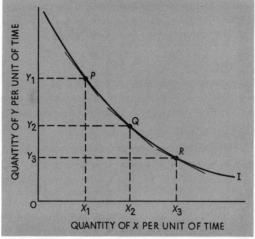

By construction $X_1X_2 = X_2X_3$; but very obviously $Y_1Y_2 > Y_2Y_3$. Hence the *MRS* is less at *R* than at *Q*. This is also shown by the absolutely decreasing slopes of the tangents at *P*, *Q*, and *R*.

3.5.c Marginal utility approach

Earlier approaches to the theory of consumer behavior, as noted above, used the concept of marginal utility. In fact, this approach is still frequently used by many theorists.

Marginal utility is based upon a concept called utility, defined as the satisfaction a person obtains from the goods and services consumed. Utility is, of course, a subjective phenomenon because each person's physiological and psychological makeup is different from every other person's.

Recall that the earliest economists who used the concept of utility assumed that utility was actually measurable and that one could assign actual numbers to the value of utility. They reasoned that the more of one good consumed, the greater the total utility associated with it. Each *additional* unit of the good consumed per unit of time adds to total utility, but each adds less than the previous unit.

Definition. Marginal utility is the addition to total utility that is attributable to the addition of one unit of a good to the current rate of its consumption. The marginal utility of good X depends not only upon its rate of consumption but upon the rates of consumption of other goods as well.

We can quite easily relate the concept of marginal utility to the marginal rate of substitution along an indifference curve. Note first that marginal utility can be either (a) the increase in utility attributable to a small increase in the rate of consumption of a commodity, holding the level of consumption of all other commodities constant; or (b) the decrease in utility attributable to a small decrease in the rate of consumption under the same assumption.

Assume now that utility (U) is measurable and depends upon the rate of consumption of two goods, X and Y. Next let the consumption of both X and Y change very slightly. We can represent the total change in utility resulting from the changes in X and Y as

$$\triangle U = [(MU \text{ of } X) \times \triangle X] + [(MU \text{ of } Y) \times \triangle Y].$$

For example, if X increases by 2 units, and the average marginal utility of each is 5, while Y increases by 3 units and the average marginal utility of each is 4, utility increases by 22 units $= (2 \times 5) + (3 \times 4)$. Or under the same marginal utility assumptions, if X increases by 4 units and Y decreases by 5 units, total utility remains constant; $(5 \times 4) + (4 \times -5) = 0$.

Since an indifference curve represents the locus of all combinations of X and Y among which the consumer is indifferent, utility must remain constant along any indifference curve. Thus, $\triangle U$ equals zero for any movement along an indifference curve. From the equation above, if for very small changes in X and Y, $\triangle U$ equals zero

$$\frac{MU_x}{MU_y} = -\left(\frac{\triangle Y}{\triangle X}\right),$$

where $(\triangle Y/\triangle X)$ is the slope of the indifference curve. Recall that the slope of an indifference curve is the marginal rate of substitution; thus we can interpret

$$MRS_{x \text{ for } y} = \frac{MU_x}{MU_y}.$$

A marginal utility interpretation of the previous hot dog–soft drink example might help. First, remember that we assume the marginal utility of any commodity is smaller the greater the rate of its consumption. Now picture a graph (or construct one for yourself) in which the number of hot dogs is plotted on the vertical axis, the number of soft drinks on the horizontal.

When the number of hot dogs is great, the marginal utility of hot dogs is relatively low. Similarly, when the number of soft drinks is low, their marginal utility is relatively high. Thus the MRS, which is the ratio of the marginal utility of soft drinks to that of hot dogs, is relatively high. Now let the football fan substitute soft drinks for hot dogs (X for Y, in the previous notation). Increasing the rate of consumption of soft drinks decreases their marginal utility, while reducing the rate of consumption of hot dogs increases theirs. Thus the substitution of soft drinks for hot dogs must lead to a decrease in the MRS of soft drinks for hot dogs.

3.5.d Summary

The concept of indifference curves is extremely important to the theory of consumer behavior and therefore to the theory of demand. Indifference curves show equally preferred combinations of goods. A higher curve designates more preferred levels of consumption. Indifference curves slope downward, reflecting the assumption that when the consumption of one good increases, the consumption of the other good must be decreased in order to keep the consumer indifferent between the two combinations.

The marginal rate of substitution is the rate at which one good is substituted for another good along an indifference curve. The MRS can be interpreted as the ratio of the marginal utilities of the two goods, marginal utility being the additional utility obtained from the consumption of an additional unit of the good. MRS diminishes as one moves downward along an indifference curve. This decrease in MRS reflects the assumption that as one has less of one good relative to a second good, the consumer is willing to give up less and less of that good in order to obtain an additional unit of the second good.

APPLICATION

Use of indifference curve theory

Although the theory of indifference curves is very useful in developing the theory of demand, measuring and plotting actual indifference curves for real people is extremely difficult. This is not to say that economists have not attempted such measurement. They have done so—with both people and animals—with varying levels of success. But the *actual measurement and graphing* of indifference curves are not really relevant methods of analysis for people who use economics in business, in government, or in other everyday decision making.

In fact, there is considerable controversy among economists at this time over the meaning of indifference curves for groups of consumers, such as an indifference curve for an entire community or state or nation. Some say such indifference curves have no meaning at all. Others say they have meaning only under very restrictive assumptions. Still others say that such community indifference curves are very useful tools of analysis under some circumstances.

Notwithstanding the tremendous difficulty of estimating indifference curves the *concept* of these curves is rather useful in decision making. A decision maker in a business must recognize that employees have subjective rates of trade-off between income and the package of working conditions. It is possible to obtain certain goals by trading off between the two types of employee benefits. For example, some of the recent Ph.D.'s in economics from our department have gone to work in business departments such as finance departments, while others have joined economics departments. The teaching load—number of classes to be taught—for young Ph.D.'s has been on average higher in business than in economics departments, but the total income earned has been somewhat lower in the economics departments. Thus there is a trade-off between the faculty working conditions and income; university officials recognize this. They also recognize that faculty are willing to trade some amenities such as preferred seating at football games and preferred parking facilities for income. All the results depend upon a comparison of utilities.

Any business must make its decisions about working conditions based on comparison of utilities. Governmental decision makers must attempt to balance utilities. Consumers of governmental products— constituents—do not want zero schools and perfect streets or perfect schools and no streets. Government officials must realize that there is a trade-off between the two that would be preferred. Even within a school system there is a trade between teaching and classroom facilities.

Finally, and perhaps most important, any student of economics must realize that all goods have some substitutes. There are very few goods—probably no goods—that you are now consuming that you would not give up some amount of in order to obtain other goods.

Don't say, I would not give up food because I would die. We did not say you would give up *all consumption* of a large group of goods. We only said that there is some group of other goods for which you would be willing to give up some amount of the food—or some type of food—you are now consuming. Any consumers will make trade-offs among goods.

In very few cases is it *essential* that someone consumes exactly the same amount of that good as is being consumed now. We can think of some examples, of course, mostly medical, such as a given amount of medicine without which the patient would die, or a weekly treatment on a kidney machine. But these absolute essentials are rare.

Therefore, do not make the mistake, unless you are trying to convert someone to your point of view, of making statements like, "It is essential that the school increase classroom space by 20 percent"; "the city must double its recreational area in 5 years." All of these "essentials" have some substitutes in the minds of consumers. The concept of the indifference curve allows us to analyze this concept of substitution. We shall return to a discussion of this below.

3.6 BUDGET LINES

Thus far in this chapter we have set forth a method to analyze what a consumer is willing to do or wishes to do. But, recall from Chapter 2 that demand indicates both what consumers are *willing* or wish to do and what they are *able* to do. We will now lay out a method to analyze what a consumer can do.

3.6.a Limited money income

If all consumers had an unlimited money income—in other words, if there were an unlimited pool of resources—there would be no problem of "economizing," nor would there be "economics." But since this utopian state does not exist, even for the richest members of our society, people are compelled to determine their behavior in light of limited financial resources. For the theory of consumer behavior, this means that each consumer has a maximum amount that can be spent per period of time. The consumer's problem is to spend this amount in the way that yields maximum satisfaction.

Continue to assume that there are only two goods, X and Y, bought in quantities x and y. Each individual consumer is confronted with market-determined prices p_x and p_y of X and Y respectively. Finally, the consumer in question has a known and fixed money income (M) for the period under consideration. M is the maximum amount the consumer can spend, and we assume that it is all spent on X and Y.[4] Thus the amount spent on X (xp_x) plus the amount spent on Y (yp_y) is equal to the stipulated money income. Algebraically,

$$M = xp_x + yp_y. \tag{3.6.1}$$

This equation can be expressed as the equation for a straight line. Solving for y—since y is generally plotted on the vertical axis—one obtains

$$y = \frac{M}{p_y} - \frac{p_x}{p_y}x. \tag{3.6.2.}$$

Equation (3.6.2) is plotted in Figure 3.6.1. The first term on the right-hand side of equation (3.6.2), $\dfrac{M}{p_y}$, shows the amount of Y that can be purchased if no X is purchased at all. This amount is represented by the distance OA in Figure 3.6.1; thus $\dfrac{M}{p_y}$ (or point A) is the ordinate intercept of the equation.

In equation $(3.6.2)$ $\left(-\dfrac{p_x}{p_y}\right)$ is the slope of the line. Consequently, the slope of the budget constraint is the negative of the price ratio. To see this, consider the quantity of X that can be purchased if Y is not bought. This amount is $\dfrac{M}{p_x}$, shown by the distance OB in Figure 3.6.1. Since the line obviously has a negative slope, its slope is given by

$$-\frac{OA}{OB} = -\frac{\dfrac{M}{p_y}}{\dfrac{M}{p_x}} = -\frac{p_x}{p_y}.$$

The line in Figure 3.6.1 is called the budget line.

---

[4] In more advanced models, saving may be considered as one of the many goods and services available to the consumer. Graphical treatment limits us to two dimensions; thus we ignore saving. This does not mean that the theory of consumer behavior precludes saving—depending upon preference ordering, a consumer may save much, little or nothing. Similarly, spending may in fact exceed income in any given period as a result of borrowing or from using assets acquired in the past. The M in question for any period is the total amount of money to be spent during the period.

FIGURE 3.6.1

BUDGET LINE

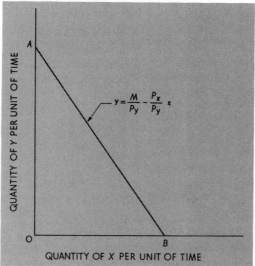

QUANTITY OF X PER UNIT OF TIME

Definition. The budget line is the locus of combinations or bundles of goods that can be purchased if the entire money income is spent. Its slope is the negative of the price ratio.

Note again our assumption that the consumer spends all income on X and Y. This implies that the bundle purchased must lie on the budget line.

3.6.b Shifting the budget line

In much of the analysis that follows, we are interested in changes in quantities purchased resulting from changes in price and money income, both of which are represented graphically by shifts in the budget line. Consider first the effect of a change in money income, the prices of the goods remaining constant.

Any given budget line represents the set of all possible consumption bundles for a consumer at a given set of relative prices and money income. If the consumer has an increase in money income at the original set of commodity prices, the set of possibilities must increase. Since the increase in money income allows the consumer to buy more goods, the budget line is pushed outward. Since the slope of the budget line is the ratio of prices, which does not change when money income changes, the slope of the line is the same. Thus an increase in money income causes an outward parallel shift in the budget line. Similarly a decrease in money income, the price ratio held constant, causes a parallel inward shift in the budget line. In Figure 3.6.2 budget line AB is associated with a lower income than budget line $A'B'$. Since the slopes of AB and $A'B'$ are equal, the price ratio remains constant as the change in money income shifts the budget line upward or downward.

Figure 3.6.3 shows what happens to the budget line when the price ratio changes, money income held constant. Assume that money income and the prices of X and Y are such that the relevant budget line is AB. The slope of the line is $-(p_x/p_y)$. Hold money income and the price of Y constant, then let the price of X increase. Since p_x increases, p_x/p_y increases also. Thus the budget line becomes steeper, in this case the line AB'. The intercept on the Y axis remains the same because M/P_y remains constant. In other words, if income and the price of Y remain constant, the consumer can purchase the same amount of Y by spending the entire income on Y regardless of the price of X. Thus we can see that an increase in the price of X rotates the budget line backward, the Y-intercept remaining fixed. Of course, a decrease in the price of X pivots the budget line outward, in Figure 3.6.3 from AB' to AB.

Alternatively and perhaps more directly the price change can be ex-

FIGURE 3.6.2

CHANGING MONEY INCOME

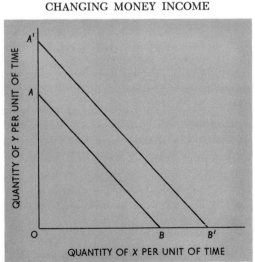

QUANTITY OF X PER UNIT OF TIME

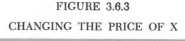

FIGURE 3.6.3

CHANGING THE PRICE OF X

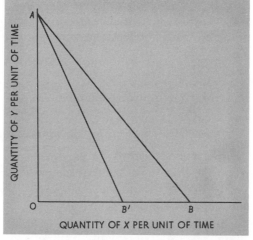

plained as follows. At the original price, P_x, the maximum purchase of X is M/P_x, or the distance OB. When the price rises to p^*, the maximum purchase of X is M/p^*, or the distance OB'. Thus an increase in the price of X is shown by pivoting the budget line clockwise around the ordinate intercept. A decrease in the price of X is represented by a counterclockwise rotation.

Relations. (a) An increase in money income, prices unchanged, is shown by a parallel shift of the budget line—outward and to the right for an increase in money income, and in the direction of the origin for a decrease. (b) A change in the price of X, the price of Y and money income constant, is shown by rotating the budget line around the ordinate intercept—to the left for a price increase, to the right for a decrease.

3.7 CONSUMER EQUILIBRIUM

All bundles of goods (combinations of X and Y) designated by the budget line are available to the consumer in the sense that his income allows him to purchase them if he wishes. This line is established by his fixed money income and the given prices of the commodities available. The consumer's indifference map shows his rank ordering of all conceivable bundles of X and Y. The principal assumption upon which the theory of consumer behavior is built is that *a consumer attempts to allocate his limited money income among available goods and services so as to maximize satisfaction or utility.* Given that assumption and the concepts developed in this chapter, it is a relatively simple matter to determine the way in which a consumer will allocate income; that is, select the most preferred bundle of goods available with the given level of income and prices.

3.7.a Maximizing satisfaction subject to a limited money income

Graphically we can visualize the consumer as being constrained by the fact that the money income permits consuming only bundles of goods along the budget line. The consumer chooses the particular bundle along the line that is on the highest attainable indifference curve. In this way the highest possible preference level is achieved.

The problem is depicted by Figure 3.7.1. The portion of the indifference map, represented by the four indifference curves drawn in that figure, indicates preferences among different combinations of goods. Similarly, the budget line, *LM*, specifies the different combinations the consumer can purchase with the limited income, assuming all income is spent on *X* and *Y*. Thus the choice of combinations is limited by the given income.

Clearly, the consumer cannot purchase any bundle lying above and to

FIGURE 3.7.1

CONSUMER EQUILIBRIUM

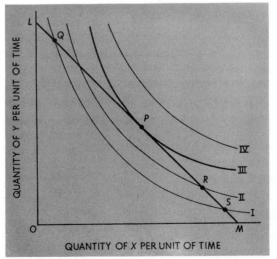

the right of budget line *LM*, and hence he cannot consume any combination lying on indifference curve IV. Some points on curves I, II, and III are attainable. Moreover, as already observed, an infinite number of indifference curves lie between curves I and III. Therefore, all points on the budget line between *Q* and *S* are touched by some indifference curve (and, if we extend the map to include curves below I, all points above *Q* and below *S* are touched by some curve). Thus each point on the budget line yields some specific level of utility. Four of the infinite number of attainable combinations on *LM* are represented by points *Q*, *P*, *R*, and *S*.

Suppose the consumption bundle is located at *Q*. Without experimenting, the consumer cannot know for certain whether *Q* represents a maximum position or not. Thus let him experimentally move to combinations just to the left and right of *Q*, along *LM*. Moving to the left lowers the level of satisfaction to some indifference curve below I. But moving to the right leads to a higher indifference curve; and continued experimentation will lead him to move at least as far as *P*, because each successive movement to the right brings the consumer to a higher indifference curve. If he continued to experiment, however, by moving to the right of *P*, the consumer would locate upon a lower indifference curve with its lower level of satisfaction. He would accordingly return to the point *P*.

Similarly, if a consumer were situated at *R*, experimentation would lead him to substitute *Y* for *X*, thereby moving in the direction of *P*. No point except *P* is optimal because each successive substitution of *Y* for *X* brings the consumer to a higher indifference curve. Hence the position of maximum satisfaction—*or the point of consumer equilibrium*—is attained at *P*, where an indifference curve is just tangent to the budget line.

As you will recall, the slope of the budget line is the negative of the price ratio, the ratio of the price of *X* to the price of *Y*. As you will also recall, the slope of an indifference curve at any point is called the *MRS* of *X* for *Y*. Hence the point of consumer equilibrium is defined by the condition that the *MRS* must equal the price ratio.

The interpretation of this proposition is very straightforward. The *MRS* shows the rate at which the consumer *is willing to substitute X* for *Y*. The price ratio shows the rate at which he *can substitute X* for *Y*. Unless these two are equal, it is possible to change the combination of *X* and *Y* purchased so as to attain a higher level of satisfaction. For example, suppose the *MRS* is two—meaning the consumer is willing to give up two units of *Y* in order to obtain one unit of *X*. Let the price ratio be unity, meaning that one unit of *Y* can be exchanged for one unit of *X*.

Clearly, the consumer will benefit by trading Y for X, since he is willing to give up two Y for one X but only has to give up one Y for one X in the market. Generalizing, unless the MRS and the price ratio are equal, some exchange can be made so as to move the consumer to a higher level of satisfaction.

> **Principle.** The point of consumer equilibrium—or the maximization of satisfaction subject to a limited money income—is defined by the condition that the MRS of X for Y must equal the ratio of the price of X to the price of Y.

3.7.b Marginal utility interpretation of equilibrium

Recall that at the beginning of this chapter we gave a rather simplified intuitive explanation of consumer equilibrium. We argued that if a consumer could give up some good and gain more satisfaction from purchasing other goods with the amount saved than would be lost because of the amount given up, such substitution would occur. We can set forth this explanation a bit more formally now using the marginal utility interpretation of indifference curves.

Recall from section 3.5 that along an indifference curve

$$MRS_{x \text{ for } y} = \frac{MU_x}{MU_y}.$$

Writing the condition for consumer equilibrium symbolically,

$$MRS_{x \text{ for } y} = \frac{p_x}{p_y}.$$

Thus in equilibrium

$$\frac{MU_x}{MU_y} = \frac{p_x}{p_y},$$

or

$$\frac{MU_x}{p_x} = \frac{MU_y}{p_y}.$$

The relation just above provides an alternative view of the condition for consumer equilibrium. Dividing the marginal utility of a commodity by its price gives the marginal utility per dollar's worth of the commodity bought. In this light we can restate the condition for consumer equilibrium as the following:

Principle. To attain equilibrium, a consumer must allocate money income so that the marginal utility per dollar spent on each commodity is the same for all commodities purchased.

This principle is certainly plausible; and explaining why it is plausible illustrates a method of analysis that is used pervasively in economic theory. Suppose at the current allocation of income, the marginal dollar spent on X yields a greater marginal utility than the marginal dollar spent on Y. That is, suppose

$$\frac{MU_x}{p_x} > \frac{MU_y}{p_y}.$$

Reallocating one dollar of expenditure from Y to X will therefore increase total utility; and it must do so until the marginal utility per dollar's worth is the same for both commodities.

Alternatively, if

$$\frac{MU_x}{p_x} < \frac{MU_y}{p_y},$$

a dollar taken away from X will reduce utility less than the increase in utility obtained from spending the dollar on additional consumption of Y. The consumer will continue to substitute away from X toward Y until the marginal utilities per dollar expenditure are equal. Thus our intuitive definition is theoretically sound.

3.7.c Zero consumption of a good

To this point the discussion has implied that the consumer chooses to consume some positive amount of both X and Y, regardless of relative prices. This circumstance obviously need not be the case. A consumer might choose to spend the entire income and purchase none of some specific good. Recall that in the introduction to this chapter we gave an intuitive explanation of the circumstances under which a consumer would purchase none of some good.

One set of theoretical circumstances under which a consumer would choose to spend the entire income on (say) good Y and none on X is depicted in Figure 3.7.2. Given the budget line LM and the indifference map represented by curves I, II, III, and IV, the highest level of satisfaction attainable from the given money income is at point L on indifference curve III. The consumer chooses to purchase OL units of Y and no X.

FIGURE 3.7.2

CORNER SOLUTION

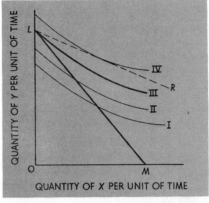

This point need not be a point of tangency at which the *MRS* equals the price ratio (although it could be such a point). Note that an equilibrium situation exists even though there is no point (at both nonnegative *X* and nonnegative *Y*) where the *MRS* equals the price ratio. Economists call such a situation a *corner solution*. Note also, however, that for a sufficiently large decrease in the price of *X* relative to the price of *Y* (say to a price ratio depicted by budget line *LR*), the budget line could become tangent to some indifference curve above III (curve IV) at a point where both *X* and *Y* are bought. Hence the consumer will purchase some positive amount of *X* if its relative price decreases sufficiently.

In other words a corner solution, in which the consumer purchases none of some good *X*, results when

$$\frac{MU_x}{p_x} < \frac{MU_i}{p_i} = \cdots = \frac{MU_j}{p_j}$$

for all goods *i, j,* etc. where the *i*th and *j*th goods are purchased in finite amounts. The consumer spends all of his income, yet the marginal utility per dollar of *X* is less than the marginal utility per dollar spent on any other good that is purchased. This is generally what we mean when we say that "we cannot afford something." Perhaps you do not own a Cadillac. You say you cannot afford one. Conceivably you could buy one (perhaps by borrowing). So if you do not own one it must be that the alternative expenditure on goods that you consume gives more utility *per dollar* than would a Cadillac, even though a Cadillac would give *more* total utility than your present automobile. Stated differently, one does not consume some good X when the $MRS_{x \, for \, y}$ (where Y is any other good that is consumed) is less than the price ratio, p_x/p_y, and total income is exhausted.

APPLICATION

Economics of philanthropy

It would be a serious mistake if you have acquired the impression, as many people have, that economic theory necessarily assumes humans are coldly calculating individuals concerned only with their personal well-being and therefore are totally uninterested in the welfare of others. This is by no means the case. In fact, we can use the simple analytical techniques developed in this chapter to examine the causes of charitable contributions.*

Begin by assuming that an individual's utility depends upon both the amount of his own consumption and the level of consumption enjoyed by other people. Let us assume, for simplicity, only two individuals, A and B. A's utility is a function of his own consumption and of B's. Assume also that it is costless for A to transfer income to B. We need not worry *why* A's utility depends partly upon B's consumption, our only interest is that it does.

Equilibrium for A is depicted by Figure 3.7.3. Indifference curve I_A is one of the family of A's indifference curves between A's own consumption and B's consumption, where B's consumption is measured along the vertical axis and A's along the horizontal. This curve is drawn to reflect A's diminishing marginal rate of substitution between his consumption and B's in the neighborhood of N. That is, around N, the smaller A's consumption becomes relative to B's, the less consumption A is willing to give up to B and remain at the same level of utility.

The budget line of A is R_bR_a. The distance $OR_b = OR_a$ is the sum of A's and B's income. This is the amount that they both could consume together. Since we assume that transfers are costless, the slope of R_bR_a is unity; that is, a dollar of income transferred from A to B costs A one dollar. Assume that initially A's income is OY_1. Thus B's income is Y_1R_a. A can reach a higher level of utility by transfer-

---

* The remainder of this application is based upon the article by Robert A. Schwartz "Personal Philanthropic Contributions," *Journal of Political Economy*, November/December 1970, pp. 1264–91.

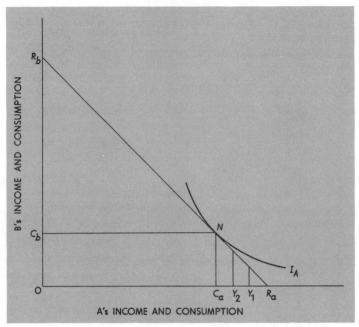

FIGURE 3.7.3

PHILANTHROPY

ring C_aY_1 to B, attaining equilibrium at point N. B now consumes OC_b and A consumes OC_a. If A's initial income were less, say OY_2, and B's were larger, A would now transfer less income to B in order to arrive at N, the point of A's highest utility level. Thus the theory is quite applicable to philanthropy.

EXERCISE

Economics of bribery

There is a large amount of literature in economics devoted to the study of externalities. An externality in consumption exists when one individual's consumption affects another individual's utility. We have just analyzed a case in which someone receives utility from increasing another person's consumption. Let us turn now to the opposite situation in which one individual's consumption of a *particular good decreases* another individual's utility.

Use the tools developed thus far to analyze graphically the following situation. You live next door to someone whose hobby is playing

FIGURE 3.7.4

BRIBERY

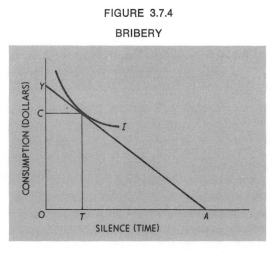

the drums. You hate the sound of drums, but this person plays them every evening. The only way to stop the drum playing is to pay your neighbor by the minute not to play the drums. There is a fixed fee per minute of silence. Show the situation graphically.

The result is depicted in Figure 3.7.4. Your total income is *OY,* and *OA* is the total amount of silence you could obtain by spending all of your income on bribery. Budget line *YA* shows the rate at which the neighbor must be bribed per minute of silence. The indifference map shows the rate at which you are willing to trade consumption for silence. The highest curve attainable is *I.* Therefore, in equilibrium you consume *OC* and pay the remainder *CY* to obtain a total amount of silence *OT.*

Clearly, this is a rather farfetched example. But economists do use similar methods to analyze the implications of externalities such as air and water pollution. One method of reducing pollution is bribing the pollutor not to pollute.

3.8 ECONOMICS OF EXCHANGE

Now we are in a position to analyze how and why markets come into existence. Markets exist because people can benefit from trade. Otherwise there would be no markets and no exchange. In fact the study of trade and exchange, and hence the study of markets, is one of the primary concerns of economists.

3.8.a Why trade takes place

To summarize the entire theory of trade, exchange takes place when individuals have different marginal rates of substitution between goods. Let us consider the following example. You and I consume only two goods, an endowment of which we each receive every week. These goods are hamburgers and milkshakes. Given my preferences and initial endowment, my marginal rate of substitution is three hamburgers for eight milkshakes. That is, I would be willing to exchange three hamburgers for eight milkshakes or eight milkshakes for three hamburgers and remain indifferent. Your *MRS* is three hamburgers for six milkshakes. Thus you would be willing to trade at the ratio of three to six.

Both of us can benefit from trade. I am willing to give up eight milkshakes to gain three hamburgers. You require only six milkshakes to induce you to give up three hamburgers. Trade could benefit us both if we trade at some rate between eight to three, my *MRS,* and six to three, your *MRS.*

Suppose we settle that I give up seven hamburgers to you in exchange for three of your milkshakes. I give up fewer hamburgers than the maximum number I would have been willing to trade in order to gain three added milkshakes. You gain one more hamburger than you would have been willing to accept for the three milkshakes. We both make deals better than we would have been willing to make, and are therefore better off than before trade.

Or, put more realistically in money terms, McDonald's is willing to exchange hamburgers of a particular type for $1.25 each. If you are willing to trade more than $1.25 for a McDonald hamburger, both you and McDonald's are made better off by the trade of $1.25 for one hamburger. The same analysis can be applied to any other type of exchange. Thus markets occur when individuals' marginal rates of substitution are not equal. In fact this is a major proposition in economics.

> **Proposition.** If two individuals have differing marginal rates of substitution, both can be made better off in the sense of attaining a more preferred level of consumption by exchange.

3.8.b Edgeworth box diagram

Economists frequently use a graphical method to analyze the above proposition. A certain amount of insight into the benefits of exchange can be gained from this graphical exposition.

Assume only two people and only two goods. Each person has an *initial endowment* of each good, but each does not necessarily have the goods in the proportion that yields greatest satisfaction. To analyze exchange, we need to develop a graphical device known as the Edgeworth box diagram, named for F. Y. Edgeworth, a famous British economist of the late 19th century.[5]

First consider Figure 3.8.1. There are two consumption goods, X and Y; these goods are available in absolutely fixed amounts. In addition, there are only two individuals in the society, A and B; they initially possess an endowment of X and Y, but the endowment ratio is not the one either would choose if allowed to specify it. This problem is graphically illustrated by constructing an *origin* for A, labeled O_A, and plotting quantities of the two goods along the abscissa and ordinate. Thus, from

FIGURE 3.8.1

CONSTRUCTING THE EDGEWORTH BOX DIAGRAM

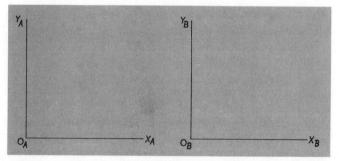

Panel A

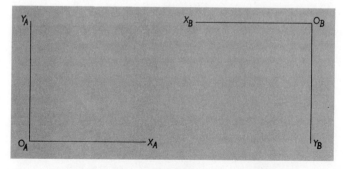

Panel B

---

[5] It has been pointed out to me by a reader of the manuscript, Professor Rodney Mabry of Clemson University, that Edgeworth had nothing to do with the development of the Edgeworth box diagram; the true originator was V. Pareto. Not being an historian of thought, I gratefully acknowledge this but yield to convention in naming the diagram.

the origin O_A, the quantity of X held by $A(X_A)$ is plotted on the horizontal axis and the quantity of $Y(Y_A)$ on the vertical axis. A similar graph for B, with origin O_B, may be constructed beside the graph for A. These two basic graphs are illustrated in panel A, Figure 3.8.1.

Next, rotate the B-graph 180 degrees to the left, so that it is actually "upside down" when viewed normally, as shown in panel B. The Edgeworth box diagram is formed by bringing the two graphs together. There could conceivably be a problem involving the lengths of the axes; if the X axes meshed, the Y axes might not. The problem does not in fact exist, however, because of our assumption concerning fixed availabilities of X and Y. $X_A + X_B$ must equal X, and $Y_A + Y_B$ must equal Y. The length of each axis measures the fixed quantity of the good it represents; when the two "halves" in panel B are brought together, both axes mesh. One thus obtains Figure 3.8.2.

The point D in Figure 3.8.2 indicates the initial endowment of X and Y possessed by A and B. A begins with $O_A x_A$ units of X and $O_A y_A$ units of Y. Since the aggregates are fixed, B must originally hold $O_B x_B = X - O_A x_A$ units of X and $O_B y_B = Y - O_A y_A$ units of Y.

3.8.c Equilibrium of exchange

As a first step toward equilibrium analysis, consider an economy in which exchange of goods takes place. If you like, you may think of the problem in the following context. There exists a small country with only

FIGURE 3.8.2

EDGEWORTH BOX DIAGRAM

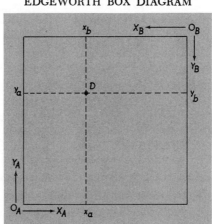

two inhabitants, A and B, each of whom owns one half the land area. A and B produce nothing; they merely gather goods of types X and Y that fall nightly. Each gathers only the goods that fall on his land; but the two types do not fall uniformly. There is a relatively heavy concentration of Y on A's property and, consequently, a relatively heavy concentration of X on B's land.

The problem of exchange is analyzed by means of the Edgeworth box diagram in Figure 3.8.3. To the basic box diagram, the dimensions of which represent the nightly scattering of goods, we add indifference curves for A and B. For example, the curve I_A shows combinations of X and Y that yield A the same level of satisfaction. In ordinary fashion, II_A represents a greater level of satisfaction than I_A; III_A than II_A; and so on. Quite generally, A's well-being is enhanced by moving toward the B origin; B, in turn, enjoys greater satisfaction the closer he moves toward the A origin.

Suppose the initial endowment (the nightly fall of goods) is given by point D; A has $O_A x_A$ units of X and $O_A y_A$ units of Y. Similarly, B has $O_B x_B$ and $O_B y_B$ units of X and Y respectively. The initial endowment places A on indifference curve II_A and B on curve I_B. At point D, A's marginal rate of substitution of X for Y, given by the slope of TT', is relatively high; A would be willing to sacrifice, say, three units of Y in order

FIGURE 3.8.3

GENERAL EQUILIBRIUM OF EXCHANGE

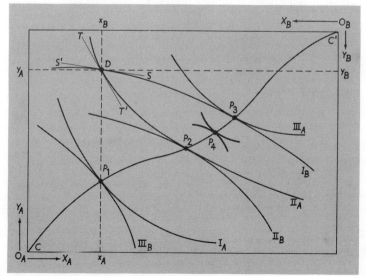

to obtain one additional unit of X. At the same point, B has a relatively low marginal rate of substitution, as shown by the slope of SS'. Or turning it around, B has a relatively high marginal rate of substitution of Y for X. B may, for example, be willing to forego four units of X to obtain one unit of Y.

A situation such as this will always lead to exchange if the parties concerned are free to trade. From the point D, A will trade some Y to B, receiving X in exchange. The exact bargain reached by the two traders cannot be determined. If B is the more skillful negotiator, B may induce A to move along II_A to the point P_2. All the benefit of trade goes to B, who jumps from I_B to II_B. Just oppositely, A might steer the bargain to point P_3, thereby increasing his level of satisfaction from II_A to III_A, B's utility level remaining I_B. Starting from point D, the ultimate exchange is very likely to lead to some point between P_2 and P_3, perhaps at a point such as P_4, at which two indifference curves are tangent. Both are therefore made better off by trade. But the skill of the bargainers and their initial endowments determine the exact location. In any case one can be made better off without causing the other to become worse off, or both can become better off in the sense of attaining a higher level of utility.

One important thing can be said. Exchange will take place until the marginal rate of substitution of X for Y is the same for both traders. If the two marginal rates are different, one or both parties can benefit from exchange; neither party need lose. In other words, the exchange equilibrium can occur only at points such as P_1, P_2, P_3, or P_4 in Figure 3.8.3. The locus CC', called the *contract curve,* is a curve joining all points of tangency between one of A's indifference curves and one of B's. It is thus the locus along which the marginal rates of substitution are equal for both traders. We accordingly have the following proposition:

Proposition. The general equilibrium of exchange occurs at a point where the marginal rate of substitution between every pair of goods is the same for all parties consuming both goods. The exchange equilibrium is not unique; it may occur at any point along the contract curve.

The contract curve is an optimal locus in the sense that if the trading parties are located at some point not on the curve, one or both can benefit, and neither suffer a loss, by exchanging goods so as to move to a point on the curve. To be sure, some points not on the curve are preferable to one or the other party than some points on the curve. But for any point not on the curve, one or more attainable points on the curve are preferable. The chief characteristic of each point on the contract curve is that a movement along the curve away from the point must benefit one party and harm the other. Every organization that leads to a point on the contract curve is said to be a *Pareto-optimal organization.*

> **Definition.** A Pareto-optimal organization is one in which any change that makes some people better off makes some others worse off. That is, an organization is Pareto-optimal if, and only if, there is no change that will make one or more better off without making anyone worse off. Thus every point on the contract curve is Pareto optimal, and the contract curve is a locus of Pareto optimality.

To summarize, the economics behind all of the graphical analysis simply says that people will trade only if the trade makes the participants better off. Only if each person's *MRS* is the same will it be impossible to make both parties better off.

APPLICATIONS

Uses of the theory of trade: Goods in kind and water rationing

We can use our concept of the Edgeworth Box to analyze the economics of government giving people goods in kind instead of money. Take food stamps, for instance. Government gives stamps that can be used to purchase food—in reality to purchase only certain kinds of good—rather than money. If individuals pay a different price for food, there is motivation for exchange. Someone with food stamps pays a different price for food than someone without. Or possibly we have two individuals both of whom receive food stamps and have other income. Unless the allocation of stamps and incomes between the two individuals is *precisely* on the contract curve, both individuals can be made better off by trade, in the sense of being able to reach higher indifference curves. Thus trade will take place. But to the extent that trade in goods—in this case food stamps—is less efficient than trade in organized markets because of transaction costs, there is waste involved in giving goods in kind.

"All well and good," some will say. Certainly there is waste involved in giving goods in kind rather than income, but if government gives income rather than goods, recipients will use some of the income to buy things that are not good for them, like liquor or drugs, and not buy desirable goods such as food for the family.

You can answer this question in the following way. Certainly income recipients may use some of the income to buy liquor or drugs, but if the government gives food stamps, the recipients can trade stamps for money in black markets. Since the transaction is illegal, food stamps yield a lower value. The stamp sellers then pay for the liquor or drugs with the money received. Since the market for stamps is less efficient than legal organized markets, the individual may give up more food to buy liquor than would have been the case if income had been given. The waste in the illegal transaction would have been the sacrifice of food.

Another application of the Edgeworth box diagram is the analysis of water rationing. During the winter of 1976–77 a serious drought occurred in the Western United States, causing considerable decreases in the water supplies of many communities. In his *Newsweek* column of March 21, 1977, the famous economist Milton Friedman discussed the approach of one such community, Marin County, California, a prosperous bedroom community north of San Francisco.

In response to the drought, Marin County rationed water to 37 gallons per person per day for a household of four. Very stiff fines were imposed for exceeding this level. Furthermore, one household could not legally sell part of its water allocation to another household. Thus no household would have the incentive to sacrifice or cut down and use less than 37 gallons of water.

We can analyze the situation with an Edgeworth box diagram in Figure 3.8.4. Let A and B be any two individuals. The origins for A and B are at O_A and O_B. The income of A is $O_A I_A$; B's income is $O_B I_B$. Each receives exactly the same amount of water; $OW_A = OW_B$. The original allocation is shown as point R. The contract curve is $O_A O_B$,

FIGURE 3.8.4

TRADE IN WATER

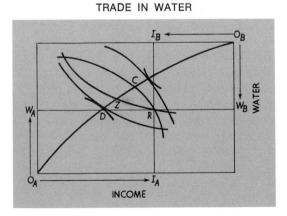

showing the locus of points of tangency between A's and B's indifference curves.

If trade were allowed both individuals could be made better off than they were at point R. Their consumption sets would move to some point on the contract curve between points Z and C. The only circumstances under which trade would not benefit both would be if the incomes of each were precisely such that point D, where the contract curve crosses $W_A W_B$, was the original allocation. This would appear to be a rather remote possibility. Otherwise trade would be preferable.

EXERCISES

Pareto optimality

Why is trade not allowed under such circumstances?

If all individuals are in equilibrium, such that the budget lines are tangent to indifference curves, why is this situation *Pareto optimal?*

The answer is that for *Pareto* optimality to exist, for every pair of individuals the marginal rates of substitution between any pair of goods must be equal. Equilibrium requires that for any two goods an individual's marginal rate of substitution must equal the price ratio. If every consumer faces the same price ratios, then all marginal rates of substitution are equal. Thus the answer requires that everyone faces the same prices.

3.9 SUMMARY

In this chapter we have developed the basic tools necessary to analyze consumer demand theory. Foremost are the concepts of indifference curves and budget lines. An indifference curve shows combinations of goods among which consumers are indifferent. Several indifference curves make up an indifference map. The slope of an indifference curve shows the rate at which a consumer is willing to substitute one good for another in order to remain at a constant level of utility. The slope is called the marginal rate of substitution.

The marginal rate of substitution can be related to marginal utility, which is the addition to total utility attributable to the addition of one unit of a good to current consumption. The marginal rate of substitution between two goods is the ratio of the two marginal utilities.

The budget line indicates the combinations that the consumer is able to purchase with a given money income. The price ratio given by the market is the slope of the budget line. An increase in money income moves the budget line outward, parallel to the old line. A change in commodity price pivots the budget line.

The consumer is in equilibrium when the budget line is tangent to the highest attainable indifference curve; in this case the MRS equals the price ratio. Expressed in terms of marginal utility, equilibrium occurs when the marginal utility per dollar expenditure (MU/P) is equal for all goods consumed.

Finally, we used indifference curves for two consumers to show why trade takes place. If the MRS between any two goods is not equal for two consumers trade can make both consumers better off.

APPLICATION

Use of equilibrium theory

We noted above that the concept of indifference curves is a useful analytical concept for decision makers even though the actual curves will not be available in all probability. The same thing is true about the concept of equilibrium. The decision in business about the relation between labor income and working conditions uses the notion of equilibrium. Employees have a particular preference pattern. Employers have a budget and a set of prices that determine what can be offered. The final contract evolves from a search for equilibrium.

In government the decision maker with a budget constraint allocates expenditure among alternatives that are ostensibly designed to give utility to consumers. The notion of a constrained maximization is behind this type of decision also. The real problem, of course, is in finding the equilibrium or something close to it.

We can use our knowledge of the theory to predict how people or groups will react to changing circumstances. For example, consider the following exercise.

EXERCISE

Inflation and changes in labor contracts

In a period of inflation both prices of goods and services (the general price level) and incomes rise, to a large extent, together. (For purposes of this problem at least assume that they do.) Would you expect during a long period of inflation that improvements in working conditions would make up an increasing or a decreasing percentage of labor contracts? Why?

It seems that the key to this exercise is the effect of inflation on the rate of income tax. Our society uses a graduated income tax. To see how inflation affects the tax paid, assume that an individual earns $15,000 a year. Because of inflation the income rises to $30-000, but the price level in the economy doubles as well. One would say at first that this person is no better or no worse off than before. Income has doubled but prices also have doubled. But, with a graduated income tax the second $15,000 is subject to a higher *marginal* tax rate than the first $15,000. Thus the person is worse off because of having to pay more than double the taxes after income doubles and prices double also.

Thus in contract bargaining individuals move into higher marginal tax brackets. They can keep less of increases in income. Improvements in working conditions—extra vacation and so on—are not subject to taxation and therefore increase in value relative to additional income. Employers then can make employees better off at a lower cost by marginally substituting these fringe benefits for increases in income. This is not to say that income does not increase. Of course it does. But we would expect some increase in the percent of non-income benefits to total benefits, income plus nonpecuniary income, in the new contract packages.

TECHNICAL PROBLEMS

1. Assume that an individual consumes three goods, X, Y, and Z. The marginal utility (assumed measurable) of each good is independent of the rate of consumption of the other goods. The prices of X, Y, and Z are respectively $1, $3, and $5. The total income of the consumer is $65 and the marginal utility schedule is as follows:

Units of good	Marginal utility of X (units)	Marginal utility of Y (units)	Marginal utility of Z (units)
1........	12	60	70
2........	11	55	60
3........	10	48	50
4........	9	40	40
5........	8	32	30
6........	7	24	25
7........	6	21	18
8........	5	18	10
9........	4	15	3
10........	3	12	1

    a. How should the consumer allocate the $65 income so as to maximize utility?

    b. Suppose income falls to $43 with the same set of prices; what combination will the consumer choose?

    c. Let income fall to $38; let the price of X rise to $5 while the prices of Y and Z remain at $3 and $5. How does the consumer allocate income? What would you say if the consumer maintained that he now does not buy X because he can no longer afford it?

2. In Figure E.3.1, suppose a consumer has the indicated indifference map and the budget line designated *LM*. You know the price of Y is $5 per unit.

    a. What is the consumer's income?

    b. What is the price of X?

    c. Write the equation for the budget line *LM*.

    d. What is the value of the slope of *LM*?

    e. What combination of X and Y will the consumer choose? Why?

    f. What is the marginal rate of substitution in equilibrium?

    g. Explain precisely in terms of *MRS* why the consumer would not choose combinations designated by *B* or *C*.

Suppose the budget line shifts to *L'M'*.

    h. At the same prices, what has happened to money income?

FIGURE E.3.1

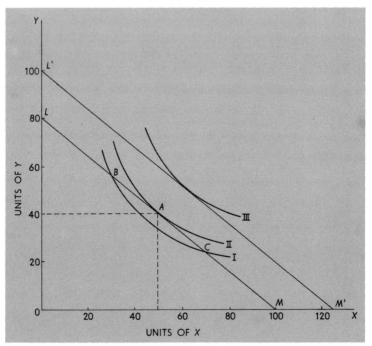

    i.   What combination is now chosen?

    j.   Draw the relevant budget line if money income remains at the original level (designated by LM), the price of Y remains at $5, but the price of X rises to $10.

    k.   Draw in an indifference curve showing the new equilibrium.

    l.   What are the new equilibrium quantities?

3.   If $\dfrac{MU_X}{MU_Y} < \dfrac{P_X}{P_Y}$, the individual would (increase, decrease) the consumption of X relative to Y. Explain your answer.

4.   Define the marginal rate of substitution and relate it to the older concept of marginal utility.

5.   In the Edgeworth diagram in Figure E.3.2 point R represents the original allocation of goods X and Y between individuals A and B. Indicate

    a.   The feasible region of exchange and why this range is feasible.

    b.   All points unacceptable to A and why.

FIGURE E.3.2

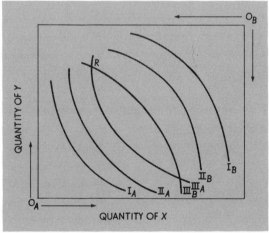

6.   An individual consumes two goods, A and B. The price of A is $5 per unit; the price of B is $7 per unit. The marginal utility of A is 10; the marginal utility of B is 21. The consumer spends the entire income on A and B.

    a.   What should the consumer do?

    b.   The marginal utility of B falls to 14; what should the consumer do now?

7.   There are two individuals, A and B. A's marginal rate of stubstitution between goods X and Y is 2X for 1Y. B's MRS is 3X for 2Y. In what direction will trade take place and between what two ratios?

8. Initially, individual A has $5X$ and $14Y$. B has $12X$ and $12Y$. For A, $MU_X = 16$ and $MU_Y = 4$; for individual B $MU_X = 20$ and $MU_Y = 10$. Is trade profitable to both? Why or why not?

9. Figure E.3.3 shows a portion of an individual's indifference map between pizzas and hamburgers. Explain in terms of MRS why you think this person likes _____ relative to _____.

FIGURE E.3.3

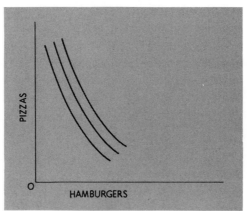

10. "If the price of X equals the price of Y, then the utility-maximizing consumer will always buy equal amounts of X and Y." Analyze.

11. Suppose the price of X is $2 and the price of Y is $6. If the marginal utility of X is 12, then the marginal utility of Y for a consumer in equilibrium is _____. Why?

ANALYTICAL PROBLEMS

1. Business executives generally receive their salary in money income and in goods in kind, such as stock options, nice offices, free trips, and so on. If the income tax is replaced by a sales tax how do you think the general ratio of money income to non-pecuniary income would change? Explain.

2. If trade must clearly make both parties better off, why are some types of trade made illegal, if such trade cannot harm an outside party (prostitution, for example)?

3. I recently served on a committee set up by the city council to put forth and evaluate the goals of the city for the next ten years. These goals were supposedly to give guidance to the city council.
   a. Can a city have goals?
   b. Why or why not?

    c. Only under what circumstances could you state unequivocally that a city was made better off by a particular activity?

    d. Two of the "goals" set forth by this committee were to force downtown merchants to beautify the downtown area and to encourage new businesses into the downtown area. Can you see any trade-off or possible contradiction here?

4. Say you are the mayor of the city discussed in question 3. You know that the city cannot raise enough money to accomplish all of the goals set forth. How would you allocate the city's money among the goals? As mayor, what is your goal?

5. Suppose you know your income for the next two years. At what rate can you trade income between years? Why? Explain why saving can be considered a good.

4

———— ··⟨∞⟩·· ————

Theory of
consumer behavior:
Changes in income
and price

———— ··◄⟨∞⟩►·· ————

4.1 INTRODUCTION

Having developed the concept of consumer equilibrium, we are now prepared to analyze the effect of changes in two important determinants of the amount demanded—the consumer's income and the price of the good. Recall from Chapter 2 that the theory of demand is concerned primarily with the effect of changes in price, other things held constant, and secondarily with changes in income, other things held constant.

In this chapter we will examine these two types of changes in some depth. We shall also analyze in depth the reasons that economists always assume that demand curves slope downward. Finally, we shall apply our tools of analysis to the theory of labor supply.

4.1.a Basic principles

The effects of changes in income and price are really rather simply analyzed. First consider the effect of an increase in money income, prices held constant. You will recall from Chapter 3 that this increase involves a parallel shift outward in the budget line. If the consumer was in equilibrium before the increase in income, after the increase there will be a new equilibrium on the higher budget line tangent to a higher indifference curve. The increase in income simply extends the set of the consumer's consumption possibilities, thereby making the consumer better off. The new equilibrium on the higher curve is attained under exactly the same conditions—the marginal rate of substitution equals the price ratio. The effect of a decrease in money income is analyzed similarly. In this case the budget line shifts downward; equilibrium is attained now on a lower indifference curve since the set of consumption opportunities is decreased.

Now recall that a change in the price of a good, money income held constant, rotates the budget line, outward for a decrease in price, inward for an increase. The adjustment principle is simple. Begin in equilibrium. Let the price of the good decrease. Since the budget line rotates outward, the set of consumption opportunities available to the individual is increased. In other words the consumer is made better off. The increase in consumption opportunities affects the new level of consumption. Economists call the effect on consumption of a consumer's being better off, the "income effect." Furthermore, the good for which the price decreased is now less expensive relative to other goods. Thus the consumer tends to substitute consumption away from other goods to the now relatively cheaper good. Economists call this effect on consumption the "substitution effect."

The combination of these two effects leads to a new equilibrium situation; the new budget line, which has rotated outward, is tangent to a higher indifference curve. The entire effect combines both income and substitution effects. After the change, the marginal rate of substitution equals the new price ratio.

The effect of an increase in price is symmetrical. The budget line rotates inward, leading to a new tangency on a lower indifference curve. The income effect follows because the consumer now has a smaller set of consumption possibilities and is therefore worse off. Since the price of the good increases relative to that of other goods, the substitution effect involves a shift in consumption away from the now more expensive good to other goods.

Thus you see that the principles involved in analyzing the effects of changes in income and prices are quite straightforward. There are, however, several implications of the theory that are made more apparent with the use of graphical analysis. Of particular interest is the relation of the principles discussed above to demand theory. We shall devote considerable space in this chapter to developing that relation and in using the analysis to see why economists assume that demand slopes downward.

4.1.b Important points developed

The basic concepts to be learned in Chapter 4 are

1. How a demand curve is derived from indifference curves and budget lines.
2. Why economists assume demand slopes downward.
3. How the slope of demand is related to the income and substitution effects.
4. How to derive the relation between income and consumption from indifference curves and budget lines.
5. How to develop labor supply theory from indifference curves and budget lines.

4.2 CHANGES IN MONEY INCOME

4.2.a Income-consumption curve

To analyze graphically the effect of changes in money income we will introduce a slightly different method of approach. As before, we plot the quantity of some good, X, along the horizontal axis. But, rather than plotting the quantity of some other good, Y, along the vertical, we plot expenditure on all goods other than X. Thus, the unit of measure along the vertical axis is dollar expenditure. In Figure 4.2.1 each indifference curve, I–IV, indicates the various combinations of X and expenditures on other goods that yield the same level of utility. Higher levels of utility are indicated by the higher numbered indifference curves. Assume that the price of X is fixed at $10 per unit and that initially the consumer has an income of $1,000, indicated by budget line $L''M''$. A consumer can spend all income on X and purchase 100 units, buy no X and spend all income on other goods, or can purchase any combination on $L''M''$. We know from Chapter 3 that equilibrium is at R on indifference curve III, indicating that the highest available level of utility from 40 units of X and $600 spent on other goods.

When we decrease income to $700 the new budget line is $L'M'$. Equilibrium is now at Q, with 30 units of X and $400 spent on other goods. An income of $400 causes the consumer to purchase 20 units of X and spend $200 on other goods. Finally, if income is increased to $1,400, $L'''M'''$ is tangent to IV at 70 units of X and $700. As income changes,

FIGURE 4.2.1

INCOME-CONSUMPTION CURVE

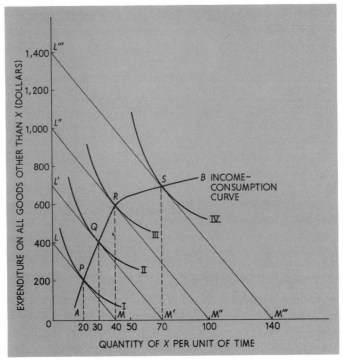

the point of consumer equilibrium changes as well. The line connecting the successive equilibria is called the *income-consumption curve,* indicated by *AB* in Figure 4.2.1. This curve shows the *equilibrium combinations* of *X* and expenditures on goods other than *X* at various levels of money income, nominal prices remaining constant throughout. That is, it shows the various equilibria corresponding to various income levels; it thus shows the effects of changes in money income at constant commodity prices.

Definition. The locus of points showing consumer equilibria at various levels of money income at constant prices is called the income-consumption curve.

4.2.b Engel curves

Now we can relate the income-consumption curve to Engel curves. Engel curves, named for a 19th-century German statistician, show the relation between money income and the consumption of some good, other things, including the price of the good, held constant. These curves are important for applied studies of economic welfare and for the analysis of family expenditure patterns.

The Engel curve derived from the income-consumption curve in Figure 4.2.1 is constructed in Figure 4.2.2. Here the quantity of good X is plotted along the horizontal axis, money income along the vertical. Point LM in Figure 4.2.2, showing that with an income of $400 the consumer purchases 20 units, is associated with point P in Figure 4.2.1. It follows that LM', 30 units of X at an income of $700, is associated with point Q. Likewise, LM'' and LM''' are equivalent to R and S respectively. As we shall see, not all income-consumption curves and Engel curves have the same general slope as this.

> **Definition.** An Engel curve is a locus of points relating equilibrium quantity of some good to the level of money income. Such curves are readily derived from income-consumption curves.

4.2.c Normal and inferior goods

Note that in Figure 4.2.1 and 4.2.2 the relation between money income and the amount of the good consumed is such that as income increases, the amount of the good consumed increases, the prices of all goods held constant. That is, in this case the income-consumption curve does not bend backward; neither does the Engel curve slope downward. Such a good is called a *normal good* over the relevant income levels. That is, more X is purchased as money income increases; the income-consumption curve and the Engel curve are positively sloped in the case of a normal good.

> **Definition.** A normal good is one for which consumption varies directly with money income at a specific set of constant prices for specified levels of money income.

In the case of a normal good the income elasticity of the good is positive. That is, $(\triangle Q/Q) \div (\triangle I/I) > 0$. Normal goods are given that name because economists in the past seemed to believe that in the majority of cases an increase in income causes an increase in the consumption of a good; they believed that this is the "normal" situation. However, an increase in income may well cause a decrease in the consumption of certain

FIGURE 4.2.2

ENGEL CURVE

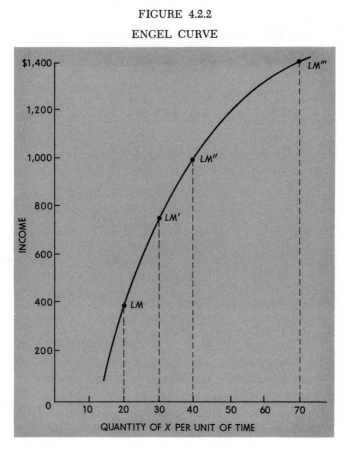

commodities at certain price ratios. These commodities are called *inferior* goods. In other words, an inferior good is a commodity for which the income elasticity is negative over the range of incomes for which it is inferior.

> **Definition.** A good is normal or inferior as its income elasticity is positive or negative. A normal good's Engel curve is positively sloped. The Engel curve for an inferior good is negatively sloped over its range of inferiority.

Figure 4.2.3 illustrates a good that is inferior over a certain range of incomes. Note that in this figure the quantity of Y, rather than expenditure on all goods other than X, is plotted on the vertical axis. The analysis

FIGURE 4.2.3

ILLUSTRATION OF AN INFERIOR GOOD

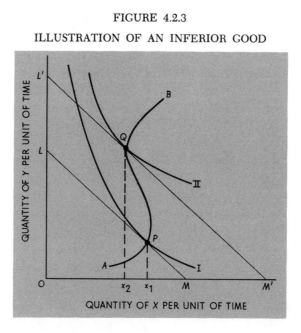

QUANTITY OF X PER UNIT OF TIME

is the same in either case. The quantity of good X is plotted along the horizontal axis.

Begin with an income shown by budget line LM. Point P, indicating Ox_1 consumed, is the point of equilibrium for the consumer. Next, let income increase to the level shown by $L'M'$, prices held constant. After the change the position of consumer equilibrium shifts from point P to point Q. The consumer is better off by being on a higher indifference curve. But the increase in income leads to a *decrease* in the consumption of X. For this reason we say that X is inferior over the range of incomes denoted by LM and $L'M'$. Over this range the income consumption curve bends backward. Since this curve bends backward, the income elasticity of demand, $(\triangle x / \triangle I)(I/x)$, is negative. We might note that over some ranges of income, the good may be normal for the consumer, such as movements from A to P and from Q to B.

We should emphasize in passing that it is clear from the above exposition that inferiority and normality—and therefore, of course, income elasticity—vary over different ranges of income. Hamburger may be a normal good for one family over a particular range of incomes. It may be an inferior good over still another range of incomes. Furthermore, the classification of goods as inferior or normal depends upon the price ratio. At one price ratio a good may have a substantially different income elas-

ticity from the income elasticity at another price ratio. We might also
note that economists frequently point out examples of inferior goods such
as margarine, hamburgers, and Volkswagens. As their income increased
many people may have reduced their consumption of these goods. Many
others may not have. Therefore it is well to remember that inferiority
and normality are not inherent properties of the goods themselves. Income
elasticities depend upon preference patterns of consumers, the price
ratio, and the range of incomes.

FIGURE 4.2.4

ENGEL CURVES

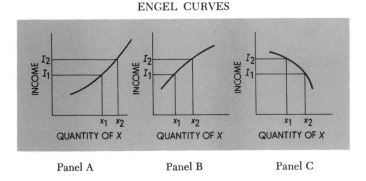

| Panel A | Panel B | Panel C |

4.2.d Shapes of Engel curves

Engel curves can have many shapes over a particular range of incomes,
depending upon several factors. Three basic types, or shapes, are shown
in Figure 4.2.4. Panel A illustrates a normal good, the consumption of
which increases but at a decreasing rate as income increases. That is, an
increase in income increases consumption of good X, but more and more
income causes smaller and smaller increases in its consumption.

Another relation is shown in Panel B. In this case increases in income
bring about larger and larger increases in X as income rises. Finally,
Panel C shows an inferior good over the relevant range. Over this range
increases in income lead to less X purchased by the consumer.[1]

Let us emphasize two points. First, Engel curves may take on various
shapes over different ranges of incomes. Perhaps at first the consumption
increases at an increasing rate with income, later increases at a decreasing
rate, and then perhaps decreases with income. The only thing we can say

---

[1] Do not make the mistake of saying the curve in A is income inelastic while that
in B is income elastic. You cannot estimate income elasticity simply by looking at the
slope of the curve. As they are drawn each curve has a range of being inelastic and
elastic.

positively is that a good cannot be inferior over the entire range of incomes.

Second, do not attribute the shapes of Engel curves solely to the properties of the goods themselves. Engel curves reflect the properties of indifference maps. It may well be true that, as some have said, food, taken as a whole, has an Engel curve shaped like the one in Figure 4.2.4, panel A. It may also be true that goods such as steaks and fine wines have curves like that in panel B. But income-consumption curves, and hence Engel curves, are derived under specific price ratios, under specific preference functions, and over specific income ranges. It certainly could be the case that with one price ratio the derived curves could have one shape, while another ratio could give rise to Engel curves with totally different shapes, even though indifference maps do not change. Or the introduction of some new goods into the possible consumer's bundle could markedly change the shape of an Engel curve. It would be quite surprising, for example, if the introduction of television did not change the Engel curve for radios. We could speculate also that the recent increase in gasoline and gas prices have changed the Engel curve for Volkswagens and gas furnaces.

APPLICATION

Theory and predictions

The ability to predict long-range consumption patterns as a society's per capita income changes is important for both government and business decision makers. For example, as a society becomes wealthier the consumption of medical care generally increases markedly. This certainly has been the case in the United States over the past several years. Governments, from local through national, have had to adapt to meet this growing consumption. Adaptation can take many forms, such as more doctors, more nurses, more hospital rooms, and so on. In order to make plans for these changes the increase in consumption must be predicted well in advance.

Certainly, businesses must make such predictions also, and of course they do. Otherwise they are not very successful. Firms that were at all medically oriented and predicted the huge increase in medical consumption were most successful.

The increase in consumers' income does not have to be so dramatic or on such a national scale for businesses to benefit by correct adaptation. A local community may experience a substantial increase in per capita income while the economy as a whole has much smaller increases or even decreases. Those businesses that predict correctly usually benefit.

This exact circumstance has been occurring in the community in which our university is located. The university has about tripled in size over the past ten years. Everyone locally knew this was happening and would continue to happen. University officials publicized the predictions. What everyone did not predict was the huge increase in the community's per capita income that accompanied the expansion. That is, such an increase in the size of the school must bring in large numbers of people. And these new people had rather high salaries compared with the earlier average income in the community. Furthermore, added students also brought added per capita income.

EXERCISES

Some predictions

What businesses would you expect to undergo great expansion and great increases in profitability over this period of rising income? Remember it does not do any good for a business to recognize a trend or pattern after everyone else does. Those who get in first are those who reap the profits before widespread entry takes place and the profits are competed away. (We will return to this phenomenon in much more detail in Chapter 7.)

In this example the great profits and the great expansion came in several areas. Restaurants became increasingly popular, particularly the more expensive restaurants. The number of places for dining out grew dramatically. House building expanded, particularly the construction of larger homes. The number of airplane flights into and out of the community doubled. The number of apartments grew more and more each year.

On the other hand, the number of department stores and clothing stores did not increase much, if at all. Many of both types opened up but went out of business during this period of economic growth. Does this mean clothing is inferior? Surely as a community becomes wealthier, people buy more and better clothing and other department store items. But the catch was that as the community became wealthier, people were more and more induced to travel to nearby large metropolitan areas, in this case Houston and Dallas, for their department store purchases. Such trips are a very superior good. Even though clothing was not an inferior good, locally purchased clothing may well have been.

This real but simplified example shows how businesses can use, and some did use, a knowledge of good business practice to benefit significantly from increased per capita income. Those who predicted early and correctly benefited most.

Now assume that you are a local government official—say a city planner—at the beginning of the expansion described above. Which public goods and services do you predict will have the greatest increase in utilization? Will the consumption of any public services decline?

Who will benefit the most from correct predictions or suffer the most from incorrect ones, government officials or local businesses? Why? From whom do you expect the best predictions?

Finally suppose that you are in business in a city experiencing declining income due to the loss of a major industry. Are there any businesses that might expand profitably during the decline? Which types?

4.3 DEMAND CURVES

The effect of price on the consumption of goods is even more important to economists than is the effect of changes in income. In this section we hold money income constant and let price change in order to analyze the fundamentals of demand theory.

4.3.a Price-consumption curves

Just as was the case for Engel curves, demand curves are derived by moving the budget line and observing the various points of tangency to indifference curves. In this case, rather than a parallel shift in the budget line, there is a rotation of the line, as was noted in the introduction to this chapter.

Figure 4.3.1 contains a portion of an indifference map for a consumer who can consume X (measured in units along the horizontal axis) and goods other than X (the total expenditure on these is measured in dollars along the vertical axis). The consumer has money income of $1,000. When X is priced at $25 per unit the consumer's budget line is LM. He can spend the entire $1,000 on other goods, spend the entire $1,000 on 40 units of X at $25 per unit, or spend at any point along LM. By the analysis developed above the consumption represented at point P, where LM is tangent to indifference curve I, is optimal. He consumes 24 units of X, thereby spending $600 on this commodity. The remaining $400 is spent on other goods.

FIGURE 4.3.1

PRICE-CONSUMPTION CURVE

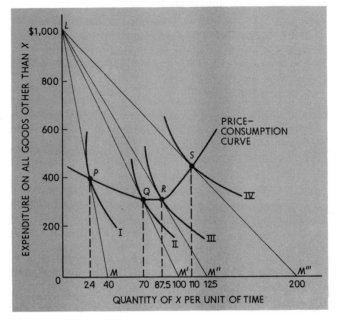

Assume that the price of X falls to $10. Now if the consumer wishes to spend all income on X, he can purchase 100 units. The budget line at the new price is LM', with a slope of -10 rather than -25. The new equilibrium point of tangency is designated by Q, at which he consumes 70 units of X at a total expense of $700 and spends the remaining $300 on other goods. If price falls to $8 per unit, other things remaining the same, the new budget line is LM'', with a slope of -8. At equilibrium point R he purchases 87.5 units of X. Note that $700 is still spent on X and $300 on all other goods. Finally the price of X falls to $5. The new budget line LM''' is tangent to indifference curve IV at point S. The maximum utility level is attained by spending $550 on 110 units of X and $450 on goods other than X. Thus, each price decrease causes the consumer to purchase more units of X. The line joining points P, Q, R, and S (and all other equilibria) is called the *price-consumption curve*. For a given money income it shows the amount of X consumed as its price changes, other prices remaining the same.

Definition. The price-consumption curve is a locus of equilibrium points relating the quantity of X purchased to its price, money income and all other prices remaining constant. In the case treated above, the price-consumption curve also shows how expenditure on all goods other than X changes as the price of X changes.

4.3.b   Derivation of demand curves from price-consumption curves

The individual's demand curve for a commodity can be derived from the price-consumption curve, just as an Engel curve is derivable from the income-consumption curve. The price-quantity relations for good X at points P, Q, R, and S, and presumably for all other points on the price-consumption curve in Figure 4.3.1, are plotted in Figure 4.3.2. The horizontal axis is the same (units of X), but the vertical axis now shows the price of X. When the price of X is given by the slope of LM ($\$25$), 24 units of X are purchased; this is indicated by point P' in Figure 4.3.2. If the price is $\$10$, 70 units are purchased (point Q'), and so forth. All other points on the curve are derived similarly. The locus of these points is called the demand curve for X.

FIGURE 4.3.2

DEMAND CURVE

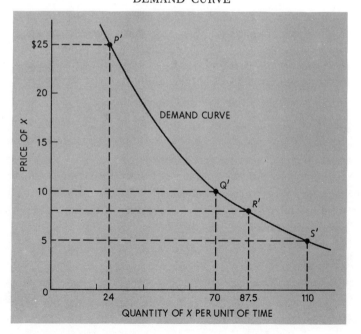

Definition. The demand curve of an individual for a specific commodity relates equilibrium quantities bought to market price, money income and nominal prices of all other commodities held constant. The slope of the demand curve illustrates the law of demand: quantity demanded varies inversely with price—income and the prices of other commodities held constant.

EXERCISE

Demand elasticity and the price-consumption curve

Using your knowledge of the relation between the change in total expenditure on a good and whether that good's demand is elastic, inelastic, or unitary, show from the shape of the price-consumption curve in Figure 4.3.1 that the demand curve in Figure 4.3.2 is elastic between \$25 and \$10, of unitary elasticity between \$10 and \$8, and inelastic between \$8 and \$5.

First recall that if the price of a good falls, total expenditure on the good increases (decreases) if the demand is elastic (inelastic). Total expenditure remains constant if the demand is of unitary elasticity. When price falls from \$25 to \$10, money income remaining constant at \$1,000, equilibrium moves from point P to Q. From the graph it is clear that the movement involves a *decrease* in expenditure on all goods other than X. Thus expenditure on X must rise and demand must be in the elastic range. The fall in price from \$10 to \$8 moves equilibrium from Q to R. Since expenditure on all other goods stays the same, with money income constant, expenditure on X must stay the same as well. Thus elasticity is unitary over the range \$10 to \$8. The fall in price from \$8 to \$5 moves equilibrium from R to S; expenditure on all other goods increases. Thus expenditure on X decreases and demand is necessarily inelastic over this range. The demand curve in Figure 4.3.2 is elastic at higher prices, becomes unitary, then becomes inelastic at lower prices.

We might note that the relation between the slope of the price-consumption curve and demand elasticity holds only when expenditure on all other goods is plotted along the vertical axis. When the quantity of some other good, say Y, is along the vertical axis the relation does not hold, unless Y stands for all other goods with a fixed price.

A demand curve can quite similarly be derived from an indifference map when the consumption of some other good rather than expenditure on all other goods is plotted along the vertical axis. Such is the case in Figures 4.3.3 and 4.3.4. Price of X falls, rotating the budget line from LM, to LM', to LM''. Equilibrium moves from $P(Ox_1$ units$)$ to $Q(Ox_2$ units$)$ to $R(Ox_3$ units$)$. Figure 4.3.4 shows the corresponding demand for the price-consumption curve in Figure 4.3.3.

FIGURE 4.3.3

PRICE-CONSUMPTION CURVE

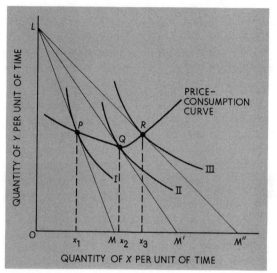

FIGURE 4.3.4

DEMAND CURVE

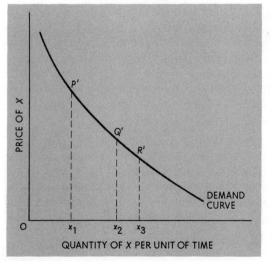

APPLICATIONS

Problems in estimation of demand and some methods of estimation

While theoretical or graphical derivation of consumer demand is rather simple, the statistical estimation of actual demand curves is quite difficult. It is, however, these real-world demands in which decision makers are actually interested. Those in business are willing to pay large amounts of money to have the demand for their products estimated. Certainly a knowledge of this type of demand is of primary importance in business decision making. Anyone in business wishes to know how sales will vary when price varies.

Governmental decision makers make many important decisions based upon statistical estimates of commodity demand curves. Estimates of demand elasticities for gasoline and petroleum had a significant impact on government policy concerning these commodities. As it turned out, in some cases the estimates proved quite accurate; in other cases the results were far off. Estimates of demand play an important role in the decision to levy taxes on certain commodities. Those working for nonprofit institutions make long-range plans based upon estimates of demand also. For example, the demand for hospital services plays an important role in the plans of hospital administrators. University presidents like to have good estimates about the demand for classroom space. We could go on and on, but the situation should be clear. Decision makers can frequently make better decisions when they have a reasonably accurate estimate of the demand for the relevant goods and services.

The problem is, however, that statisticians simply do not have available the indifference curves of individuals. They must use actual data. Furthermore, in theory we hold everything but price and quantity constant when deriving demands; in actual investigations economists may have strong reason to believe that other things have changed during the time over which they have collected their data. It is not enough to go out into the world and gather data on price and quantity sold, plot these data, and from those plotted points estimate a demand curve. A series of price-quantity observations collected over time may give the series of points plotted in Figure 4.3.5. The line drawn through the points appears to fit the data rather well. Its positive slope, however, is not evidence that the market demand for X is upward sloping. The points plotted in the figure may well designate different points of equilibrium. Supply and demand could have shifted many times during the period of observation because of changes in other variables. Each indicated point would then be a

FIGURE 4.3.5

PRICE-QUANTITY OBSERVATIONS
FROM A TIME SERIES

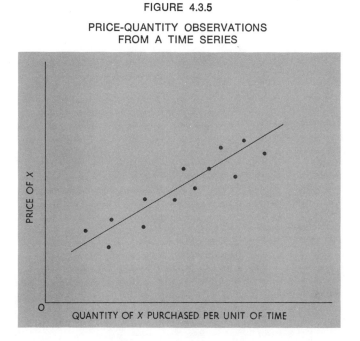

point of equilibrium. Without knowledge of the way that these other variables change and the way that they affect supply and demand one cannot really say what the line indicates. For example, supply and demand may have shifted over time in the way illustrated by Figure 4.3.6. S_1 and D_1 determine equilibrium point A, S_2 and D_2 determine B, and so forth. From five observations we observe only points A through E. We cannot tell simply from the observations how these points were generated.

Even though some observed points actually indicate an inverse relation between price and quantity, these points do not necessarily set forth a demand curve. Again they may simply be points of equilibrium. There are, however, some techniques that economists and statisticians have used to estimate actual demands from actual data.

One obvious extension of the technique of estimating demand solely from price-quantity data is to consider statistically those variables that would have been held constant in a controlled experiment. This technique is called multiple regression. The economist or statistician sets up a model of equations with two or more independent variables. He or she solves the model to obtain estimating equations. One example of this type is

$$Q_D = b_0 + b_1 P + b_2 W + b_3 P_0,$$

FIGURE 4.3.6

CHANGING EQUILIBRIA OVER TIME

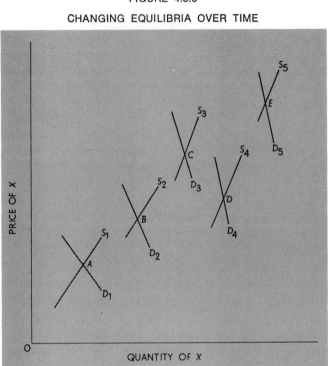

where Q_D is the total quantity demanded, P is per-unit price of a good, W is an average wage rate, and P_0 is some index of related prices. The b's are the parameters to be estimated by multiple regression techniques. (Such techniques are generally taught in beginning statistics classes.) In this way the effect of changes in W and P_0 can be isolated while one attempts to analyze the effect of P on Q_D. Of course, the effect of any other variables that affect supply and demand is not isolated. This omission could cause misleading interpretation. Another problem is the frequent difficulty of obtaining sufficient and accurate data so that meaningful results can be obtained.

In using the above method the economist must assume that the relations are reasonably linear and that the estimating equation specifies what is actually happening. The problems concerned with making such types of estimates make up an entire branch of economics. This branch is known as econometrics—the use of statistics in economic theory. In any case you should be aware that such techniques are available. Many government agencies and large businesses employ their own group of econometricians. Private firms of econometricians are available to answer questions for smaller businesses.

An interesting, though expensive and difficult technique for estimating demand and demand elasticity is the controlled market experiment. The experimenter attempts to hold everything constant during the experiment except for the price of the good. Many such experiments have been undertaken to gain information for the agricultural sector of the economy.

Those carrying out these market experiments display the products in several different grocery stores over a period of time. They make sure that there are always sufficient amounts available at each price to satisfy demand. In this way the effect of changes in supply is removed. There is generally no advertising. During the period of the experiment, price is changed in reasonably small increments over a range, and sales are recorded at each price. In this way many of the effects of changes in other things can be removed, and a reasonable approximation of actual demand is estimated. We must mention again, however, that this is a difficult and expensive process.

As we noted above, in market experiments to determine demand, advertising is generally omitted. Frequently, however, retail merchants are interested in the effect of both price and advertising. One such controlled experiment was carried out by the Agricultural Experiment Station of Oregon State University.* A grocery chain of 20 stores participated in the experiment, which lasted about five years.

The experiment was designed to determine whether sales revenue was higher from advertising a particular good, in this case fish, with or without a price reduction. Clearly a store advertises a good in the hope of increasing revenue from that good. But if in conjunction with the ad, the price of the good is reduced, revenues may be either larger or smaller than if the good is advertised without a price decrease. The result as you know would depend upon price elasticity in connection with advertising.

Over the five-year period, several types of fish were advertised in the 20 stores. Sometimes there was no price reduction. Other times the advertising was done in connection with price reductions that varied over the relevant range. In this way the retailers learned the price response for various items. The results were rather surprising (to me at least). For some fish—for example, salmon—advertising with a price discount created more revenue than advertising without a price

---

* *Fresh Fish Sales as a Function of Promotion in a Portland, Oregon, Grocery Chain,* Agricultural Experiment Station, Oregon State University, October 1972. Special Report 372.

decrease; for others—sole and snapper—revenue from advertising was greater without a price discount than with one.

We put in this example only to show that there are many ways to estimate the effect of price changes on sales under various circumstances and there are many groups, public and private, that specialize in such estimation. This example is simply a means of showing the application of statistical methods to economic theory to make business decisions.

An alternative method of derivation, the questionnaire or survey approach, is a much cheaper method but far less reliable. Potential or actual consumers are simply questioned about how much of certain goods they *would* buy at several prices. Or what do they consider a "reasonable" price? These surveys may provide some useful indirect information, but the imprecision and ambiguity is, as you probably would expect, extremely high. What consumers say they would do or would buy often differs from how they would actually act. In fact, consumers may not even know their future reactions. What people being questioned say may also depend upon the images they wish to convey to the questioner. That is, they may not wish to appear miserly and, therefore, say price would not affect their purchases. According to marketing experts, these techniques are not very reliable.

A relatively new technique, laboratory experiments, is a compromise between market experiments and surveys. In some types of laboratory experiments volunteers are paid to simulate actual buying conditions without going through real markets. Volunteer "consumers" are given money to go on simulated market trips. The experimenter changes relative prices between trips. After many "shopping trips" by many "consumers" an approximation to demand is obtained. The volunteers have the incentive to act as though they are really shopping, because there is always the probability that they may keep their purchases. We might note that in every case about which we have read, demand was deduced to be downward sloping.

Going a step further, some economists have conducted experiments about consumer behavior—with the help of psychologists—in mental institutions and in drug centers, by setting up token economies, which incidentally are supposed to have therapeutic value. Patients receive tokens for jobs performed. They can exchange these tokens for goods and services. The experimenters can change prices and incomes and thus generate demands and Engel curves. These are compared with the theoretical properties of such curves. These types of experiments are in very early stages. Some economists are going even further by emulating psychologists and conducting economic experiments on animals.

These applications are not meant to teach you how to estimate actual demands. This is the task of your marketing and econometrics classes. In these classes they actually show how estimates are made. But in order to do such actual estimating one should have acquired a thorough foundation in the theoretical underpinnings of demand theory. The purpose of this chapter is to provide that foundation.

4.4 SUBSTITUTION AND INCOME EFFECTS

Let us now turn to a more complete analysis of why demand curves slope downward. Recall from the introduction that there are two effects of a price change. If price falls (rises) the good becomes cheaper (more expensive) relative to other goods, and consumers substitute toward (away from) the good. This is the substitution effect. Also, as price falls (rises) consumers become better (worse) off. Since the set of consumption opportunities increases (decreases), the consumer changes the level of consumption; the direction of change is not self-evident. This effect is called the income effect. Let us analyze each effect in turn, then combine the two in order to see why demand is assumed to slope downward.

4.4.a Substitution effect

The substitution effect of a price change is defined as the change in the consumption of a good resulting from a price change, while the consumer is forced to stay on the same indifference curve. Obviously this is a purely theoretical concept designed to permit insight into the theory of demand.

Consider Figure 4.4.1 panel A. Assume LM is the original budget line, giving an equilibrium at point A on indifference curve I. The equilibrium consumption of X is Ox_1. Let the price of X *decrease* so that the new budget line is LM'. We know from our theory that the consumer will now move to a new equilibrium tangency on the new budget line LM'.

But suppose we conduct the following experiment. After the decrease in the price of X we reduce the consumer's money income just enough to force tangency on the original indifference curve I. That is, at the new price ratio given by the slope of LM' reduce income so that a budget line with the same slope (same price ratio) as LM' is tangent to I. This new

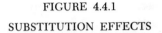

FIGURE 4.4.1

SUBSTITUTION EFFECTS

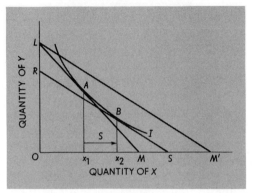

Panel A

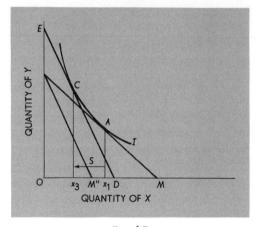

Panel B

budget line is shown as RS, parallel to LM' and tangent to I. With the new budget line RS showing the new price ratio the consumer maximizes at point B, consuming Ox_2 units of X. The consumer is neither better nor worse off. Thus there is no income effect. The movement from A to B, or the change in consumption from Ox_1 to Ox_2, is the pure substitution effect, designated by the arrow labeled S.

Note that considering only the substitution effect along an indifference curve, a decrease in price must lead to increased consumption of the good. That is, a fall in the price of X reduces the slope of the budget line. Because of the typical slope of indifference curves, the less steeply sloped budget line must become tangent to the original indifference curve at a greater quantity of X.

Panel B shows the substitution effect for an *increase* in the price of X. As above, begin with budget line LM tangent to indifference curve I at point A. Ox_1 of good X is consumed in equilibrium. The price of X now rises, causing the budget line at the given money income to rotate to LM''. Again we know that, money income held constant, the new equilibrium will now be along LM''.

Now we *increase the consumer's income* at the new price ratio, shown by the slope of LM'', until a budget line with the new slope is just tangent to the original indifference curve I. This is shown by the budget line ED, tangent to I at point C. In this case the consumption of X is Ox_3 units. Thus the pure substitution effect in this case is the movement from A to C, or the change from Ox_1 units of X to Ox_3, designated again by the arrow labeled S.

Considering the substitution effect only, the *increase* in the price of X causes a reduction in the consumption of X. This must always be the case. An increase in the price of X makes the budget line steeper. The new point of tangency must come where the indifference curve is steeper. Thus after a price decrease tangency must come at a lower consumption of X, using normally sloped indifference curves.

We have established the following proposition:

Proposition. The substitution effect is the change in the consumption of a good after a change in price, when the consumer is forced by a change in money income to consume at some point on the original indifference curve. Considering the substitution effect only, the amount of the good consumed must vary inversely with its price. That is, utility held constant, $(\Delta X/\Delta P_x)<0$.

4.4.b Income effect

We now have established the direction of the substitution effect. But we cannot be as certain about the income effect. In Figure 4.4.2 begin with budget line LM. The consumer is in equilibrium at point P on indifference curve I, consuming Ox_1 of X. Next let the price of X fall, causing the budget line to rotate outward to LM'. As before, we can isolate the substitution effect by reducing money income and forcing the new budget line at the new price ratio to move back until a new line with the same slope as LM' is just tangent to I. Such a budget line is AB, tangent to I at Q, where the consumer chooses Ox_2 units of X. Thus in this case the substitution effect of the price decrease shows an increase in the consumption of X from Ox_1 to Ox_2, shown as S in Figure 4.4.2.

Now that we have isolated the substitution effect, let us return the money income to the original level. This simply involves a shift of the budget line from AB back to LM'. Assuming that the good X is normal, the increase in money income from the level shown by AB to that shown by LM' causes the consumption of X to increase. This result is shown by the movement from Q on indifference curve I to R on indifference curve II; or the increase in X from Ox_2 to Ox_3. This is the income effect. The income effect causes more X to be consumed and hence reinforces the substitution effect, when the good is normal.

From our previous analysis we can see that the total effect of the decrease in price that rotated the budget line from LM to LM', is the movement from P to R, or the increase from Ox_1 to Ox_3. The total effect is broken up into the substitution effect, the distance x_1x_2, plus the income effect, the distance x_2x_3, resulting from returning the money income theoretically taken away when isolating the substitution effect.

In this example the income effect was added to the substitution effect

FIGURE 4.4.2

SUBSTITUTION AND INCOME EFFECTS FOR A
DECREASE IN THE PRICE OF X

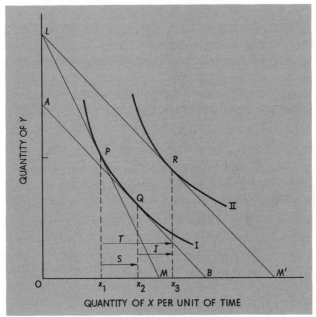

because the good was assumed normal. Had the good been inferior, however, the shift from *AB* back to *LM′* would have caused a reduction in the consumption of *X;* that is, a decrease from Ox_2. Such a situation is shown in Figure 4.4.3, in which *X* is inferior over the relevant range. Again begin with budget line *LM;* equilibrium is again at *P*, with Ox_1 being consumed. The decrease in the price of *X* as before rotates the budget line to *LM′*, and as before the pure substitution effect of the decrease in price is the increase from Ox_1 to Ox_2, or the movement from *P* to *Q*. Next let the income be returned for the inferior good. As the budget line shifts from *AB* back to *LM′* the consumption of *X* is reduced from Ox_2 to Ox_3 by the return of the money income. Thus the income effect is the movement from *Q* back to *R*. The total effect is the change in *X* from Ox_1 to Ox_3. But the total effect is less than the substitution effect alone because the income effect offsets to some extent the substitution effect. In other words, the decrease in price makes the consumer better off. Since the good is inferior, the shift between indifference curves, considered alone, causes less *X* to be consumed.

Note that the total effect is still negative; a lower price of *X* increases

FIGURE 4.4.3

SUBSTITUTION AND INCOME EFFECTS FOR AN INFERIOR GOOD

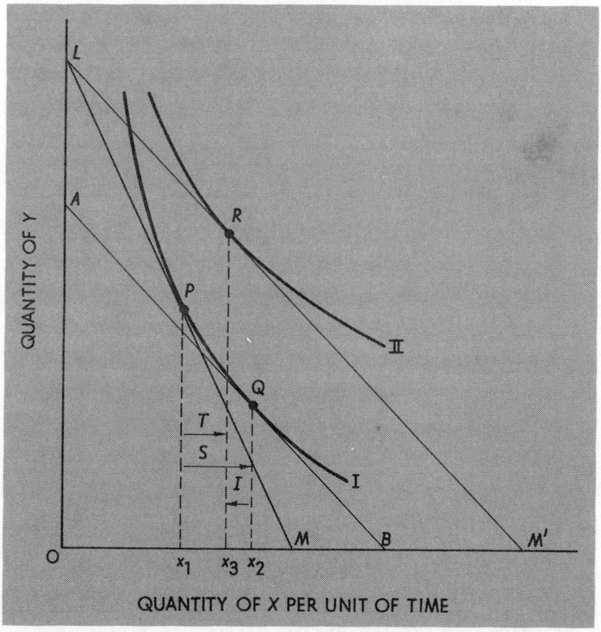
L
A
R
P
Q
II
I
T
S
I
M
B
M′
O
x_1
x_3
x_2
QUANTITY OF Y
QUANTITY OF X PER UNIT OF TIME

the consumption of X. But this change results from the substitution effect, since the income effect for an inferior good partially offsets the substitution effect.

Let us review this somewhat complicated analysis by briefly considering the effects of a price increase. First, take the case of a normal good, illustrated in Figure 4.4.4.

The original price ratio is indicated by the slope of LM. The consumer attains equilibrium at point P on indifference curve II, purchasing Ox_1 units of X. When the price of X rises, as indicated by shifting the budget line from LM to LM', the consumer moves to a new equilibrium position at R on indifference curve I. At this point he purchases Ox_3 units of X. The total effect of the price change is indicated by the movement from P to R, or by the reduction in quantity demanded from Ox_1 to Ox_3. In other words, the total effect is $Ox_1 - Ox_3 = x_1x_3$. This is a negative total effect because quantity demanded is reduced by x_1x_3 units when price increases.

Coincident with the price rise the consumer is given an amount of additional money just sufficient to compensate for the loss in real income otherwise sustained. That is, he is given a compensatory payment just sufficient to make him choose to consume on indifference curve II under

FIGURE 4.4.4

SUBSTITUTION AND INCOME EFFECTS
FOR A NORMAL GOOD
IN CASE OF A PRICE RISE

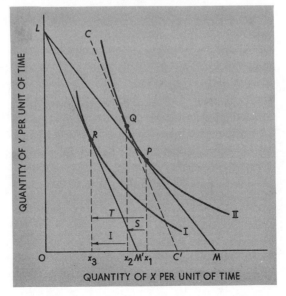

the new price regime. This new imaginary budget line is CC'; it is tangent to the original indifference curve II at point Q, but it reflects the new price ratio.

The substitution effect is shown by the movement from P to Q, or by the reduction in quantity demanded from Ox_1 to Ox_2. Now let the consumer's real income *fall* from the level represented by the fictitious budget line CC'. The movement from Q to R (the decrease in consumption from Ox_2 to Ox_3) indicates the income effect. Since CC' and LM' are parallel, the movement does not involve a change in relative prices. It is once more a real income phenomenon since the reduction in quantity demanded measures the change in purchases attributable exclusively to the decline in real income, the change in relative prices already has been accounted for by the substitution effect. Note that X is a normal good; the decrease in real income causes a decrease in consumption. In this case the income effect reinforces the substitution effect, as is always the case for a normal good.

Turn now to the situation in which the good is inferior. In Figure 4.4.5 an increase in price rotates the budget line from LM to LM'. Following the now familiar analysis, the consumer moves from point P to point R, decreasing consumption of X from Ox_1 to Ox_3 (the total effect). The substitution effect, derived by giving the consumer just enough additional money income to compensate for the decrease in real income occasioned by the price rise, is P to Q (from Ox_1 to Ox_2). The income effect is from Q to R (an *increase* in consumption from Ox_2 to Ox_3). This partial offset to the substitution effect is to be expected since X is an inferior good; a decrease in income causes an increase in the consumption of X.

We have established an additional proposition:

Proposition. Considering the substitution effect alone, an increase (decrease) in the price of a good causes less (more) of the good to be demanded. For a normal good the income effect—from the consumer's being made better or worse off by the price change—adds to or reinforces the substitution effect. The income effect for an inferior good offsets or takes away from the substitution effect to some extent.

4.4.c Why demands slope downward

In the case of a normal good, it is quite clear why price and quantity demanded are negatively related. From the substitution effect alone a decrease in price is accompanied by an increase in quantity demanded, and an increase in price decreases quantity demanded. As we have

FIGURE 4.4.5

SUBSTITUTION AND INCOME EFFECTS FOR AN
INFERIOR GOOD IN CASE OF A PRICE RISE

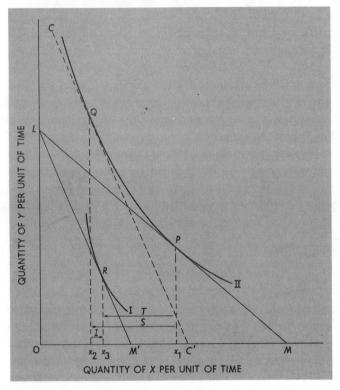

shown, for a normal good the income effect must add to the substitution effect. Thus both effects push quantity demanded in the same direction, and demand must be negatively sloped.

But in the case of an inferior good the income effect operates in the
opposite direction from, and to some extent offsets, the substitution effect.
In the analysis set forth in the previous subsection we have hedged a
little bit by saying that in the case of an inferior good the income effect
partially offsets the substitution effect. Thus in these cases demand is still
downward sloping. You might ask if under some circumstances the income effect could dominate or more than offset the substitution effect,
thereby causing price and quantity demanded to be directly rather than
inversely related?

In other words, in Figure 4.4.3 could the indifference map be such that
the income effect is so great that the equilibrium point on budget line

LM' falls to the left of Ox_1 rather than at R? In other words, in this case could not the income effect dominate the substitution effect, causing demand to slope upward?

Theoretically at least, such a circumstance is possible. In fact economists call such theoretical cases in which the domination of the income effect for an inferior good causes an upward sloping demand *Giffen's Paradox,* named for a 19th-century British civil servant who collected data on the effect of price changes.

But just because such cases are theoretically possible does not mean that they are very likely or occur frequently, or even that they occur at all in the real world. Some economists have noted that one way a young economist could advance rapidly in the profession is by discovering a Giffen good. No one has yet, to our knowledge, done so.[2] Thus such cases involving positively sloped demands are probably just theoretical curios. They certainly are not important in the real world.

In fact, it is easy to see logically that in most, if not all, conceivable cases the substitution effect would tend to dominate the income effect. In the first place an increase in the price of a good makes this good more expensive relative to all other goods. In the sense that all goods compete for a consumer's income, all other goods are substitutes. Furthermore, it would be extremely unusual if a good did not have reasonably close substitutes. People can and do change consumption patterns in response to changes in relative prices by substituting to and from other goods.

Moreover, it would be an unusual case in which an increase in the price of a good consumed reduced substantially a consumer's real income. Furthermore, the effect of the probably slight reduction in real income would be felt not only in the case of the good with the increase in price *but it would be spread over all other goods as well.* Thus the impact of the change in real income from a price change on *any single good* would be rather small if not minute. It, therefore, would appear that the slight change in real income from most relevant price changes in the case of inferior goods, combined with that slight change in real income being spread over all goods, make it extremely unlikely that the income effect from a change in the price of an inferior good would overcome the substitution effect and cause demand to slope upward.

---

[2] Some colleagues, who are doing experimental work, have made a convincing argument that under certain extraordinary circumstances they could force a rat's demand for a certain type of food to be positively sloped. While they have convinced me it can be accomplished, I am not convinced that results will be of particular importance for real-world analysis.

Economists feel so strongly, based upon theory and evidence, that they speak of the law of demand.

Law of Demand. Quantity demanded varies inversely with price, money income and other influences remaining constant.

APPLICATION

Psychological pricing

Friends in the marketing department have pointed out several examples from the business world that supposedly violate the law of demand. Evidence of these alleged departures is that some goods have sold better at higher prices than at lower prices. Marketing experts call such departures from the law of demand "psychological pricing." Let us take a look at a few examples, then analyze them.

One example pointed out is a new nasal spray that did not sell well when introduced at a price lower than the price of well-known national brands. An increase in the price of the new spray increased sales. Another case of a firm's raising price to increase sales involved the pantyhose manufactured by a national hosiery firm. The particular brand of pantyhose sold better when the price was increased to the range at which competition was selling.

The marketing literature also points out other examples, such as a car wax, the sales of which increased after a price increase. There was a marketing experiment in which a particular brand of ink was displayed at 25¢ and 15¢. Everything but the price and the name was the same. The ink sold better at 25¢ than at 15¢.* There are many other examples available.

The question is, do these and similar empirical examples mean that the law of demand does not hold under these circumstances? The answer is, "No, these examples imply no such thing." The problem is one of ignorance.† Again ask yourself the question, Is there anything you buy that you would be willing to buy more of if the price rises? Your answer is probably no; but you may well judge

---

* For these and other instances, see chapter 10, "Demand Curve Estimation and Psychological Pricing," in F. C. Sturdivant et al., *Managerial Analysis in Marketing* (Glenview, Ill.: Scott, Foresman, 1970).

† Do not equate ignorance with stupidity. Ignorance means lacking knowledge about something. Even the smartest people are ignorant about many, many things, possibly through lack of interest. If I value the use of my time more in some other alternative than in learning about the diet of the ancient Incas, I will remain ignorant in that area. As in all things, overcoming ignorance has a cost.

quality by price when you are uncertain (ignorant) about product quality. This is not irrational behavior; in fact, it is quite easy to explain why this type of behavior (products that sell more at higher than at lower prices) does not violate the law of downsloping demand.

First of all, your time is valuable. Since time is scarce, no one takes the time to become an expert on every item available. While you are shopping around gaining information about products, you could be working or consuming leisure. The time that you spend shopping has value in the sense that you are allocating time (a scarce resource) away from other activities. Thus, economists say that the time spent shopping has an opportunity cost, and the total cost of a good is the price of that good plus the value of the time spent shopping for it.

Secondly, people note from past experience that frequently, although not always, price and quality are directly related. Thus, price is often used in lieu of quality research as an indicator of product quality. This would be expected when the monetary saving expected from buying the lower rather than the higher-priced item is low compared to the cost (in time) of gaining information that might save a little money. When absolute price variations among products are low relative to income, as would be expected in the case of relatively low-priced items, one would expect people to do less systematic research and to judge quality more by prices. The absolute price variation among higher-priced goods is greater. Since the absolute difference is greater for higher-priced than for lower-priced goods, the cost of judging quality by price is greater relative to the cost of systematic quality research for higher-priced goods. Thus, as one would expect, consumers do depend more upon research and less upon price as an indicator of quality when purchasing high-cost (relative to income) items, such as housing, automobiles, and major household appliances. In other words, as the cost of taking price as an indicator of quality rises, people do it less.

Furthermore, as the returns to quality research rise, we should expect people to rely more on research and less on price as an indicator of quailty. This again would be the case for higher-priced goods where the cost of making a purchasing mistake is greater. The penalty for misjudging quality in an automobile is greater than that for misjudging a 25¢ bottle of ink. All of the examples given above are for low-priced goods. One would guess that if the price of the goods in these examples had been increased much above the going price, sales would have fallen substantially. The ink at $1 a bottle would not have sold well when other brands were selling at around 25¢. In almost every example about which I have heard, the lower-priced good was well below the average price of similar goods, leading consumers to think they were not as good. In each case the price was increased only to about the "going" price, never well above, or the price increase was accompanied by a vigorous marketing campaign.

Finally, when consumers believe that quality differences among different brand names are great they will tend to buy higher-priced brands than when they expect little quality difference. That is, when consumers believe they will gain little quality at higher prices they tend to pay lower prices. Marketing experiments on brands of razor blades, floor wax, cooking sherry, mothballs, salt, aspirin, and beer tend to verify this hypothesis.‡

Thus, we can easily explain apparent exceptions to the law of demand. If consumers *know* two goods are exactly alike in every way (including prestige) and choose the higher-priced good, it would be an exception. For some goods, the imputed quality is judged by price when the cost of other research on quality is high relative to expected return. These are different goods at different prices in the minds of some consumers, and the cases cited are not violations of the law of demand.

----

‡ See Sturdivant et al., *Managerial Analysis in Marketing* for a description of such experiments.

4.5 LABOR SUPPLY AND SOME APPLICATIONS

The tools developed in this chapter can be easily adapted to analyze the theory of labor supply. We can consider that a person's willingness to supply a certain amount of his labor time is the same as that individual's demanding leisure time. Thus the analytical tools pertaining to demand theory are applicable to labor supply and the economic problems associated with labor supply.

4.5.a Derivation of labor supply from indifference curves

Figure 4.5.1, panel A contains a portion of an individual's indifference map between income and leisure. Instead of depending strictly upon the quantity of goods, utility is now regarded as a function of income and leisure. Note from the shape of the indifference curves that we have assumed that both income and leisure are considered desirable by the

FIGURE 4.5.1

INDIFFERENCE CURVE ANALYSIS OF LABOR SUPPLY

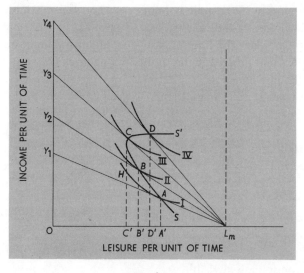

Panel A

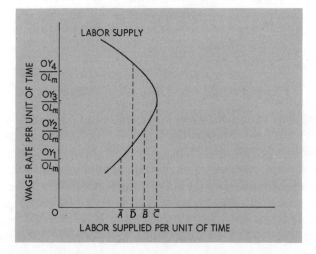

Panel B

individual; that is, one does not become satiated with leisure within the relevant range.

Before considering the problem of how the consumer maximizes utility, a word of explanation about the unit of measurement for leisure and the vertical line at L_m is in order. The unit of measurement along the horizontal axis can be hours per day, days per year, or any other period of time. Obviously if the unit is hours per day, the maximum time for leisure is 24 hours. If the unit is days of leisure, the maximum is 7 per week or 365 per year. The line L_m indicates the maximum attainable units of leisure per time period. If the individual chooses OC' units of leisure per period, he also chooses $C'L_m$ for work; or if he chooses OL_m of leisure, he does not work at all. The unit of measurement chosen for the horizontal axis clearly specifies the unit for the vertical. For example, when leisure is designated as hours per day, the vertical axis must measure income per day. Each indifference curve specifies the various combinations of income and leisure that yield the same level of satisfaction. For example, the consumer considers OC' leisure (and hence $C'L_m$ work) and income $C'H$ equivalent to OA' leisure (and hence $A'L_m$ work) and income $A'A$, since both points lie on the same indifference curve. The slopes of the curves indicate the rates at which an individual is willing to trade leisure for income. We assume for analytical convenience that both income and leisure are continuouly divisible.

The budget lines are determined by the payment per unit of time. If the unit is hours per day, the budget line is determined by the individual's hourly wage rate; if days per year, by the earnings per day. Consider budget line Y_1L_m. If the individual works the entire time period (say 24 hours per day) and consequently takes no leisure, he could make OY_1 per time period. Assuming specialization in leisure and no work, income is zero. The slope of the budget line is the relevant wage rate or payment per unit of time. The "cost" of a unit of leisure is the sacrificed earnings for that period of time.[3] Y_2L_m, Y_3L_m, and Y_4L_m are the relevant budget lines for higher wage rates, OY_2/OL_m, OY_3/OL_m, and OY_4/OL_m, respectively.

With a given wage rate, the highest attainable level of utility is given by the point where the relevant budget line is tangent to the indifference curve. An individual with the wage rate indicated by the slope of Y_1L_m achieves the highest attainable level of utility at point A. He chooses OA' leisure, $A'L_m$ work, and receives an income of $A'A$. If the wage rises to that level designated by budget line Y_2L_M, the highest attainable level of

---

[3] For simplicity we assume a constant wage rate regardless of the amount of time worked. Certainly "overtime" work might be at overtime pay or a second job could be taken at a lower wage than the primary job. We also assume that the individual is free to choose the amount of time he works; sometimes this may not be the case.

utility is at B, where the individual works $B'L_m$ for an income of $B'B$ and enjoys OB' leisure time. Points C and D indicate the equilibria leisure, work, and income for the other two budget lines, and SS' connects these and all intermediate equilibria. Thus, SS' indicates the amount of time the individual is willing to work (or the amount of labor he is willing to supply) at each of a series of wages.

Note that at relatively low wages the individual is willing to work more, or to consume less leisure, as the wage rate increases. Since an increase in potential earnings causes leisure to cost more (in lost earnings), he chooses less leisure and more work. After point C, however, further increases in the wage rate induce more leisure and less work. Leisure still costs the individual more as he moves from C to D, but the income effect means that the individual chooses to consume more leisure with the increased earnings (an exercise at the end of this chapter will help clarify this last relation).

Just as we can derive demand and Engel curves from price-consumption and income-consumption curves, we can derive a labor supply curve from curves such as SS'. Figure 4.5.1, panel B, shows the labor supply curve derived from the indifference map in panel A. The distance $O\bar{A}$ in panel B equals $A'L_m$ in panel A and is the amount of work associated with wage rate OY_I/OL_m, and so on. Since SS' bends backward at C, the labor supply curve bends backward at $O\bar{C}$.

APPLICATIONS

Some effects of an income tax minimum guaranteed income

Many times we cannot obtain a definitive answer to important policy questions by just using basic economic theory. We can only get the answer "It depends," or "The theory does not say," or "It's an empirical question." This is still, of course, a legitimate use of theory. Certainly a theory is useful to show those who assert "obvious" answers that the answers are not so apparent.

We take two important policy questions as examples. These questions are even now being analyzed by governmental policy makers, because the solutions are certainly important for policy purposes. These problems are the effect on the incentive to work of an increase in the rate of income tax and the imposition of a government-supported guaranteed minimum income.

Turn first to the income tax, the results of which are much easier

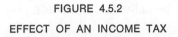

FIGURE 4.5.2

EFFECT OF AN INCOME TAX

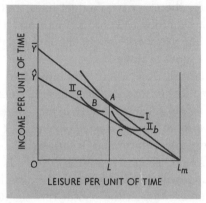

to analyze. Begin analysis under the assumption of no income tax. Consider the individual depicted by Figure 4.5.2. Before the income tax the income-leisure budget line is $\overline{Y}L_m$; the individual attains equilibrium on indifference curve I at A, working LL_m and consuming OL units of leisure per period of time.

The imposition of an income tax rotates the budget line downward to $\hat{Y}L_m$. The new budget line is very close to the old at low incomes, reflecting low taxation. Since high incomes are taxed more, the new line is further below the old at high incomes. Note that the before-tax income-leisure trade-off is the same. But the after-tax line rotates downward.

As Figure 4.5.2 indicates, the individual may choose to work more or work less. Points B or C on indifference curves II_a or II_b are equally possible, depending upon the indifference map. If point B is the new equilibrium, more work time is chosen; if point C is chosen, less work time and more leisure are chosen. Certainly other points on $\hat{Y}L_m$ are possible as well. Thus our theory does not give a definitive answer. As noted, the solution must be empirical in nature.

Let us turn now to another implication of a possible governmental policy and analyze the effect of a guaranteed minimum income. Many discussions of guaranteed minimum income ignore the problem of work incentives. In its most familiar form a guaranteed minimum income would allow people to work, but those who are unable to earn the minimum income would receive the difference between what they earn and the designated minimum from the government. It has been asserted that a person who could not make the minimum income would not work, but that anyone who could make more would choose

FIGURE 4.5.3

INDIFFERENCE CURVE ANALYSIS OF A
MINIMUM GUARANTEED INCOME

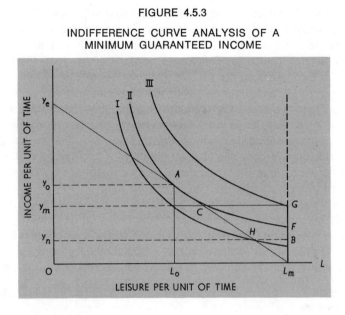

to work. We can analyze the theoretical aspects of the problem rather simply.*

Consider an individual with an indifference map for leisure and earnings depicted by curves I, II, and III and earning possibilities shown by budget line Y_eL_m in Figure 4.5.3. Following the type of analysis previously developed, we can see that equilibrium is at income OY_o, leisure OL_o, and work time L_oL_m per period of time. Now suppose the government declares that income OY_m per period is a "necessary" income. No one should receive less. The government will make up any difference between what one earns and OY_m, assuming, of course, that one earns less than OY_m. Since the individual under consideration is earning more than OY_m, the question is whether the minimum will affect him or not.

Note the way that the guaranteed minimum changes the set of possible incomes. The budget line from C to Y_c remains the same, but since the individual can have at least Y_m no matter how much he works and no matter what his wage rate, the income possibility line changes at point C. The new line becomes Y_eCGL_m. The individual can now attain the highest possible level of utility on indifference curve III by choosing OL_m leisure and no work. Since III is clearly

* This analysis is based upon an article by C. T. Brehm and T. R. Saving, "The Demand for General Assistance Payments," *American Economic Review,* December 1964, pp. 1002–18.

higher than II, the utility-maximizing individual will move from A to G even though he could earn more than the guaranteed minimum.

Under the circumstances, three factors could change and cause the person to choose to work some portion of the time. First, the minimum income could be decreased to some level below the intersection of indifference curve II with the perpendicular at L_m; for example, OY_n-may be the new minimum income. Then the person would choose point A on II. Second, the wage or potential earnings rate could increase enough to induce him to work. A sufficient increase would raise the budget line at least enough for it to become tangent to indifference curve III. Third, the individual might not consider welfare payments as desirable as equal payments for work.

In any case the answer must be reached empirically. Many types of tests have been done or are even now being carried out in order to reach a solution. However, no real conclusion has been reached yet. This example does show rather well how theory must be combined with statistical analysis to obtain answers to some problems.

4.5.b   Price search and the wage rate

We now have the analytical tools to address a question or problem that may have bothered you in this and the preceding chapter. Perhaps you have thought that people do not in fact merely respond to fixed, market-determined prices. People "shop around" for bargains, for lower prices. Stores advertise their lower prices. Because of the prevalence of price search it may be thought that non-fixed prices refute our theory. No such thing. For many, many economic problems the assumption of given prices is a useful one, which does not affect the theory's ability to make accurate predictions. For other problems the assumption of price search is useful, and this assumption enables one to solve other problems. We can use the simplified theory developed here to analyze the problem of the way in which price search affects consumer behavior.

Assume a consumer with a fixed wage rate. For some goods there are fixed prices. For others consumers feel that by searching (that is, shopping around) they can find lower prices. For example, they know that they can buy some good, say X, at p_{xo} (perhaps some catalog price). They also know that stores often reduce the price of X, and that prices differ among stores from time to time. They believe that the more time spent in price search, up to a point, the lower the price they will have to pay for a unit of X; that is, for the consumer $\triangle p_x / \triangle S_x < 0$, where S_x is the time spent in price search for X and, once again, $\triangle$ is "the change in." The problem is to determine the amount of time spent shopping for X.

To begin, note that searching for lower prices is not without cost. As we have emphasized, the total amount of time available is limited. Furthermore, the cost of a unit of time spent shopping is the wage rate, to extend the above analysis.

The expected return from a unit of price search is the amount that consumers believe they will save on a particular purchase by shopping around for a lower price. Certainly one would expect that the greater the known or average price of the product before any shopping is done, the greater the possible saving from price search. No matter how much you search, you could not reduce the price of a ten-cent candy bar more than ten cents. For a higher-priced item like a car the saving may be substantial.

Thus we would deduce that a consumer would price search as long as the expected gain from a unit of price search exceeds the cost of the time spent searching—the wage rate. If the expected gain is less than the value of time, the consumer would choose work or leisure. Thus the theory tells us that consumers will engage in more price search for a good the higher the average price of that good, and the more efficient they are in searching (that is, the higher the return to search). They will engage in less price search for a specific good the higher the wage rate (that is, the higher the cost of search). There have been several empirical studies that were found consistent with the theory.

Here we simply note that the assumption of variable prices can easily be handled in our theoretical structure. But we often omit this assumption in the interest of convenience and simplicity, when we are interested in other problems in economics.

APPLICATION

Implications of price search

Several studies have been done and are now in process concerning a very important national problem concerned with price search. These studies are based upon a theory similar to that set forth here. They concern the price effect of requiring gasoline stations to display gasoline prices prominently, so motorists can observe these prices from the street. Some areas, in the hope that such mandatory posting will drive down gasoline prices, already have such requirements. Others are contemplating such a move.

The conclusion is not quite clear. What do you believe would be the effect? There seem to be two opinions. First there are those who feel mandatory price posting would make price search much easier and less time-consuming. It takes time to drive into several stations and look at the prices on the pumps. Once in the station, many motorists feel it is simply not worth their time to leave and go into several other stations in order to save one or two cents a gallon. But with price search easier and less time-consuming, higher-priced stations would either be driven out of business or be forced to lower price. Thus, say the advocates of this position, gasoline prices would fall. Our theory seems to point in this direction.

There are certain opponents of this position. They say the price search theory is well and good, but they also say that mandatory posting would allow stations to collude. Owners of some stations would see that other stations are obtaining higher prices and would raise their own prices. The mandatory posting of prices would make price-fixing agreements easier to enforce. Price cutting would be more easily detected than when prices are not posted. Therefore, say those opposed to mandatory posting, gasoline prices would on average rise rather than fall.

We must note that this important policy question is still being debated. What is your opinion now? Carry it one step further. If mandatory posting can lower gasoline prices, why not force mandatory posting of all prices? Would you as a person in business be in favor of or opposed to such a move?

4.6 SUMMARY

The basic principles of consumer behavior and demand have now been developed. The fundamental point of this chapter is that if consumers behave so as to maximize satisfaction from a limited money income, quantity demanded (with one relatively unimportant exception) will vary inversely with price. Furthermore, an Engel curve is a locus of points relating equilibrium quantity to the level of money income at a specified set of relative prices. The Engel curve slopes upward if the good is normal over that range. If the good is inferior the curve bends backward. The substitution effect of a price change upon the consumption of that good is always negative; that is, quantity demanded varies inversely with price, considering the substitution effect only. If the good is normal, the income effect reinforces the substitution effect. If the good is inferior, the income effect to some extent offsets the substitution effect. The decision concerning the allocation of time between labor time and leisure can be analyzed with the same tools used to derive demand curves.

EXERCISE

An effect of better job opportunities for women

Over the past few years there have been great strides made in increasing the job opportunities for women. Women are more and more frequently finding jobs opening to them that were previously open exclusively, or almost exclusively, to men. The pay for women relative to men has been rising. This trend seems likely to continue.

The question is how will this trend be expected to affect the birthrate? Use your theory to analyze this question. Do not neglect either the substitution effect or the income effect.

Turn first to our labor-leisure theory. While carrying, giving birth to, and bringing up a child would probably not be considered as truly leisure time activities, they are, for a woman who is doing them, substitute activities for work. Thus the cost of a woman's time in child raising is the lost income from work that could have been done during this time. As the opportunities and potential incomes for women increase, the cost of having children increases also. A woman who works as a typist in an office gives up much less to raise a child than a woman who is a vice president in that company or one who is a professor in a university.

One would think then, considering the cost alone, that the birthrate would fall from this situation as the cost rises and families substitute goods for children. But as women's opportunities and incomes increase, the income of the family increases also. If children are an inferior good, this increase would also cause the birthrate to fall. But if children are a normal good, the higher income might increase the demand for children and offset the substitution or cost effect. Thus the situation is indeterminate.

Many analysts say, however, that even if children are normal goods, the income effect is spread over many other goods and in the case of children would not offset the higher cost of children. Moreover, they say that the income would fall during the time spent raising children, which would further reduce the income effect. Others say that men are tending to increase the amount of time they spend raising children, reducing the cost to women. What do you think will happen?

TECHNICAL PROBLEMS

1. Consider Figure E.4.1. Begin with the consumer in equilibrium with an income of $300 facing the prices $P_X = \$4$ and $P_Y = \$10$.

FIGURE E.4.1

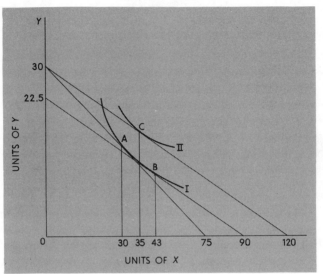

a. How much X is consumed in equilibrium?
    Let the price of X fall to $2.50, nominal income, and P_Y remaining constant.
b. What is the new equilibrium consumption of X?
c. How much income must be taken from the consumer to isolate the income and substitution effects?
d. The total effect of the price decrease is _____. The substitution effect is _____. The income effect is _____.
e. The good X is _____, but not _____.
f. Construct the consumer's demand curve for X with nominal money income constant; with real income (utility) constant.

2. Figure E.4.2 shows an individual's indifference map between leisure and income. Ignore indifference curve III for now and assume that curves I and II make up the map. The unit of time is one day of 24 hours. The wage rate is $3 per hour.
    a. How much does the individual choose to work? How much leisure does he consume?
        Let the wage rate rise to $5 an hour.

FIGURE E.4.2

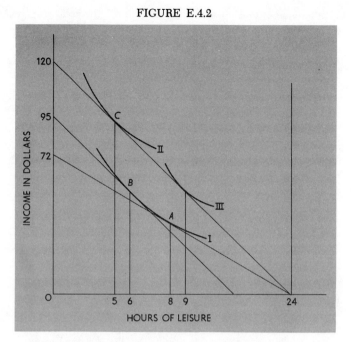

b. Ignoring III, what are his work and leisure time?
    Suppose at the wage rate of $5 the individual was taxed just enough to
    make him choose a point on the original indifference curve, I.
c. What is the substitution effect for the wage change from $3 to $5?
d. Return the taxed income; what is the income effect?
e. What is the total effect?
f. In this example leisure is a (normal, inferior) good, and the income
    effect (offsets, reinforces) the substitution effect.
g. Derive the associated supply curve for labor.
    Now let the relevant indifference map be I and III.
h. Derive the new supply of labor curve.
i. Now the total effect of a wage increase from $3 to $5 is _____, the
    substitution effect is _____, and the income effect is _____.
j. Leisure is now a (normal, inferior) good.
k. What can you say about the classification of leisure and a backward
    bending supply of labor?
l. Draw an indifference curve IV tangent to the budget line associated
    with $5 so that leisure is a normal good but the supply of labor is not
    backward bending.

3. Use indifference curves to analyze the effect of the following policies on the quantity demanded of some good, X.
   a. Government gives the individual $500.
   b. Government places a 5-percent tax on good X only.
   c. Government places a 5-percent tax on both goods.

4. An individual can choose between income and leisure as depicted in Figure E.4.3. The maximum amount of time available in the period is OT. The first wage rate is indicated by the slope of MT; the new higher rate by the slope of RT. Regardless of the wage rate the person works just long enough to earn income OI.

FIGURE E.4.3

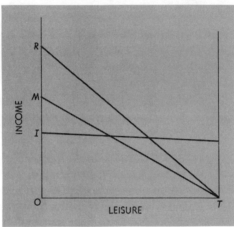

a. Draw in the indifference curves at the two points of equilibrium.
b. Is leisure a normal or an inferior good to the individual? Prove graphically.

5. Graphically derive a demand curve for a normal good. Start with indifference curves between goods X and Y. Let the price of X fall. Identify the income and substitution effects of this price decline on the graph. Identify two points on the resulting demand curve, showing where you got each of the points. Explain each step. Draw and label your diagrams clearly.

6. Draw an income consumption curve and an Engel curve for good X, assuming that the price of X is $10 and the price of Y is $25, by examining incomes of $100, $200 and $300. Show your work. (Use conventionally shaped indifference curves.)

7. Suppose the following table represents points on one indifference curve.

Point	Quantity of pizzas	Quantity of hamburgers
A	10	1
B	8	3
C	6	6
D	4	10
E	2	15

a. Draw this indifference curve, putting quantity of pizzas on the vertical axis and quantity of hamburgers on the horizontal axis. Label points *A, B, C, D,* and *E.*

b. Does this indifference curve show diminishing *MRS?* Defend your answer by calculating the *MRS* between points *A* and *B* and between *B* and *C.*

8. A person's marginal rate of substitution between *X* and *Y* ($\Delta Y/\Delta X$) is 4. The person is in equilibrium with the price of *X* at $12 and the price of *Y* is $3. The price of *X* rises to $15 and the price of *Y* rises to $5. Income is varied to restrict the consumer to the same indifference curve. Does the consumer substitute more *X* for *Y* or more *Y* for *X?* Explain.

9. Economists admit that people have greatly differing taste patterns. But they say that for any two goods consumed by any two people picked at random, the marginal rates of substitution must be equal even though tastes differ. How can this be so?

10. We did not cover this point specifically in the text, but the derivation should give some insight into income and substitution effects.

Begin with a consumer in equilibrium. Let the price of the good plotted on the horizontal axis decrease. The good is inferior, so the income effect will to some extent offset the substitution effect, which is of course negative. Show the situation graphically, using indifference curves and pivoting budget lines, in which the income effect of the inferior good more than offsets the substitution effect.

ANALYTICAL PROBLEMS

1. Family size in the United States decreased for 50 years after 1900 while per capita income increased. Given constant tastes, children must be an inferior good. Evaluate.

2. A higher sales tax has been imposed on all automobiles in a particular state. *Every one* of the automobile salesmen in the state would have been opposed to the tax increase. Evaluate the conclusion under the following conditions:

a. The tax is a fixed dollar amount per car sold.

b. The tax is a given percentage of the purchase price.

    c. The tax is progressive, the percentage increasing with the price of the automobile.

3. Charitable contributions are deductible from income taxes. How would an increase in the tax rate affect charitable contributions? (Hint: consider both income and substitution effects.)

4. Suppose you are a government official given the job of estimating how a guaranteed annual income would affect labor force participation. You have a very large budget. How would you carry out this research?

5. For the entire United States assume that real per capita income rises over the next few years. Assume also all *relative* prices remain the same. Draw what you think would be the appropriate Engel curve for the following commodities. Explain why you drew them with the shape you did. Restrict yourself if you wish to the three shapes set forth in Figure 4.2.4.

    a. Toyotas and Pintos
    b. Cadillacs and Lincolns
    c. Water
    d. Fish
    e. All food
    f. College education
    g. Television sets
    h. Black and white television sets

6. If you manage a grocery store, how could you tell whether the price of a given item is too high or too low? What does "too high or too low" mean?

7. The material relevant to this question is taken up in a later chapter, but you can probably deal with it rather well right now. How would you answer someone who asserts that any air pollution at all is bad; there should be absolutely none? How would you answer the person who asserts that nothing should be done about any air pollution; it costs too much to prevent it?

5

Theory of production

5.1 INTRODUCTION

Now that we have completed demand theory, we have developed half of the theory of price. Let us turn to the other half of the theory, the theory of supply.

The basic foundation of the theory of supply is production theory. Production in a general sense refers to the creation of any good or service that people will buy. While we generally speak of production as being carried out by business firms, the theoretical structure is equally applicable to production of goods and services by agencies of government or by nonprofit institutions, such as hospitals and private universities.

One can speak just as well about a doctor producing medical care as a city government producing police protection. Ford Motor Company produces automobiles, the Corps of Engineers produces dams, and Stanford produces educated people. Most of the principles developed in this chapter apply to the production of either goods or services by private firms, branches of government, or nonprofit institutions.

We will, however, generally in this chapter concentrate upon the production of goods by business firms, only because it is simpler to specify the precise inputs and to identify the quantity of output. It is far easier to specify the number of automobiles produced by Ford or the amount of wheat produced by some specific farmer than it is to measure the amount of education produced by your school in a year or the amount of defense produced by the federal government. But keep in mind at all times that the basic principles also apply to production by agencies other than private business firms and to services as well as to goods.

5.1.a Production possibility curves and the theory of production

The theory of production illustrates the economic problem faced by every society, the problem of scarcity. Recall our discussion in Chapters 1 and 2 in which we introduced the problem of scarcity. In order for a society to gain additional goods and services of one type it must give up goods and services of other types.

Scarcity, the reason for such trade-offs, results from the fact that goods and services are produced by factors of production such as labor, capital, natural resources, and so on. At any time in any society these inputs or factors of production are limited. The limit is at a higher level for very rich societies, but the limit is still there. The basic point is that in order to have some additional amounts of certain goods, the society must use inputs to produce these additional goods. Where do the added inputs come from? They must be taken away from the production of other goods and services. Consequently these other goods must be given up.

If society is to get more cotton, then resources such as land and farm machinery must be withdrawn from the production of other crops. If government wishes to build more roads, labor and machinery must be taken from the construction of other things—houses, offices, and so on. Thus the entire concept of scarcity is based upon this notion of production and the use of scarce inputs to carry out production. The problem of giving up some goods (or the inputs needed to produce these goods) in order to use the inputs to produce other goods exists in all economies regardless of their social makeup. The most totalitarian dictatorship, the most free democracy, and all societies in between face the same problem.

This problem is best illustrated with the concept of a production possibility frontier. This frontier illustrates the way societies must make trade-offs among different goods and services—publically or privately produced.

To analyze the concept of a limit or a frontier to the available goods and services, let us for analytical simplicity assume that a society can

FIGURE 5.1.1

PRODUCTION POSSIBILITIES CURVE

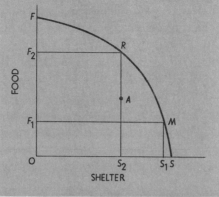

produce and consume only two goods—call them food and shelter. Society's finite resources can be used to produce these two goods in many different combinations.

Figure 5.1.1 shows a hypothetical production possibility frontier or curve of a typically assumed shape. The curve *FRMS* shows the combinations of the two goods possible for the society with the given amount of productive resources available. The figure shows that if society chooses to produce no shelter it can have *OF* units of food per period; or if it chooses to produce no food, it can consume *OS* units of shelter. Similarly, it can choose any other point on the curve, such as *R*, with OF_2 units of food and OS_2 units of shelter, or *M*, with a combination of OF_1 and OS_1 food and shelter.

Furthermore, the society could consume any combination inside of the curve *FRMS*, such as the combination indicated by point *A*. But at interior points such as *A*, society is not using all of its resources, or it is not using the resources efficiently. In this case, the society producing at *A* could increase its food consumption to OF_2 without giving up any shelter, it could increase shelter with no sacrifice of food, or it could increase its consumption of both goods, moving to some point on *FRMS*. Scarcity exists simply because the society cannot consume any combination outside of the curve.

The shape of the curve reflects certain assumptions about the way in which the output of some goods can be substituted for other goods. In the first place it is obvious that the production possibilities curve slopes downward. This negative slope reflects the fact that in order to have more of one good, society must give up some portion of the other good. Note also that the curve decreases at a decreasing rate. For example, if the society decreases its food production from OF to OF_2 units, it can increase shelter from zero to OS_2. On the other hand if there is very little food being produced, say OF_1, and society moves from OF_1 to zero food, it gains only the very slight increase in shelter from OS_1 to OS. We have drawn the distance OF_1 to equal the distance F_2F. It is easily seen that the increase in shelter from an equal decrease in food diminishes greatly as the amount of shelter rises relative to the amount of food. Clearly the situation holds for decreases in shelter relative to increases in food.

The changes in the production of goods described above reflect the fact that resources are better adapted to one type of production than to another. As the output of a good rises, less suitable resources must be used to increase its output. Even though we have been concerned here with only two goods, the same principles apply in a multiple-good world.

This chapter and the next deal with the theories of production and cost. As you go through these theories—and they are related quite closely—relate the concepts developed in these theories to this fundamental principle of scarcity, as illustrated by the production possibility frontier.[1]

5.1.b Important points developed

The basic concepts to be learned in Chapter 5 are

1. How output varies with the services of one variable input.
2. The principle under which variable inputs can be substituted to produce output.
3. How to maximize the level of output obtainable at a given level of cost.
4. How to minimize the cost of producing a given level of output.
5. The principles and results of technological change.

---

[1] Those students who have already gone through consumer theory will note many similarities between the concepts discussed there and the theory of production. Several users of this text have pointed out that they choose to cover production and cost theory before consumer theory. Therefore, we will not dwell on these similarities in this and the next chapter. We will, however, discuss briefly the similarities and differences after we have developed the theory here. Those who have not yet covered consumer behavior may omit those brief sections without any loss of continuity. For those students who have already studied consumer behavior theory the relations should be rather obvious.

5.2 PRODUCTION FUNCTIONS

Production processes typically require a wide variety of inputs. They are not as simple as "labor," "capital," and "materials"; many qualitatively different types of each are normally used to produce an output. With a given state of technology, the quantity of output depends upon the quantities of the various inputs used. This relation is more formally described by a *production function* associating physical output with physical rates of input.

> **Definition.** A production function is a schedule (or table, or mathematical equation) showing the maximum amount of output that can be produced from any specified set of inputs, given the existing technology or "state of the art." In short, the production function is a catalog of output possibilities.

A hypothetical example of a very simple production function is the production of a student's course grade from study time. This might take the form of a table such as

Expected grade	Minimum study time (hours)
A	10
B	6
C	3
D	1
F	0

This table relates the expected grade to the minimum time allocated to study. Note that a student could study more than the required time for a grade but receive no higher grade if he does not advance completely into the next category. Five hours of study still produce only a C. The production function could take the form of a simple equation such as

$$G = 10T,$$

where G is the numerical grade and T is time spent studying. These functions make product (grade) depend only on one input (study time). Other functions relate output or product to two or more inputs. Still more complicated functions relate several different outputs to several different inputs. We will be dealing primarily with one output produced by either one or two inputs. The principles apply to more than two inputs, however.

5.2.a Short and long runs

In analyzing the process of production it is convenient to introduce an important distinction: classification of inputs as fixed or variable. Accordingly, a *fixed input* is defined as one the quantity of which cannot readily be changed when market conditions indicate that a change in output is desirable. To be sure, no input is ever *absolutely* fixed, no matter how short the period of time under consideration. But frequently, for the sake of analytical simplicity, we hold some inputs fixed, reasoning perhaps that while these inputs are in fact variable, the cost of immediate variation is so great as to take them out of the range of relevance for the particular decision at hand. Buildings, major pieces of machinery, and managerial personnel are examples of inputs that generally cannot be rapidly augmented or diminished. A *variable input,* on the other hand, is one the quantity of which may be changed quite readily in response to desired changes in output. Many types of labor services and the inputs of raw and processed materials fall in this category.

For the sake of analysis economists introduce a distinction between the short and long runs. The *short run* refers to that period of time in which the input of one or more productive agents is fixed. Therefore, changes in output must be accomplished exclusively by changes in the use of variable inputs. Thus if producers wish to expand output in the short run, they must usually do so by using more hours of labor service with the existing plant and equipment. Similarly, if they wish to reduce output in the short run, they may discharge certain types of workers; but they cannot immediatley "discharge" a building or a diesel locomotive, even though its use may fall to zero.

In the long run, however, even this is possible, for the *long run* is defined as that period of time (or planning horizon) in which all inputs are variable. The long run, in other words, refers to that time in the future when output changes can be accomplished in the manner most advantageous to the producer. For example, in the short run a producer may be able to expand output only by operating existing plant for more hours per day. In the long run, it may be more economical to install additional productive facilities and return to the normal workday.

5.2.b Fixed or variable proportions

Our attention here is restricted mainly to production under conditions of *variable proportions*. The ratio of input quantities may vary; the producer, therefore, must determine not only the optimal level of output to produce but also the optimal proportion in which to combine inputs.

There are two different ways of stating the principle of variable proportions. First, variable proportions production implies that output can be changed in the short run by changing the amount of variable inputs used in cooperation with the fixed inputs. Naturally, as the amount of one input is changed, the others remaining constant, the *ratios* change. Second, when production is subject to variable proportions, the *same* output can be produced by various combinations of inputs—that is, by different input ratios. This may apply only to the long run, but it is relevant to the short run when there is more than one variable input.

Most economists regard production under conditions of variable proportions as typical of both the short and long run. There is certainly no doubt that proportions are variable in the long run. When making an investment decision a producer may choose among a wide variety of different production processes. As polar opposites, an automobile can be practically handmade or it can be made by assembly line techniques. In the short run, however, there may be some cases in which output is subject to fixed proportions.

Fixed-proportions production means that there is one, and only one, ratio of inputs that can be used to produce a good. If output is expanded or contracted, all inputs must be expanded or contracted so as to maintain the fixed input ratio. At first glance this might seem the usual condition: one man and one shovel produce a ditch, two parts hydrogen and one part oxygen produce water. Adding a second shovel or a second part of oxygen will not augment the rate of production. In such cases the producer has little discretion about what combination of inputs to employ. The only decision is how much to produce.

In actuality, examples of fixed proportions production are hard to come by. Certainly some "ingredient" inputs are often used in relatively fixed proportions to output. Otherwise the quality of the product will change. There is so much leather in a pair of shoes of a particular size and style. Use less leather, and we have a different type of shoe. There is so much tobacco in a cigarette and so on. In many cases the producer has little choice in this regard. But shoes and cigarettes can be produced in many ways using many different combinations of labor and machinery. In fact, there is even a certain amount of substitution possible among ingredient inputs. In any case we will in general direct our attention to those aspects of production over which the producer has some control. Thus we concentrate here basically on production under variable proportions.

ASIDE

Fixity of ingredient inputs

Just in passing we should emphasize that this fixity of ingredient inputs is really only a short-run problem. Historically, when these "necessary" ingredients have become very high priced or practically impossible to obtain, businesses, generally under the lure of profits, have invented new processes, discovered new ingredients, or somehow overcome the problem of a given production function and increasingly scarce ingredients.

The history of businesses is full of such examples. Prior to World War II American tire manufacturers knew that raw rubber—a necessary input for many products—was going to be impossible to obtain in the event of war. Synthetic rubber was thought impossible. But less than one year after an eminent chemist presented at a chemistry conference a paper explaining why it was impossible to produce synthetic rubber at any reasonable price, Du Pont was manufacturing synthetic rubber and selling it at a price lower than that at which raw rubber could be obtained. Prior to that Du Pont had developed nylon, partly because silk would be unavailable for stockings.

During the early days of the industrial revolution in England, charcoal, which was made from wood, was a necessary ingredient in the production of steel. The problem was that English mills were producing so much steel that the country was running out of trees. During this period the British newspapers constantly predicted that the manufacturing center of the world would move to Germany and Sweden, both of which had plenty of trees. But as wood became more expensive manufacturers discovered that coke, made from coal, was better for steel production; England happened to be sitting on gigantic coal deposits.

W. P. Gramm, a colleague of ours, recently pointed out in *The Wall Street Journal* that the oil crisis of 1973–74 was really the *second oil crisis* faced by the United States.* The first was the whale

---

* See "The Energy Crisis in Perspective," *The Wall Street Journal,* November 30, 1973.

oil crisis of the middle 19th century. During that period whale oil was absolutely necessary for lighting and lubrication; but the whales were disappearing under the pressure of increased hunting. The real price of whale oil quadrupled over a short period of time. Possibly spurred on by these higher prices people discovered oil and how to use it for lighting and lubrication. Whales became almost redundant for oil production, and the price of whale oil fell drastically.

There are many other such historical examples of technological changes replacing a "necessary" ingredient input when this input became too scarce. Even now the search continues for substitutes for scarce raw materials. One firm is testing a battery that may well power small and medium-sized automobiles. In fact the battery is now, we are told, able to power an automobile 50 miles per hour. It is too expensive to use presently; in the near future, perhaps not. Other firms are working on cheaper substitutes for gas.

In any case, these brief passing remarks are not part of the basic theoretical structure of production theory. They are important to note, however, in the context of our discussion about fixed-proportion ingredient inputs. Probably, in the long run, no input has to be used in fixed proportion.

5.3 PRODUCTION WITH ONE VARIABLE INPUT

To clarify analysis we first introduce some simplifying assumptions in order to cut through the complexities of dealing with hundreds of different inputs. Thus our attention is focused upon the essential principles of production. More specifically, we assume that there is only one variable input, which can be combined in different proportions with fixed inputs to produce various quantities of output. Note that these assumptions also imply the assumption that inputs may be combined in *various* proportions to produce the commodity in question.

5.3. a Total, average, and marginal product: Arithmetic approach

Assume that a firm with a fixed plant can apply different numbers of workers to get output according to columns 1 and 2 of Table 5.3.1. Columns one and two define a production function over a specific range.

They specify the product per unit of time for different numbers of workers in that period. The total output rises up to a point (nine workers), then declines. The *total output* is the *maximum* output obtainable from each number of workers with the given plant.

Average and marginal product are obtained from the production function. The *average product* of labor is the total product divided by the number of workers (here it rises, reaches a maximum at 15, then declines thereafter). *Marginal product* is the additional output attributable to using one additional worker with a fixed plant (or with the use of all other inputs fixed). It first rises, then falls, becoming negative when an additional worker reduces total product.

Note that we speak of the marginal product of labor, not of the marginal product of a particular laborer. We assume all workers are the same, in the sense that if we reduce the number of workers from eight to seven, total product falls from 88 to 84 regardless of which of the eight workers is released. Thus, the order of hiring makes no difference; the third worker adds 20 units no matter who is hired.

Note also from the Table that when average product is rising (falling) marginal product is greater (less) than average. When average reaches its maximum, average equals marginal (at 15). This result is not a peculiarity of this particular table; it occurs for any production function in which the average product peaks. An example should illustrate this point. If you have taken two tests on which you have grades of 70 and 80, your average grade is 75. If your third test grade is higher than 75, say 90, your average rises, to 80 in the example. The 90 is the *marginal addition* to your total grade. If your third grade is less than 75, the marginal addition is below average and the average falls. This is the rela-

TABLE 5.3.1

TOTAL, AVERAGE, AND MARGINAL PRODUCTS OF LABOR

Number of workers	Total output per unit of time	Average product	Marginal product
1..............	10	10	10
2..............	25	12.5	15
3..............	45	15	20
4..............	60	15	15
5..............	70	14	10
6..............	78	13	8
7..............	84	12	6
8..............	88	11	4
9..............	90	10	2
10..............	88	8.8	−2

tion between all marginal and average schedules. In production theory, if each additional worker adds more than the preceding worker, average product rises; if each additional worker adds less than the preceding worker, average product falls.

The short-run production function set forth in Table 5.3.1 specifies a very common assumption in production theory. Marginal and average products first increase then decrease with marginal becoming negative after a point. Marginal reaches a peak before the peak of average is attained. At the peak of average, marginal equals average. These relations mean that total product at first increases at an increasing rate, then increases at a decreasing rate, and finally decreases. The graphical exposition in the next sub-section will illustrate these points.

However, while this shape is frequently assumed for a short-run (one variable input) production function, it is not the only shape assumed. We summarize in the following:

Definition. The average product of an input is total product divided by the amount of the input used. Thus, average product is the output-input ratio for each level of output and the corresponding volume of input. The marginal product of an input is the addition to total product attributable to the addition of one unit of the variable input to the production process, the fixed inputs remaining constant.

5.3.b Total, average, and marginal product: Graphical approach

The short-run production function in Figure 5.3.1 shows the maximum output per unit of time obtainable from different amounts of the variable input (labor), given a specified amount of the fixed inputs and the required amounts of the ingredient inputs. In Figure 5.3.1 and thereafter in this section, we assume that both the output and the variable input are continuously divisible. This assumption sacrifices little realism yet adds a great deal of analytical convenience. As you will see the product curve in this figure embodies the same assumptions about production given in subsection 5.3.a; both average and marginal product rise then fall, marginal product equaling average product at the maximum point of the latter.

In the Figure, Ox_0 is the *maximum* amount of output obtainable when OL_0 workers are combined with the fixed and ingredient inputs. Likewise, OL_1 workers can produce a maximum of Ox_1, and so forth. Certainly the specified numbers of inputs could produce less than the amount

FIGURE 5.3.1

DERIVATION OF AVERAGE PRODUCT
FROM TOTAL PRODUCT

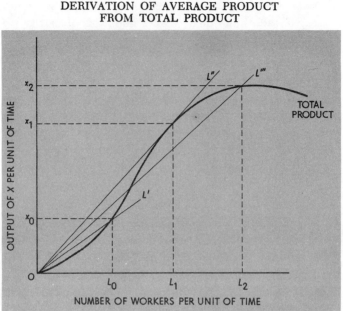

indicated by the total product curve but not more than that amount. First, total output increases with increases in the variable input up to a point, in this case OL_2 workers. After that so many workers are combined with the fixed inputs that output diminishes when additional workers are employed. Second, production at first increases at an increasing rate, then increases at a decreasing rate until the maximum is reached.

The average product of OL_0 workers is Ox_0/OL_0, the slope of the ray from the origin, OL'. In like manner, the average product of any number of workers can be determined by the slope of a ray from the origin to the relevant point on the total product curve; the steeper the slope, the larger the average product. It is easy to see that the slopes of rays from the origin to the total product curve in Figure 5.3.1 increase with additional labor until OL'' becomes tangent at OL_1 workers and Ox_1 output, then decrease thereafter (say, to OL''' at OL_2 workers). Hence typical average product curves associated with this total product curve first increase and then decrease thereafter.

As with average product, we can derive a marginal product curve from a total product curve. In Figure 5.3.2, OL_0 workers can produce Ox_0 units of output and OL_I can produce Ox_1. L_0L_1 additional workers in-

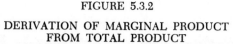

FIGURE 5.3.2

DERIVATION OF MARGINAL PRODUCT
FROM TOTAL PRODUCT

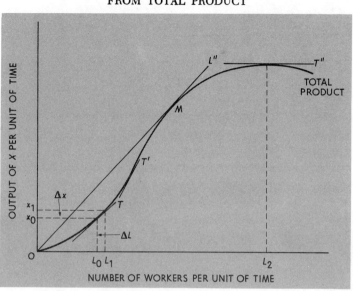

crease total product by $x_0 x_1$. Marginal product is therefore $x_0 x_1 / L_0 L_1$ or $\triangle x / \triangle L$, where the symbol $\triangle$ denotes "the change in." Let L_1 become very close to L_0; hence x_1 is very close to x_0; $\triangle x / \triangle L$ approaches the slope of the tangent T to the total product curve. Therefore, at any point on the total product curve, marginal product, which is the *rate of change of total product,* can be *estimated* by the slope of the tangent at that point.

On inspection we see that marginal product first increases; note that T' is steeper than T. It then decreases, OL'' at point M being less steep than T'. Marginal product becomes zero when OL_2 workers are employed (the slope of T'' is zero) and then becomes negative. At point M the slope of the tangent OL'' is also the slope of the ray from the origin to that point. As noted above, average product attains a maximum when a ray from the origin is tangent to the total product curve. Therefore, marginal product equals average product at the latter's maximum point. To repeat, so long as marginal product exceeds average product, the latter must rise; when marginal product is less than average product, the latter must fall. Thus, average product must attain its maximum when it is equal to marginal product.

FIGURE 5.3.3

TOTAL, AVERAGE, AND MARGINAL PRODUCTS

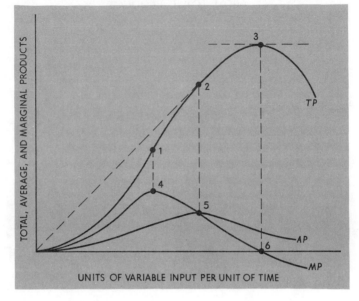

Figure 5.3.3 illustrates all these relations. In this graph one can see not only the relation between marginal and average products but also the relation of these two curves to total product.

Consider first the total product curve. For very small amounts of the variable input, total product rises gradually. But even at a low level of input it begins to rise quite rapidly, reaching its maximum slope (or rate of increase) at point 1. Since the slope of the total product curve equals marginal product, the maximum slope (point 1) must correspond to the maximum point on the marginal product curve (point 4).

After attaining its maximum slope at point 1, the total product curve continues to rise. But output increases at a decreasing rate, so the slope is less steep. Moving outward along the curve from point 1, the point is soon reached at which a ray from the origin is just tangent to the curve (point 2). Since tangency of the ray to the curve defines the condition for maximum average product, point 2 lies directly above point 5.

As the quantity of variable input is expanded from its value at point 2, total product continues to increase. But its rate of increase is progressively slower until point 3 is finally reached. At this position total product is at a maximum; thereafter it declines. Over a tiny range around point 3, additional input does not change total output. The slope of the total product curve is zero; thus marginal product must also be zero. This is shown by the fact that point 3 and 6 occur at precisely the same input value. And since total product declines beyond point 3, marginal product becomes negative.

Most of the important relations have so far been discussed with reference to the total product curve. To emphasize certain relations, however, consider the marginal and average product curves. Marginal product at first increases, reaches a maximum at point 4 (the point of diminishing marginal physical returns) and declines thereafter. It eventually becomes negative beyond point 6, where total product attains its maximum.

Average product also rises at first until it reaches its maximum at point 5, where marginal and average products are equal. It subsequently declines, conceivably becoming zero if total product itself becomes zero. Finally, one may observe that marginal product exceeds average product when the latter is increasing and is less than average product when the latter is decreasing.

5.3.c Law of diminishing marginal physical returns

The slope of the marginal product curve in Figure 5.3.3 illustrates an important principle, the law of diminishing marginal physical returns. As the number of units of the variable input increases, other inputs held constant, after a point the marginal product of the variable input declines. When the amount of the variable input is small relative to the fixed inputs (the fixed inputs are plentiful relative to the variable input), more intensive utilization of fixed inputs by variable inputs may increase the marginal output of the variable input. Nonetheless a point is reached beyond which an increase in the use of the variable input yields progressively less additional returns. Each additional unit has, on average, fewer units of the fixed inputs with which to work.

Principle (the law of diminishing marginal physical returns). **As the amount of a variable input is increased, the amount of other (fixed) inputs held constant, a point is reached beyond which marginal product declines.**

This is a simple statement concerning physical relations that have been observed in the real economic world. While it is not susceptible of mathematical proof or refutation, it is of some worth to note that a contrary observation has never been recorded. That is why it is called a law.

Psychologists have even found that the law holds true for consecutive study time.[2]

5.3.d Three stages of production

Economists use the relations among total, average, and marginal products to define three stages of production, illustrated in Figure 5.3.4. Stage I covers that range of variable input use over which average product increases. In other words, stage I corresponds to increasing *average returns* to the variable inputs. Stage III is defined as the range of negative marginal product or declining total product. Additional units of variable input during this stage of production actually cause a decrease

FIGURE 5.3.4

STAGES OF PRODUCTION

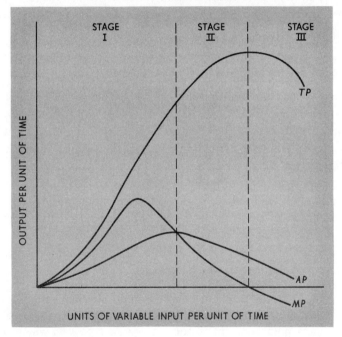

[2] Do not make the common mistake, however, of saying that you stopped studying because diminishing returns set in. The term "diminishing returns" is frequently heard in noneconomic usage and is almost as frequently misused. Diminishing returns may set in with the first unit of study time, but you may continue studying. You cease studying when the marginal utility of the (expected) increase in grade (or of the pleasure of studying) from an additional unit of study time is less than the expected marginal utility of using that time for something else.

in total output. Even if units of the variable input were free, a rational producer would not employ them beyond the point of zero marginal product because their use entails a reduction in total output. Stage II includes the range over which marginal product is positive and less than average product.

The concept of a single variable input is quite important in developing the more advanced theory of production and particularly in deriving demands for factors of production. It is not a really important real-world concept since it would be difficult to visualize a firm using only one variable input. Thus we shall postpone our examples and applications until the theory has been extended a little further.

5.4 PRODUCTION WITH TWO OR MORE VARIABLE INPUTS

Here we consider the more general case of several variable inputs. For graphical purposes we concentrate upon only two inputs; but all of the results hold for more than two. One may assume either that these two inputs are the only variable inputs or that one of the inputs represents some combination of all variable inputs other than one.

5.4.a Production isoquants

When analyzing production with several variable inputs we cannot simply use several sets of average and marginal product curves such as those discussed above. Recall that these curves were derived holding the use of all other inputs constant and letting the use of only one input vary. Thus when the amount of one variable input changes, the total, average, and marginal product curves of all other variable inputs shift. In the case of two variable inputs, increasing the use of one increases the amount of this input that is combined with the other input. This increase would probably cause a shift in the marginal and average product curves of the other input. For example, an increase in capital would quite possibly result in an increase in the marginal product of labor over a wide range of labor use.

This proposition is shown graphically in Figure 5.4.1. We show only the situation in which labor is in stage II. TP_0 in panel A and AP_0 and MP_0 in panel B are the original total, average, and marginal product curves of labor for a fixed amount of another factor, say capital. If the amount of capital increases, the three curves increase to TP_1, AP_1, and MP_1. This means that for each amount of labor over the relevant range total, average, and marginal products are greater. For example, for OL units of

FIGURE 5.4.1

TOTAL, AVERAGE, AND MARGINAL PRODUCTS FOR TWO
DIFFERENT AMOUNTS OF THE FIXED FACTOR

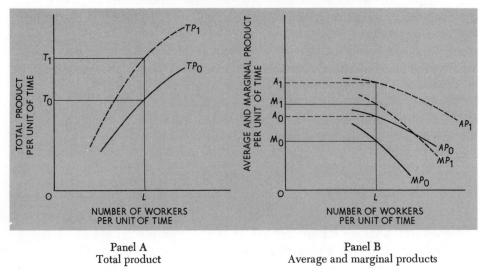

Panel A   Panel B
Total product   Average and marginal products

labor, an increase in capital increases total product from OT_0 to OT_1,
average product from OA_0 to OA_1, and marginal product from OM_0
to OM_1.

If both labor and capital are variable, each factor has an infinite set of
product curves, one for every amount of the other factor. Therefore another tool of analysis is necessary when there is more than one variable
factor. This tool is the *production isoquant*.

An isoquant is a curve or locus of points showing all possible combinations of inputs physically capable of producing a given level of output.
An isoquant that lies above another designates a higher level of output.

Figure 5.4.2 illustrates two isoquants of the shape typically assumed in
economic theory. Capital use is plotted on the vertical axis and labor use
on the horizontal. Isoquant I shows the locus of combinations of capital
and labor yielding 100 units of output. The producer can produce 100
units of output by using 10 units of capital and 75 of labor, or 50 units of
capital and 15 of labor, or by using any other combination of inputs on I.
Similarly, isoquant II shows the various combinations of capital and labor
that can produce 200 units of output.

Isoquants I and II are only two of an infinite number of isoquants that
are possible. In fact there are an infinite number of isoquants between I
and II because there are an infinite number of possible production levels

between 100 and 200 units, provided, as we have assumed, that the product is continuously divisible.

5.4.b Properties of isoquants

Isoquants have several important properties. First, as shown in Figure 5.4.2, isoquants slope downward over the relevant range of production. This negative slope indicates that if the producer decreases the amount of capital employed, more labor must be added in order to keep the rate of output constant. Or if labor use is decreased, capital must be increased to keep output constant. Thus the two inputs can be substituted for one another to maintain a constant level of output.

Great theoretical and practical importance is attached to the rate at which one input must be substituted for another in order to keep output constant. This rate at which one input is substituted for another along an isoquant is called the *Marginal Rate of Technical Substitution* (*MRTS*). It is defined as

$$MRTS = -\frac{\triangle C}{\triangle L},$$

FIGURE 5.4.2

TYPICAL ISOQUANTS

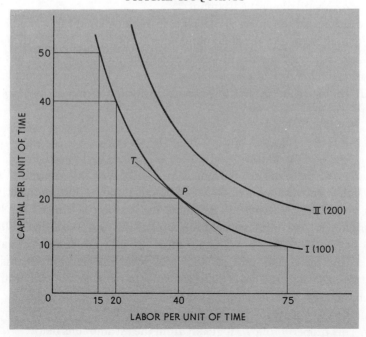

where C is the amount of the input measured along the vertical axis, capital, and L is the amount measured along the horizontal, labor. The minus sign is added in order to make $MRTS$ a positive number, since $\triangle C / \triangle L$, the slope of the isoquant, is negative.

Over the relevant range of production the marginal rate of technical substitution diminishes; that is, as more and more labor is used relative to capital, the absolute value of $\triangle C / \triangle L$ decreases along an isoquant. This can be seen in Figure 5.4.2. If capital is decreased by 10 units from 50 to 40, labor must be increased by only 5 units, from 15 to 20, in order to keep the level of output at 100 units. But if capital is decreased by 10 units from 20 to 10, labor must increase by 35 units, from 40 to 75, to keep output at 100 units.

The fact that the marginal rate of technical substitution diminishes means that isoquants must be concave from above; that is, in the neighborhood of a point of tangency the isoquant must lie above the tangent. This relation is seen at point P in Figure 5.4.2. The slope of the tangent T shows the rate at which labor can be substituted for capital in the neighborhood of point P, maintaining an output of 100 units. For very small movements along an isoquant, the negative of the slope of the tangent is the marginal rate of technical substitution. It is easy to see that the slope of the tangent becomes less and less steep as the input combination moves downward along the isoquant.

The concept of diminishing $MRTS$ is stressed again in Figure 5.4.3. Q, R, S, and T are four input combinations lying on the isoquant I. Q has the combination OK_1 units of capital and one unit of labor; R has OK_2 units of capital and two units of labor; and so on. For the movement from Q to R, the marginal rate of technical substitution of capital for labor is, by the formula,

$$- \frac{OK_1 - OK_2}{1 - 2} = OK_1 - OK_2.$$

Similarly, for the movements from R to S and S to T, the marginal rates of technical substitution are $OK_2 - OK_3$ and $OK_3 - OK_4$, respectively.

Since the marginal rate of technical substitution of capital for labor diminishes as labor is substituted for capital, it is necessary that $(OK_1 - OK_2) > (OK_2 - OK_3) > (OK_3 - OK_4)$. Visually, the amount of capital replaced by successive units of labor will decline if, and only if, the isoquant is concave from above. Since the amount *must* decline, the isoquant must be concave from above.

One final property of isoquants is that they cannot intercept one another. This property follows logically from the assumptions made.

FIGURE 5.4.3

DIMINISHING MARGINAL RATE OF
TECHNICAL SUBSTITUTION

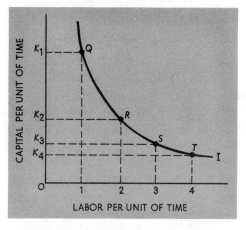

5.4.c Relation of *MRTS* to marginal products

For very slight movements along an isoquant the marginal rate of technical substitution equals the ratio of the marginal products of the two inputs. The proof is quite straightforward.

Let the level of output, Q, depend upon the use of two inputs, L and K. Assume that L and K are both allowed to vary slightly, and consider how Q must vary. As an example, suppose the use of L increases by 3 units and that of K by 5. If, in this range, the marginal product of L is 4 units of Q per unit of L and that of K is 2 units of Q per unit of K, the change in Q is

$$\triangle Q = (4 \times 3) + (2 \times 5) = 22.$$

In other words, when L and K are allowed to vary slightly, the change in Q resulting from the change in the two inputs is the marginal product of L times the amount of change in L plus the marginal product of K times its change.[3] Put in equation form

$$\triangle Q = MP_L \triangle L + MP_K \triangle K.$$

---

[3] Note that we have really violated our assumption about marginal product somewhat. The marginal product of an input is defined as the change in output per unit change in the input, *the use of other inputs held constant*. In this case we allow both inputs to change; thus the marginal product is really an approximation. But we are speaking only of *slight* or very small changes in use. Thus the violation of the assumption is small and the approximation approaches the true variation for very small amounts.

Along an isoquant Q is constant; therefore $\triangle Q$ equals zero. Setting $\triangle Q$ equal to zero and solving for the slope of the isoquant, $\triangle K/\triangle L$, we have

$$-\frac{\triangle K}{\triangle L} = \frac{MP_L}{MP_K} = MRTS.$$

Since, as noted, along an isoquant K and L must vary inversely, $\triangle K/\triangle L$ is negative.[4]

Using the relations developed here the reason for diminishing $MRTS$ is easily explained. As additional units of labor are added to a fixed amount of capital the marginal product of labor diminishes. Furthermore, as shown in Figure 5.4.1, if the amount of the fixed input is diminished the marginal product of labor diminishes. Thus two forces are working to diminish the marginal product of labor: (a) less of the other input causes a downward *shift* of the marginal product of labor curve; and (b) more units of the variable input (labor) cause a downward movement *along* the marginal product curve. Thus, as labor is substituted for capital the marginal product of labor must decline. For analogous reasons the marginal product of capital increases as less capital and more labor is used. With the quantity of labor fixed, the marginal product of capital rises as fewer units of capital are used. But simultaneously there is an increase in labor input, thereby shifting the marginal product of capital curve upward. The same two forces are present in this case: a movement along a marginal product curve and a shift in the location of the curve. In this situation, however, both forces work to increase the marginal product of capital. Thus, as labor is substituted for capital, the marginal product of capital increases.

ASIDE

Similarity to the theory of consumer behavior

Those of you who have covered the theory of consumer behavior have certainly noted several analogies between that theory and the theory of production that we have developed thus far. First, of course, an isoquant in production theory is similar to an indifference curve in consumer theory. The shapes of the curves are similar. Sec-

---

[4] It is possible that as more and more labor is used relative to capital and labor goes into stage III, the isoquant bends upward. Or as more and more capital is used relative to labor and capital goes into stage III, the isoquant bends backward. Since both of these regions involve one input in stage III, production does not take place in that area. Thus we shall ignore these noneconomic regions.

ond, the marginal rate of substitution in consumption (*MRS*) is analogous to the marginal rate of technical substitution in production (*MRTS*). Similarly, *MRS* equals the ratio of the marginal utilities of the two goods, and *MRTS* equals the ratio of the marginal products. Finally an indifference curve map is similar to an isoquant map. The basic difference is that we can assign an actual number (quantity of output) to an isoquant whereas no cardinal number (units of utility) can be assigned to indifference curves.

5.5 OPTIMAL COMBINATION OF RESOURCES

So far the theory of production has been analyzed from the standpoint of individual producers. However, nothing has been said about the *optimal* way in which they should combine resources. Any desired level of output can normally be produced by a number of different combinations of inputs. Our task now is to determine the specific combination a producer should select. We shall see in this section that a firm attains the highest possible level of output for any given level of cost or the lowest possible cost for producing any given level of output when the marginal rate of technical substitution for any two inputs equals the ratio of input prices.

5.5.a Input prices and isocosts

Inputs, as well as outputs, bear specific market prices. In determining the optimal input combination producers must pay heed to relative input prices if they are to minimize the cost of producing a given output or maximize output for a given level of cost.

Input prices are determined, as are the prices of goods, by supply and demand in the market. For producers who are not monopsonists or oligopsonists (that is, the sole purchaser or one of a few purchasers of an input), input prices are given by the market and their rates of purchase do not change them even though many producers as a group can change them. Let us now concentrate upon a producer who is a perfect competitor in the input market facing parametrically given input prices.

Let us continue to assume that the two inputs are labor and capital, although the analysis applies equally well to any two productive agents. Denote the quantity of capital and labor by K and L, respectively, and their unit prices by r and w. The total cost, $\bar{C}$, of using any volume of K

and L is $\bar{C} = rK + wL$, the sum of the cost of K units of capital at r per unit and of L units of labor at w per unit.

To take a more specific example, suppose capital costs \$1,000 per unit ($r = \$1,000$) and labor receives a wage of \$2,500 per man-year ($w = \$2,500$). If a total of \$15,000 is to be spent for inputs, the equation above shows that the following combinations are possible: $\$15,000 = \$1,000\ K + \$2,500\ L$, or $K = 15 - 2.5\ L$. Similarly, if \$20,000 is to be spent on inputs, one can purchase the following combinations: $K = 20 - 2.5\ L$. More generally, if the fixed amount $\bar{C}$ is to be spent, the producer can choose among the combinations given by

$$K = \frac{\bar{C}}{r} - \frac{w}{r} L.$$

This equation is illustrated in Figure 5.5.1. If \$15,000 is spent for inputs and no labor is purchased, 15 units of capital may be bought. More generally, if $\bar{C}$ is to be spent and r is the unit cost, $\bar{C}/r$ units of capital may be purchased. This is the vertical axis *intercept* of the line. If one unit of labor is purchased at \$2,500, two and five tenths units of capital must be sacrificed; if two units of labor are bought, five units of capital must be sacrificed; and so on. Thus, as the purchase of labor is increased, the purchase of capital must decrease if cost is held constant. For each additional unit of labor, w/r units of capital must be foregone. In Figure 5.5.1, $w/r = 2.5$. Attaching a negative sign, this is the *slope* of the line.

The solid lines in Figure 5.5.1 are called *isocost curves* because they show the various combinations of inputs that may be purchased for a stipulated amount of expenditure. In summary:

Relation.   At fixed input prices, r and w for capital and labor, a fixed outlay $\bar{C}$ will purchase any combination of capital and labor given by the following linear equation:

$$K = \frac{\bar{C}}{r} - \frac{w}{r} L.$$

This is the equation for an isocost curve, whose intercept ($\bar{C}/r$) is the amount of capital that may be purchased if no labor is bought and whose slope is the negative of the input price ratio (w/r).

5.5.b Production of a given output at minimum cost

Whatever output producers choose to produce, they wish to produce it at the least possible cost. Or whatever expenditure the entrepreneur wishes to make, the highest output possible with that expenditure is

FIGURE 5.5.1

ISOCOST CURVES FOR $r = \$1,000$ AND $w = \$2,500$

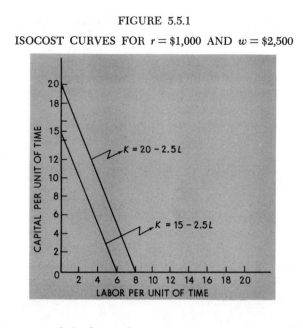

desired. To accomplish this task, production must be organized in the most efficient way. The basic principles can be shown with the following problem:

Problem. Suppose that Transport Service must produce a certain output of cargo and passenger service per year. The Service is confronted with the following combinations of aircraft and mechanics that can be used to yield this required output over its route pattern.

Combination	Number of aircraft	Number of mechanics
No. 1............	60	1,000
2............	61	920
3............	62	850
4............	63	800
5............	64	760
6............	65	730
7............	66	710

If the annual cost resulting from the operation of another aircraft is $250,000, and if mechanics cost them $6,000 each annually, which combination of aircraft and mechanics should Transport Service use to minimize its cost? By trial and error a solution of combination No. 4 is obtained. Or, we could use the following method. Begin at combination 1. An additional airplane would cost $250,000, but 80 mechanics could be released at a saving of $480,000. A move to 2 would be beneficial. By moving to 3, the firm would save $420,000 in mechanics' salaries and add $250,000 in aircraft expenses. Following the same line of reasoning, the firm could save cost by moving to combination 4. It would not move to 5 since the $240,000 saved is less than the $250,000 added.

Let us analyze the problem graphically. Suppose at given input prices r and w an entrepreneur wishes to produce the output indicated by isoquant I in Figure 5.5.2. Isocost curves KL, $K'L'$, and $K''L''$ represent the infinite number of isocost curves from which the producer can choose at the given input prices. Obviously he chooses the lowest one that enables him to attain output level I. That is, he produces at the cost represented by isocost curve $K'L'$. Any resource expenditure below that, for example, that represented by KL, is not feasible since it is impossible to produce output I with these resource combinations. Any resource combinations above that represented by $K'L'$ are rejected because the entrepreneur wishes to produce the desired output at *least* cost. If combinations A or B are chosen, at the cost represented by $K''L''$, the producer can reduce costs by moving along I to point E. Point E shows the optimal resource combination, using OK_0 units of capital and OL_0 units of labor.

Equilibrium is reached when the isoquant representing the chosen output is just tangent to an isocost curve. Since tangency means that the

FIGURE 5.5.2

OPTIMAL INPUT COMBINATION TO
MINIMIZE COST SUBJECT TO
A GIVEN LEVEL OF OUTPUT

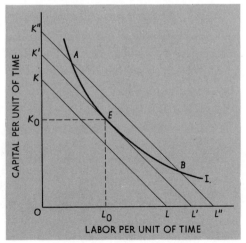

two slopes are equal, least cost production requires that the marginal rate of technical substitution of capital for labor be equal to the ratio of the price of labor to the price of capital. The market input-price ratio tells the producer the rate at which one input can be substituted for another *in purchasing*. The marginal rate of technical substitution shows the rate at which the producer *can substitute in production.* So long as the two are not equal, a producer can achieve a lower cost by moving in the direction of equality.

> **Principle.** To minimize cost subject to a given level of output and given input prices, the producer must purchase inputs in quantities such that the marginal rate of technical substitution of capital for labor is equal to the input-price ratio (the price of labor to the price of capital). Thus

$$MRTS = \frac{MP_L}{MP_K} = \frac{w}{r}.$$

We can analyze the equilibrium condition in another way. Assume the equilibrium condition did not hold, or specifically that

$$\frac{MP_L}{MP_K} < \frac{w}{r}.$$

In other words,

$$\frac{MP_L}{w} < \frac{MP_K}{r}.$$

In this case the marginal product of an additional dollar's worth of labor is less than the marginal product of an additional dollar's worth of capital. The firm could reduce its use of labor by one dollar, expand its use of capital by less than one dollar, and remain at the same level of output but with a reduced cost. It could continue to do this so long as the above inequality holds. Eventually MP_L/w would become equal to MP_K/r since MP_L rises with decreased use of labor and increased use of capital, and MP_K falls with increased capital and decreased labor. By the same reasoning it is easy to see that firms substitute labor for capital until the equality holds if the inequality is reversed.

5.5.c Production of maximum output with a given level of cost

The most realistic way of examining the problem is to assume that the entrepreneur chooses a level of output and then chooses the input combination that permits production of that output at least cost. As an alternative we could assume that the entrepreneur can spend only a fixed amount on production and wishes to attain the highest level of production consistent with that amount of expenditure. Not too surprisingly, the results turn out the same as before.

FIGURE 5.5.3

OUTPUT MAXIMIZATION FOR A
GIVEN LEVEL OF COST

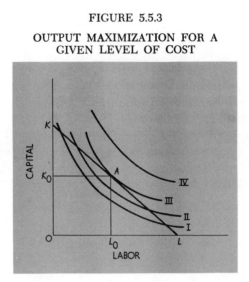

This situation is shown in Figure 5.5.3. The isocost line KL shows every possible combination of the two inputs at the given level of cost and input prices. Four isoquants are shown. Clearly at the given level of cost, output level IV is unattainable. Neither level I nor level II would be chosen since higher levels are possible. Thus the highest level of output attainable with a given level of cost is produced by using OL_0 labor and OK_0 capital. At point A the highest possible isoquant, III, is just tangent to the given isocost. Thus in the case of output maximization the marginal rate of technical substitution of capital for labor equals the input-price ratio (the price of labor to the price of capital).

Principle. In order either to maximize output subject to a given cost or to minimize cost subject to a given output, the entrepreneur must employ inputs in such amounts as to equate the marginal rate of technical substitution and the input-price ratio.

APPLICATIONS

Uses of equilibrium theory in decision making

The concepts just developed are among the most applicable and useful tools for decision makers. Business and governmental decision makers use this type of analysis frequently in making important decisions. This would be expected because of the frequency of situations in which people are given a budget and are instructed to maximize something. Or just as frequently they are given an objective and are told to minimize the cost of attaining that objective. Let us look at a few examples to see how the theory applies to daily decision making.

Agricultural agents, many of whom have training in agricultural economics, frequently must give advice such as how to blend fertilizers so as to give the maximum yield for a given level of cost. These fertilizers are a blend of several ingredients. The agent knows the general farming conditions and, equally important, the prices of the various ingredients. The formulas used are basically the same as those set forth here. In essence the blend must be such that the marginal expected yield per dollar's worth is the same for each ingredient. Certainly the numerical solution is probably done by a computer, but the conditions are the same. Other very similar agricultural problems involve blending feeds so as to minimize the cost of a given weight gain in cattle or other stock. The same principles hold.

Businesses often hire efficiency experts in order to reduce the cost of running an office or increase the output from a particular plant operating at a given cost. Perhaps in reorganizing an office the expert would recommend reducing the number of secretaries and adding more dictaphones and copiers. Why such a recommendation? Clearly it was thought that the marginal product per unit of expenditure on secretaries was lower than the marginal products per unit of expenditure on dictaphones and copiers. The recommendation in the case of the factory would involve different inputs such as labor and machinery, but the solution is similar. You can certainly think of other business applications.

But the same method of analysis applies to nonprofit organizations. These organizations have objectives but have to operate within a budget also. Take, for example, a great medical center, perhaps the heart center in Houston with the famous heart surgeon Dr. Denton Cooley. The hospital administration must meet a budget, but it wishes to perform as many safe heart operations as possible. Clearly there is some optimal operation mix consisting of Dr. Cooley, other assisting doctors, and equipment technicians. If you were told that Dr. Cooley and a few of the other most competent doctors were doing all of the work—preparing the patient, doing the operating, tending to the patient afterward—you could probably suggest that changes would decrease the cost of an operation and more operations could be performed. Additional nurses or less thoroughly trained doctors could perform some of the more routine tasks at which their marginal productivity per dollar expenditure was higher. This would free the most skilled doctors for more operations.

The administrators, regents, and faculty of our university are currently debating an issue involving similar principles. Possibly officials of your school are also. With the growth of the university these officials are trying to decide how to give more education or training (however that is defined) within a given budget. The debate concerns substitution among very large classrooms with classes taught by very experienced professors, hiring more junior professors who teach smaller classes, using more graduate student teachers, and so on. Clearly there is a certain amount of added productivity per expenditure in each case. Of course, the really difficult thing in this case is how to measure the educational output of a university. How do you compare the returns from being taught in a large class by a professor or in a small class by a teaching assistant? Notwithstanding the measurement problem, the fundamental determinants in the decision-making process are the same as those set forth in the theory.

Turning to other types of governmental decisions, we have the strategic and tactical decisions of the military. The navy, for example, has many options for attack—aircraft, submarines, cruisers. There is the problem of substitution among these weapons in order to obtain the maximum striking power from a given budget. The air force can use airplanes or missiles for defense. Here the problem may be to minimize the cost of a given level of air defense by substituting missiles for aircraft. Again the principles are the same.

You can probably think of many more applications just as valid. Any time there is a given budget to carry out a specified task using two or more inputs or a given task that is to be done at minimum cost, the same theory applies. In all cases efficiency is attained when the marginal product per dollar expenditure on each input is the same. This type of analysis using the tools developed above occurs every day in many areas and in many jobs.

5.5.d Expansion path

The expansion path in production theory shows the way in which factor proportions change when output changes, the factor-price ratio

FIGURE 5.5.4

EXPANSION PATH

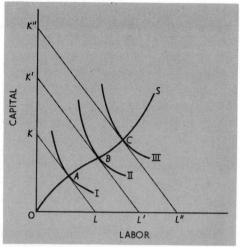

held constant. In Figure 5.5.4 the curves I, II, III are isoquants depicting a representative production function; KL, $K'L'$, and $K''L''$ represent the least cost of producing the three output levels. Since the factor-price ratio does not change, they are parallel.

To summarize: first, factor prices remain constant. Second, each equilibrium point is defined by equality between the marginal rate of technical substitution and the factor-price ratio. Since the latter remains constant, so does the former. Therefore, OS is a locus of points along which the marginal rate of technical substitution is constant. But it is a curve with a special feature. Specifically, it is the locus along which output will expand when factor prices are constant. We may accordingly formulate this result as a

> **Definition.** The expansion path is the curve along which output expands when factor prices remain constant. The expansion path thus shows how factor proportions change when output or expenditure changes, input prices remaining constant throughout. The marginal rate of technical substitution remains constant also since the factor-price ratio is constant.

As we shall see in the next chapter the expansion path gives the firm its cost structure. That is, the expansion path shows the optimal input combination for each level of output at the given set of input prices.

Thus it gives the minimum cost of producing each level of output from the cost associated with each tangent isocost curve.

In Figure 5.5.4 the two inputs, capital and labor, are called normal inputs because as higher levels of output are produced, more of each input is used. In other words, the expansion path is positively sloped.

An output is called "inferior" if over a range of outputs the use of this input declines as production increases. Over this range the expansion path is negatively sloped. In Figure 5.5.5 labor is inferior over the range of production between the outputs shown by I and II. At the lower output given by I, OL_0 labor is used; labor is reduced to OL_1 when the higher output represented by II is produced.

If capital had been the inferior input, the expansion path would have bent downward as capital becomes inferior. Clearly both inputs cannot be inferior at the same time. No firm could increase output by reducing all inputs, therefore reducing total cost.

As mentioned at the beginning of this chapter a production function could possibly be characterized by production under fixed proportions. In this case, all inputs must be used in the same proportion regardless of output. For example, if 2 units of labor and 5 of capital are necessary to produce 100 units of output, 200 units of output require 4 labor and 10 capital, 300 units require 6 labor and 15 capital, and so on. If labor is limited to 2 units, no matter how much capital is added beyond 5 units, only 100 units of output can be produced.

Figure 5.5.6 shows a set of isoquants and the expansion path for a fixed-

FIGURE 5.5.5

EXPANSION PATH: ONE INPUT INFERIOR

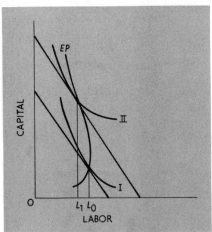

FIGURE 5.5.6

PRODUCTION WITH FIXED PROPORTIONS

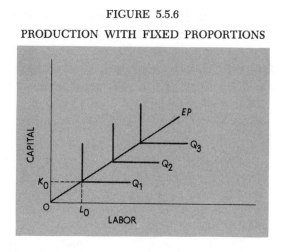

proportions production function. The isoquants for outputs Q_1, Q_2, and Q_3 form right angles. Take output level Q_1; this output is produced by OK_0 capital and OL_0 labor. If labor remains at that level while capital is increased, no more output can be produced. Neither can an increase in labor increase output while capital remains fixed. Furthermore, Q_2 and Q_3 and all other outputs require labor and capital to be used in the same ratio, OK_0/OL_0. This ratio is the slope of the expansion path, which is a straight line passing through the corner of each isoquant.

Before concluding this section we should note in passing a production concept that will be of considerable importance in the next chapter when we analyze cost in the long run. This concept is the relation of proportional changes in all inputs to the change in output—called returns to scale.

We have noted in the case of fixed-proportions production functions if *all inputs* are increased by k percent, output increases by k percent also. This phenomenon is called constant returns to scale.

But returns to scale are sometimes spoken of when dealing with variable-proportions production functions. Begin at a specific point on the expansion path. If the use of all inputs is increased by k percent and output increases by *more than* k percent, we are in the range of *increasing returns to scale*. If the use of all inputs increases by k percent and output increases by *less than* k percent, we are in the range of *decreasing returns to scale*. Finally, if a specific percentage increase in the use of all inputs leads to the same percentage increase in output, this denotes *constant returns to scale*.

Do not deduce from this discussion of returns to scale that with variable-proportions production functions firms actually expand output by increasing input use in exactly the same proportion. As we have seen above the very concept of variable proportions means that they do not necessarily expand in the same proportions; the expansion path may twist and turn in many directions. But, as noted, this concept of returns to scale is of great importance in the theory of cost, and therefore it should be at least mentioned in the theory of production.

ASIDE

Similarity to consumer behavior theory

Those of you who have already covered Chapters 3 and 4 have obviously noted additional similarities between consumption and production theory. In consumption theory equilibrium occurs where the marginal rate of substitution equals the ratio of commodity prices; in production theory equilibrium occurs where the marginal rate of technical substitution in production equals the ratio of the input prices. The isocost curve is analogous to the budget line, as is the expansion path to the income-consumption curve.

5.6. SUBSTITUTION EFFECT AND TECHNOLOGICAL CHANGE

In Section 5.5 we showed how the optimal or most efficient combination of inputs is derived for each level of output. Two things can occur and change the optimal level of input use for a given level of output: The prices of the inputs can change and technological change can occur. Under either circumstance the firm would probably, though not necessarily, change the input ratio.

5.6.a Input prices change

First let us analyze the substitution effect of a change in input prices. As we would expect, when the ratio of input prices changes, firms would substitute away from the relatively more expensive input toward the relatively cheaper input.

In Figure 5.6.1 let the output level be that given by isoquant Q. The original set of input prices is that given by the slope of isocost curve CL.

FIGURE 5.6.1

CHANGING INPUT PRICES

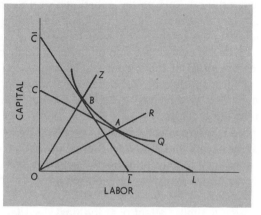

Cost minimization occurs at point A; the ratio of input use is given by the slope of the ray OR. Now the price of labor rises relative to the price of capital. The budget line is now $\bar{C}\bar{L}$, the steeper slope of which reflects an increase in the price of L relative to the price of C. Thus tangency, and hence efficiency, must occur at a steeper part of the isoquant, reflecting that if output remains constant, capital, the now relatively cheaper input, is substituted for labor, now relatively more expensive. Equilibrium occurs now at point B on Q; the higher capital-to-labor ratio is shown by the steeper slope of the ray OZ. If the price of capital rises relative to that of labor, the isocost becomes less steep and efficiency would then call for labor to be substituted for capital. Considering the substitution effect alone, the firm always substitutes away from the input that becomes relatively more expensive when the price ratio changes.[5]

APPLICATION

Substitution effects in response to changes in relative prices

There have been many dramatic changes in input proportions in response to changes in the relative prices of inputs. A historical ex-

---

[5] We do not have in production theory a concept analogous to the income effect from a price change in consumption theory. There is an output effect, but this is not completely straightforward at this level of economic theory. A change in the price of an input can either increase or decrease a firm's level of output, the direction depending upon several factors.

ample is a change beginning about 50 or 60 years ago, but lasting for a long period of time: the change from rail transportation of freight to truck transportation. This partial substitution or switch in proportions came in large measure due to the decrease in the price of petroleum relative to the price of coal over these many decades. However, in the 1970s the cost of gas and oil is rising relative to the price of coal, and a reversal of the process is taking place, although not necessarily in transportation. Businesses in many sections of the country are changing from gas to coal in anticipation of a relative increase in the price of gas.

As labor became relatively more expensive, there has been a marked change in retailing methods. Stores are becoming more and more self-service as counter and display space is being substituted for labor. Some grocery stores are even requiring customers to bag their own groceries.

We have seen a similar effect over the past decades in the home. As we have mentioned, the job opportunities and salaries for women have improved. Now the labor of the housewife is becoming relatively more expensive, in terms of lost earnings. We are witnessing a substitution in housework away from pure labor and toward labor-saving devices, for example, microwave ovens. Perhaps you can think of many other examples, from history or more recently, of a shift in input use in response to a change in relative prices.

We see the same type of substitution among various countries. For example, agricultural methods vary greatly from one country to another. I once had a friend from France who insisted that American farmers were extremely inefficient, compared to French farmers. She pointed out that French farmers planted crops much closer together and thus got a higher yield per acre than American farmers; French farmers fertilized more carefully and weeded much better, thereby growing larger vegetables. Americans even harvested by machine, she said, thereby wasting a great deal. Could you explain to her why French farmers were no more efficient than Americans?

Clearly the key point is that in the United States land is cheaper relative to labor, whereas in France labor is cheaper relative to land. Thus in France farmers use a lot of the relatively cheap labor and try to conserve the relatively expensive land. They do this by planting crops close together, and so on. Farmers in the United States use a lot of land and capital to save on the relatively expensive labor.

We continually hear that Americans have wasted oil and are therefore to blame for the energy problem. Address yourself to this problem. If we had not used so much oil—driving fast in large cars, for example—in response to the relatively low price of oil, what would we have wasted? Probably some relatively higher-priced resource, such as time, perhaps historically the scarcest of all resources?

5.6.b Technological change

A change in technology also can change input proportions. Technological change essentially involves a shift of the isoquant map toward the origin. This downward shift in the isoquants simply means that at given input prices, each level of output can be produced at a lower cost (on a lower isocost curve) than was possible prior to the change in the level of technology. Thus technological change involves an improvement in the state of knowledge—the knowledge of how to organize factors of production more efficiently. In terms of the production function, any given set of inputs in the relevant range can produce more output after the improvement in technology.

Technological change can, as noted, alter input proportions. Consider Figure 5.6.2. The given ratio of input prices is given by the slope of budget line CL. Let isoquant Q represent some level of production. At the given input price ratio, cost minimization occurs at A; the slope of the ray OR gives the capital-labor ratio.

Technological change from an improvement in knowledge shifts the isoquant representing output level Q toward the origin. It is now possible to produce Q with less capital and less labor. The isoquant representing an output of Q can shift in three possible ways, as shown by the three

FIGURE 5.6.2

TECHNOLOGICAL CHANGE

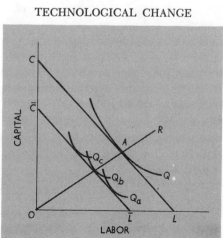

isoquants Q_a, Q_b, and Q_c. These three possible isoquants represent the same level of output after technological change as did isoquant Q before the change.

Let input prices remain constant; suppose Q shifts to Q_b. Isocost $\overline{CL}$ gives cost minimization precisely at the original capital-labor ratio. True, there is less of each input used, but the proportions remain the same. If Q is shifted to Q_a the use of labor relative to capital is increased. On the other hand if Q shifts to Q_c, the use of capital increases relative to labor. Economists call these technological changes neutral, labor-using, and capital-using.[6] Or sometimes the two non-neutral changes are referred to as capital-saving (rather than labor-using) and labor-saving (rather than capital-using). Thus, technological change over a given range of output can mean that for any output level, capital is substituted for labor, labor is substituted for capital, or the proportion remains constant.

APPLICATION

Some effects of technological change

Although the problem of unemployment is a topic classified as part of macroeconomic theory (the economy as a whole) not microeconomic theory (the subject of this text) we really should discuss briefly the relation between labor-saving technological change and unemployment. For more than 200 years many groups have resisted technological change in some areas on the grounds that such change would be labor saving and cause unemployment. In a sense they were wrong in resisting this type of technological chance, in another sense they were right.

In the first place, just because any given level of output is produced more efficiently with a higher capital/labor ratio, such change does not mean that less *total* labor is employed in the industry. Do not forget that any technological change lowers the cost of producing any level of output. Thus the amount of labor used per-unit-of-output may fall, but *total labor employed may increase* because output increases. That is, cost falls; the forces of competition increase supply, which in turn drives down price. The increased output may require more labor.

On the other hand, the output effect may not offset the substitution effect. The use of labor in the industry may fall—even though the

---

[6] We might note in passing that there are certain other definitions of neutral and capital- or labor-using technological change.

wage rate could rise because labor is working with more capital. Economists generally say, true, but the reduction in labor can in the long run be spread over other occupations and in effect shift the production possibility frontier outward. Yet in the short run there is the problem—academic to those not directly affected, tragic to those who are—that some technological change causes some workers to become obsolete in their professions.

This brings us to another point of analysis that is quite possibly more macroeconomic than microeconomic in nature. This point concerns whether technological change induces changes in factor proportions or whether changes in input prices induce technological change.

Certainly we have seen changes in technology that are quite labor saving; some examples may be automatic elevators replacing elevator operators, ship loading and unloading equipment replacing stevadores, photocopiers replacing secretaries, paint sprayers replacing painters, computors replacing mathematicians, and possibly televised lectures replacing college professors.

But, were these spontaneous labor-saving technological changes or induced changes? That is, it may well have been that as one type of labor became or is becoming relatively expensive, the change in the input price ratio induced not only a change in the input proportion but also additional research devoted to finding technological change that would reduce the use of the resource that was becoming increasingly higher priced. This must have been the case for many advances in technology. Therefore it is extremely difficult to separate the substitution effect due to a change in relative prices from the change in technology induced by changes in relative prices.

An example of one of the simplest cost-reducing technological changes in history might establish the problem of distinguishing between the two types. When the Du Pont's began the production of gunpowder in the United States, all gunpowder producers had a serious problem; from time to time their factory simply blew up. This obviously represented a substantial business setback. The same thing happened to the Du Pont's a few times.

But after a while Du Pont began separating production into many distinct, widely separated plants rather than producing in one factory, as was the custom at the time. Then an explosion only closed down a small part of the operation. Production continued in all of the other parts of the establishment. Certainly this innovation, simple as it may have been, changed input uses drastically, but it was done in response to a problem of costs.

We could go on and on about the effects and inducements of

technological change, but this subject is really a problem for a class in industrial organization or possibly economic history.

5.7 SUMMARY

This chapter has set forth the basic theory of production and the optimal combination of inputs under a given set of input prices. The basic concepts upon which production theory is based are given in the following definitions:

Definition. A production function is a schedule, table, or equation showing the maximum output that can be obtained from any given combination of inputs.

Definition. An isoquant is the locus of points showing combinations of inputs physically capable of producing a given level of output. An isocost line shows all combinations of inputs that can be purchased at some given level of expenditure. The slope of the isoquant, the marginal rate of technical substitution, shows the rate at which one input can be substituted for another while maintaining the same level of output. The slope of the isocost line, the ratio of input prices, shows the rate at which the market allows inputs to be substituted.

The optimal combination of inputs is determined by the following:

Relation. The firm minimizes the cost of producing any given level of output or maximizes the output that can be produced at any given level of cost when the marginal rate of technical substitution equals the ratio of input prices.

Relation. Two circumstances can change the input ratio used to produce a given output, relative input prices can change and technology can change. It is frequently difficult to separate the two effects.

We have briefly mentioned in this chapter the relation between production theory and cost. We will in the next chapter develop this relation further.

ASIDE

Estimating production functions

While the estimated form of past production functions for real firms or real industries is not of particular relevance for a course in price theory, we might note that there have been a multitude of such studies made over the past 50 years. How these studies are made may be of some tangential interest in case you wish to have one done for your business or for those goods or services in which you are interested. There are several methods econometricians have used to make such estimates. They have gathered data over time for different firms about the amount of labor, capital, and other inputs used to produce different outputs. They have also gathered similar data from several firms in the same industry during a relatively short time period. They have carried out experiments and used questionnaires to gather data.

There are many shortcomings to each method of approach. However, the great difficulty of obtaining reliable data either over time or across firms and the problem of measuring capital are the major reasons why many estimates may be somewhat unreliable. Notwithstanding these points there have been many estimates made of various production functions. We will not go into any of these types of studies here. The subject is more appropriate to a statistics or econometrics class.

TECHNICAL PROBLEMS

1. Fill in the blanks in the following table.

Usage of the variable input	Total product	Average product	Marginal product
4........		20	—
5........			15
6........	102		
7........			10
8........		15	
9........	126		
10........		12	

2. Below are hypothetical data for a manufacturer, possessing a fixed plant, who produces a commodity that requires only one variable input. Total

product is given. Compute and graph the average and marginal product curves. Save your basic calculations because they form the basis for a subsequent problem in Chapter 6.

Units of variable input	Total Product	Average product	Marginal product
1.................	100		
2.................	250		
3.................	410		
4.................	560		
5.................	700		
6.................	830		
7.................	945		
8.................	1,050		
9.................	1,146		
10.................	1,234		
11.................	1,314		
12.................	1,384		
13.................	1,444		
14.................	1,494		
15.................	1,534		
16.................	1,564		
17.................	1,584		
18.................	1,594		

After completing the table and graph, answer the following questions:

a. When marginal product is increasing, what is happening to average product?

b. Does average product begin to fall as soon as marginal product does? That is, which occurs first, the point of diminishing marginal or average returns?

c. When average product is at its maximum, is marginal product less than, equal to, or greater than average product?

d. Does total product increase at a decreasing rate: (i) when average product is rising? (ii) when marginal product is rising? (iii) when average product begins to fall? (iv) when marginal product passes its maximum value?

e. When average product equals zero, what is total product?

3. You are an efficiency expert hired by a manufacturing firm that uses two inputs, labor (L) and capital (K). The firm produces and sells a given ouput. You have the following information

$$P_L = \$4, \ P_K = \$100, \ MP_L = 4, \ MP_K = 40$$

a. Is the firm operating efficiently?

b. Should it increase or decrease the quantity of labor relative to capital or the quantity of capital relative to labor to produce the given output? Explain your answer.

4. A firm can produce a certain amount of a good using three combinations of labor and capital. Labor costs $2 per unit, capital $4 per unit. The three methods are:

	A	B	C
Labor (units)	5	6	2
Capital (units)	7	5	9

   a. Which method should be chosen?

   b. The price of labor rises to $4 while the price of capital falls to $3, which method should be chosen?

   c. Under the second price structure (part *b*) the labor is done by you and you hire capital at $3; now which method should be chosen? Why? Can you even answer this? What information would you need?

5. Assume that a curve is drawn showing along the horizontal axis the amounts of a factor *A* employed in combination with a fixed amount of a group of factors called *B*, and along the vertical axis the amount of physical product obtainable from these combinations of factors.

   a. How can you find (geometrically) the amount of *A* for which the average physical product per unit of *A* is a maximum?

   b. How can you find (geometrically) the amount of *A* for which the marginal physical product of *A* is a maximum?

   c. Between the two points defined in questions (*a*) and (*b*), will the marginal physical product of *A* increase or decrease as more of *A* is used?

   d. Between these two points, will the average physical product per unit of *A* increase or decrease as more of *A* is used?

   e. At the point defined in (*a*), will the marginal physical product of *A* be higher or lower than the average physical product per unit of *A*? Give reasons.

   f. At the point defined in (*b*), will the marginal physical product of *A* be lower or higher than the average physical product per unit of *A*? Give reasons.

   g. How can you find (geometrically) the amount of *A* for which the marginal physical product of *A* is zero?

6. An expansion path can be derived under the assumption either that firms attempt to produce each output at minimum cost or that they attempt to gain maximum output at each level of cost. The paths are identical in both cases. Explain.

7. In Figure E.5.1 *LM* is the isocost and *I* is a isoquant. Explain precisely

FIGURE E.5.1

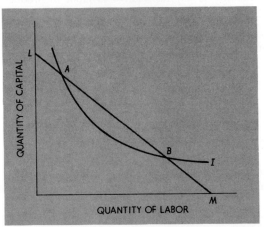

why combinations A and B are not efficient. Explain in terms of the relation of the ratio of the marginal products to the ratio of the input prices.
Explain in these terms why the direction of substitution in each case,
labor for capital or capital for labor is optimal. Using the ratio of input
prices given by LM find and label the least-cost combination of labor and
capital that can produce the output designated by I. In the above terms
explain why this combination is optimal.

8. Explain precisely why MP exceeds (is less than) AP when AP is rising
   (falling).

9. In Figure E.5.2 the isoquant turns upward at OL units of labor. Explain
   this upward turn in terms of labor going into stage III; i.e., negative marginal product.

FIGURE E.5.2

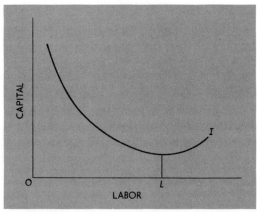

ANALYTICAL PROBLEMS

1. Why do we say that a student should not stop studying after reaching diminishing returns?

2. Make the decision, if you can, as to which is the more efficient use of resources in the following cases. Explain.
   a. Unloading a ship by hand or using a mechanical crane.
   b. Shipping a package by air or shipping it by rail.
   c. Painting a building, using painters and brushes or using automatic sprayers.

3. An efficiency expert who recently examined a power company's plant said that he believed the mill was being operated inefficiently. When the president of the company asked for examples the efficiency expert said that for one thing the crane operators who were unloading coal from barges were dropping an average of about 10 percent of the coal into the river. If you were the president of the company would you necessarily consider this circumstance evidence of inefficiency? Why or why not? What questions would you ask?

4. Economic studies have shown that education has had little impact on farmers in underdeveloped countries, while other studies have shown that education is an important variable affecting agricultural output in the United States. If these studies are accurate, can you explain why the situations might exist?

5. Several years ago the United States was sending engineers and other technical experts to the more underdeveloped countries in order to advise these countries on the latest technological methods in manufacture and in agriculture. They also assisted these underdeveloped countries in instituting these modern technological methods of farming and manufacturing. Can you explain why in many, many of these countries the advice and help were utter failures, causing great cost to the poorer countries? Why do you think in many instances the "old fashioned" methods worked better?

6. If over a long period of time in a country, considerable capital-using technological change occurs in agriculture, would you expect the birthrate to rise or fall for farm families? Why or why not?

7. This is a tough one. Even with nonregulated gas prices some areas of the North would have gas shortages (in the sense of not enough gas to heat all buildings to the desired temperature). These shortages occur very seldom; only when there is an extremely unseasonable cold spell. There is simply not enough gas stored. Are the city officials to blame for not having adequate pipe and storage facilities? Explain. If you did not get this one, try the next question.

8. In the city in which I live it snows about once every 10 to 12 years. Since the city has no equipment suitable for snow removal, schools, businesses, and so forth must close down for a day or two. There are wrecks caused by the snow. Are the mayor and city council inefficient or negligent for not having snow removal equipment for the city in order to spare the people from the inconvenience caused by the snow? Explain.

9. Explain why the marginal product of any input might become negative; that is, why would additional units of the input cause output to fall. Do not answer that the firm hires inferior inputs. Assume all units of the input are alike.

10. Recently the speed limit was reduced to 55 miles per hour. The trucking industry competes with other means of transport in the time and cost of moving freight. Can you explain the increase of CB radios as a technological change in response to a change in relative prices?

6

Theory of cost

6.1 INTRODUCTION

As we noted in Chapter 5 the important feature of production theory is the effect of production and input prices on the cost of producing something. The cost of producing or supplying goods and services is, as we shall see, the most important determinant of supply. This chapter develops the underlying theory of cost from the theory of production. It first sets forth the theory of cost in the long run when all inputs are variable, then turns to cost in the short run when some costs are fixed.

6.1.a Opportunity costs

A really important feature of cost theory is the concept of opportunity cost. Quite frequently people ignore opportunity cost when discussing the cost of something. They generally consider that cost simply means the price that must be paid for the item in question. To people in business the cost of producing a good usually means the number of dollars that must be paid for enough raw material, labor, machinery, and other inputs to produce the good. In economics, however, cost means somewhat more.

Consider the cost of attending college for one year. As a first approximation one might say that attending college for one year costs the year's tuition, room, board, book purchases, and incidental expenses. Using that approach it would appear that the cost of attending a particular college is essentially the same for any two students. Under certain circumstances that may not be quite correct. Assume that there are two students at the same school paying approximately the same tuition, board, and so forth. One student, however, is an exceptional baseball player who has been offered a major league contract with a large bonus. The *real* cost to him of attending college is not just the sum of his expenses; it is also what he had to give up to attend college. He must *sacrifice* or *give up* the amount he could have made by playing baseball in order to attend college.

The other student must also sacrifice something in addition to his direct outlays for expenses. Assuming that he is not so athletically inclined, perhaps his best alternative earning possibility might lie in working as a bank teller if he does not attend college. Thus he must sacrifice this amount of potential income. Since bank tellers generally do not receive a large bonus for signing with a bank, the athlete must sacrifice a greater amount; hence the *real* cost of attending college is greater for him than for the nonathlete. The athlete's *best alternative* is greater, so his real total cost is greater.

Or, recall that in previous chapters of this text we included the value of a person's time spent shopping for a good in the price of that good. In setting out the production possibilities curve we emphasized that the cost of having more of one good is the amount of some other good that must be given up. We use a similar type of analysis when discussing the cost of production. Throughout this chapter we shall attempt to stress the importance of this concept of opportunity cost.

ASIDE

Opportunity costs to society

In his book on language, *Strictly Speaking,* Edwin Newman points out one of the more famous current cliches in the English language: "If we can fly men to the moon, why can't we eliminate the ghetto?" Or "If we can fly men to the moon, why can't we improve our school system?" Or "If . . . , why can't we do something I want done?"

The answer is the opportunity cost. Government is faced with such costs just as firms and individuals are. Government must make decisions among alternative uses of resources. Thus, we (society, government) did not devote more resources to ghettos or schools partly because we (?) chose to fly men to the moon. The cost of the trips was the resources or, better, the things that could have been produced had government or individuals used these resources in other ways. The answer to the "If. . . Why" question is "We could have done it, but we chose to use the resources to do the other thing." The cost is what was given up.

6.1.b Social and private costs

Economists are interested principally in the social cost of production of a good, which is simply the goods and services the society gives up to get that good. In other words the social cost is the opportunity cost.

There is a close relation between the opportunity cost of producing a specific commodity and a calculation the producer of that commodity must make. The use of resources to produce X rather than Y entails a social cost; there is a private cost as well because the entrepreneur must pay a price to get the resources used. The producer must pay a certain amount to the owners of the resources in order to bid these resources away from alternative uses. These payments are *explicit* costs to the firm. Entrepreneurs incur some *implicit costs* also, and a complete analysis of costs must take these implicit costs into consideration.

To aid in analyzing the nature of implicit costs, consider two firms that produce good X and are in every way identical, with one exception. Both use identical amounts of the same resources to produce identical amounts of X. The first entrepreneur rents the building in which the good is produced. The second inherited the building and therefore pays no rent. Whose costs are higher? An economist would say both are the same, even though the second entrepreneur makes lower payments to outside factors of production. The reason costs are the same is that using the building to produce X costs the second entrepreneur the amount of income he could have received had he leased it at the prevailing rent. Since these two buildings are the same, presumably the market rental would be the same. In other words, a part of the cost incurred by the second entrepreneur is the payment from himself as entrepreneur to himself as the owner of a resource (the building). Similarly the implicit cost would also include what entrepreneurs could make in the best alternative use of their time and capital in another occupation had they not been associated with their firm.

Definition. The implicit costs incurred by entrepreneurs in producing a specific commodity consist of the amounts that could be earned in the best alternative use of their time and of any other of their resources currently used to produce the commodity in question.

Implicit costs are thus charges that must be added to explicit costs in order to obtain total private costs. They are a true opportunity cost.

6.1.c Important points to be developed

The basic concepts that you will learn in this chapter are

1. The fundamentals of long-run total, average, and marginal cost curves and what these curves look like.
2. The fundamentals of short-run total, average, and marginal cost curves and what these curves look like.
3. The relations between long-run cost curves and short-run cost curves.
4. The relation between cost curves and the expansion path.
5. The importance and effect of opportunity costs.
6. The importance of the cost of time.

6.2 PLANNING HORIZON AND LONG-RUN COSTS

Let us begin our analysis of costs by assuming that an individual considers establishing a firm in a particular industry. The individual is called an entrepreneur. An entrepreneur is one who commits himself to costs (which are known) to produce an output, which he hopes consumers will purchase at a price that covers costs of production. The device for carrying out production is called a firm.

Since the entrepreneur is beginning the firm, it is in the long run. Recall from Chapter 5 that the long run is not some date in the future. The long run means that all inputs are variable to the firm. Therefore, one of the first things it must decide is the *scale* of operation or the *size* of the firm. To make this decision the entrepreneur must know the cost of producing each level of output. We begin our analysis of cost with the long run rather than the short run because the scale of the firm must be determined before an entrepreneur must decide upon different output levels from a fixed plant.

6.2.a Derivation of cost schedules from a production function

Let us assume for analytical purposes that the individual knows the firm's actions will not affect the price that must be paid for the resources used. Further, assume that he can estimate the production function for each level of output in the feasible range. Using the methods described in Chapter 5, the entrepreneur derives an expansion path. Assuming that the firm uses only two inputs, labor and capital, the characteristics of the derived expansion path are given in columns 1 through 3 of Table 6.2.1. Labor costs $5 per unit and capital, $10 per unit. Column 1 gives seven output levels and columns 2 and 3 give the optimal combinations of labor and capital for each output level at the prevailing input prices.

Column 4 shows the total cost of producing each level of output. For example, the least-cost method of producing 300 units requires 20 units of labor and 10 of capital. At $5 and $10, respectively, the total cost is $200. It should be emphasized that column 4 is a *least cost schedule* for various rates of production. Obviously the entrepreneur could pay more to produce any output by using less efficient productive processes or by paying some factors of production more than their market prices. The firm could not, however, produce an output at a cost lower than that given.

As noted above, the lowest total cost of producing any output consists of two components, the explicit costs and the implicit costs. The explicit costs, given in Table 6.2.1, are the payments entrepreneurs must make to the factors of production. The implicit costs are the market values of the resources they own and use in production, including the wages they

TABLE 6.2.1

DERIVATION OF LONG-RUN COST SCHEDULES

1	2	3	4	5	6
	Least cost usage of		Total cost at $5 per unit of		Marginal
Output	Labor (units)	Capital (units)	labor $10 per unit of capital	Average cost	cost (per unit)
100.......	10	7	$120	$1.20	$1.20
200.......	12	8	140	.70	.20
300.......	20	10	200	.67	.60
400.......	30	15	300	.75	1.00
500.......	40	22	420	.84	1.20
600.......	52	30	560	.93	1.40
700.......	60	42	720	1.03	1.60

pay to themselves. We could assume in Table 6.2.1 that the entrepreneur owns the capital. We could assume that implicit costs are zero. Or, we might just ignore them here. In any case, when entrepreneurs plan, they must consider the payments to themselves since they cost what they could receive for the services of their resources had they not chosen to use them in the firm.

Two important cost schedules, derived from column 4 are average cost, shown in column 5, and marginal cost, shown in column 6. Average cost is simply the total cost of producing a given level of output divided by that output. Column 5 reflects an important assumed characteristic of average costs: average cost first declines, reaches a minimum, then rises.

Marginal cost is the change in total cost divided by the change in output; $MC = \triangle C / \triangle Q$. Moving from 100 to 200 units of output raises the total cost from \$120 to \$140. Twenty dollars divided by 100 gives a per-unit marginal cost of 20 cents. Thus we can see arithmetically how the production function is related to the three important cost functions. Note that marginal cost first decreases then increases.

Let us now summarize the situation graphically. Consider Figure 6.2.1, in which we assume that output is produced by two inputs, K and L. The known and fixed input prices give the constant input price ratio, represented by the slope of the isocost curves $I_1I'_1$, $I_3I'_3$, etc. Next, the known production function gives us the isoquant map, partially represented by x_1, x_3, etc., in Figure 6.2.1.

As is familiar from Chapter 5, when all inputs are readily variable (that is, the long run), the entrepreneur will choose input combinations that minimize the cost of producing each level of output. This gives us the expansion path $OP'Q'R'S'$. Given the factor-price ratio and the production function, the expansion path shows the combinations of inputs that enable the entrepreneur to produce each level of output at the least possible cost.

Now let us relate this expansion path to a long-run total cost ($LRTC$) curve of a shape frequently assumed by economists. Figure 6.2.2 shows graphically the least-cost curve for the good X, the expansion path of which was derived in Figure 6.2.1. The least cost of producing Ox_1 is Oc_1, of Ox_2 it is Oc_2, and so on.

The points P, Q, R, and S in Figure 6.2.2 correspond exactly to the points P', Q', R', and S' respectively in Figure 6.2.1. For example, the cost, Oc_1, of producing Ox_1 units of output in Figure 6.2.2 is precisely the cost of using OK_1 units of capital and OL_1 units of labor to produce the out-

FIGURE 6.2.1

THE EXPANSION PATH AND LONG-RUN COST

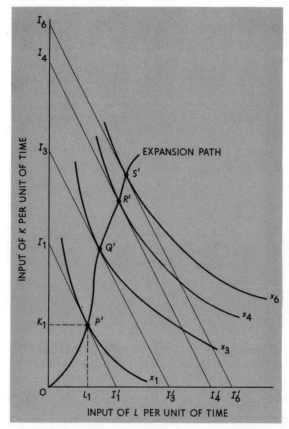

put Ox_1 at the optimal combination represented by P' in Figure 6.2.1. We assume that the implicit costs of production are included in the curve.[1] It is important to note that the firm may use different amounts and combinations of resources. Nothing is fixed except the set of techno- logical possibilities, or state of the arts, and the prices at which the firm can purchase resources. Thus, completely different production processes may be used to achieve minimum cost at (say) Ox_1 and Ox_2 units of out-

---

[1] Note that since the cost curve begins at the origin and not at some positive amount on the vertical axis, we tacitly assume that the entrepreneur can readily vary the amount of his time and other resources he "invests" in the business. That is to say, the implicit costs are as readily variable as the explicit cost when one is consider- ing the long run, or planning horizon. It is only in the short run, as we shall see be- low, that implicit costs may be fixed.

FIGURE 6.2.2

LONG-RUN TOTAL COST CURVE

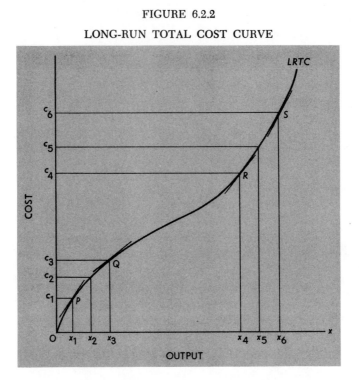

put. This "planning horizon" in which nothing is fixed to the entrepreneur except factor prices and technology is called the long run, and the associated curve that shows the minimum cost of producing each level of output is called the *Long-Run Total Cost Curve.*

Definition. Long-run total cost is the least cost at which each quantity of output can be produced when no resource is fixed in quantity or rate of use.

The shape of the long-run total cost ($LRTC$) curve depends exclusively upon the production function and prevailing factor prices. The schedule in Table 6.2.1 and the curve in Figure 6.2.2 reflect some of the commonly assumed characteristics of long-run total costs.

Two characteristics are apparent on inspection. First, costs and output are *directly related;* that is, the curve has a positive slope. It costs more to produce more, which is just another way of saying that resources are scarce or that one never gets "something for nothing" in the real economic world. The second characteristic is that costs first increase at a decreasing rate and then at an increasing rate.

Recall from Table 6.2.1 that the cost of producing an *additional* 100 units at first decreases and then increases. For example, the first 100 units add $120 to cost, the second 100 units add $20 to cost, but the third 100 units add $60. Each 100 units thereafter adds more to costs than the preceding 100.

Figure 6.2.2 is constructed to reflect that incremental costs first fall then rise. It is constructed so that $x_1x_2 = x_2x_3$, whereas c_1c_2 is clearly greater than c_2c_3. This means that the added total cost is greater when the entrepreneur moves from Ox_1 to Ox_2 than when output increases from Ox_2 to Ox_3. On the other hand, $x_4x_5 = x_5x_6$ but c_4c_5 is less than c_5c_6; over this range the additional cost incurred by producing more output increases. Alternatively stated, the slope at P (indicated by the tangent at that point) is greater than the slope at the larger output corresponding to Q. Incremental or marginal costs decrease over this range, even though total costs increase. The slope at R is less steep than that at S, indicating that incremental costs are increasing over this range.

6.2.b Long-run average and marginal costs

Now we are prepared to examine graphically the relation between the long-run total cost curve and the long-run average and marginal cost curves. Recall the definitions used with Table 6.2.1:

Definition. Average cost is the total cost of producing a particular quantity of output divided by that quantity.

Definition. Long-run marginal cost is the addition to total cost attributable to an additional unit of output when all inputs are optimally adjusted. It is thus the change in total cost as one moves along the expansion path or the long-run total cost curve.

The average and marginal costs in Table 6.2.1 first fell then increased; the minimum marginal cost was attained at a lower level of output than the level at which minimum average cost was reached. As we shall show, these are the results forthcoming from the generally assumed long-run total cost curves such as that shown in Figure 6.2.2.

Figure 6.2.3 shows graphically the relation between total cost (Panel A) and average cost (Panel B). Since average cost is total cost divided

FIGURE 6.2.3

DERIVATION OF AVERAGE TOTAL COST CURVE

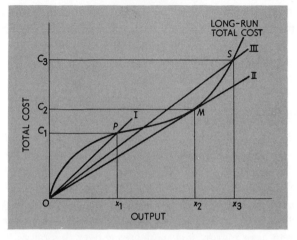

Panel A
Long-run total cost

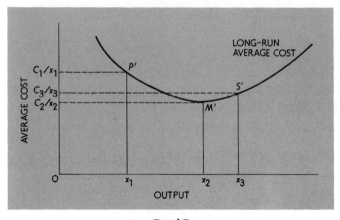

Panel B
Long-run average cost

by the corresponding output, the average cost of a particular quantity is given by the slope of a ray from the origin to the relevant point on the total cost curve. For example, in panel A the cost of producing Ox_1 is Oc_1. Average cost, Oc_1/Ox_1, is given by the slope of the ray designated I at point P. Average cost at Ox_1 is plotted in Panel B at point P'. (Note that the vertical scales of the two graphs differ; the horizontal scales are the same.)

From inspection of the long-run total cost curve it is clear that the slope of a ray to any point on the curve decreases as output increases from zero to Ox_2. Thus average cost must fall as output increases from zero to Ox_2. This is shown in Panel B. As output increases thereafter from Ox_2, the slope of a ray to any point on the total cost curve increases. For example, at Ox_3 the average cost is given by the ray III at point S. Average cost of Ox_3, Oc_3/Ox_3, is plotted at point S' in Panel B. Thus minimum average cost is reached at Ox_2, where the ray II is tangent to the cost curve at M. Average cost is plotted at M'. Average cost rises thereafter.

Relations. For the generally assumed total cost curve, long-run average cost (*LRAC*) first declines, reaches a minimum, where a ray from the origin is tangent to the total cost curve, and rises thereafter. These relations are all shown in Figure 6.2.3.

The derivation of long-run marginal cost is illustrated in Figure 6.2.4. Panel A contains a total cost curve (*LRTC*) shaped similar to that in Figure 6.2.3. As output increases from Ox' to Ox'', one moves from point P to point Q and total cost increases from Oc' to Oc''. Marginal cost, the additional cost of producing one more unit of output, is thus

$$MC = \frac{Oc'' - Oc'}{Ox'' - Ox'} = \frac{QR}{PR}.$$

As P moves along *LRTC* toward point Q, the distance between P and Q becomes smaller and smaller, and the slope of the tangent T at point Q becomes a progressively better estimate of QR/PR. For movements in a tiny neighborhood around point Q, the slope of the tangent is marginal cost at output Ox''.

As one moves along *LRTC* through points such as P and Q the slope of *LRTC* diminishes until point S is reached at output Ox_m. Therefore the marginal cost curve (*LMC*) is constructed in panel B so that it decreases (as the *slope* of *LRTC* decreases) until output Ox_m is attained and increases thereafter (as the *slope* of *LRTC* increases).

One point should be noted. As indicated in Figure 6.2.3, the slope of the ray II gives minimum *LRAC*. But at this point ray II is tangent to *LRTC*, hence the slope of II also gives *LMC* at point M. Thus $LMC = LRAC$ when *LRAC* attains its minimum value. Ray II in Figure 6.2.4, panel A, also illustrates this point. Since the slope of *LRTC* is less than the slope of a ray from the origin to any point on the curve to the left of M, *LMC* is less than *LRAC* from the origin to Ox_m. Since the slope of

FIGURE 6.2.4

DERIVATION OF MARGINAL COST CURVE

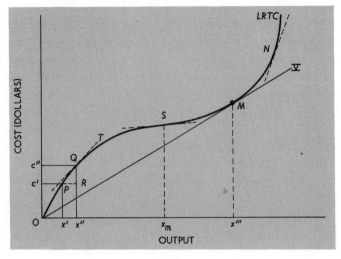

Panel A
Long-run total cost

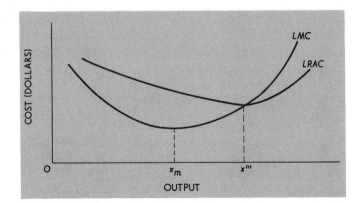

Panel B
Long-run marginal cost

LRTC is greater than the slope of a ray from the origin to any point on the curve to the right of M, say at point N, *LMC* is greater than *LRAC* at outputs larger than Ox_m.

Following a line of reasoning similar to that set forth in the theory of production, the relations between marginal and average costs would be expected. If an additional unit of output adds more to cost than the average cost, the average must increase. Thus average increases when marginal is greater than average. When the marginal cost is less than average, an additional unit of output adds less than the average; consequently average must fall under this circumstance. When another unit adds exactly the average, average and marginal are equal.

> **Relations.** (1) *LRTC* rises continuously, first at a decreasing rate then at an increasing rate. (2) *LRAC* first declines, reaches a minimum, then rises. When *LRAC* reaches its minimum, *LMC* equals *LRAC*. (3) *LMC* first declines, reaches a minimum, and then increases. *LMC* lies below *LRAC* over the range in which *LRAC* declines; it lies above *LRAC* when *LRAC* is rising.

6.2.c Economies and diseconomies of scale

Thus far we have concentrated exclusively upon describing the generally assumed shapes of the long-run cost curves and have not analyzed the economic forces behind them. These forces are economies and diseconomies of scale.

Recall from Chapter 5, our discussion of increasing and decreasing returns to scale. When all inputs are increased in the same proportion and output increases but in a smaller proportion, the result is *decreasing* returns to scale. Alternatively, when all inputs are increased in the same proportion and output increases in a greater proportion, we have *increasing* returns to scale.

It requires a much more sophisticated mathematical proof than is appropriate here, but there is a specific relation between returns to scale and the shape of the long-run average cost curve.[2] With constant input prices, over the range of increasing returns to scale, the average cost curve declines; thus, we speak in this case of economies of scale. Over the range

---

[2] See C. E. Ferguson, *The Neoclassical Theory of Production and Distribution,* Cambridge University Press, 1969, pp. 79–83, for the derivation of a measure of increasing and decreasing proportions. See pp. 158–63 for the relation to cost functions.

of decreasing returns to scale, the long-run average cost curve is rising; over this range we say that the cost function is subject to diseconomies of scale. We must note that this relation applies even when cost curves are not derived, by increasing all factors proportionally. In fact, in the case of variable proportions, inputs are not increased in the same proportion; some are even decreased as output increases. Again we must emphasize that the proof is too mathematical for this text.

In any case, under variable proportions economies of scale cause long-run average cost to decline. As the size of plant and the scale of operation are larger, certain economies of scale are usually realized. That is, after adjusting *all* inputs optimally, the unit cost of production is reduced as the size of output is increased.

Adam Smith gave one of the chief reasons for this: specialization and division of labor. When the number of workers is expanded, fixed units remaining fixed, the opportunities for specialization and division of labor are rapidly exhausted. The marginal product curve rises, to be sure; but not for long. It very quickly reaches its maximum and declines. When workers and equipment are expanded together, however, very substantial gains may be reaped by division of jobs and the specialization of workers in one job or another.

Proficiency is gained by concentration of effort. If a plant is very small and employs only a small number of workers, each worker will usually have to perform several different jobs in the production process. In doing so he or she is likely to have to move about the plant, change tools, and so on. Not only are workers not highly specialized but a part of their worktime is consumed in moving about and changing tools. Thus important savings may be realized by expanding the scale of operation. A larger plant with a larger work force may permit each worker to specialize in one job, gaining proficiency and decreasing or eliminating time-consuming interchanges of location and equipment. There naturally will be corresponding reductions in the unit cost of production.

Technological factors constitute a second force contributing to economies of scale. If several different machines, each with a different rate of output, are required in a production process, the operation may have to be quite sizable to permit proper "meshing" of equipment. Suppose only two types of machines are required, one that produces and one that packages the product. If the first machine can produce 30,000 units per day and the second can package 45,000, output will have to be 90,000 per day in order to utilize fully the capacity of each type of machine.

Another technological element is the fact that the cost of purchasing and installing larger machines is usually *proportionately* less than the cost of smaller machines. For example, a printing press that can run 200,000 papers per day does not cost 10 times as much as one that can run 20,000 per day—nor does it require 10 times as much building space, 10 times as many people to work it, and so forth. Again, expanding size tends to reduce the unit cost of production.

A final technological element is perhaps the most important of all: as the scale of operation expands there is usually a qualitative, as well as a quantitative, change in equipment. Consider ditchdigging. The smallest scale of operation is one laborer and one shovel. But as the scale expands beyond a certain point one does not simply continue to add workers and shovels. Shovels and most workers are replaced by a modern ditchdigging machine. In like manner, expansion of scale normally permits the introduction of various types of automation devices, all of which tend to reduce the unit cost of production.

Thus two broad forces—specialization and division of labor and technological factors—enable producers to reduce unit cost by expanding the scale of operation.[3] These forces give rise to the negatively sloped portion of the long-run average cost curve.

But why should it ever rise? After all possible economies of scale have been realized, why doesn't the curve become horizontal?

The rising portion of *LRAC* is usually attributed to diseconomies of scale, which generally implies limitations to efficient management. Managing any business entails controlling and coordinating a wide variety of activities—production, transportation, finance, sales, and so on. To perform these managerial functions efficiently the manager must have accurate information; otherwise the essential decision making is done in ignorance.

As the scale of plant expands beyond a certain point, top management necessarily has to delegate responsibility and authority to lower echelon employees. Contact with the daily routine of operation tends to be lost, and efficiency of operation declines. Red tape and paper work expand;

---

[3] This discussion of economies of scale has concentrated upon physical and technological forces. There are financial reasons for economies of scale as well. Large-scale purchasing of raw and processed materials may enable the buyer to obtain more favorable prices (quantity discounts). The same is frequently true of advertising. As another example, financing of large-scale business is normally easier and less expensive; a nationally known business has access to organized security markets, so it may place its bonds and stocks on a more favorable basis. Bank loans also usually come easier and at lower interest rates to large, well-known corporations. These are but examples of many potential economies of scale attributable to financial considerations.

management is generally not as efficient. This increases the cost of the managerial function and, of course, the unit cost of production.

Note that in all of our discussion of economies and diseconomies of scale we have implied production under variable proportions. But we must emphasize that the relation between the slope of long-run average cost and increasing and decreasing returns to scale in production still applies.

It is very difficult to determine just when diseconomies of scale set in and when they become strong enough to outweigh the economies of scale. In businesses where economies of scale are negligible, diseconomies may soon become of paramount importance, causing LRAC to turn up at a relatively small volume of output. Panel A, Figure 6.2.5, shows a long-run average cost curve for a firm of this type. In other cases, economies of scale are extremely important. Even after the efficiency of management begins to decline technological economies of scale may offset the diseconomies over a wide range of output. Thus the LRAC curve may not turn upward until a very large volume of output is attained. This case, typified by the so-called natural monopolies, is illustrated in panel B, Figure 6.2.5.

In many actual situations, however, neither of these extremes describes the behavior of LRAC. A very modest scale of operation may enable a firm to capture all of the economies of scale; however, diseconomies may not be incurred until the volume of output is very great. In this case, LRAC would have a long horizontal section as shown in panel C. Some economists and businesspeople feel that this type of LRAC curve describes many production processes in the American economy. For analytical purposes, however, we will assume a "representative" LRAC, such as that illustrated in Figure 6.2.4.

FIGURE 6.2.5
VARIOUS SHAPES OF LRAC

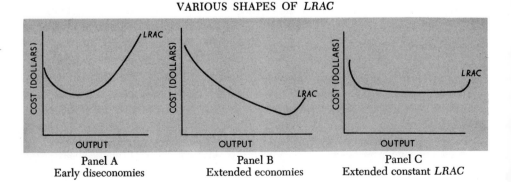

Panel A   Panel B   Panel C
Early diseconomies   Extended economies   Extended constant LRAC

6.2.d Summary

The conventional definition of the long run is "a period of time (not calendar time) of such length that all inputs are variable." Another aspect of the long run has also been stressed, an aspect that is, perhaps, the most important of all. The long run is a *planning horizon*. All production, indeed all economic activity, takes place in the short run. The long run refers to the fact that economic agents, consumers and entrepreneurs, can plan ahead and choose many aspects of the short run in which they will operate in the future. Thus, in a sense the long run consists of all possible short run situations among which an economic agent may choose.

APPLICATION

Estimating cost curves

Many estimates have been made of the cost curves of various industries. Frequently these studies are designed to find the point at which minimum long-run average cost is attained for firms in an industry. Most of these studies have used engineering data and the assumption that factors of production are available at a constant price.

But when we examine actual industries, we observe that firms in the same industry frequently vary greatly in size. This leads us to believe that the cost curves differ among firms in an industry. Some extremely small firms survive beside veritable giants, with many sizes of firms in between. If there is no single scale for firms in an industry, any attempt to measure an industry cost curve must consider the effect of having many sizes of firms in the industry. Once the industry costs have been estimated one can predict what size or range of sizes is optimal—that is, least cost. An interesting method of estimating industry costs and the point of minimum average cost is called the "survivor technique." Let us look at the results of two such studies.*

The survivor principle is based upon the following assumption: all firms in the industry are classified by size, and the share of total industry output is calculated; if the relative share of any class falls,

---

* This discussion is based upon two related papers: George J. Stigler, "The Economies of Scale," *Journal of Law and Economics,* October 1958, pp. 54–71, and T. R. Saving, "Estimation of Optimum Size by the Survivor Technique," *Quarterly Journal of Economics,* November 1961, pp. 569–607.

that class is relatively inefficient, and is more inefficient the faster the share is falling. In this way economists can consider not merely the technological composition of a firm's costs but also the ability of the firm to solve its other problems—labor relations, innovation, regulation, and so on. In this way one can tell the range over which economies of scale are attainable and points, if any, at which diseconomies are reached.

Examples of this method are G. J. Stigler's studies of the steel and automobile industries.† In the steel industry during the 1930s and 1940s very small firms and the largest firms experienced a decline in relative share. Intermediate firms, in size classes from 2½ to 25 percent of the industry's capacity, grew or retained their share. The smallest sizes lost shares most rapidly. It appears then that over the period of measurement the long-run average cost curve for the part of the steel industry that was measured looked somewhat like the curve in panel C, Figure 6.2.5. This change in distribution for the steel industry is shown in Table 6.2.2. Of course, this method cannot estimate how much higher than the minimum are the costs of the declining firms.

The analysis was extended from firm size to *plant size*. It was found that the share of the smallest plants—up to almost one percent of industry capacity—declined, with no tendency toward decline for plants above this size, even the very largest. It appears that the diseconomies of large firm size were due to diseconomies of multiplant operation and not to diseconomies of large plants.

The trend of the passenger automobiles industry from 1936 to 1955 differed somewhat from that of steel. Over this span of time the smallest automobile companies—under five percent of industry capacity—experienced a declining share. During periods of inflation with price control the data revealed diseconomies for the largest class, but substantial economies otherwise. That is, the long-run average cost is shaped like that in panel C during inflation, but it does not rise at large size in other times. The petroleum industry from 1947 to 1954 showed essentially the same characteristics as steel in both firm size and plant size. The range of firm sizes from one half of one percent to ten percent of industry capacity contained all classes in the optimal range.

After examining these specific industries, Stigler investigated 48 manufacturing industries to isolate the most important determinants of the optimum-size firm. In the past, economists had said that influences such as large advertising expenditures, complicated technology, research, and large plant size caused industries to be char-

† Stigler, "The Economies of Scale," p. 54–71.

TABLE 6.2.2

DISTRIBUTION OF OUTPUT OF STEEL INGOT CAPACITY
(by relative size of company)

Company size (percent of industry total)	1930	1938	1951
1. Percent of industry capacity			
Under ½	7.16	6.11	4.65
½ to 1	5.94	5.08	5.37
1 to 2½	13.17	8.30	9.07
2½ to 5	10.64	16.59	22.21
5 to 10	11.18	14.03	8.12
10 to 25	13.24	13.99	16.10
25 and over	38.67	35.91	34.50
2. Number of companies			
Under ½	39	29	22
½ to 1	9	7	7
1 to 2½	9	6	6
2½ to 5	3	4	5
5 to 10	2	2	1
10 to 25	1	1	1
25 and over	1	1	1

Source: This table was taken from the article by G. J. Stigler (p. 58), cited at the end of this section. The original sources cited in that paper were *Directory of Iron and Steel Works of the United States and Canada,* 1930, 1938, and *Iron Age,* January 3, 1952.

acterized by large-scale firms. After the optimum ranges of sizes for all industries were determined, the average assets of these firms were computed. This average-size firm was regressed on advertising, technology and research, and plant size.‡ Advertising expenditure had no significant effect on average optimum size. The other two variables were quite significant. The range of optimal sizes were quite wide, indicating strong evidence that many *industry* (but *not* necessarily *firm*) cost curves are saucer-shaped as in panel C.

One frequently hears that very large-scale plants are necessary for survival in manufacturing industries today. There are supposedly economies of large-scale production in manufacturing that make for large plant size. Evidence based upon the survivor technique does not verify this allegation.

T. R. Saving used this technique to investigate the minimum, the average, and the range of optimum sizes for plants in 89 manufacturing industries.§ The data show wide variation in both average

---

‡ The ratio of chemists and engineers to total employment was used as a proxy variable for technology.

§ Saving, "Estimation of Optimum Size by the Survivor Technique," pp. 569–607.

and minimum optimum sizes. The magnitudes, however, are quite small relative to total industry size. For example, 72 percent of all industries showed minimum optimal plant size—that is, they exhausted all economies of scale—at plant sizes that produced less than one percent of the industry's total output. Ninety-eight percent had an average optimal size below ten percent of total, and 55 percent showed average optimal sizes at less than one percent. The ranges of optimal size tended to be small compared to the industry's size; 81 percent had ranges that were below five percent of total. The ranges, however, were large compared to average optimal size. It appears then that economies of scale in plant size are rapidly exhausted in expansion.

After estimating optimum plant sizes, Saving looked at the causes of large or small average firm size relative to size of the industry. He hypothesized that average firm size is affected by the optimum plant size and the extent of multi-plant operation (as measured by the average number of plants per firm in the industry). Both variables significantly affected average firm size, accounting for about 87 percent of the variation, but the average number of plants was found to be a far more significant determinant. These economies may be more important than plant economies. That is, the optimum-size plant is usually not so large as to cause industries to be characterized by a few, very large firms.

Next the determinants of optimum firm size were analyzed to examine why industries differ so greatly in the points at which plant economies of scale end and diseconomies begin. The hypothetical determining variables were (1) industry size, (2) rate of growth of the industry, (3) complexity of the productive process, and (4) the extent of capital intensiveness. These four variables explained approximately 50 percent of the variation in minimum and average plant size in the 89 industries tested. The two most important variables in both tests were, in order of importance, industry size and capital intensiveness as measured by the capital-to-labor ratio. They accounted for about 80 percent of the explained variation. The rate of growth of the industry was not significant at all. The complexity of the productive process, measured by the proportion of chemists and engineers to total labor force, was not highly significant but was more significant in the case of the average optimum plant size than the minimum. The only important variables affecting the range of optimal plant sizes—that is, the length of the horizontal portion of industry long-run average cost—were the mean optimum plant size and the size of the industry.

Certainly there may be biases in the survivor technique from imperfections in data, but other methods of cost estimation must also use imperfect data. In any case this technique gives some interesting insight into the nature of industry costs and the extent of long-run economies and diseconomies of scale.

Of course the cost curve of primary interest to business decision makers is the cost structure of a particular firm, or of a specific project of the firm. This estimation involves a different technique. Certainly engineering data would be of utmost importance, if one considers building a new plant or an entirely new operation. This can be obtained through consultation. Prices of inputs, particularly labor costs, are usually obtainable, at least over a range. Certainly the best tool of analysis is a lot of experience in the particular business.

6.3 THEORY OF COST IN THE SHORT RUN

Once entrepreneurs have investigated all possibilities open to them, they can decide upon a specific scale of output and hence build a plant of such size as to produce this output at the least possible cost. For economic theory, this may be regarded as either *money* cost or *resource* cost because, in the final analysis, they are the same (except in one situation, which is discussed in the last chapter of the book).

6.3.a Short-run total cost

Prior to investing money resources in buildings, machinery, and so on, the amounts of all resources are variable. That is, the use of each type of resource can be determined so as to obtain the most efficient (that is, least cost) combination of inputs. But once money resources have been congealed into buildings, machinery, and other *fixed* assets, their amounts cannot be readily changed, although their rates of utilization can be decreased by allowing fixed assets to lie idle (note, however, that idle assets cost as much as, perhaps more than, utilized assets). To summarize, in the *short run* there are certain resources whose amounts cannot be changed when the desired rate of output changes, while there are other resources (called variable inputs) whose use can be changed almost instantaneously.[4]

---

[4] It is not quite precise to say that the inputs of some resources cannot be changed. Certainly the firm could scrap a very expensive piece of capital equipment, buy another one twice as large, and have it installed before lunch, *if it is willing to*

FIGURE 6.3.1

SHORT- AND LONG-RUN TOTAL COST

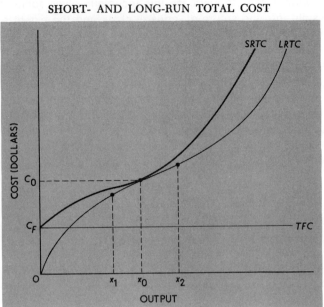

Suppose an entrepreneur, whose $LRTC$, or planning horizon, is that indicated in Figure 6.3.1, builds a plant to produce Ox_0 units of output at total cost OC_0. Since the inputs of certain resources are fixed, the cost to the firm of these resources is fixed also. We can now examine the effect of varying output when the use of certain resources cannot be changed. The firm operates in the short run—that period of time in which the input of one or more factors of production is fixed, hence the cost of these factors to the firm is fixed also. Since output can be changed in the short run only by changing variable inputs, the cost of these inputs is a variable cost. The sum of the variable and the fixed costs at any level of output is the *total cost* of producing that output.

Definition. Total fixed cost is the sum of the short-run explicit fixed costs and the implicit cost incurred by an entrepreneur.

---

pay the price. In fact the firm can probably change any input rather rapidly, given, once more, its willingness to pay. The short run is thus a convenient but important analytical device. It is frequently helpful in analyzing problems to assume that some inputs are fixed for a period of time. Moreover, it does not deviate too much from reality to make this assumption since entrepreneurs often consider certain resources as fixed over a period of time. The student should not be overly concerned about the time factor in the short and long run. The fixity of resources is the important element.

Definition. Total variable cost is the sum of the amounts spent for each of the variable inputs used.

Definition. Total cost in the short run is the sum of total variable and total fixed cost.

Consider the short-run total cost curve ($SRTC$) in Figure 6.3.1. This is the curve indicating the firm's total cost of production for each level of output when the input of certain resources is fixed. One characteristic of this curve is that $SRTC$ (OC_0) equals $LRTC$ at output level Ox_0. This equality is apparent when we remember that the plant was built (and the input of all resources chosen) so as to produce Ox_0 at the least possible cost. Short-run cost at Ox_0 is therefore also the lowest attainable cost for this output.

A second characteristic of short-run total cost shown by $SRTC$ is that for every output other than Ox_0, the output that the plant was built to produce optimally, short-run total cost exceeds long-run total cost. At outputs such as Ox_1 and Ox_2, for example, $SRTC$ could not by definition be lower than $LRTC$ because $LRTC$ is defined as the *least cost possible* for every level of output. Since moving from Ox_0 to other outputs such as Ox_1 or Ox_2 in the short-run is done with some resources fixed at a level that is probably non-optimal at these new outputs, one would assume that $SRTC$ is higher than $LRTC$ at these other outputs. It seems reasonable to assume also that the further the firm gets from Ox_0, the more $SRTC$ exceeds $LRTC$.

A third characteristic of $SRTC$ is that at zero output cost is positive; here it is OC_F. Since we have fixed the input of some resources, the firm must pay these resources the same amount at all outputs. Figure 6.3.1, therefore, shows both components of short-run total costs: (1) total fixed costs (TFC) OC_F, which must be paid regardless of output, and (2) total variable costs (TVC), the difference between $SRTC$ and OC_F. TVC changes as output changes, since variable costs are the payments to the resources that the firm can vary with output.

6.3.b Average and marginal costs

The short-run total cost of production, including implicit cost, is very important to an entrepreneur. However, one may obtain a deeper understanding of total cost by analyzing the behavior of the short-run average costs and marginal cost. The method used in deriving these curves is similar to that used to derive long-run average and marginal costs.

We assume a specific short-run situation such as that developed in sub-section 6.3.a. First, consider average fixed cost (AFC).

Definition. Average fixed cost is total fixed cost divided by output.

Since average fixed cost is a constant amount divided by output, average fixed cost is relatively high at very low output levels and falls continuously as output decreases, approaching the horizontal axis as output gets very large.

Now we examine average variable cost (AVC), a concept completely analogous to long-run average costs, since all costs are variable in the long run.

Definition. Average variable cost is total variable cost divided by output.

Having spent considerable time developing the concept of long-run average cost, we need not spend much time deriving the average variable cost curve, since the two techniques are similar.

Figure 6.3.2 shows how AVC is derived from TVC. As is true of all "average" curves, the average variable cost associated with any level of output is given by the slope of a ray from the origin to the corresponding point on the TVC curve. As may easily be seen from panel A, the slope of a ray from the origin to the curve steadily diminishes as one passes through points such as P; and it diminishes until the ray is just tangent to the TVC curve at point Q, associated with output Ox_2. Thereafter the

FIGURE 6.3.2

DERIVATION OF THE AVERAGE
VARIABLE COST CURVE

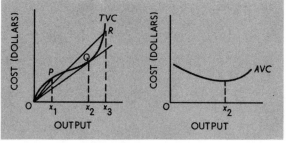

Panel A   Panel B
Total variable cost   Average variable cost

slope increases as one moves from Q toward points such as R. This is reflected in panel B by constructing AVC with a negative slope until output Ox_2 is attained. After that point, the slope becomes positive and remains positive.

Although the U-shapes of AVC and long-run average cost are similar, the reasons for their decline and rise are different. The explanation for the curvature of AVC lies in the short-run theory of production. Total variable cost at any output consists of the payments to the variable factors of production used to produce that output. TVC, therefore, equals the sum of the number of units of each variable input (V) multiplied by unit price (P) of that input. For example, at output Q produced by n variable inputs, $TVC = P_1V_1 + P_2V_2 + P_3V_3 + \cdots + P_nV_n$. For the one-variable case, $TVC = PV$. Average variable cost is TVC divided by output (Q), or

$$AVC = \frac{TVC}{Q} = \frac{PV}{Q} = P\left(\frac{V}{Q}\right).$$

The term (V/Q) is the number of units of input divided by the number of units of output. In Chapter 5, we defined the average product (AP) of an input as total output (Q) divided by the number of units of input (V). Thus

$$\frac{V}{Q} = \frac{1}{(Q/V)} = \frac{1}{AP},$$

and

$$AVC = P\frac{V}{Q} = P\frac{1}{(Q/V)} = P\left(\frac{1}{AP}\right).$$

Thus average variable cost is the price of the input multiplied by the reciprocal of average product. Since, by the law of variable proportions, average product normally rises, reaches a maximum, then declines, average variable cost normally falls, reaches a minimum, then rises.

Figure 6.3.3 shows the derivation of short-run average total cost (ATC), which may be called average cost or unit cost.

Definition. Average total cost is total cost divided by output.

Exactly the same analysis used for AVC holds for panels A and B, which show the derivation of ATC from TC. The slope of the ray diminishes as one moves along TC until point Q' is reached. At Q' the slope of the ray is at its minimum, so minimum ATC is attained at output level Ox_2'. Thereafter the slope of the ray increases continuously, and the ATC curve has

FIGURE 6.3.3

DERIVATION OF THE AVERAGE TOTAL COST
OR UNIT COST CURVE

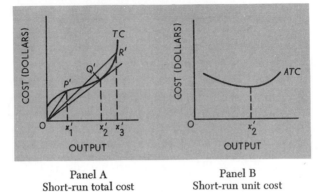

Panel A   Panel B
Short-run total cost   Short-run unit cost

a positive slope. (Note: the output level Ox_2' *does not* represent the same quantity as Ox_2 in Figure 6.3.2. As we shall see, AVC reaches its minimum at a lower output than that at which ATC reaches its minimum.)

ATC may also be computed by an alternative method. Since $TC = TFC + TVC$,

$$ATC = \frac{TC}{Q} = \frac{TFC + TVC}{Q} = \frac{TFC}{Q} + \frac{TVC}{Q} = AFC + AVC.$$

Thus one may calculate average cost as the sum of average fixed and average variable cost.

This method of calculation helps to explain the shape of the average total cost curve. Over the range of values for which AFC and AVC both decline, ATC, the sum of AFC and AVC, must obviously decline as well. But even after AVC turns up, the decline in AFC causes ATC to continue to decline. Finally, however, the increase in AVC more than offsets the decline in AFC; ATC therefore reaches its minimum and increases thereafter. We will show this graphically below.

Finally, let us examine marginal cost in the short run.

Definition. Marginal cost is the change in total cost attributable to a one-unit change in output.

The definitions of long- and short-run marginal cost that we have given are virtually identical. The concepts are not quite the same, however. Long-run marginal cost refers to the change in cost resulting from a change in output when *all inputs are optimally adjusted.* Short-run marginal cost, on the other hand, refers to the change in cost resulting from a change in output when *only the variable inputs change.* Since the fixed inputs cannot be changed in the short run, input combinations are not optimally adjusted. Thus the short-run marginal cost curve reflects suboptimal adjustment of inputs.

Although the concept of marginal cost differs slightly between the long run and the short run, the process of deriving marginal cost is similar. The marginal cost of, say, the second unit produced is the increase in the total cost caused by changing production from one unit to two units; or, $MC_2 = TC_2 - TC_1$. Since only variable cost changes in the short run, however, the marginal cost of producing an additional unit is the increase in variable cost. Thus the marginal cost of the second unit is also $MC_2 = TVC_2 - TVC_1$.

The derivation of marginal cost is illustrated in Figure 6.3.4. Panel A shows the short-run total cost curve TC. As output increases from Ox_1 to Ox_2, one moves from point P to point Q, and total cost increases from Oc_1 to Oc_2. Marginal cost is thus QR/PR. As before, the slope of the tangent T at point Q becomes a progressively better estimate of MC (QR/PR) as the distance between P and Q becomes smaller and smaller. Thus for small changes, the slope of the total cost curve is marginal cost.

As TC increases, the slope decreases (MC decreases) until point S is reached at output Ox_3. Thereafter the slope increases (MC increases).

FIGURE 6.3.4

DERIVATION OF THE MARGINAL COST CURVE

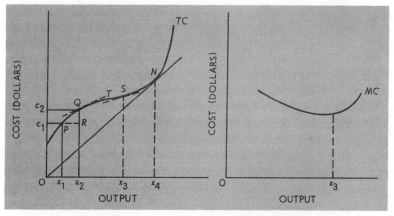

| Panel A | Panel B |
| Short-run total cost | Short-run marginal cost |

The MC curve is constructed in panel B so that it decreases until output Ox_3 is attained, and increases thereafter.

Just as average variable cost is related to average product, marginal cost is related to marginal product. As before, consider the one-variable case in which $TVC = PV$. Thus, if P is fixed

$$MC = \frac{\triangle VC}{\triangle Q} = \frac{\triangle(PV)}{\triangle Q} = P\frac{\triangle V}{\triangle Q},$$

where again $\triangle$ means "the change in." But, recall that marginal product is $MP = \triangle Q/\triangle V$. Therefore,

$$MC = P\left(\frac{1}{MP}\right).$$

From this relation, as marginal product rises, marginal cost falls; when marginal product declines, marginal cost rises.

One final point concerning the relation of short-run marginal and average cost curves should be noted. As already implied, and as Figure 6.3.5 again illustrates, TC and TVC have the same slope at each output level. TC is simply TVC displaced upward by the constant amount TFC (see Figure 6.3.5).

At output Ox_0 the tangent (T) to TVC has the same slope as the

FIGURE 6.3.5

RELATION OF MC TO VARIABLE AND TOTAL COSTS

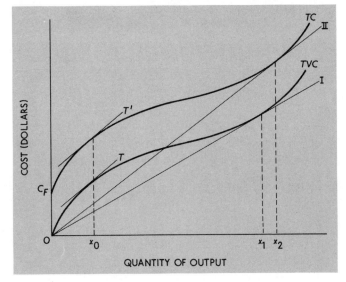

tangent (T') to TC. Since the slopes of the two tangents at output Ox_0 are equal, MC at Ox_0 is given by the slope of either curve. The same holds true for any other output level. The slope of ray I from the origin gives minimum AVC. But at this point (output Ox_1) ray I is just tangent to TVC; hence its slope also gives MC at output Ox_1. Thus $MC = AVC$ when the latter attains its minimum value. Similarly the slope of ray II gives minimum ATC (at output Ox_2). At this point the ray is tangent to TC; thus its slope also gives MC at output Ox_2. Consequently $MC = ATC$ when the latter attains its minimum value. Finally, as is easily seen from Figure 6.3.5, AVC attains its minimum at a lower output than the output at which ATC attains its minimum.

The properties of the average and marginal cost curves, as derived in this section, are illustrated by the traditionally assumed set of short-run cost curves shown in Figure 6.3.6. The curves indicate the following:

Relations. (a) AFC declines continuously, approaching both axes asymptotically, as shown by points 1 and 2 in the figure. (b) AVC first declines, reaches a minimum at point 4, and rises thereafter. When AVC attains its minimum at point 4, MC equals AVC. As AFC approaches asymptotically the horizontal axis, AVC approaches ATC asymptotically, as shown by point 5. (c) ATC first declines,

FIGURE 6.3.6

TYPICAL SET OF COST CURVES

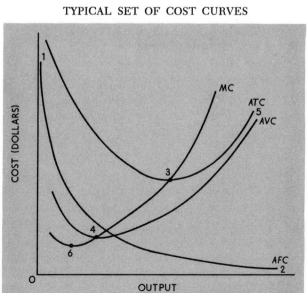

TABLE 6.3.1

SHORT-RUN COST SCHEDULES

1 Output	2 Total cost (dollars)	3 Fixed cost (dollars)	4 Variable cost (dollars)	5 Average fixed cost	6 Average variable cost	7 Average total cost	8 Marginal cost (per 100 units)	9 Marginal cost (per unit)
100......	6,000	4,000	2,000	40.00	20.00	60.00	2,000	20.00
200......	7,000	4,000	3,000	20.00	15.00	35.00	1,000	10.00
300......	7,500	4,000	3,500	13.33	11.67	25.00	500	5.00
400......	9,000	4,000	5,000	10.00	12.50	22.50	1,500	15.00
500......	11,000	4,000	7,000	8.00	14.00	22.00	2,000	20.00
600......	14,000	4,000	10,000	6.67	16.67	23.33	3,000	30.00
700......	18,000	4,000	14,000	5.71	20.00	25.71	4,000	40.00
800......	24,000	4,000	20,000	5.00	25.00	30.00	6,000	60.00
900......	34,000	4,000	30,000	4.44	33.33	37.77	10,000	100.00
1,000......	50,000	4,000	46,000	4.00	46.00	50.00	16,000	160.00

reaches a minimum at point 3, and rises thereafter. When *ATC* attains its minimum at point 3, *MC* equals *ATC*. (*d*) MC first declines, reaches a minimum at point 6, and rises thereafter. *MC* equals both *AVC* and *ATC* when these curves attain their minimum values. Furthemore, *MC* lies below both *AVC* and *ATC* over the range in which the curves decline; it lies above them when they are rising.

6.3.c Numerical example of short-run cost schedules

Table 6.3.1 illustrates numerically the characteristics of the cost curves we have thus far analyzed graphically. As seen in this table, average fixed cost decreases over the entire range of output. Both average variable and average total cost first decrease, then increase with average variable cost attaining a minimum at a lower output than that at which average total reaches its minimum. Marginal cost per 100 units is the incremental increase in total cost and variable cost. Marginal cost (per unit) is below average variable and average total when each is falling and is greater than each when *AVC* and *ATC* are rising.

APPLICATIONS

Benefit-cost analysis in decision making

A really crucial point in the economics of decision making, and one that we shall be making again and again, is that in the short run the decision maker ignores fixed costs and relies on marginal costs: *fixed costs are irrelevant in the short run.*

This rule is critical in running your own business. It is also vastly important for those who work for someone else, in business, in government, or for nonprofit firms. The reason for such importance is the vast number of decisions that take the form of benefit-cost analysis. In most cases these are *marginal benefits* and *marginal costs*.

To illustrate, let us examine why airlines sometimes put on flights that make losses when all costs are considered, or why trucking companies sometimes make seemingly unprofitable hauls. The reason is that the marginal benefit exceeds the marginal cost. It may be that a particular flight has so little passenger and freight demand that the total cost of the flight exceeds the total revenue when the cost of the plane is spread over this extra flight. But if the plane would be idle anyway, the real cost of the additional flight is the added labor and fuel costs, the added wear and tear on capital, and any other costs that would not be encountered if the flight was not made. In other words *only the marginal costs matter.* If these marginal costs are expected to be less than the expected additional revenues from making the additional flight, the trip will be made (if regulatory board permission is received, which is another story). Exactly the same line of reasoning applies to the trucking companies' decisions about additional hauls.

Employees who manage departments or divisions of firms frequently use the same line of reasoning. Say you manage a department in a large department store. How do you convince your store manager that you need more advertising (always say "need" rather than want; "need" sounds much more crucial than "want").* You know more advertising will increase sales and therefore your income. Convince the manager that the *additional returns from the additional sales will exceed the additional cost of additional advertising.* Use the same argument when you wish more sales help or more of any resource, like floor space, that will increase sales. Managers of offices or branches of plants can use much the same argument.

Many, many governmental decisions are based upon marginal benefit–marginal cost analysis. For example, government agencies operate under a fixed budget; with this budget they are assigned the task of carrying out certain operations—possibly building roads and highways. Obviously, there are more projects desired at any one time than can be undertaken with a given budget. Thus the leading candidates for funding are analyzed as to the marginal benefit and the marginal cost involved in each. Theoretically (that is, political implications aside), those projects that should be undertaken are those in which the marginal gain exceeds the marginal cost by the greatest amount.

Even politicians make campaign decisions based upon marginal cost considerations. If you plan to run for an elected office, your campaign funds will no doubt be limited—probably far below your desired level. Since you cannot saturate each area with expenditure, you will have to compare the marginal cost of political advertising (TV, etc.) with the marginal benefits in expected votes.

Possibly you will work for a nonprofit organization, a school, or a hospital. Decision-making using marginal cost is certainly relevant in any of these occupations. A hospital administrator, for example,

---

* Keep track of the number of times political figures at all levels of government use the term *need* when they really mean they want it. Need, which implies necessity, seems a little out of place when used in ways such as, "Houston needs three new golf courses and a swimming pool" or "the nation needs to keep Yellowstone Park free from environmental decay," or "the State of Texas needs legalized paramutuel betting at horse races."

would argue for additional facilities on the basis of a comparison between the marginal cost and the marginal gain, measured not necessarily in money income under these circumstances but in more
patients treated, better care per patient, and so on. School administrators use the same type of approach. Based on personal
experience, I should warn you that such economically based arguments of marginal analysis may not always work if the upper level
of management does not understand marginal analysis. Recently, I
sent through a request for two new faculty members to be added
to the economics department. Departmental income is based upon
departmental student enrollment. The written request "proved" that
the additional new faculty would cost less than the additional income from being able to offer the new classes. Thus, the department
could teach more students at a lower net expenditure. The Dean,
who is an economist himself, approved the request. The top administration, who were not economists, turned it down on the basis
that fixed salary expenditure is already "too high." Moral: when
using these arguments, hope that your superiors have had training
in economics also, or give them some training in economics.

6.4 RELATIONS BETWEEN SHORT-RUN AND LONG-RUN AVERAGE AND MARGINAL COSTS

Figure 6.3.1 showed the relation between short-run and long-run total
cost curves. Recall that the two curves are tangent at the output for which
the short-run is optimal. At every other level of output the short-run cost
exceeds long-run cost.

Figure 6.4.1 shows a long-run average and marginal cost curve. Three
short-run situations are indicated by the three curves $SRAC_1$-MC_1, $SRAC_2$-
MC_2, and $SRAC_3$-MC_3. $SRAC_1$ and MC_1 are the short-run curves for the
plant size designed to produce output Ox_s optimally. Since the short-run
total cost curve is tangent to the long-run total cost curve at this output,
the two average cost curves are tangent at this output also. Recall that
marginal cost, $\triangle C/\triangle Q$, is shown by the slope of the total cost curve.
Thus long-run marginal cost equals short-run marginal cost at the output
given by the point of tangency, Ox_s. Finally, short-run marginal cost
crosses short-run average cost at the latter's minimum point. Note that
because Ox_s is on the decreasing portion of $LRAC$, $SRAC_1$ must be decreasing also at the point of tangency.

$SRAC_3$ and MC_3 show another short-run situation. Here tangency

FIGURE 6.4.1

LONG-RUN AND SHORT-RUN AVERAGE AND MARGINAL COSTS

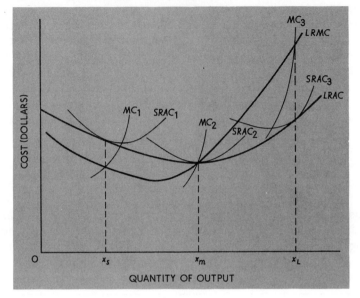

occurs at Ox_L on the increasing part of $LRAC$. Thus $SRAC_3$ is increasing at this point also. Again the two marginal curves are equal at Ox_L, and MC_3 crosses $SRAC_3$ at the minimum point on the latter.

Finally, $SRAC_2$ is the short-run curve corresponding to the output level at which long-run average cost is at its minimum. At output level Ox_m the two average curves are tangent. The two marginal costs MC_2 and $LRMC$ are equal at this output and since the two average curves attain their minimum at Ox_m, the two marginal curves equal the two average cost curves. Thus all four curves are equal at output Ox_m.

In the situation shown in Figure 6.4.1 the firm must operate with one of the three sizes, large, medium, or small. But in the long run, it can build the plant whose size leads to least average cost for any given output. Thus it regards the long-run average cost curve as a planning device, because this curve shows the least cost of producing each possible output. Entrepreneurs therefore are normally faced with a choice among quite a wide variety of plants. In Figure 6.4.2 six short-run average and marginal cost curves are shown; but this is really far from enough. Many curves could be drawn between each of those shown. These six curves are only representative of the wide variety that could be constructed.

These many curves generate *LAC* as a planning device. Suppose the entrepreneur thinks the output associated with point *A* in Figure 6.4.2 will be most profitable. The plant represented by SAC_3, will be built because it will allow production of this output at the least possible cost per unit. With the plant whose short-run average cost is given by SAC_1, unit cost could be reduced by expanding output to the amount associated with point *B* (Ox_2), the minimum point on SAC_1. If demand conditions were suddenly changed so this larger output were desirable, the entrepreneur could easily expand and would add to profitability by reducing unit cost. Nevertheless, when setting future plans the entrepreneur would decide to construct the plant represented by SAC_2 because the firm could reduce unit costs even more. It would operate at point *C*, thereby lowering unit cost from the level at point *B* on SAC_1.

FIGURE 6.4.2

AVERAGE AND MARGINAL COST CURVES

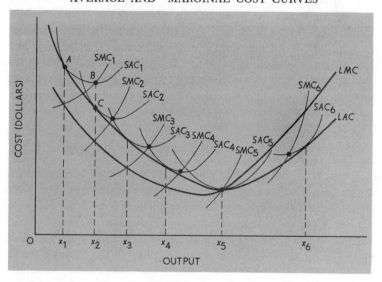

The long-run planning curve, *LAC*, is a locus of points representing the least unit cost of producing the corresponding output. The entrepreneur determines the size of plant by reference to this curve, selecting the short-run plant that yields the least unit cost of producing the volume of output desired.

Figure 6.4.2 illustrates the following:

Relations. (a) *LMC* intersects *LAC* when the latter is at its minimum point. One, and only one, short-run plant has minimum *SAC* that coincides with minimum *LAC* (SAC_5). SMC_5 equals *LMC* at this common minimum. (b) At each output where a particular *SAC* is tangent to *LAC,* the relevant *SMC* equals *LMC.* At outputs below (above) the tangency output, the relevant *SMC* is less (greater) than *LMC.*(c) For all *SAC* curves the point of tangency with *LAC* is at an output less (greater) than the output of minimum *SAC* if the tangency is at an output less (greater) than that associated with minimum *LAC.*

APPLICATION*

Economics of pollution

Up to here we have simply assumed that all costs of production are private costs to the firm. This situation may not apply in all cases, however. More and more one important exception to this assumption is becoming an issue and a point of conflict between business and government. This problem is the existence of pollution. Since many of you will work at jobs that deal with one side or the other of the pollution controversy, we will briefly analyze the problem of pollution.

We can think of pollution as being an input in the production process. A plant or a mine uses factors of production to produce a product. As part of the production process impurities such as smoke, or sulphur dioxide, or sewage are released into the air or water. The firm bears little cost of waste disposal. Others with no connection to the firm bear a social cost from having to breath impure air or by not being able to swim or fish in the stream. Thus the social cost is not necessarily equal to the private cost of production.

The problem is that no one owns the air or the water. If someone owned the air and could enforce the property rights, then the firm could be charged for smoke emission and an optimal amount of smoke would exist. But, if no one owns the air, some branch of government frequently takes upon itself the task of reducing pollution.† Since some of you will be dealing with the problem, think

---

* This application deals with social cost, a concept we will deal with again in the final chapter. Some professors may wish to delay this application until that chapter.

† In some cases with which we are familiar government has taken it upon itself to force a firm to stop polluting its own property. The pollution took place out of sight of any persons not on the firm's property.

how you would handle it. What would you do about the smoke-belching factory and the smoke-breathing residents of the area?

Frequently the answer given is simply to tell the factory to cut it out: stop polluting. But zero pollution is not necessarily optimal pollution. Since you have come this far in the theory of production and cost you are probably thinking—compare the marginal costs and marginal benefits from pollution reduction.

In the first place pollution elimination or reduction is certainly not costless. Expensive equipment must be installed, sometimes output is reduced, some firms have been put out of business by environmental regulations. The cost of the produced product will be increased. In any case, reducing pollution, if the firm continues producing, takes resources away from alternative uses. This then is the opportunity cost.

But the benefit to society may well be worth it. One must look at the benefits from reducing pollution. These benefits are extremely difficult to measure, however. How can one put a price on the value of a 20-percent increase in air purity? We could compare the market value of property—say homes—that are affected by smoke from the factory with the value of equivalent homes that are not in a smoky area. Even this method has shortcomings.

People buy homes in smoke-damaged areas partly because these areas are being damaged. Why would someone choose to live in a polluted area? Because land or homes in these areas are less desirable and are therefore less expensive. People trade some discomfort for some monetary saving. Some families choose to live near airports and bear the noise, because of the less expensive property.

Thus the market has allocated some of the cost of pollution. Of course, those who own property prior to establishment of the polluting firm do suffer a net loss, if they are not reimbursed for the lower property value. Thus pollution elimination would in these cases restore the property to the original value. But, when ownership was established with full knowledge of the effect of pollution, its elimination would compare benefits to cost when the owner made the purchase in full expectation of the decreased value because of pollution.

We might note in passing that more and more local governments are making sophisticated econometric studies to estimate the costs of and benefits from pollution reduction. We recently completed a study for the Ministry of Natural Resources in Ontario, Canada, that showed the recent pollution regulations in the Ontario mining industry reduced investment in mining in Ontario between 4 and 11 percent. The total measurable economic benefit was not as clear.

This is really a growing area in economics. More and more studies will be made by both government and business, and there is a great deal that we have to learn about the economics of pollution, particularly about measuring the costs and benefits. In any case, this may represent an opportunity for some of you to make a real contribution to progress. The field is wide open.

6.5 COST AND THE VALUE OF TIME

We have discussed to some extent the relation between the value of time and the wage rate. The cost of not working is the income that is lost. If a person does not sell an hour of labor time, that hour is lost forever.

But not selling a physical asset is a different story. If you own a pool of oil and do not pump out the oil this year, you can pump it in the future. Thus there is another aspect of cost theory, the cost of holding an asset. This type of cost is becoming an increasingly important topic because of the growing emphasis being placed on the conservation and stockpiling of natural resources.

Let us first set forth the basic theory of the cost of holding an asset. If someone owns a sterile asset[5] worth one dollar and the relevant rate of interest is 10 percent, that person should hold the asset until the next period if the price of the asset is expected to rise above $1.10. If the price expected in the next period is less than $1.10, the asset should be sold, because the value of a dollar invested now at the market rate of interest will be $1.10 in the next period. To generalize, a business would withhold the sale of a sterile asset, including a mineral, if it expected the value of the asset to increase at a rate greater than the relevant rate of discount. Otherwise, the business would maximize wealth by selling the asset and investing the returns.

Thus the cost of holding an asset for one period is the lost return from not having sold the asset and invested the returns. The return from holding an asset is the amount that the asset appreciates in value while being held.

The cost of holding an asset two years is the sacrificed return on the value of the asset in the first year plus the sacrificed return in the second year. To illustrate, assume an asset is worth $100 now; the interest rate is

---

[5] A sterile asset is an asset that yields no return while being held. A ton of coal is sterile. A cow is not. A painting is not sterile, if it gives enjoyment while being held.

10 percent. At the end of the first year an investment of $100 at a 10 percent interest rate is worth

$$\$100 \times (1 + .10) = \$110.$$

If the investment is continued, at the end of the second year it is worth

$$\$100 \times (1 + .10) \times (1 + .10) = \$110 (1 + .10) = \$121.$$

At the end of the third year the value is

$$\$100 (1 + .10)^3 = \$133.10.$$

To generalize, at the end of t years the value is

$$\$100 (1.1)^t,$$

and to generalize even further an investment of A dollars at an interest rate of r at the end of t years is worth

$$A(1 + r)^t.$$

Thus this theory has broad application for business decision making. Consider the following exercise:

EXERCISE

Use of the interest rate in decision making

Suppose you own a building that will sell today for $100,000. You can lease the building to someone for $5,000 a year for five years. The total lease value of $25,000 is payable immediately. You estimate that even with inflation the wear and tear from the leasor's using the building will exactly offset any appreciation in value. Thus the building will sell for $100,000 in five years. If the interest rate you can receive with certainty is 7 percent, should you lease or sell? Ignore any transaction costs and taxation.

Solution:

If you sell the building now and invest the amount at 7 percent, in five years the investment is worth $140,000 since

$$\$100,000 (1 + .07)^5 = \$140,000.$$

If you receive the $25,000 rent receipts now and invest at 7 percent, the investment will be worth $35,000 in five years because

$$\$25,000 (1 + .07)^5 = \$35,000.$$

Thus by leasing, then selling in five years the return is $135,000. Clearly you maximize by selling now.

Suppose the interest rate is only 3 percent. In this case

$$\$100,000 \ (1.03)^5 = \$116,000,$$

and

$$\$25,000 \ (1.03) = \$29,000.$$

Thus by leasing you will have $129,000 in five years in contrast to $116,000. You should lease. The decision, as you can see, depends greatly on the rate of interest.

Clearly, this was a very simple problem in the sense that the two alternatives were so straightforward. But the simplicity does allow us to cut straight to the major point, the effect of the rate of interest. The rate of interest determines the cost of holding an asset for sale in the future. The higher the rate of interest the higher the cost. Thus we should emphasize strongly that the interest rate used in private and governmental decisions is a measure of what else can be done with scarce resources.

To get some idea of the rate at which the value of a resource must increase in order to make holding on to it for future sale economically feasible, consider the following simplified example. Suppose that the value of a resource at the present time, year zero, is $100. Let us assume a time horizon of 25 years. Figure 6.5.1 shows the way in which the $100 appreciates over the 25 years under the assumption of four different rates of interest, 3 percent, 6 percent, 8 percent, and 10 percent. In Figure 6.5.1 time is plotted on the horizontal axis and the value of the investment is plotted along the vertical axis. The rates of appreciation for each rate of interest are shown. Note how the effect of an increased rate of interest begins quickly and compounds geometrically. In order for holding to be economically feasible, its sale price would have to increase more rapidly than the rate shown by the relevant graph, since at each of these plotted interest rates the curves show the break-even price required for holding the sterile asset to be more profitable. The power of compound interest is often underestimated. As an example, had the Dutch West India Company, which bought Manhatten Island from the Indians for $24 worth of beads in 1626, borrowed the money at 8 percent interest the value of the debt would be $12.94 trillion in 1976. This is much more than the value of all of the capital in the United States today. In fact had

FIGURE 6.5.1

POWER OF COMPOUND INTEREST

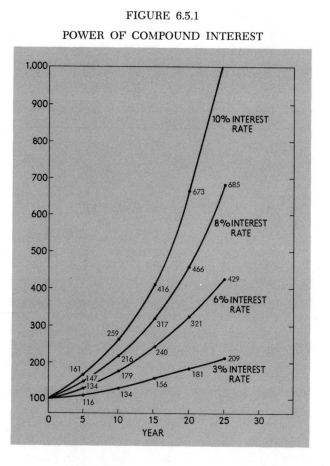

the relevant interest rate been 8 percent in 1626, Manhatten Island would have been a terrible long-term investment. Think of the current value had the Indians invested the $24 at 8 percent.

APPLICATION*

The interest rate and resource conservation

Conservation of natural resources and resource stockpiling recently has been receiving considerable interest. All aspects of the

---

* This and some of the previous analysis is based upon a study done by Gerhard Anders, W. P. Gramm and S. C. Maurice, *Economics of Conservation* (International Institute for Economic Research, Los Angeles, Spring, 1978).

resource conservation question are being hotly debated not only in academic circles but also in the popular media.

Of course, the topic of natural resource conservation is not new. Conservation has received a certain amount of attention throughout history. At the end of the 19th century ardent conservationists were extremely vocal and had a significant impact on public policy in the United States. Many articles thereafter, both in the popular and academic press, have dealt with the problem of conservation. The emphasis in most cases throughout the period is that natural resources were being exploited far too rapidly and government must intervene in order to save resources for future generations. But within the past few years the interest in conservation and exploitation of natural resources has increased astonishingly. This interest is based in part, though not solely, upon the recent oil embargo.

In the case of conservation we have an excellent historical case study in the conservation movement during the early part of the 20th century. We can apply the theory developed in this section to analyze resource conservation over this period.

Obviously a private firm would have the incentive to hold back exploitation of a resource if the resource is expected to increase in value more rapidly than would the investment of the return from extracting and selling the resource now. Clearly the decision depends on the interest rate, which, as we noted, is the value of what else can be done with capital resources.

The relation between the rate of interest and the decision about whether to sell an asset now or hold it until later is fundamental for business decision making. Certainly businesses are interested in making profits, and more profits are preferred to less, other things equal. One might question, however, whether such analysis applies to government, which obviously has objectives or motivations other than economic considerations. While government may have motives other than purely economic motives, the above economic analysis applies to governmental decision making for two extremely important reasons.

In the first place, whatever a government wishes to do and whatever the motivation, the cost to society of carrying out the decision must be considered or taken into account when making decisions. For example, increasing welfare benefits has costs to society, even though the increase in benefits is not motivated purely on economic grounds. The same thing applies to increases in the military budget or other programs carried out by governmental agencies. Even though increasing the military budget may be carried out for other than purely economic reasons, the cost of the increased budget must be considered and compared with alternative uses of the funds. Thus any project of government involves a cost, which is the loss of the resources in alternative uses. This cost is the opportunity cost of the project.

The same type of cost consideration must also apply to stockpiling or conservation of natural resources, even though holding resources in the ground rather than extracting them involves no out-of-pocket costs to the government treasury and even though the delayed extraction is ordered from purely noneconomic motivations. No matter what the motivation, economic or otherwise, the decision to hold resources involves opportunity costs and these costs may not be inconsiderable.

If the value of the resource increases less rapidly than the rate at which an investment of the value of the resource increases, society loses economically by witholding extraction. That is, the value of the resource must increase at a rate greater than the relevant rate of interest or there is a social cost involved. The *difference* between the rate of increase in the value of the resource and the interest rate is the cost to society of withholding the extraction. On the other hand, if the value of the resource conserved grows at a more rapid rate than the relevant rate of interest over the time period of conservation, society is in fact better off economically for having postponed exploitation of the resource. If these circumstances occur, society benefits economically from a withholding activity, which may have been motivated by noneconomic considerations.

In conservation decisions, government decision makers should recognize that the true cost of withholding extraction of resources is as real a cost as the price of a good purchased, even when the motivation for conservation is noneconomic.

The key variable in the process of analyzing the decision to delay extraction is the break-even price. As noted, the break-even price is the value in some future year that would be obtained from investing the sale price of a unit of the resource in the present year at the relevant rate of interest. For example, suppose the value of a unit of a resource today is $7 and the relevant rate of interest is a constant 5 percent a year. The value of $7 invested for 9 years is

$$\$7.00 \, (1 + .05)^9 = \$10.85$$

Thus $10.85 is a "break-even" price in the following sense: Stockpiling or conservation of units of the resource would have been economically feasible, if the value of the resource has risen to an amount in excess of $10.85. Otherwise, if the interest rate is 5 percent, selling the resource at $7 and investing would have been preferable economically.

Even though the motive for stockpiling is for reasons entirely divorced from economic interest, the break-even price gives a good indication of the cost of the stockpiling. For example, if the price in the future period happens to be $9 per unit, the cost is the difference between the break-even price and the actual price, in this case $1.85 per unit stockpiled. Of course, if the price in the future period exceeds $10.85 then society benefits to the extent of the difference, even though the motivation is noneconomic. In any year the ratio of the break-even price to the actual price indicates whether or not society does or does not benefit economically by stockpiling.

The second important reason for applying economic analysis to the governmental decision to withhold extraction of resources concerns long-term resource conservation. The resource conservation movement is and has been involved basically in plans to make future generations better off economically by postponing far into the future the extraction of some natural resources. The amount extracted now will not be available later; thus later generations will, it is alleged, be impoverished if present generations use up resources at the market-determined rate of extraction.

The above analysis indicates the logical method of measuring the cost or benefits of long-term conservation of resources. If the real value of the resource appreciates less rapidly over time than the relevant rate of interest, the future generation would be made better off economically if the philanthropic generation exploits the resources and invests the return at the market rate of interest. On the other hand, if increasing scarcity causes the value of the natural resource to appreciate more rapidly than the interest rate, the later generations benefit more by having inherited the resources in the ground. Again when a society considers conservation as a method of endowing future generations, it cannot neglect the cost of the endowment; that cost is the lost opportunity of investing the return from the resources at the going rate of interest. The endowing generation bears the cost of foregoing income from using the resources. The endowed generation bears a cost when it could have been made better off if the previous generation had exploited the resource and invested the returns in capital for the later era. Which program would leave future generations better off—leaving resources or exploiting the resources and investing—is an economic question that can be estimated empirically.

Just as an aside, the question of long-term resource conservation brings up an additional problem. There is the distinct possibility that technological change will make the conserved resource obsolete. In this case early generations sacrifice in order to benefit future generations. But then the future generations have little or no use for the resource that the earlier group gave up. Secondly, there is the high probability that the earlier generation sacrifices in order to make a vastly richer generation even richer. If, for example, Americans in 1830 had stockpiled whale oil to protect the Americans of the 1970s against the loss of a lighting fuel, not only would such a fuel be technologically obsolete today but a relatively poor generation would have made a sacrifice attempting to make a relatively rich generation even richer.

To summarize, the value of a natural resource in the ground in any period is the price at which the resource would sell minus the cost of extraction. If the decision criterion for conservation is to make some future generation better off than it would otherwise be, the decision to force production holdbacks would be uneconomical when the value of the conserved resources increases at a rate less rapid than the relevant rate of discount. Otherwise, as noted, exploitation and investment of the returns would maximize the wealth of the future generation. We will concern ourselves here only with the economic feasibility of conservation or stockpiling decisions regardless of motivation, in order to isolate the social costs of such decisions.

Table 6.5.1 shows the results of long-term stockpiling for 14 resources. Column *1* lists the particular resource. Column *2* gives the purchase price in 1900 (or in three indicated years the price in the earliest available years). Column *2* shows the price in 1975.† Suppose stockpiling of the resource had been enforced in the earliest year, 1900 in all but three cases. Column *4a* shows what the price would have had to have been in 1975 to make the enforced conservation economically feasible if the relevant rate of interest had been the rate paid for AAA corporate bonds.

Take the second resource, bauxite, for example. If the price of a unit of bauxite, $3.87, had been invested and reinvested each year at the AAA bond rate for that year, the value of that investment in 1975 would have been $111.20 or 741 percent of the actual price. Thus the cost of stockpiling rather than investing was $111.20 − $15.00 = $96.20. Or if the 1900 generation had wished to make the 1975 generation better off, they could have done it better by selling

---

† Technically, the real price is price less extraction costs. If these varied in the same way over time the conclusion is the same. In the study cited in the footnote above, price and cost were found to have varied in about the same way.

TABLE 6.5.1

PURCHASE PRICE IN 1900, SALE PRICE IN 1975,
AND BREAK-EVEN PRICES IN 1975

1	2	3	4a	4b
			Break-even	
	Purchase	Purchase	$R = AAA$	
	price	price		
Resource	1900	1975	Dollars	Percent
Aluminum	$32.72	$ 39.80	939.90	2,361
Bauxite	3.87	15.00	111.20	741
Coal	1.04	18.75	29.90	159
Copper	0.17	0.64	4.80	745
Crude				
petroleum	0.62*	7.52	14.30	191
Gold	20.67	162.25	593.70	366
Iron ore	4.00	18.62	114.90	617
Lead	4.41	21.60	126.70	587
Lime	3.68†	22.18	89.00	401
Magnesium	1.81‡	0.82	22.60	2.758
Nickel	27.00	210.50	775.60	368
Silver	61.33	443.00	1,761.70	398
Tin	30.00	346.00	861.70	249
Zinc	4.40	39.10	126.40	323

Note: Series begins in *1905; †1904; ‡1918.

the resource and investing the returns. Column 4b shows the percent of this "break-even" price to the actual price in 1975. In every case the break-even price was higher. In all but two cases, coal and oil, the break-even price was more than double the actual price. For other interest rates the percent of break-even to actual price was higher.

This result does not say that conservation or stockpiling is undesirable. We only wish to show how the theory allows us to estimate the cost and benefit of such a policy. It is a tool to evaluate future policy. The cost of conservation is seldom mentioned in the literature on the subject, but such analysis allows us to estimate whether or not a particular policy really does what it was designed to do—make future generations better off.

6.6 SUMMARY

The physical conditions of production and resource prices jointly establish the cost of production. If the set of technological possibilities changes, the cost curves change. Or if the prices of some factors of production change, the firm's cost curves change. Therefore, it should be emphasized that cost curves are generally drawn under the assumptions of *constant factor prices and a constant technology.*

We have distinguished between cost in the short run and in the long run. Except for one output level, cost is always higher in the short run than in the long run. As we emphasized, the really crucial cost, as far as decision making is concerned, is marginal cost. This concept is frequently used in cost-benefit analysis.

While the cost of production is important to business firms and to the economy as a whole, it is only half the story. Cost gives one aspect of economic activity; to the individual businessperson it is the obligation to pay out funds; to the society as a whole it represents the resources that must be sacrificed to obtain a given commodity. The other aspect is revenue or demand. To the individual entrepreneur revenue constitutes the flow of funds from which the obligation may be met. To society, demand represents the social valuation placed on a commodity.

Thus both demand and cost must be taken into consideration. It is to this combination of demand and cost that we turn in Chapter 7.

APPLICATION

Time and the cost of travel

Why does one person fly from Washington to New York, another take a train, and yet another drive? Do not say solely differences in income, or that one person can afford to fly and another cannot. Many rich old people take the train, while middle-income people and poor students choose to fly. The answer lies in the different valuations of time among people. A paper by Reuben Gronau used simple consumer behavior theory to analyze the problem and to estimate the demand for passenger transportation.* Gronau incorporated time into the cost of a trip. In his model the price of a trip, Π, consists of two parts, the money cost and the cost of the time spent traveling:

$$\Pi = P + KT$$

where P is the dollar cost of the trip, T is the time spent traveling, and K is the traveler's valuation of a unit of his time, perhaps his wage rate. Assume someone values time at $10 an hour. A particular trip

---

* This application is based upon Reuben Gronau "The Effect of Traveling Time on the Demand for Passenger Transportation," *Journal of Political Economy,* March/April 1970, pp. 377–94. For a general analysis of the importance of time in behavior theory, see G. S. Becker, "A Theory of the Allocation of Time," *Economic Journal,* September 1965, pp. 493–517.

takes 2 hours by air and 15 by rail. If air fare is $150 and rail is $80, the total cost of flying is $170 and of traveling by rail, $230.

The demand for trips is a function of their total cost, and the cost of other inputs, such as hotel, meals, etc. Also, the demand for trips depends upon the demand for visits, which in turn depends upon whether the visit is for business or pleasure, and upon income. For now, we will ignore everything except the choice of method of transportation. In the example above, the traveler chooses air. We will ignore fear of flying, pleasure from sightseeing by car, and so on. We will assume that a consumer plans a visit, then chooses the cheapest method of travel.

Gronau attempted to estimate statistically the variables that determined which mode of transportation would be used for a particular trip. First, he estimated the relation of miles traveled to time spent traveling and to the money price of the fare for four different methods of transportation: air, rail, bus, automobile. Using these equations he then found the points at which consumers, who choose the cheapest (total) methods of transportation, would switch from one method to another. For example, if V is the value in dollars per hour of a traveler's time, he would prefer air to rail transportation if

$$V > \frac{1.45 + 0.1741M}{-3.15 + .02331M},$$

where M is the distance in miles of the trip. He prefers air to bus if

$$V > \frac{3.48 + .02742M}{-2.88 + .02631M},$$

and he prefers rail to bus when

$$V > \frac{2.03 + 0.1001M}{.27 + .00300M}.$$

(If you assign a value to your time, you can use these inequalities to determine the most economical method of transportation for your next trip.) It was found that an increase in distance increased the time differentials between any two methods of transportation more than the price differentials. Thus, passengers would tend to use the faster method of travel as the distance of a trip increased. The "switching points" between automobile transportation and any other method of transportation depend, of course, upon the number of passengers making the trip. Some examples will show the various relations. Air is cheaper than rail transportation for a trip of 150 miles if the value of one's time exceeds $11.80 an hour. Air is cheaper than bus if the valuation of time exceeds $7.10 an hour. Rail is preferred to bus if the valuation is over $5.30 an hour. Thus, for a 150-mile trip people whose time is worth less than $5.30 an hour go by bus, those whose time valuation is between $5.30 and $11.80 take a train, and if the time valuation exceeds $11.80, they fly, if cost is the sole consideration. Air saves no time over rail for trips less than 135 miles. Only one who values time less than $1.00 an hour will always travel by bus. As Gronau points out in conclusion the decision by some railroads to stop passenger services to distances beyond 200 miles and the decline in the passenger share of railroads is quite consistent with the model.

EXERCISE

Airline discounts

Using the methods of this section, answer the following question true or false, and defend your answer. Airlines give discounts to students who fly, because they love students, and they believe that students add a lot of class to the flights.

Solution. Probably false. While students may add class to flights, this is probably not the reason for student discounts. The demand of students for flights is probably much more responsive to price changes than the demand of business persons, when the *total* cost of the trip is considered. An example may explain. Assume a particular flight costs $100 and takes three hours. If a business person values his or her time at $100 an hour, the total cost of the trip is $400. If the student's time is worth $20 an hour, the trip costs $160. A decrease of $40 in the price of a ticket reduces the business person's cost 10 percent while the student's cost falls 25 percent. Thus, one would expect students to be much more responsive to price cuts in tickets than travelers flying on business. We will discuss price discrimination (charging different people different amounts) in Chapter 8 below.

TECHNICAL PROBLEMS

1. Return to Problem 2 at the end of Chapter 5. Total product is given; and you have computed average and marginal product. You are now given the following information.

   Total fixed cost (total price of fixed inputs) is $220 per period.
   Units of the variable input cost $100 per unit per period.

   Using this information, complete the following table:

Units of variable input	Product			Cost			Average cost			Marginal cost
	Total	Average	Marginal	Fixed	Variable	Total	Fixed	Variable	Total	
1......	100									
2......	250									
3......	410									
4......	560									
5......	700									
6......	830									
7......	945									
8......	1,050									
9......	1,146									
10......	1,234									
11......	1,314									
12......	1,384									
13......	1,444									
14......	1,494									
15......	1,534									
16......	1,564									
17......	1,584									
18......	1,594									

A. Graph the total cost curves on one sheet and the average and marginal curves on another.

B. By reference to table and graph, answer the following questions.

    1. When marginal product is increasing, what is happening to:

        a. Marginal cost?

        b. Average variable cost?

    2. When marginal cost first begins to fall, does average variable cost begin to rise?

    3. What is the relation between marginal cost and average variable cost when marginal and average product are equal?

    4. What is happening to average variable cost while average product is increasing?

    5. What is average variable cost when average product is at its maximum? What happens to average variable cost after this point?

    6. What happens to marginal cost after the point it equals average variable cost?

        a. How does it compare with average variable cost thereafter?

        b. What is happening to marginal product thereafter?

        c. How does marginal product compare with average product thereafter?

    7. What happens to total fixed cost as output is increased?

    8. What happens to average fixed cost as:

        a. Marginal product increases?

      b. Marginal cost decreases?

      c. Marginal product decreases?

      d. Marginal cost increases?

      e. Average variable cost increases?

  9. How long does average fixed cost decrease?

  10. What happens to average total cost as:

      a. Marginal product increases?

      b. Marginal cost decreases?

      c. Average product increases?

      d. Average variable cost decreases?

  11. Does average variable cost increase:

      a. As soon as the point of diminishing marginal returns is passed?

      b. As soon as the point of diminishing average returns is passed?

  12. When does average cost increase? Answer this in terms of:

      a. The relation of average cost to marginal cost.

      b. The relation between the increase in average variable cost and the decrease in average fixed cost.

2. Assume that the labor—the only variable input of a firm—has the average and marginal product curves shown in Figure E.6.1. Labor's wage is $2.00 per unit of labor.

    a. At how many units of labor does average variable cost reach its minimum? _____

    b. What is average variable cost at this output? _____

    c. At what level of output does marginal cost attain its minimum? _____

    d. What is marginal cost at this output? _____

    e. Suppose fixed cost is $1,000. What is average total cost when average product is 200 and decreasing? _____

FIGURE E.6.1

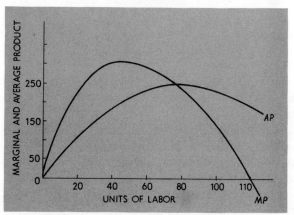

f. At the same fixed cost, what is average total cost when marginal product is 100 and falling? _____

3. Discuss the essential differences between the law of variable proportion and returns to scale.

4. Why do long-run average cost curves first fall, then rise? Why do short-run average cost curves first fall, then rise?

5. Assuming the long-run total cost curve in Figure E.6.2, answer the following questions:

   a. When output is OQ_0, average cost is the ratio _____ and is (greater than, less than, equal to) marginal cost.

   b. At output OQ_2 average cost is the ratio _____ and marginal cost is the ratio _____.

   c. Answer part (a) for output levels OQ_1 and OQ_3.

FIGURE E.6.2

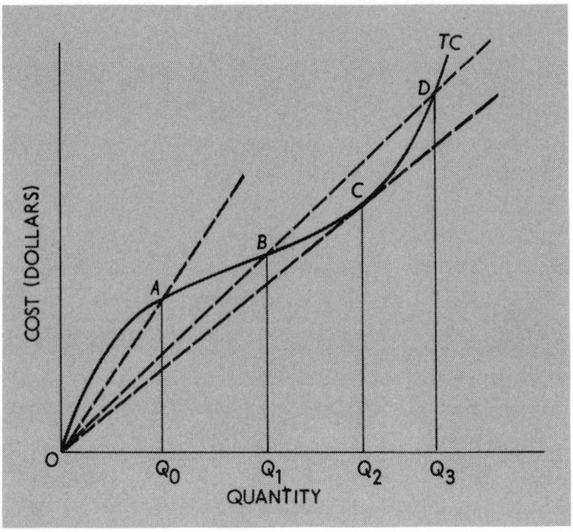

6. In Figure E.6.3, LAC and LMC make up a firm's planning horizon. SAC_1, SAC_2, and SAC_3 are the only three plant sizes available. These are called Plant 1, Plant 2, and Plant 3.

   a. Draw accurately the short-run marginal cost curves associated with each plant. Recall the relation between short- and long-run marginal costs.

   b. Plant 1 is designed to produce _____ units optimally, Plant 2 is designed to produce _____ units optimally, and Plant 3 is designed to produce _____ units optimally.

   c. The firm would produce in Plant 1 any output below _____. It would produce any output between _____ and _____ in Plant 2.

FIGURE E.6.3

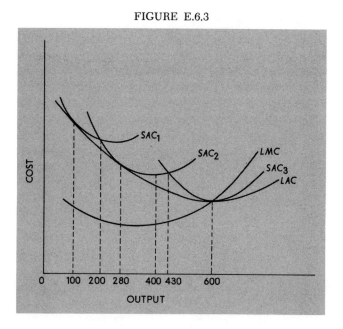

d. SAC_2 attains its minimum at 400 units. Suppose there was another plant (say, 4) that could produce 400 optimally. Would the average cost curve associated with this plant attain its minimum above, below, or at 400 units?

e. The lowest possible per unit cost is attained at _____ units in Plant _____. Why would the firm not use this plant to produce every other output since this is least cost?

7. Consider the average and marginal curves shown in Figure E.6.4. Label properly the four curves, *LAC, LMC, SAC,* and *SMC.*

FIGURE E.6.4

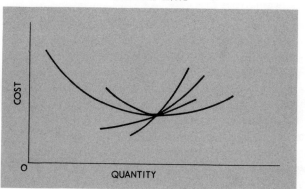

8. Fill in the blanks in the following table:

Units of output	Total cost	Fixed cost	Variable cost	Average fixed cost	Average variable cost	Average total cost	Marginal cost
1....		$100	$ 900				
2....					$850		
3....							$700
4....					$800		
5....						$900	
6....							$1,500
7....			$7,900				
8....						$1,300	
9....	$14,000						

9. Why does short-run marginal cost rise more rapidly than long-run marginal cost beyond the point at which they are equal?

ANALYTICAL PROBLEMS

1. You are hired as an economic consultant to a firm that produces and sells wine. Over a relevant period the wine gets better as it ages; therefore, the longer it ages, the higher the price the wine maker can get for the wine. Explain precisely the method that you would use in order to advise the wine maker how long to age the wine before putting it on the market. Assume you have all the required technical information.

2. You are the adviser to the president of a university. A wealthy alumnus buys, then gives a plot of land to the university, which plans to use the land as an athletic field. The president says that as far as the land is concerned it does not cost the university anything to use the land as an athletic field. What do you say?

3. Why do economists call opportunity costs real costs? Do you think businesses are really concerned about these? How would you go about gathering evidence to see if business persons are really concerned with the opportunity cost of using their own resources in their businesses?

4. If you had a little trouble with the last part of question 3, try this one, then go back. Compute the *total cost* of your attending school this year—this is the cost paid by you, your parents, or anyone else. Now suppose you were asked to take a job in Washington as a governmental adviser at the beginning of this academic year. The job is for one year. What is the *least* payment that would have induced you to drop out of school for one year and take the job? Now do you believe opportunity costs are real costs? Or could college tuition, board, books, etc., become so high that you would drop out of school? Does this set of circumstances differ from the situation of an "outrageously" large long-term contract being offered to you in Washington and inducing you to quit school?

5. Does it cost a doctor more to treat a rich person than a poor person? Explain. What information would you need to answer the question?

6. Suppose you are a lawyer representing a person whose spouse was killed at work through proven negligence of the employer. The firm obviously cannot measure and therefore compensate for the grief of the survivor. It will compensate for the *economic* loss because of the lost earnings of the deceased, who incidentally was 50 years old at death. Mandatory retirement is 65 years old. The firm is willing to make a flat cash settlement now if you can show the *economic* loss. What information do you need? How would you figure the economic loss if you had the information?

7. Suppose you could somehow measure the output of education from a college or university. Why might the long-run average cost curve at first show economies of scale? Why after some size might diseconomies set in? How can you account for the fact that some of our most distinguished universities are rather small, in terms of number of students, while other very distinguished universities are extremely large? How do you measure "distinguished?" The last part of this question may be very difficult to answer.

8. We frequently hear several terms used by businesspersons. What do they mean in economic terminology?
   a. Spreading the overhead.
   b. A break-even level of production.
   c. The efficiency of mass production.

9. Assume the average price of oil is $10 a barrel and the interest rate is 10 percent. The government wants to stockpile oil in reservoirs (assume they are free). What is the cost of stockpiling this oil over the next 10 years? What if the interest rate is only 4 percent?

10. How much does it cost you to keep money in a checking rather than a savings account? If there is this cost, why do people keep money in a checking account? What would cause people to keep less in a savings account and more in checking?

11. There is considerable debate in Congress at the present time about the president's proposal to eliminate some water projects, mainly dams. If you were assigned the task, how would you go about estimating the marginal benefits and marginal costs of building a dam? What information would you need? Do you think it is readily available? This is a hard question.

7

Theory of price in perfectly competitive markets

7.1 INTRODUCTION

In Chapter 2 we showed how demand and supply interact to determine prices and quantities sold in markets. Chapters 3 and 4 established the fundamentals of demand. This chapter will develop the basic determinants of supply. The foundations of supply theory are the concepts discussed in Chapters 5 and 6—the theories of production and cost.

Thus Chapters 3 through 6 supply the framework upon which the theory of the firm is based. *Demand* establishes the revenue side of business operation. *Production and cost* establish the supply conditions. Brought together, revenue and cost for the individual business firm and demand and supply for the entire market determine the market price and output of the firm and industry. Furthermore, as we shall see in this and subsequent chapters, these forces also determine the allocation of resources among industries.

7.1.a Principle of profit maximization

The fundamental point of this chapter is the way in which firms determine their output, both in the long run and the short run. The basic analysis is really rather simple. We shall summarize the fundamentals here before going into the more rigorous formal analysis below.

Our entire theoretical structure is based upon the simple assumption that entrepreneurs try to maximize profits. That is, other things remaining the same, they prefer more profit to less, profit being the difference between revenue and cost. This assumption does not mean that a businessperson may not seek other goals. Nonetheless, one who ignores profits or prefers less profit to more, other things equal, would be rather unusual. In any case, a business generally cannot remain in business very long unless some profits are earned. To be sure, there have been several criticisms of the profit-maximizing assumption; but this assumption is the only one providing a general theory of firms, markets, and resource allocation that is successful both in explaining and predicting firm behavior. In short the profit maximization assumption is used, first because it works well, and second because it describes to some extent the way that firms behave.

The basic principles of profit maximizing are really quite simple. The firm will increase any activity so long as the *additional* revenue from the increase exceeds the *additional* cost of the increase. The firm will cease to expand the activity if the *additional* revenue is less than the *additional* cost.

Suppose that the activity or choice variable is the firm's level of output. As the firm increases its level of output each added unit adds to the total revenue of the firm. The change in revenue per unit change in output is called *marginal revenue*. As the firm increases its level of output, each unit increase in output increases the firm's total cost. As you will recall from Chapter 6, the added cost per unit increase in output is called *marginal cost*.

Thus the firm will choose to expand output so long as the added revenue from the expansion (marginal revenue) is greater than the added cost of the expansion (marginal cost). The firm would choose not to increase output if the marginal cost of the increase is greater than the marginal revenue from the increase.[1] Profit maximization is therefore based upon the following principle:

Principle. Profit is the difference between revenue and cost. If an increase in output adds more to revenue than to cost, the increase in output adds to profit. If the increase in output adds less to revenue

---

[1] There is one extremely minor exception to this rule of behavior. The exception will be mentioned later in the text.

than to cost, the increase in output subtracts from profit. *The firm, therefore, chooses the level of output at which marginal revenue equals marginal cost.* This level maximizes total profit.

If the firm has some market power and consequently must lower price in order to sell more, then the marginal revenue from an increase in output is less than price. This situation provides the framework for the next chapter. Here we are concerned with the special case in which the price of the produced commodity is given to the firm by the market. In this special case, marginal revenue equals price. That is, if the firm is a cotton farm, and the price of cotton is $500 per bale of cotton, the marginal revenue from each additional bale of cotton is $500. The owner of the farm would increase cotton production as long as the marginal cost of each additional bale is less than $500. It would not increase production if each additional bale costs more than $500 to produce.

EXERCISE

A profit maximization problem

Suppose that a firm's engineers come up with the following marginal cost curve: the first unit produced adds $1 to cost, the second adds $2, the third $3, and so on. Fixed cost is $10; the price of the commodity is $25.50 per unit. How many units should the firm produce? Clearly an output of 25 is optimal. Each unit sold adds $25.50 to revenue. Each unit through the 25th adds less than $25.50 to cost. The 26th adds more to cost, $26, than it does to revenue. Thus the firm produces and sells 25 units. Note that fixed cost is irrelevant in the decision-making process, once the decision is made to produce any output.

This very simplified explanation provides the theoretical structure for a powerful predictive and explanatory theory. This theory is the theory of perfect competition. Throughout the formal exposition of the theory do not forget that most of the structure is based upon the very simple notion that the firm maximizes profit by producing the output at which marginal revenue equals marginal cost.

Let us note in passing that the term "profit" means return over and above *all costs,* including explicit costs and the entrepreneur's opportunity cost. Recall from Chapter 6 that opportunity cost is included in total cost.

Thus, if the owner manages the firm, the wages that could be earned in another occupation are included in cost.

Or let us take another example. Suppose the entrepreneur has invested his or her own resources in capital used in the firm's production process. The return that could be earned from the use of the capital is an opportunity cost and is included in costs. Economists frequently refer to the opportunity cost of using the entrepreneur's capital as a "normal profit" or "normal return." This is a cost. Any return over and above the "normal" return is called "pure profit" or economic profit.

To illustrate, suppose the entrepreneur has $1 million worth of capital invested in the firm. Suppose also that the normal or going return in the economy is 6 percent per year. If the entrepreneur earns 10 percent per year, the normal profit, included in cost, is 6 percent; the pure or economic profit is the additional 4-percent return. In this text when we use the term *profit* we shall mean pure or economic profit, over and above the normal return on the entrepreneur's resources.

ASIDE

Why firms exist

It has been pointed out to me, quite correctly I believe, that many texts, earlier editions of this one included, treat the business firm much too mechanically. Students are given the impression that firms are merely institutions or monsters forced upon society; and we are forced to live with them. Some firms may well be monsters; we have all dealt with some we thought were monsters at the time. Certainly firms want profit, but to obtain this profit they must perform a social function.

Therefore, before developing the theory of firms' behavior we should at least discuss briefly why firms exist at all. Recall that in the introductory chapter we pointed out that economists, for analytical purposes, frequently divide the economy into two sectors—households and business firms. Households sell their resources to firms in exchange for income with which they can purchase the goods produced by firms.

An economy could, of course, function without firms; and some have. Households could produce practically everything that they consume, as in the past many frontier households have virtually had to do. Clearly this method of production is less efficient in the sense that the society loses the advantage of specialization and trade.

But we could go one step further and let households specialize in one part of production and trade their products in the marketplace. Trade would result in the market rather than all resources being assembled under a single management. But, there would be large transportation and transaction costs involved in such a method. Some people would discover that it is more efficient to bring together all of the resources and have them cooperate in the production of goods and services. This form of organization would give the advantages of specialization and division of labor. If there were economies of scale (recall the discussion in Chapter 6), then this cooperative form of organization would produce at a lower cost and drive out other organizational forms of production.

But mere cooperation of resources does not necessarily make a firm efficient. To show why, let us take a very simplified example. Suppose four of us chipped in and bought a boat in order to enter the fishing business. We agree to split the profits equally. Fishing is hard work. I know that if I goof off a little, I will catch fewer fish than if I fished hard all of the time. But every fish that I *do not catch* while loafing costs me only one fourth of the value of that fish, because its value would have been divided into four parts. Thus, since the cost of goofing off is lower than if I received the entire value of my product, i will goof off more. If I have this incentive to loaf, so then do the other three partners. Thus production falls off. The same situation would probably hold in a factory or on a farm.

Someone would see the advantage of beginning a firm, in the sense used here. This person would contract with resource owners for a fixed amount of their resources per period in return for a fixed payment per period. This individual would then claim any residual; or would suffer the loss, if such results. The residual claimant would assume the task of monitoring the resource owners to see that these resource owners fulfill their contracts.

Of course, we could go one step further and postulate that the firm owner or owners actually hired other individuals to monitor the hired resource owners. These hired monitors are called managers. Depending upon the size of the firm, the persons who contract with the owners of resources may choose to perform the monitoring tasks themselves.

In any case, firms of various types arise in an economy because they have been able to organize production more efficiently than other types of institutions set up to organize production. Generally, we think of the owners of capital doing the task of contracting with other resources and either hiring managers (monitors) or carrying out the task themselves. While this may be the more prominent form of organization, in many countries the labor-managed firm is a frequently used form of organization. Sometimes, but less frequently seen, is the consumer-managed firm.

Thus various types of firms arise in an economy because they are efficient. This is not to say that various branches of government do not produce goods and services. This other form or organization is introduced for several reasons, which need not be discussed here. Likewise, nonprofit organizations produce goods and services also. But as we attempted to show in Chapters 5 and 6 much of the same production and cost theory applies to production under these forms of organization also. We will in this chapter also point out that the basic analysis developed here is still useful for analyzing many problems of the "noncompetitive" government sector.

But the point here is that most production takes place in business firms. These are not merely forced onto a helpless society. The institution of business firms exists because it is an efficient form for organizing production. If some other form of organizing production is discovered, that form of organization will replace the business firm. Until then, economics texts will treat production of goods and services as generally being organized in firms.

7.1.b Important points developed

The basic concepts to be learned in Chapter 7 are

1. What determines the level of output for competitive firms in the short run and in the long run.
2. What factors determine the supply curve for a competitive firm and industry.
3. Why most supply curves are upward sloping.
4. How profits are competed away in the long run and how long-run equilibrium is attained.

7.2. PERFECT COMPETITION

The theory of the firm set forth in this chapter is based upon the exacting concept of *perfectly competitive markets*. Perfect competition forms the basis of the most important and widely used model of economic behavior. The essence of perfect competition is that neither buyers nor producers recognize any competitiveness among themselves; no *direct* competition among economic agents exists.

The theoretical concept of competition is diametrically opposed to the businessman's concept of competition. For example, someone in business might maintain that the automobile industry or the cigarette industry is quite competitive since each firm in these industries must consider what its rivals will do before it makes a decision about advertising campaigns, design changes, quality improvements, and so forth.

That type of market is far removed from what the economist means when speaking of perfect competition. Perfect competition permits no personal rivalry (that is, personal in the sense that the firm considers the reaction of competitive firms in determining its own policy). All relevant economic magnitudes are determined by impersonal market forces.

Several important conditions define perfect competition. Taken together, these conditions guarantee a free, impersonal market in which the forces of demand and supply, or of revenue and cost, determine the allocation of resources and the distribution of income. The first of these conditions or assumptions has been discussed in section 7.1 above. This assumption is that firms attempt to maximize profits. There are five additional restricting assumptions.

7.2.a Free markets

We assume that each market is free and operates freely in the sense that no external control of market forces exists. One form of external control is governmental intervention—for example, farm crop controls, public utility regulations, or presidential threats to manufacturers. All such controls establish artificial market conditions to which business firms must adjust. Another type of control is collective behavior or collusion of firms in a market. Such behavior limits the free exercise of market forces.

While many markets are not free in the sense used here, a large number are. The object is to analyze the efficiency of resource allocation in free markets. In cases in which the market is not free, one may draw inferences concerning the relative efficiency of free, as opposed to controlled, markets. Thus the perfectly competitive market serves as a yardstick to measure the performance of other types of market structures.

Furthermore, we can use the competitive theory to analyze the consequences of externally imposed interferences with the free market. That is, we can use the competitive theory to generate equilibrium conditions in the absence of interferences. Then we impose such an interference—for example, some governmental regulation—and see how this change affects the equilibrium. Thus, while the basic theory assumes free markets, external constraints can be imposed in order to study the results of the constraint.

7.2.b Small size, large numbers

Perfect competition requires that every economic agent be so small, relative to the market as a whole, that it cannot exert a perceptible influence on price. From the standpoint of buyers this means that each consumer taken individually must be so unimportant he cannot obtain special considerations from the sellers. Perhaps the most familiar special consideration is the rebate, especially in the area of transportation services. But there can be many others, such as special credit terms to large buyers, or free additional services. None of these can prevail if the market is perfectly competitive.

From the seller's standpoint, perfect competition requires that each firm be so small it cannot affect market price by changes in output. If all producers act collectively, changes in quantity will definitely affect market price. But if perfect competition prevails, each producer is so small that individual changes will go unnoticed. In other words, the actions of any individual firm do not affect market supply.

7.2.c Homogeneous product

A closely related provision is that the product of each seller in a perfectly competitive market must be identical to the product of every other seller. This ensures that buyers are indifferent as to the firm from which they purchase. Product differences, whether real or imaginary, are precluded by the existence of perfect competition.

In this context the word "product" has a much more detailed meaning than it does in ordinary conversation, where one might regard an automobile or a haircut as a product. For us, this is not adequate to describe a product: every changeable feature of the good must be included. When this is done it is possible to determine whether the market is characterized by a homogeneous, or perfectly standardized, commodity. If it is not, the firm that has a slightly differentiated product has a degree of control over the market for its product and, therefore, over the price of its specific variety; it can thus affect market price by changes in output. This condition is incompatible with perfect competition.

7.2.d Free mobility of resources

Another precondition for perfect competition is that all resources are perfectly mobile—that each resource required can move in and out of the market very readily in response to pecuniary signals.

The condition of perfect mobility is an exacting one. First, it means that labor must be mobile, not only geographically but among jobs. Next, free mobility means that the inputs are not monopolized by an owner or producer. Finally, free mobility means that new firms (or new capital) can enter and leave an industry without extraordinary difficulty. If patents or copyrights are required, entry is not free. Similarly, if vast investment outlays are required, entry certainly is not easy. In short, free mobility of resources requires free and easy entry and exit of firms into and out of an industry—a condition very difficult to realize in practice.

7.2.e Perfect knowledge

Consumers, producers, and resource owners must possess perfect knowledge if a market is to be perfectly competitive. If consumers are not fully cognizant of prices, they might buy at higher prices when lower ones are available. Then there will not be a uniform price in the market. Similarly, if laborers are not aware of the wage rates offered, they may not sell their labor services to the highest bidder. Finally, producers must know costs as well as price in order to attain the most profitable rate of output.

But this is only the beginning. In its fullest sense, perfect knowledge requires complete knowledge of the future as well as the present. In the absence of this omniscience, perfect competition cannot prevail.

The discussion to this point can be summarized by the following:

Characteristics. Perfect competition is an economic model of a market possessing the following characteristics: each economic agent is so small relative to the market that it can exert no perceptible influence on price; the product is homogeneous; there is free mobility of all resources, including free and easy entry and exit of business firms into and out of an industry; and all economic agents in the market possess complete and perfect knowledge. Furthermore, markets are free and firms attempt to maximize profits.

7.2.f Conclusion

Glancing at the requirements above should immediately convince one that no market has been or can be perfectly competitive. Even in basic agricultural markets, where most of the requirements are frequently satisfied, the requirement of perfect knowledge is not met. One might therefore reasonably ask why such a palpably unrealistic model should be considered at all.

The answer can be given in as much or as little detail as desired. For our present purposes, it is brief. First, generality can be achieved only by means of abstraction. Hence, as we stressed in Chapter 1, no theory can be *perfectly* descriptive of *real-world* phenomena. Furthermore, the more accurately a theory describes one specific real-world case, the less accurately it describes all others. In any area of thought a theoretician does not select assumptions on the basis of their presumed correspondence to reality; the conclusions, not the assumptions, are tested against reality.

This leads to a second point of great, if somewhat pragmatic, importance. The conclusions derived from the model of perfect competition have, by and large, permitted accurate explanation and prediction of real-world phenomena. That is, perfect competition frequently works as a theoretical model of economic processes even though it does not accurately describe any specific industry.[2] The most persuasive evidence supporting this assertion is the fact that despite the proliferation of more sophisticated models of economic behavior, economists today probably use the model of perfect competition in their research more than ever before.

7.3 DEMAND FACING A PERFECTLY COMPETITIVE FIRM

Recall from our previous analysis of consumer behavior that demand is a list of prices and the quantities demanded by a consumer or a group of consumers at each price in the list per period of time. The demand curves for products are generally assumed to be downward sloping. The

---

[2] Furthermore, the assumptions do not imply that the model of perfect competition is not relevant in predicting the consequences of a disturbance in an economy containing industries that comprise a few interdependent firms (economists call such industries oligopolistic). The competitive model is a useful approach to many problems in which the conditions differ from the assumptions set forth here.

entrepreneur or owner of an individual competitive firm sees the demand for the product produced by that firm in a much different way.

This difference follows from two of our assumptions about competitive firms—first, each firm produces a homogeneous product and, second, each firm is very small relative to the size of the total market for the product. Thus, since no firm, acting alone, can affect market price, each firm takes the market price, as set by total industry supply and demand, as given. Any firm can sell all it wants at the going market price. If the market price of the product is $10 each, the marginal revenue from each additional unit sold is $10. The marginal revenue curve is therefore a horizontal line at $10. Such a curve is shown in Figure 7.3.1; the marginal revenue equals the price, $10, at any relevant output.

The horizontal marginal revenue curve at the market price is called the *demand* for the product of a perfectly competitive firm. This is the demand facing the firm because each firm can sell all it wishes at the going market price. This conclusion follows even though the demand curve faced by the industry for the commodity is downward sloping.

We use Figure 7.3.2 to illustrate the entire process. Panel A shows equilibrium in the market. Supply and demand have the "typically" assumed shapes. Equilibrium price is OP_0 and quantity demanded and supplied is Ox_0. The marginal revenue for every firm in the industry is therefore OP_0. The demand curve for any firm in this perfectly competitive industry is shown in panel B. Each producer knows that changes in the firm's volume of output will have no perceptible effect upon market price. A change in the rate of sales per period of time will change the firm's revenue, but it will not affect market price.

FIGURE 7.3.1

MARGINAL REVENUE-DEMAND FACING A
PERFECTLY COMPETITIVE FIRM

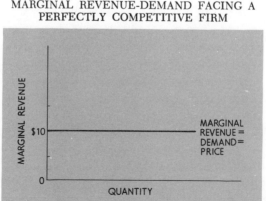

FIGURE 7.3.2

DERIVATION OF DEMAND FOR A PERFECTLY COMPETITIVE FIRM

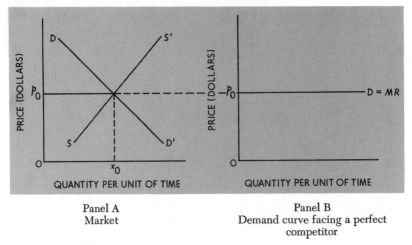

Panel A   Panel B
Market   Demand curve facing a perfect
                                                competitor

The producer in a perfectly competitive market, therefore, does not have to reduce price in order to expand the rate of sales. Any number of units per period of time can be sold at the market equilibrium price. If the firm charges a higher price, it could sell nothing. A lower price would result in a needless loss of revenue.

Since price remains constant, each additional unit sold increases total revenue by its (constant) price. Therefore, the demand curve and the marginal revenue curve are identical for a producer in a perfectly competitive market. For this reason, the curve in panel B is labeled $D = MR$. When the demand curve is horizontal, demand is said to be perfectly elastic.

Alternatively, recall from Chapter 2 that demand elasticity depends upon the number and closeness of substitutes. The product of a perfectly competitive firm has perfect substitutes—the products of all other firms in the industry. We would expect then that the demand elasticity for a firm's output would be infinite.

The results of this section may be summarized as follows:

Relations. The demand curve (also called the average revenue curve) facing a producer in a perfectly competitive market is a horizontal line at the level of the market equilibrium price. The output decisions of the seller do not affect market price. In this case, the demand and marginal revenue curves are identical (that is, $D = AR =$

MR); demand is perfectly elastic and the coefficient of price elasticity approaches infinity.

EXERCISE

Effect of supply change on agricultural prices

There is a local morning "RFD" television program originating from Waco, Texas. This program is devoted to farm and ranch news and information. On one recent program the announcer reported that farmers were receiving very good cotton prices for their crops this year. But, he said that unluckily production had been substantially off this year, so farmers were not receiving full benefit from the high prices. Use your knowledge of economics to criticize this statement.

The announcer implied that cotton prices happened to be higher than usual but that production independently happened to be reduced. Clearly the output of one cotton farmer could not affect the price of cotton in the market. But if one farmer's production was off, probably because of adverse weather conditions, many other farmers, faced with essentially the same weather conditions, have a reduction in production also. Thus the total supply is reduced; price is driven upward and the output of any one farmer can be sold at a higher price, even though market demand remains constant.

In terms of Figure 7.3.2 supply shifts upward and to the left of SS' in panel A. Price is driven above OP_0. In panel B each farm's marginal revenue curve rises above OP_0. But, the production of each farm is below the desired level. Thus the reduced production led to the increased price; these are not independent events. Whether *total* revenue in the cotton market increases or decreases depends upon the elasticity of demand for cotton in the market. (Why?)

Use a similar type of analytical technique to analyze the immediate effect of the U.S. government buying wheat in order to sell it to the Russians.

7.4 SHORT-RUN PROFIT MAXIMIZATION

Let us turn now to the output decision of a firm in the short run. Recall from Chapter 6 that in the short run the firm has fixed costs, a fixed amount that must be paid regardless of output, and variable costs, which vary with the level of output. In the short run the firm, given its production function and the prices of inputs, must make two decisions. The first decision is whether to produce or to close down; if the first decision is to produce rather than close down, the second decision concerns the proper level of output. We analyze these decisions first with a numercial example.

7.4.a Numerical example

Suppose a hypothetical firm faces a short-run cost situation shown in Table 7.4.1. Let the given market price of the firm's product be $42 per unit. Thus the marginal revenue for each unit produced and sold is $42. From the marginal cost schedule, shown in column 7, we see that if the firm produces at all, it will produce eight units of output. That is, each additional unit of output through eight units adds less to cost than the marginal revenue received for that unit. The firm would not produce the ninth unit, which adds $45 to cost but only $42 to revenue. The total profit is 8 × $42 = $336 minus a total cost of $210. This yields a profit of $126 for the period. Since the entrepreneur's opportunity cost is included in the total cost of production, the $126 represents an "above normal" profit, sometimes, as mentioned above, called "pure" profit or "economic" profit. In any case, it represents a return over the opportunity cost. The reader should verify arithmetically that $126 is the maximum obtainable profit.

Now let price fall to $33. Using the same method of increasing output as long as marginal revenue exceeds marginal cost, we see that the profit-maximizing output is now six units. With total revenue of 6 × $33 = $198 and a total cost of $135, the firm now earns a profit of $63. Again it can

TABLE 7.4.1

SHORT-RUN COSTS

(1) Rate of output and sales (units)	(2) Fixed cost	(3) Variable cost	(4) Total cost	(5) Average variable cost	(6) Average total cost	(7) Marginal cost
0....	$30.00	$ —	$ 30.00	$ —	$ —	$ —
1....	30.00	5.00	35.00	5.00	35.00	5.00
2....	30.00	15.00	45.00	7.50	22.50	10.00
3....	30.00	30.00	60.00	10.00	20.00	15.00
4....	30.00	50.00	80.00	12.50	20.00	20.00
5....	30.00	75.00	105.00	15.00	21.00	25.00
6....	30.00	105.00	135.00	17.50	22.50	30.00
7....	30.00	140.00	170.00	20.00	24.29	35.00
8....	30.00	180.00	210.00	22.50	26.25	40.00
9....	30.00	225.00	255.00	25.00	28.33	45.00
10....	30.00	275.00	305.00	27.50	30.50	50.00

be verified arithmetically that this output does in fact yield maximum profit when commodity price is $33.

Finally let us assume that market price decreases to $12. Marginal revenue exceeds price for each of the first two units of production. The third unit costs $15 to produce but only yields $12. Therefore, if the firm produces at all, it will produce two units. Total revenue is $24; total cost is $45, resulting in a loss of $21. Should the firm produce at a loss? The answer is yes, because the $21 loss is $9 less than the $30 fixed cost that must be paid if the firm closes down in the short run. In other words, if the firm produces nothing in the short-run, revenue is zero, and cost is $30. By producing two units and selling at $12 each, the $24 would cover all of the $15 variable cost, leaving $9 left over to apply to fixed cost. The net loss is $21, compared to a loss of $30 at zero production. The reader should verify that the $21 loss is the minimum loss possible at a price of $12.

To be sure, the firm would not and could not go on for a very long period of time suffering a loss in each period. In the long run the firm would leave the industry if it could not cover costs, including opportunity cost at any level of output. Or it would change its short-run situation if all costs could be covered at some optimal level of output in the long run. We shall postpone long-run analysis until we analyze the short-run situation graphically. Let us first see how our theory of loss minimization might apply to actual business decision making.

APPLICATION

Decision making and marginal analysis

Many businesses are from time to time faced with the decision of whether to extend the number of hours that they operate during the week. Restaurants, once opened only 16 hours a day, choose to stay open all night. Stores extend the number of evenings that they stay open. Service stations change the number of hours that they operate. What factors influence the decision to stay open additional hours?

The answer is simple. The manager compares the expected marginal revenue with the expected marginal cost of staying open. Fixed costs are not spread over the additional hours of operation. They are irrelevant in this type of decision.

For example, suppose a restaurant is open 16 hours but is contemplating staying open an additional 8 hours a day. The expected monthly addition to revenue is $6,000; the expected monthly addition to cost is \$5,000. Thus staying open all night increases yearly profit to the firm by \$12,000. If the total fixed cost of the restaurant is, say, \$8,000, none of this cost *is spread* over the nightly operation in making the decision. Regardless of the fixed cost, the marginal changes are all that matter. Fixed cost is ignored. If, for example, the all-night operation is expected to add only \$4,500 a month to revenue, the restaurant would not extend its hours.

7.4.b Graphical exposition of short-run equilibrium

Figure 7.4.1 shows a set of typical short-run cost curves, marginal cost (MC), average total cost (ATC) and average variable cost (AVC). Average fixed cost is omitted for convenience and because it is irrelevant for decision making. The given market price is Op_0. Therefore, the marginal revenue is the horizontal line at p_0. The firm produces where short-run marginal cost equals marginal revenue, point E at output Ox_m. Producing another unit would add more to costs than the firm would receive from the sale of that unit; MC exceeds MR. The firm would not stop short of output Ox_m, however, since at lesser outputs producing another unit adds more to revenue than to cost; MR exceeds MC. Total cost is the area Oc_0Rx_m; total revenue is the area Op_0Ex_m; profit is the difference, the area c_0p_0ER. The firm makes a positive profit over and above opportunity cost.

Note that at point L in Figure 7.4.1 marginal cost also equals price.

FIGURE 7.4.1

SHORT-RUN EQUILIBRIUM

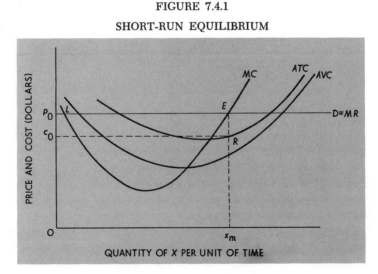

That is not, however, a point of equilibrium since the firm would not choose to produce this output under the circumstances depicted. In the first place, average cost exceeds price at this output so losses would occur, whereas at some other outputs profits could be realized. Second, the firm could clearly gain by producing an additional unit. Price is greater than marginal cost; thus the firm would be motivated to increase output.[3]

7.4.c Profit, loss, and the firm's short-run supply curve

The equality of price and short-run marginal cost guarantees either that profit is a maximum or that loss is a minimum. Whether a profit is made or a loss incurred can be determined only by comparing price and average total cost at the equilibrium rate of output. If price exceeds unit cost, the entrepreneur enjoys a short-run profit; on the other hand, if unit cost exceeds price, a loss is suffered.

Figure 7.4.2 illustrates four possible short-run situations for the firm. First, the market established price may be Op_1; the firm settles at point A where $MC = Op_1$, produces Ox_1 units, and, since ATC is less than price,

FIGURE 7.4.2

PROFIT, LOSS, OR CEASING PRODUCTION IN THE SHORT RUN

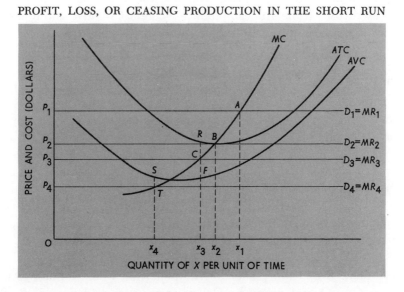

---

[3] Economists say that $MC = P$ is the *necessary* or first order condition for profit maximization and that the second order condition is that where $MC = P$, MC must be positively sloped. The two conditions together are *necessary* and *sufficient* for profit maximization.

receives a profit. Second, market price may be Op_2. MC now equals price at point B; the firm produces Ox_2. Since B is the lowest point on ATC, the firm makes neither profit nor loss, but it does cover opportunity cost, which is included in ATC. Third, if price is Op_3, the firm produces Ox_3; price equals MC at C. Because average cost is greater than price at the optimal output, total cost is greater than total revenue, and the firm suffers a loss. That loss is CR times Ox_3.

When demand is $D_3 = MR_3$, there is simply no way the firm can earn a profit. At every output level average total cost exceeds price. If output were either smaller or greater than Ox_2 units per period of time, the loss would be greater. As we noted above, the firm would not necessarily close down in the short run even though losses result. Recall that a firm incurring a loss in the short run will continue to produce if, and only if, it loses less by producing than by closing the plant entirely. Remember there are two types of costs in the short run: fixed costs and variable costs. The fixed costs cannot be changed and are incurred whether the plant is operating or not. Fixed costs are unavoidable in the short run and are the same at zero output as at any other.

Therefore, at zero output total revenue would be zero also and total cost would be the total fixed cost. The loss would thus be the amount of total fixed costs. If the firm can produce where $MC = MR$, and if at this output total revenue is greater than total variable cost, a smaller loss is suffered when production takes place. The firm covers all of its variable cost and some revenue is left over to cover a part of fixed cost. The loss is that part of fixed cost not covered and is clearly less than the entire fixed cost.

Returning to Figure 7.4.2 one can see more easily why the firm in the short run would produce at C and not shut down. The firm loses CR dollars per unit produced. However, variable cost is not only covered but there is an excess of CF dollars per unit sold. The excess of price over average variable cost, CF, can be applied to fixed costs. Thus, not all of the fixed costs are lost, as would be the case if production were discontinued; the amount CF times Ox_3 can be applied to fixed costs. Although a loss is sustained, it is smaller than the loss associated with zero output.

Suppose, however, that market price is Op_4; demand is given by $D_4 = MR_4$. If the firm produces, its equilibrium would be at T where $MC = Op_4$. Output would be Ox_4 units per period of time. Here the average variable cost of production exceeds price. Not only would the firm lose all of its fixed costs, it would also lose ST dollars per unit on its variable costs as well. The firm could improve its earnings situation by producing nothing and losing only fixed cost. Thus when price is below average variable cost at every level of output, the short-run equilibrium output is zero.

As shown in Chapter 6, average variable cost reaches its minimum at the point at which marginal cost and average variable cost intersect. If price is less than the minimum average variable cost, the loss-minimizing output is zero. For price equal to or greater than minimum average variable cost, equilibrium output is determined by the intersection of marginal cost and price.

Principles: (1) Marginal cost tells *how much* to produce, given the choice of a positive output; the firm produces the output for which $MC = P$. (2) Average variable cost tells *whether* to produce; the firm ceases to produce if price falls below minimum AVC. (3) Average total cost tells how much profit or loss is made if the firm decides to produce; profit equals the difference between P and ATC multiplied by the quantity produced and sold.

Using the principles just discussed, it is possible to derive the short-run supply curve of an individual firm in a perfectly competitive market. The process is illustrated in Figure 7.4.3. Panel A shows the marginal cost curve of a firm for rates of output greater than that associated with minimum average variable cost. Suppose market price is Op_1, the cor-

FIGURE 7.4.3

DERIVATION OF THE SHORT-RUN SUPPLY CURVE OF AN
INDIVIDUAL PRODUCER IN PERFECT COMPETITION

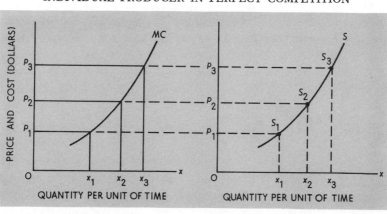

Panel A	Panel B
Positions of short-run equilibria for the firm	Equilibrium quantities supplied by the firm

responding equilibrium rate of output is Ox_1. Now, find on panel B the point associated with the coordinates Op_1, Ox_1. Label this point S_1; it represents the quantity supplied at price Op_1.

Next, suppose price is Op_2. In this case, equilibrium output would be Ox_2. Plot the point associated with the coordinates Op_2, Ox_2 on panel B—it is labeled S_2. Similarly, other equilibrium quantities supplied can be determined by postulating other market prices (for example, price Op_3 leads to output Ox_3 and point S_3 on panel B). Connecting all the S-points so generated one obtains the short-run supply curve of the firm, the curve labeled S in panel B. But by construction, the S-curve is precisely the same as the MC curve. The following is thus established:

Proposition. The short-run supply curve of a firm in perfect competition is precisely its marginal cost curve for all rates of output equal to or greater than the rate of output associated with minimum average variable cost. For market prices lower than minimum average variable cost, equilibrium quantity supplied is zero.

7.4.d Short-run industry supply curve

In earlier chapters it was shown that market demand is simply the horizontal sum of the demand curves of all buyers in the market. Deriving the short-run industry supply curve is not always such an easy matter.

As you will recall from Chapter 6, the short-run marginal cost curve of a firm is derived under the assumption that the unit prices of the variable inputs are fixed; no change by the individual firm acting alone can change a factor's unit cost to the firm. This seems a reasonable assumption under perfect competition because one firm is usually so small, relative to all users of the resource, that variations in its rate of purchase will not affect the market price of the resource. In other words, many resource markets are more or less perfectly competitive, at least on the buying side. Thus production, and therefore resource use, can frequently be expanded in one firm without affecting the market price of the resource.

But when *all* producers in an industry *simultaneously* expand output there may be a marked effect upon the resource market. For example, one small textile manufacturer could probably expand production by 10 percent or even 100 percent without affecting the world price of raw cotton. The few additional bales purchased would not have a significant effect on the total demand for raw cotton. If all textile manufacturers in the United States simultaneously attempt to expand output by 10 percent, however, the demand for cotton would probably increase substantially and the resulting increase in the price of cotton would be significant. When all manufacturers attempt to increase output, raw cotton prices are bid up; and the increase in the price of a variable factor of production (raw cotton) causes an increase in all firms' cost curves, including marginal cost.

As a consequence, the industry supply curve usually cannot be obtained by summing horizontally the marginal cost curves of each producer. As industry output expands, input prices normally increase, thereby shifting each marginal cost curve upward and to the left. A great deal of information would be required to obtain the exact supply curve. However, one may generally presume that the industry supply curve is somewhat more steeply sloped and somewhat less elastic when input prices increase in response to an increase in industry output. In this case, the concept of a competitive industry supply curve is less precise. Nonetheless, doubt is not cast upon the basic fact that in the short run, quantity supplied varies directly with price. The latter is all one needs to draw a positively sloped market supply curve. Finally, we should emphasize that price equals each firm's marginal cost at each and every point along a competitive industry's supply curve, even though cost curves of individual firms do shift.

7.4.e Summary of firm in the short run as industry output expands

The firm operates in the short run, a period in which some costs are fixed regardless of the level of production. The firm will produce some positive output in the short run so long as price can cover all of average variable cost and at least some portion of average fixed cost. The price to the firm is its marginal revenue because each unit sold adds its price to the firm's revenue. Equilibrium output is that at which marginal revenue equals marginal cost. Therefore, the firm's short-run supply curve is its marginal cost above average variable cost.

If price equals marginal cost above average total cost, a pure profit above opportunity cost is earned. Profit is price minus ATC times output. If price equals marginal cost between ATC and AVC, the loss to the entrepreneur is ATC minus price times output. If price falls below minimum AVC, the firm produces nothing and loses all of its fixed cost, per time period.

Industry short-run supply is not necessarily the summation of the supply curves of all firms. Any firm can change output without changing the prices of inputs; all firms changing output together will probably affect the prices of some inputs. Thus industry supply would probably be more inelastic than the horizontal sum of all firms' supplies.

APPLICATION

More marginal analysis and decision making

One should not suppose that our short-run marginal analysis is applicable solely to the firm's output decision. Exactly the same method of approach as that set forth in our theory can be easily applied and is applied to many other types of daily business decision-making processes. Let us consider a simplified example.

First, consider the type of problem frequently faced by agricultural economists who work for state agricultural extension services. These extension services advise farmers and ranchers about new and efficient agricultural methods. Suppose there has been a new fertilizer developed. The scientists have tables of technical data about the potential yield under almost all different circumstances. But the agricultural economists need other data in order to recommend specific amounts of the fertilizer in specific situations. These additional data are the price of the new fertilizer and the price of the specific product.

The computer shows the following technical situation for a given wheat farmer applying the fertilizer to the crop.

(1) 100 pounds fertilizer per acre	(2) Expected yield per acre (bu.)	(3) Marginal yield per acre (bu.)
0..........	120	
1..........	150	30
2..........	174	24
3..........	194	20
4..........	209	15
5..........	220	11
6..........	226	6
7..........	230	4
8..........	230	0

Columns 1 and 2 show the expected wheat crop per acre estimated for various amounts of fertilizer per acre. The economist, knowing that marginal yield per acre is the important variable, computes column 3, from column 2. The expected price of wheat is $5 per bushel; the price of fertilizer is $35 per 100 pounds. How much fertilizer per acre should the economist recommend in this situation? Everything but the amount of fertilizer remains constant.

Additional fertilizer should be used as long as the marginal return per 100 pounds exceeds the marginal cost per 100 pounds. The marginal return per 100 pounds of fertilizer is the price per bushel of wheat times the marginal yield per 100 pounds of fertilizer. Thus the first 100 pounds of fertilizer adds $150 per acre to revenue, the second $120, the third $100. The marginal cost is $35 per 100 pounds of fertilizer. The recommendation is for 500 pounds of fertilizer per acre. Each 100 pounds through 5 adds more than $35 to revenue. The sixth adds only $30 and should not be applied unless the price of fertilizer falls below $30.*

---

* In a sense this problem applies more to input demand theory, to be covered in a later chapter. But, the analytical method is a useful approach, and the student cannot get too much practice using marginal analysis.

We do not wish to give the impression that the marginal cost-marginal revenue analysis is applicable only to the decisions of a profit-maximizing firm. Since many economics and business students go to work for institutions that are not concerned with profit maximization—for example, local, state, and federal governments, schools, hospitals, the military, and so on —we should provide a few examples of the way our theory applies in these types of situations.

APPLICATION

Marginal analysis and crime prevention

Our marginal analysis is quite applicable to the economics of crime prevention. Suppose a local government is interested in reducing some criminal activity such as theft. We choose theft because it is easier to put a monetary value on the loss from theft than from other crimes such as murder, rape, or prostitution. The local government produces a product called "theft prevention." Theft prevention costs society. Clearly, the city government could spend nothing on theft prevention. Or it could spend an inordinant amount, possibly putting two or three policemen on every corner, and decrease theft practically to zero. Obviously there is an optimal situation somewhere in between these extremes.

One government rule is that the scale of theft prevention produced by government should be set at a point at which the additional return from preventing theft (marginal revenue) is not less than the additional expenditure necessary to gain that return (marginal cost). In other words, society should not spend an additional $100 to prevent $50 worth of crime. On the other hand, if society wishes to spend an additional $100 preventing crime, it should spend it where the return in preventing crime is greatest, as long as the return exceeds $100.* While this analysis does not give the entire solution, this approach is the first step in a complete analysis. As we shall see below, the marginal cost–marginal revenue approach provides a useful approach to decision making in many other areas of governmental policy.

---

* Even the theft situation is complicated by the measurement problem. Theft does not necessarily mean a net loss to society. If I steal $100 from you, it is a transfer from you to me. I gain $100, while you lose the same amount. Unless one makes utility comparisons society as a whole is no better or worse off. We return to this problem below. For a superb analysis of the economics of law enforcement see George J. Stigler, "The Optimum Enforcement of Laws," *Journal of Politicial Economy,* May/June 1970, pp. 526–36.

7.5 LONG-RUN EQUILIBRIUM OF A COMPETITIVE FIRM

In the short-run the firm is limited by past decisions. In the long-run all inputs are variable; the firm is not bound by the past. The long-run may be the planning stage, prior to entry into the industry. Or a firm operating in the short-run may be at a scale such that it is not obtaining maximum possible profits. It would then readjust its scale and enter the long run. Once the plans have congealed the firm operates in a short-run situation again. It operates in the short run until it makes another long-run change in the scale of operation.

7.5.a Profit maximization in the long run

In the long run, just as in the short run, the firm attempts to maximize profits. We use exactly the same approach, except in this case there are no fixed costs; all costs are variable. As before, the firm takes a market-determined commodity price as given. This market price is also the firm's marginal revenue. As above, the firm would increase output as long as the marginal revenue from each additional unit is greater than the marginal cost of that unit. It would not expand when marginal cost exceeds marginal revenue.

To illustrate, let us take the long-run situation shown in Table 7.5.1. In deciding the size plant to build, the entrepreneur attempts to achieve maximum profit, which is the difference between the total receipts from selling the product (total revenue) and the total cost of producing it. The third and fourth columns of Table 7.5.1 show the long-run revenue and cost schedules of a hypothetical firm planning to enter an industry. Columns one and two show the market price and the attainable rates of output from which total revenue (price times output) is derived. Clearly, maximum profit is $7.50, attained at an output of either seven or eight units. The entrepreneur would build his plant to produce either output. The seeming indeterminancy of the rate of output is attributable to the discrete data used in this hypothetical example.

We can examine these relations using demand, long-run average cost, and long-run marginal cost. Table 7.5.2 shows the relevant schedules for the situation set forth in Table 7.5.1; it indicates the same profit-maximizing condition as before (any differences are because of rounding errors). Maximum profit again corresponds to seven or eight units of output. Unit profit is maximized at seven units of output, but this is immaterial inasmuch as the entrepreneur is concerned with total profit. Equilibrium is clearly where marginal cost equals marginal revenue equals price.

So long as the firm can sell an additional unit for more than the marginal cost of producing that unit, it can increase profit by producing one more. If the price is less than marginal cost the firm should not produce

TABLE 7.5.1

REVENUE, COST, AND PROFIT

Market price	Rate of output and sales	Total revenue	Total cost	Profit (TR − TC)
$5.......	1	$ 5	$17.00	$−12.00
5.......	2	10	18.50	− 8.50
5.......	3	15	19.50	− 4.50
5.......	4	20	20.75	− 0.75
5.......	5	25	22.25	+ 2.75
5.......	6	30	24.25	+ 5.75
5.......	7	35	27.50	+ 7.50
5.......	8	40	32.50	+ 7.50
5.......	9	45	40.50	+ 4.50
5.......	10	50	52.50	− 2.50

TABLE 7.5.2

MARGINAL REVENUE, MARGINAL COST, AND PROFIT

Output and sales	Marginal revenue or price	Marginal cost	Average cost	Unit profit	Total profit
1......	$5.00	$17.00	$17.00	$—12.00	$—12.00
2......	5.00	1.50	9.25	— 4.25	— 8.50
3......	5.00	1.00	6.50	— 1.50	— 4.50
4......	5.00	1.25	5.19	— 0.19	— 0.75
5......	5.00	1.50	4.45	+ 0.55	+ 2.75
6......	5.00	2.00	4.04	+ 0.96	+ 5.75
7......	5.00	3.25	3.93	+ 1.07	+ 7.50
8......	5.00	5.00	4.06	+ 0.94	+ 7.50
9......	5.00	8.00	4.50	+ 0.50	+ 4.50
10......	5.00	12.00	5.25	— 0.25	— 2.50

that unit, because it costs more to produce than would be gained from its sale.

Let us examine these relations graphically. In Figure 7.5.1 LAC and LMC are the long-run average and marginal cost curves. The demand curve indicates the market price (p_0), which is marginal revenue. As long as price is greater than long-run average cost the firm can make a profit above the opportunity cost. Thus any output between Ox_0 and Ox_1 yields some profits. These levels of output are sometimes called break-even points.

FIGURE 7.5.1

PROFIT MAXIMIZATION BY THE MARGINAL APPROACH

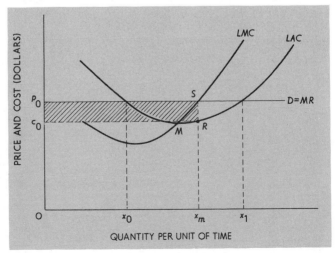

Maximum profit occurs at point S where marginal revenue equals long-run marginal cost. The firm would not under these circumstances try to produce at point M, the minimum point of long-run average cost. At M marginal revenue exceeds marginal cost; the firm can gain by producing more output. In Figure 7.5.1 total revenue (price times quantity) is given by the area of the rectangle Op_0Sx_m. Total cost (average cost times quantity) is the area Oc_0Rx_m. Total profit ($TR - TC$) is the shaded area c_0p_0SR.

To summarize, the firm will plan to operate at a scale or size such that long-run marginal cost equals price. This is the most profitable situation with the given market price. Of course, if market price changes, the point of long-run profit maximization will change also.

7.5.b Zero and negative profit situations

If firms in a competitive industry are in fact making above-normal returns, there is strong reason to believe that the price in the market will in fact fall. Profits attract new firms into the industry. This increased supply drives down price. In fact, price may even be driven below long-run average cost, at least temporarily.

Figure 7.5.2 shows such a situation. Price (Op_L) lies below LAC at every output; no positive profit can result. The minimum loss at a positive output occurs at Ox_L, where LMC equals Op_L. This loss is given by the area of the rectangle $p_Lc_0L'R$, the difference between total cost and total revenue. Firms would no longer wish to enter the industry under these

FIGURE 7.5.2

ZERO AND NEGATIVE PROFIT SITUATIONS

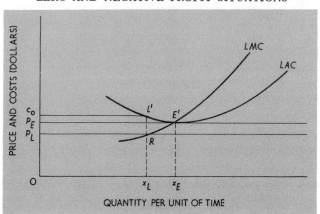

circumstances. In fact, under the assumption that all firms have similar cost curves, firms already in the industry would be induced to exist.[4]

If an increase in the number of firms increases supply and lowers price, a decrease in the number of firms must decrease supply and raise price. Firms would be motivated to leave the industry until market price rises sufficiently to eliminate losses. Let us assume that price rises to Op_E in Figure 7.5.2. After firms have had sufficient time to adjust optimally, all profit above opportunity cost is eliminated. Price equals marginal cost at Ox_E. At this output, price also equals average cost; hence total cost equals total revenue. At any other positive output average cost is above price, and losses result.

While no profit results at Ox_E, no firm is induced to leave the industry since each covers its opportunity cost—that is, the amount the entrepreneur could make in any alternative occupation. Neither is any other firm induced to enter since it would earn only its opportunity cost, which it presumably earns already. Each firm is in profit-maximizing equilibrium, since long-run marginal cost equals marginal revenue; of course, this maximum pure profit is zero. The industry is also in long-run equilibrium because price equals long-run average cost for each firm. Since profit is zero, no firm is induced to enter and none is induced to leave.

> **Principles.** Long-run equilibrium of a competitive industry involves several equilibrium conditions. Each firm in the industry must be in long-run (and short-run) profit-maximizing equilibrium; marginal revenue equals long-run marginal cost. The entry or exit of firms must compete away all pure profit. Then all firms must produce the quantity at which price equals the minimum long-run average cost.

7.5.c Graphical exposition of long-run equilibrium

Consider a firm in a short-run situation in which it incurs a loss. In looking to the long-run the enterpreneur has two options: liquidate the

---

[4] The student might note that we violate our assumption of perfect knowledge by positing that enough firms enter to drive the price down to Op_L. Why would a firm with perfect knowledge enter knowing full well it would make losses? We could assume that demand suddenly falls and drives price to Op_L. The explanation given, however, is more consistent with the model of long-run industry equilibrium to be analyzed later in this chapter.

The reason we know all firms are making losses is that the firms in the industry are operating in the short run and, except for the one point at which they are equal, short-run average cost is everywhere greater than long-run average cost. Thus if price is less than LAC it is also at least as far below SAC, if not further.

business and transfer resources to a more profitable alternative or construct a plant of a more suitable or profitable size and remain in the industry. Furthermore, even a firm in a profitable short-run situation may build at a more appropriate size in the long-run in order to make even more profits. But if profits are obtainable in the industry, new firms enter. This adjustment of the number of firms in the industry in response to profit motivation is the key element in establishing long-run equilibrium.

The process of attaining long-run equilibrium in a perfectly competitive industry is illustrated in Figure 7.5.3. Suppose each firm in the industry is identical. Its size is represented by SAC_1 and SMC_1 in panel B. The market demand curve is given by DD' in panel A, and the market supply is $S_1S'_1$. Market equilibrium establishes the price of Op_1 per unit and total output and sales of OX_1 units per period of time. At price Op_1 each plant is built to produce Ox_1 units (the output at which $Op_1 = LMC$) at least possible cost (x_1B). Each firm receives a profit of AB per unit of output. The number of firms multiplied by Ox_1 (each firm's output) equals OX_1 (total output). Although each firm is in equilibrium, the industry itself is not. As we saw earlier the appearance of *pure economic profit*, a return in excess of that obtainable elsewhere, attracts new firms into the industry, expanding industry supply (say) to $S_2S'_2$ and re-

FIGURE 7.5.3

LONG-RUN EQUILIBRIUM ADJUSTMENT IN A
PERFECTLY COMPETITIVE INDUSTRY

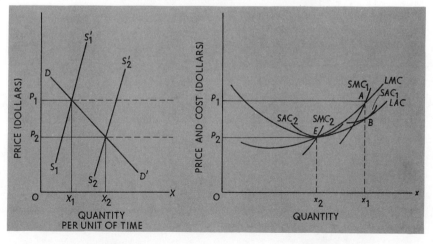

Panel A	Panel B
Long-run market equilibrium	Long-run equilibrium adjustment of a firm

ducing market price. The process of new entry might be very slow, or it might be very fast. It depends primarily upon the liquid assets in other industries. In any event, as time elapses, new firms will enter the industry, thereby shifting the supply curve to the right.

When each firm adjusts optimally to the new market price, the output of each will be smaller. The larger number of firms accounts for the increase in output from OX_1 to OX_2 in panel A. Now all firms produce the output at which Op_2 equals LMC at output Ox_2. The number of old firms plus the number of new entrants times Ox_2 equals OX_2. Since the new price equals LMC and SMC_2 at E, the minimum LAC and the minimum SAC_2, neither profit nor loss is present for any firm. Both the industry and its firms are in long-run equilibrium.

The long-run equilibrium position of a firm in a perfectly competitive industry is explained by Figure 7.5.4. As we have seen, if price is above Op, each established firm can adjust plant size and earn a pure profit. New firms are attracted into the industry, shifting the supply curve to the right. Price falls, and hence the horizontal demand curve facing each firm, old and new, falls also. All firms readjust. If "too many" firms enter, market price and each firm's horizontal demand curve may fall below

FIGURE 7.5.4

LONG-RUN EQUILIBRIUM OF A FIRM IN A
PERFECTLY COMPETITIVE INDUSTRY

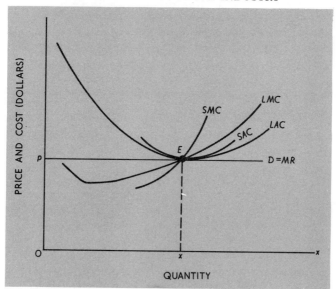

Op. Each firm incurs a loss. As their plants and equipment depreciate, some firms will leave the industry, thereby causing the market supply curve to shift to the left. Market price and, accordingly, the horizontal individual demand curves rise.

So long as the cost curves do not change, the only conceivable point of long-run equilibrium occurs at point E in Figure 7.5.4. Each firm in the industry receives neither profit nor loss. There is no incentive for further entry because the rate of return in this industry is the same as in the best alternative. But for the same reason there is no incentive for a firm to leave the industry. The number of firms stabilizes, each firm with a short-run plant represented by SAC and SMC. Note, however, that the entrepreneur is covering opportunity costs, since these are included in the cost curves. We say the firm earns "normal" profit, but not pure profit.

Firms will enter or leave the industry if there is either pure profit or pure loss. Therefore, since the position of long-run equilibrium must be consistent with *zero* profit (and zero loss), it is necessary that price equal average cost. For a firm to attain its individual equilibrium, price must be equal to marginal cost. Therefore, price must equal both marginal and average total cost. This can occur only at the point where average and marginal cost are equal, or at the point of minimum average total cost.

The statement, so far, could conceivably apply to any SAC and SMC. However, unless it applies only to the short-run plant that coincides with minimum long-run average cost, a change in plant size would lead to the appearance of pure profit, and the wheels of adjustment would be set in motion again.

7.5.d Long-run equilibrium and rent

Some students may object to the model of long-run equilibrium at the minimum point of each firm's long-run average cost curve on the grounds that the model is based upon the assumption that each firm is exactly like every other firm; that is, each firm's cost curve is the same as that of every other firm. We have made that assumption for simplicity; theory does not require it. To see why the assumption is not necessary, one must understand that any differences in cost are due to differences in the productivity of one or more resources. Assume that all firms except one are alike; that firm, because of (say) a more favorable location, has a lower cost curve. The owner of that location (who could be the owner of the firm) could raise the rent to the firm (if the firm's owner, the opportunity cost would rise) up to the point at which the firm's pure profit disappears. The firm would be motivated to pay the rent since the owner of the firm would continue making the equivalent of the best alternative. If the firm did not pay that rent, some other firm would.

Thus the cost of the previously lower-cost firm would tend to rise because of increased rent. It would not, of course, rise above those of other firms because any higher rent would occasion losses; hence no firm would pay it. The same type of argument applies to the superiority of other specialized resources, including the superiority of management. If a superior manager, even a manager-owner, could lower the firm's costs, that manager could presumably lower the costs of other firms as well. The hiring price would be bid up, or if the owner of the resource is the owner of the firm, the opportunity cost would rise. At equilibrium all firms' long-run average cost curves would, therefore, reach their minimum points at the same cost (albeit not necessarily at the same output), and no firm would make pure profit or loss (although some might have differing factor payments or rents).

We might also note that firms with even higher cost structure are generally "waiting in the wings" to enter the industry if demand increases and drives up prices sufficiently to cover their costs. These higher-cost firms could cover opportunity cost only at a higher price. But if price increases enough to induce their entry the owners of resources that cause the firms already in the industry to have lower costs than the new firms will receive increased rents. Or some firms that were just making normal profits prior to the increase in price may begin to enjoy above-normal profits, which will in the long run be dispersed as rents to the resources responsible for lower costs.

Just within the past few years we have seen oil fields that were closed down because pumping from them was unprofitable begin pumping again profitably, because of the increase in the price of oil. If the price of oil increases still more we may see firms extracting oil from oil shale, an operation until now unprofitable. The higher price could make such extraction profitable. We shall return to this concept below when dealing with increasing-cost industries.[5]

---

[5] We have simplified the theory of rent to a very large degree. The primary reason for introducing this concept at all is simply to familiarize the student with the use of this term.

APPLICATION

Some evidence supporting the theory

The theory developed in this chapter predicts that when profit is "abnormally" high in one sector of the economy, firms will enter that business, drive down prices, and eliminate the above-normal profit, so long as entry is reasonably free. However, we frequently hear about the vast profits being made in some businesses over long periods of time even in the face of free entry. Admittedly no industry exhibits all the characteristics of perfect competition, but the logic of the theory should fit much of the economy. Some major industries in which we hear of "excessive" or "exorbitant" profit over a long period are the defense industries. During times of war or preparation for war the "war profiteers" are allegedly free from competition, otherwise their profits would be competed away. On the other hand, possibly the defense industries do fit our theory.

When we hear of the profits in the defense establishment we might wonder why investors, induced by these profits, do not change some of their capital from non-defense-oriented industry to defense. The resulting increase in capacity, according to our theory, would drive down prices and eliminate the excess profit. The defense industries allegedly have been prospering since World War II. Surely that is sufficient time for entry to have taken place. Only three explanations seem possible. First, government prevents entry. Second, risks are greater in defense industry than elsewhere, and the larger returns are necessary to compensate for increased risk. Third, the allegation is not correct. It does not seem logical that government, the purchaser, would protect a monopoly position in defense. Therefore, let us examine the evidence to obtain a solution.

In a paper by George J. Stigler and Claire Friedland considerable evidence in this area was presented.* The first piece of evidence is the report of 40 major defense contractors on their rates of return from both defense and commercial or non-defense business. From 1958 through 1961, the average return from defense contracts exceeded the average return from non-defense. Furthermore, the average defense-oriented return was greater than the average return of the Federal Trade Commission–Securities and Exchange Commission listing of the returns for 3,500 companies. From 1962 through 1968 the average defense rate of return of the 40 defense contractors was less

---

* George J. Stigler and Claire Friedland, "Profits of Defense Contractors," *American Economic Review*, September 1971, pp. 692–94.

than both the return of these firms from commercial business and the average rate of return of the (FTC–SEC) 3,500 companies. In the last year of the sample, 1968, the defense return averaged 6.8 percent while the 3,500-firm average return was 10.2 percent. Note that the latter years included the period of the vast Viet Nam buildup.

The relative performances of all stocks and the stocks of the major defense contractors point in essentially the same direction. Investments in the defense contractors were almost twice as profitable as the average return from investment in all stocks on the New York Stock Exchange during the 1950s. During the 1960s investments in the major defense contractors did approximately as well as the average investment in all stocks. The correlation of stock market performance with the ratio of defense to total sales shows a positive relation in the 1950s and no significant relation for the leading defense contractors of 1959 for the 1960s.

From the evidence, it appears that the profitability of defense industries was higher than normal in the 1950s but that entry (or something) competed away the above-normal profits in the 1960s. We do not know if entry into defense is blocked, but there is some evidence that the defense industry is riskier than non-defense. Stigler and Friedland found a positive correlation between instability of sales over time for a company and the company's share of business devoted to defense. It seems, however, that defense industry has performed in somewhat the way we would predict: early excess profits were competed away in the long run.

7.6 CONSTANT- AND INCREASING-COST INDUSTRIES

The analysis thus far has been in large part based upon the tacit assumption of "constant cost," in the sense that expanded resource use by the industry does not entail an increase in resource prices. To carry the analysis further, and to make it more explicit, both constant- and increasing-cost industries are examined in this section. The phenomenon of decreasing cost is not examined inasmuch as it is not only inconsistent with all the requirements of perfect competition, but it is in all probability an empirical rarity.

7.6.a Constant-cost industries

Long-run equilibrium and long-run supply price under conditions of constant cost are explained by Figure 7.6.1. Panel A shows the long- and

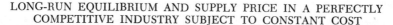

FIGURE 7.6.1

LONG-RUN EQUILIBRIUM AND SUPPLY PRICE IN A PERFECTLY
COMPETITIVE INDUSTRY SUBJECT TO CONSTANT COST

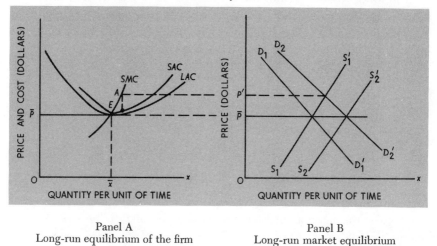

| Panel A | Panel B |
| Long-run equilibrium of the firm | Long-run market equilibrium |

short-run conditions of each firm in the industry, while panel B depicts the
market as a whole. $D_1D'_1$ and $S_1S'_1$ are the original market demand and
supply curves, establishing a market equilibrium price of $O\bar{p}$ dollars per
unit. We assume that the industry has attained a position of long-run
equilibrium, so the position of each firm in the industry is depicted by
panel A—the price line is tangent to the long- and short-run average cost
curves at their minimum points.

Now suppose demand increases to $D_2D'_2$. With the number of firms
fixed, the price will rise to Op' and each firm will move to short-run equilibrium at point A. However, at point A each firm earns a pure economic
profit inasmuch as price exceeds average cost. New entrants are thereby
attracted into the industry; the industry supply curve shifts to the right.
In this case we assume that all resources used are so general that increased use in this industry does not affect the market price of resources.
As a consequence, the entrance of new firms does not increase the costs of
existing firms; the LAC curve of established firms does not shift, and new
firms can operate with an identical LAC curve. Long-run equilibrium adjustment to the shift in demand is accomplished when the number of
firms expands to the point at which $S_2S'_2$ is the industry supply curve
with a given number of firms in the industry.

In other words, since output can be expanded by expanding the
number of firms, each producing $O\bar{x}$ units per period of time at average

cost $O\bar{p}$, the industry has a constant long-run supply price equal to $O\bar{p}$ dollars per unit. If price were above this level, firms of size represented by SAC would continue to enter the industry in order to reap the pure profit obtainable. If price were less than $O\bar{p}$, some firms would ultimately leave the industry to avoid the pure economic loss. Hence in the special case in which an expansion of resource use does not lead to an increase in resource price, the long-run industry supply price is constant. This is precisely the meaning of a constant-cost industry.

Exercise. The student should carry out the same type of analysis for a decrease in demand.

7.6.b Increasing-cost industries

An increasing-cost industry is depicted in Figure 7.6.2. The original situation is the same as in Figure 7.6.1. The industry is in a position of long-run equilibrium. $D_1D'_1$ and $S_1S'_1$ are the market demand and supply curves, respectively. Equilibrium price is Op_1. Each firm operates at point E_1, where price equals minimum average cost—both long- and short-run cost. Thus each firm is also in a position of long-run equilibrium.

Let demand shift to $D_2D'_2$ so that price rises to a much higher level. The higher price is accompanied by pure economic profit; new firms are consequently attracted into the industry. The use of resources expands, but now we assume resource price increases with expanded resource use. The cost of inputs therefore increases for the established firms as well as for the new entrants. As a result, the entire set of cost curves shifts upward, say, to a position represented by LAC_2 in panel A.[6]

Naturally, the process of equilibrium adjustment is not instantaneous. The LAC curve gradually shifts upward as new entrants gradually join the industry. The marginal cost curves of all firms shift to the left as new firms enter and bid up factor prices. Thus two forces tend to work in opposite directions upon the industry's supply curve. Shifting marginal cost to the left tends to shift the industry's supply curve to the left. However, new firms enter the industry, and this entry tends to shift industry supply to the right. The forces causing a shift to the right (entry) must dominate those causing a shift to the left (rise in marginal costs); other-

---

[6] As Figure 7.6.2 is constructed, the minimum point on LAC shifts to the left as LAC shifts upward. In fact, minimum LAC can correspond to either a smaller or a larger output. The analysis underlying the exact nature of the shift involves an advanced concept not treated in this text.

wise total output could not expand as dictated by the increase in market price.

To see why supply must shift to the right after an increase in demand, let us assume that the opposite happens. In Figure 7.6.2 demand, as before, shifts to $D_2D'_2$. In the short run price and quantity increase along with profits. The profits attract new firms, which, upon entering, bid up resource prices. All cost curves rise as indicated in panel A. Suppose, however, that the leftward shift in all marginal cost curves dominates the tendency for an increase in supply caused by entry. Therefore, the new supply curve would lie somewhere to the left of $S_1S'_1$. If demand remains $D_2D'_2$, price must be greater than Op_2; firms must be making pure profits; entry must continue. If the same process reoccurs, price will rise further, costs will rise, profits will continue, and entry will be further encouraged. Thus a leftward shift in supply is not consistent with equilibrium. At some point the entry of new firms must dominate the increase in costs, and supply must shift to the right, though not by as much as it would in a constant-cost industry, since under constant costs no shift in marginal costs occurs.

The process of adjustment must continue until a position of full long-run equilibrium is attained. In Figure 7.6.2, this is depicted by the intersection of $D_2D'_2$ and $S_2S'_2$, establishing an equilibrium price of Op_2 dollars per unit. Each firm produces at point E_2, where price equals mini-

FIGURE 7.6.2

LONG-RUN EQUILIBRIUM AND SUPPLY PRICE IN A PERFECTLY COMPETITIVE INDUSTRY SUBJECT TO INCREASING COST

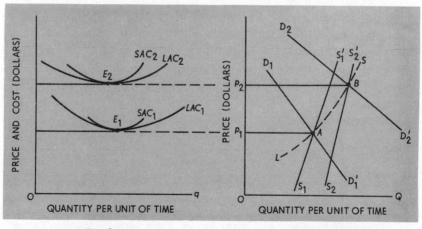

Panel A
Long-run equilibrium of the firm

Panel B
Long-run market equilibrium

mum average cost. The important point to emphasize is that in constant-cost industries new firms enter until price returns to the unchanged level of minimum long-run average cost. For industries subject to increasing cost, new firms enter until minimum long-run average cost shifts upward to equal the new price.

In the transition from one long-run equilibrium to the other, the long-run supply price increases from Op_1 to Op_2. This is precisely what is meant by an increasing-cost industry. In keeping with this, the long-run industry supply curve is given by a line, LS, joining such points as A and B in panel B. Thus an increasing-cost industry is one with a positively sloped long-run supply curve. Alternatively stated, after all long-run equilibrium adjustments are made, an increasing-cost industry is one in which an increase in output requires an increase in long-run supply price.

Recall also in our above discussion of rents, we noted that possibly because of scarce resources, industry expansion could take place only through the entry of higher-cost firms, perhaps because less productive resources are used. Until now we have assumed all firms are alike, and the only reason for cost to rise is because resource prices are bid up. But, if expansion takes place through the entry of higher-cost firms, we have an increasing-cost industry as well. Demand increases; firms that would have been previously unprofitable enter. The lower-cost firms earn pure profits, which are competed away by rents to the scarce resources. The final equilibrium price is therefore higher than before, but each firm is operating at the minimum point on long-run average cost. The lower-cost firms have their cost curves pushed up by rents. For simplicity, without loss of analytical usefulness, economists generally assume in the theory of perfect competition that all firms are identical.

As we noted above it would be hard to visualize a decreasing-cost industry because it is difficult to picture a resource or factor of production whose price is decreased because of increased use. Thus, decreasing-cost industries probably have little empirical relevance. As we noted also, a decreasing-cost industry is not even consistent with all of the assumptions of perfect competition.

ASIDE

Effects of technological change

One would suspect that many students are taking exception to the last paragraph, and to the opening paragraph of this section, in which we stressed that because decreasing-cost industries are rare, perhaps nonexistent, we did not analyze them. But everyone can think of many examples, over the past decades, of products that decreased dramatically in price while experiencing significant gains in sales and quality. One of the most recent examples is the hand-calculator industry. Prices dropped greatly as sales increased. The computer industry experienced the same phenomenon. Earlier, color TV sets dropped in price as sales increased; this was also the case with many household appliances.

These and other cases *are not examples of decreasing-cost industries* in the sense discussed above, in which an increase in output reduced the prices of some inputs because of increased use. Thus,

FIGURE 7.6.3

EFFECT OF TECHNOLOGICAL CHANGE

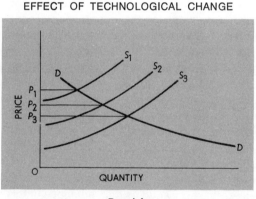

Panel A

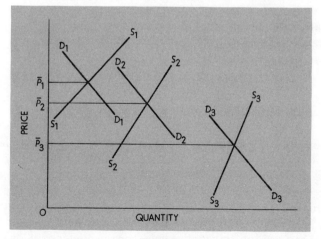

Panel B

industry costs would have dropped, and a decreasing-cost industry would have resulted. This is not the case in the above and other examples.

Technological change, one of the subjects of an earlier chapter, is in most, if not all, such cases the proper explanation. Recall that technological change lowers firms' costs and consequently increases industry supply. Two possible situations are depicted in Figure 7.6.3. In panel A the demand for the product, *DD,* remains constant over a reasonably long period of time. Begin with a long-run supply of S_1. Thus a price of Op_1 results. If technological change occurs, the isoquant map shifts toward the origin, causing a reduction in costs. Supply increases to S_2, lowering price to Op_2. Clearly, equilibrium output increases. Technological change continues (induced, spontaneous, or otherwise), increasing supply to S_3, reducing price to Op_3, and increasing output. The situation could continue.

In panel B, the demand for the product increases from D_1D_1 to D_2D_2 to D_3D_3. But, because of technological change, not because of a reduction in factor prices from increased factor use, supply increases even more, from S_1S_1 to S_2S_2 to S_3S_3. These shifts cause price to fall from $O\bar{p}_1$ to $O\bar{p}_2$ to $O\bar{p}_3$. We note that output increases also in this case. Supply does not increase because of reduced input prices from increased use but from technological change, which improves the production process and lowers costs; or in some instances the technological change could have occurred in the factor market, causing a reduction in an input's price.

Let us stress that these are not examples of decreasing long-run supply. The long-run supply curves derived above in this section were derived under the assumption that technology remains constant. In the situations depicted in Figure 7.6.3 and in the examples given here, and probably in most of the examples you can think of, it is the change in technology that is responsible for the shift in supply. Thus we have no theoretical contradiction.

The results of this section can be summarized as follows:

Relations. Constant or increasing cost in an industry depends upon the way in which resource prices respond to expanded resource use. If resource prices remain constant, the industry is subject to constant cost; if resource prices increase, the industry is one of increasing cost. The long-run supply curve for a constant-cost industry is a horizontal line at the level of the constant long-run supply price. The long-run industry supply curve under conditions of increasing cost is positively sloped, and the long-run supply price increases as long-run equilibrium quantity supplied expands. We can also have an increasing-cost industry if expansion can take place only with the entry of firms with a higher cost structure.

7.7 SOME PROBLEMS AND APPLICATIONS

As we noted above it is not necessary for economics or business majors to be employed by a profit-maximizing firm in order for them to be able to use economic theory in their jobs. An increasing number of students with training in economics are going to work for various branches of government. Governmental employees, from beginners to senior officials, are expected to predict the economic consequences of some governmental action. Government officials at all levels make decisions and take actions that have far reaching repercussions. It is the business of many governmental employees to predict these consequences. We now give some examples of analyses that have been used in the past.

An important predictive problem that has received increased attention recently is the expected effect of eliminating the percentage depletion allowance for the oil industry. Until recently the tax treatment for oil differed from that applicable to manufacturing. While manufacturing was subject to an ordinary depreciation on capital for tax purposes, oil firms were permitted to deduct a percentage of gross revenue, not to exceed 50 percent of total profits. (This description is an overly simplified version of a very complex process.) The percentage depletion allowance for oil was recently eliminated. What will be the long-run impact on the industry and on society as a whole?

APPLICATION

Effects of elimination of depletion allowance in the oil industry

Over two decades ago a University of Chicago economist, A. C. Harberger, testified before a congressional subcommittee about the effects of a percentage depletion allowance in the oil industry.* Har-

---

* This application is based upon the following two papers: A. C. Harberger, *"The Tax Treatment of Oil Exploration,"* in *Proceedings of Second Energy Institute,* Washington, D.C., American University Press, and A. C. Harberger, "The Taxation of Mineral Industries," in *Federal Tax Policy for Economic Growth and Stability* (Washington, D.C.: Government Printing Office, 1955). These papers have been reprinted as chapters 11 and 12 in Harberger's *Taxation and Welfare* (Boston: Little, Brown, 1974).

berger used the model of long-run competitive equilibrium along with industry data to make his prediction. He compared investment in the oil industry with capital investment in a typical manufacturing industry not subject to percentage depletion. Each investment was assumed to yield identical streams of income.

Under competition, Harberger pointed out, investments would be undertaken until above-normal profits from the investments were competed away. That is, the costs of the investment would in the long run equal the expected returns. But he also said that the relevant returns would be the returns after all taxation. Thus far in our theory we have ignored taxation. But, no matter what the before-tax revenue, it is the after-tax returns that the entrepreneur really cares about.

Harberger assumed two identical streams of income, but theoretically subjected the streams to two different tax treatments—ordinary depreciation and percentage depletion. He estimated how much investment would be undertaken in each circumstance, assuming that investment would be undertaken until after-tax returns are driven to the normal rate. Using estimates for a range of tax rates, Harberger obtained a range of estimates that compared the extent of investment under the two tax treatments.

These estimates showed that investment would be between 36 and 92 percent higher under percentage depletion in order to obtain the same stream of income. The average estimate was that investment would be about 62 percent higher under depletion.

Thus we can perhaps use Harberger's estimates in order to predict the effect of the elimination of percentage depletion. To the extent that the range of estimates is reasonably accurate, we would expect exploration and investment to fall in the long run below what it would have been under depletion. That is, in the long run investment would have been 36 to 92 percent higher. To the extent that domestic output depends on investment, domestic production should be below what it would have been. This result may or may not be socially desirable, but it is at least a prediction. For our purpose it shows how one can use the competitive model to make predictions about policy.

Another really crucial economic problem at this time is related to oil also. This problem is the prediction about what will occur if the price ceiling on "old oil" is repealed. Old oil is oil from wells in production prior to 1972. "New oil" is oil from recent wells and imported oil. By 1977 new oil was selling at the market-determined price of about $11 a barrel, and old oil was selling at a governmentally fixed ceiling price of about half that much.

At this time there is considerable debate about whether or not the federal government should eliminate the ceiling price on old oil and permit the market to determine the equilibrium price. Opponents of deregulation say that elimination of the ceiling would drive up the price of old oil and hence raise the *average* price of crude to the refinery. If the costs at the refinery rise, the price of products such as gasoline will be driven up. Old oil now accounts for about 35 percent of domestic production. How would you analyze the problem? Based on the information given, do you agree with those opposed to or those in favor of deregulation?

APPLICATION

Analysis of ceiling price on crude petroleum

Two years ago a young graduate student worked on this problem while serving in a summer internship at the Federal Energy Administration.* The student reached the following conclusion:

First, assume that the quantity of old oil is fixed by pumping capacity at all prices. That is, the supply of old oil is a vertical line. The total quantity supplied of oil at any price is the quantity of new oil that would be forthcoming at the price (supply of new oil is assumed upward sloping) plus the fixed amount of old oil supplied.

Figure 7.7.1 shows the situation graphically.† The amount of old oil supplied is OQ_0 regardless of price. S_n is the supply curve for new oil. Industry supply is ΣS. With a given demand by the refineries for crude oil of D, the price is OP in the absence of a ceiling price, and OQ is sold in the market. Next, let a ceiling price of P be placed upon old oil only. Clearly, supply is still $Q_0A\Sigma S$. *There is no decrease in the quantity supplied of old oil. Therefore, there is no change in the price of new oil.* An additional barrel of oil still costs the refinery OP. Thus, the *marginal cost* of an increase in gasoline production remains constant, and consequently there is no change in the price of

---

* The results of this research are in a paper by Chris W. Paul II, "The Effect of Deregulating Crude Oil Prices on the Pump Price of Gasoline," to be published in *The American Economist*. We might note in passing that the presence of oil entitlements complicates the situation to some extent and changes the conclusion somewhat. We will not complicate the problem any further now.

† Figure 7.7.1 is reproduced from the work cited above.

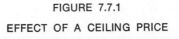

FIGURE 7.7.1

EFFECT OF A CEILING PRICE

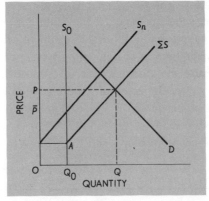

gasoline, other things remaining the same. For this reason eliminating the ceiling would have no effect on the price of gasoline.

There is a wealth transfer from the producers of old oil to the refinery because of the reduced average cost of oil and the reduced price of old oil. But, the *marginal cost* of producing more gasoline does not change since the price of additional crude does not change.

Even if the supply of old oil is upward sloping the conclusion is not changed much. In this case the total quantity of oil supplied is decreased when a ceiling price is imposed on old oil. Thus the price of new oil is increased; this higher price of new oil increases the marginal cost of gasoline, therefore raising the price of gasoline. Consequently, deregulation would lower the price of gasoline.

EXERCISE

Analyze the latter situation graphically.

7.8 FURTHER EFFECTS OF CEILING PRICES

Suppose the demand for coal at the retail level is elastic over the relevant price range. Further, suppose the government feels that the price of coal is too high. It therefore places a price ceiling or maximum on coal at the mine. What will happen to the price of coal at the retail level? Will total receipts of retailers increase or decrease?

As a first step let us consider what happens at the mine (or mining area). Assume for analytical purposes that coal mining is a perfectly competitive, increasing-cost industry. Assume also that before the imposition of the ceiling price, the industry was in long-run equilibrium; each firm produced the quantity at which $P = LAC$ and therefore enjoyed no pure profit. Figure 7.8.1 shows the market demand and supply for coal at the mine. Demand $(D_mD'_m)$ is the demand curve of retailers for coal at the mine. It is derived holding the demand for coal from retailers and other factors constant (we assume that individual consumers cannot purchase coal directly from the mine).

The long-run industry supply curve, $S_mS'_m$, is the type of supply curve developed above. It is the locus of long-run equilibria for the mining industry. Since we assume an increasing-cost industry, $S_mS'_m$ is upward sloping. The equilibrium price at the mine is OW_c and equilibrium quantity is OQ_c.

Figure 7.8.2 shows demand and supply conditions at retail. $D_rD'_r$ is the consumers' demand for coal. $S_rS'_r$, based upon a given cost of coal at the mines to retailers (Fig. 7.8.1, OW_c), is the retailers' supply curve. Since coal is an input for the retailers, the supply curve for coal at retail should shift when the price of coal at the mines changes, just as a change in the price of any factor of production changes the supply of the product produced. Specifically, when the price at the mine falls, other things remaining the same, the retail supply curve should shift to the right. That is, if retailers can buy coal cheaper, they would be willing and able to supply more retail coal at every retail price. Begin with equilibrium in

FIGURE 7.8.1

SUPPLY AND DEMAND AT THE MINE

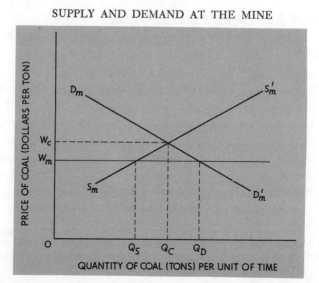

FIGURE 7.8.2

DEMAND AND SUPPLY AT RETAIL

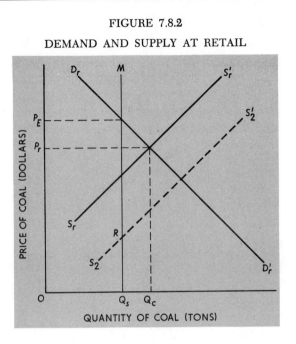

QUANTITY OF COAL (TONS)

the retail market occurring at a price of OP_r (given a price at the mine of OW_c) and a quantity sold of OQ_c, obviously the same as OQ_c in Figure 7.8.1 because the retailers sell all that they buy.

Returning to Figure 7.8.1, assume that the government sets the ceiling price OW_m. Quantity demanded by retailers at the new price is OQ_D. The new price is below OW_c (the price at which neither profit nor loss occurs); thus firms begin to make losses and some leave the industry. Since we assume that mining is an increasing-cost industry, the exit of firms and the decrease in quantity produced lower factor prices and hence lower the long-run average and marginal cost curves of the remaining firms in the industry. Figure 7.8.3 shows the process. Long-run average and marginal costs fall from LAC_1 and LMC_1 to LAC_2 and LMC_2. The minimum point on LAC_2 equals the ceiling price OW_m. Each remaining firm now produces Oq_m (the new equilibrium output) rather than Oq_c, but there are fewer firms, none of which makes pure profit. The new quantity supplied by the industry, indicated in Figure 7.8.1, is OQ_S.[7] Thus a shortage (excess demand) of Q_SQ_D occurs at the

---

[7] Figure 7.8.3 is drawn under the assumption that the fall in resource prices caused by the exit of firms from the industry shifts the minimum point on LAC to the right. It could, as noted above, just as easily have shifted it to the left.

FIGURE 7.8.3

COST CURVES OF AN INDIVIDUAL FIRM

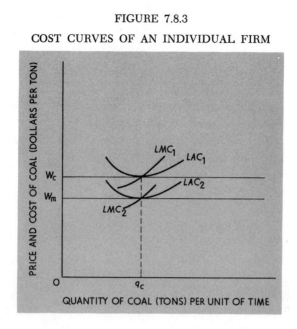

mines since retailers now wish to purchase OQ_D, but the mines are only willing to sell OQ_S. The mining industry must find some method of allocation (rationing, first come first served, favoritism, and so on) in order to determine which retailers get the available supply. In any case, only OQ_S is available to the retailers.

Now according to our analysis, the lower price of coal at the mine should cause supply at retail to shift to $S_2S'_2$ (Figure 7.8.2). Retail price should fall and the quantity of coal sold should increase as determined by the intersection of $D_rD'_r$ and $S_2S'_2$. But remember that only OQ_S is produced, so only OQ_S can be sold. The curve $S_2S'_2$ specifies the quantities that retailers are *willing* to sell at the mine price of OW_m; the vertical line MQ_S indicates the maximum amount retailers are *able* to sell at that price. Thus, the curve S_2RM shows the quantities that retailers are *willing and able* to sell at each retail price when the mine price is fixed at OW_m.

The intersection of supply and demand now occurs at the price OP_E, clearly higher than the old price. The quantity sold is OQ_S. After the ceiling price at the mine is imposed, consumers pay a higher price for less coal. Since demand was assumed to be elastic, retailers receive less total revenue.

Exercise. Analyze the problem under the assumption that mining is a constant-cost industry.

7.9 SUMMARY

Up to this point the salient feature of perfect competition is that, in long-run market equilibrium, market price equals minimum average cost. This means that each unit of output is produced at the lowest possible cost, either from the standpoint of money cost or of resource use. The product sells for its average (long-run) cost of production; each firm accordingly earns the going rate of return in competitive industries, nothing more or less.

It should be emphasized that firms do not choose to produce the quantity with the lowest possible long-run average cost simply because they believe this level of production is optimal for society and they wish to benefit society. The firms are merely trying to maximize their profits. Given that motivation, the market *forces* firms to produce at that point. If society benefits, it is not through any benevolence of firms but through the functioning of the market. Another point that also warrants emphasis is that the theory of perfect competition is not designed to describe specific real-world firms. It is a theoretical model that is frequently useful in explaining real-world behavior and in predicting the economic consequences of changes in the different variables contained in the model. The conclusions of the theory, not the assumptions, are the crucial points when analyzing economic problems.

Other important points of the theory of perfect competition are summarized in the following

Relation. In the short run the firm produces the quantity at which short-run marginal cost equals price, so long as price exceeds average variable cost. Therefore, marginal cost above average variable cost is the firm's short-run supply. If all input prices are given to the industry, industry short-run supply is the horizontal summation of all marginal cost curves. If the industry's (although not the individual firm's) use of the inputs affects the prices of some inputs, industry supply is less elastic than this horizontal summation. In the long run the entry and exit of firms force each firm to produce at minimum LAC, where $LAC = LMC = SAC = SMC$. Profit is zero at this output, although each entrepreneur earns opportunity cost. In a constant-cost industry long-run industry supply is a horizontal line at the level of the firm's minimum long-run average cost. If the industry's use affects the prices of some inputs directly, the industry's long-run supply curve increases with output.

APPLICATION

Some extensions of the theory

Probably the most important feature or most distinguishing characteristic of the perfectly competitive firms is based on the assumption that each firm is so small relative to the total market that any specific firm, acting alone, cannot affect the market price of the commodity. Certainly all firms acting together either in response to some external stimulus or in collusion do affect market price and frequently the prices of some factors of production. But the individual firm has no perceptible effect.

This characteristic of the competitive firm also goes a long way in explaining aspects of competitive behavior other than the output decision of the firm. The same characteristic also explains certain aspects of individual behavior.

In making any decision a firm or an individual weighs the marginal effect on the cost that the firm or the individual must pay to carry out an activity for the public good against the marginal effect of that activity on the total benefit. It may be that the marginal increase in cost is rather small, but if the marginal effect on the total benefit is smaller, the activity will not be carried out. In the case of competitive firms or of individuals acting alone their actions would generally have no *perceivable* effect on the total benefit.

For example, this characteristic of competitive behavior in large part explains why appeals for voluntary actions, supposedly in the public interest, but not necessarily in the interest of the firm or the individual, seldom accomplish what the appealer wishes, in the case of either competitive firms or individuals.

Consider the following example. Suppose that scientists discover that a certain insecticide used by most farmers is harming much of the wildlife in a particular state. As is frequently the case, the governor pleads for farmers to change to a nonharmful brand of insecticide that presumably would not harm wildlife. Now, clearly, the original harmful insecticide is more productive, i.e., leads to lower cost, or farmers would have been using some other brand voluntarily. The question is, would farmers have any reason to comply with the governor's request, even knowing that the original brand of insecticide harms wildlife? Probably not! Why not?

In the first place farmers must realize that each one, acting alone, probably has no effect, or an infinitesimal effect, on total wildlife killed or damaged, even though all farmers acting together would have an effect. Thus no farmer would have the incentive to bear higher costs that have zero effect, even though each farmer deplores the fact that wild animals are being damaged or killed. Even if a farmer did decide to comply with the plea, the higher costs in the long run would drive the operation out of business. Furthermore, each farmer, being competitive, knows that the particular brand of insecticide used has no effect on the farm's sales or the price that can be obtained for the product. The output of any one farm is indistinguishable from the output of any other farm. In this case voluntary actions by any individual farmer would not help sales or the public. Either a tax would have to be levied or a law passed.

We can apply the same analysis to water or air pollution. If no one owns the water or air (we will return to the effect of property rights in the final chapter) any firm can pollute at zero cost. If each firm knows that there are so many firms polluting that its own polluting activity has practically a zero effect on total pollution, appeals for voluntary restraint would have little or no effect on the total. Every firm knows that reducing the amount of pollution would raise costs but would have no effect on the price of the product. Knowing the increase would have no effect on the price of the product, no firm would raise costs voluntarily. Therefore no firm would have the incentive to reduce pollution voluntarily. (Again if someone owned the water and could charge for polluting, firms would reduce pollution, but this is a problem that belongs in the section on property rights, and will be addressed in the final chapter).

In fact, if any competitive firm is doing a social "bad," whatever that is, it would have little incentive to cease doing "bad," if its actions alone have only an infinitesimal effect on the total amount of "bad" and zero effect on sales, but would raise costs. In fact, even if owners of the competitive firms are earning rents on some of their resources, and therefore would not be driven out of business from the increased cost, few owners would be willing to sacrifice income knowing the sacrificed income has no effect on total "bad."

Similar analysis applies to the behavior of individuals in response to appeals for voluntary actions in the alleged social interest. Take, for example, the recent national reduction in the speed limit to 55 miles per hour. Would governmental appeals to reduce speed in order to conserve the nation's energy have worked? What do you think?

As you well know by now, time is valuable. I know and you know that if either one of us drives the largest "gas guzzling" automobile 24 hours a day all year at 90 miles per hour, it would have absolutely no effect on the nation's total gasoline consumption. For each individual, slowing down would merely cost valuable time but would have no perceivable effect on total consumption. There would be few volunteers. We see now, even with the law, the penalty for speeding is so small that the 55-mile-per-hour driver on the expressways of the nation is a rarity. There has been, thus far, only slight reduction in average speed.

What about recent appeals by the president to keep homes colder in winter and use less air conditioning in the summer in order to conserve the nation's gas and electricity? If all homes complied, certainly the total use would decline. But any household knows that the temperature of its home has absolutely no effect on national energy use. Why bear discomfort if the discomfort has no perceivable effect on the total?

Frequently during water shortages in cities (often caused by too low prices) the city officials ask households to cut down water use voluntarily. Again, everyone knows that his or her own use of water has no effect on the city's water use, so why comply?

During World War II, the government imposed price controls and rationing in the case of many goods. National appeals were made to consumers not to deal with black markets in the nation's interest. Yet we are told there was considerable trade in black markets. Appeals to patriotism did not work well during a period in which the nation experienced the greatest period of national purpose and patriotism in its entire history. Why should appeals to national purpose work any better now?

There is little difference in the case of appeals to boycott certain products, the producers of which some people believe are doing "bad." Again any household is a perfect competitor in affecting the price and sales of that product. Why not buy some product you want when your purchasing it has no effect. Certainly you can think of other examples.

But, I'll bet you are thinking right now that consumer boycotts have succeeded in driving some firms out of business or in forcing them to change some activity. Some households do keep their temperatures lower in winter and higher in summer in response to the president's appeal. Of course, competitive firms generally cannot do something voluntarily that raises costs but does not affect price when other firms do not, because they would be driven out of business. But individuals can voluntarily comply with an appeal that lowers their utility or causes them to bear costs. Why would they do so, however, if their actions have no perceivable effect on the total?

The only answer is social pressure, or the feeling of pleasure one gets from sacrificing, ostensibly for the national good. I know that my vote has never had any effect on the outcome of any election in which I have voted; and the probability is, I would think, zero that my vote will ever have an effect. Yet I vote in practically every election purely for the pleasure of voting for a "good guy" or voting against a "bad guy." I also vote because of social pressure.

If it becomes "chic" to keep one's home below 62 degrees in winter, possibly because that is the temperature in the White House, people may do so. They may fear being ostracized if someone comes into their home and the temperature is 80 degrees. If it is the "social thing to do" many people will refuse to serve grapes or lettuce, the objects of recent boycotts, at meals.

But these social fads and opportunities for chicness are generally soon replaced by other social fads. Voluntary activities usually do not work well in the long run. The only sure way to reduce a "bad" is to increase sufficiently the price of doing "bad." The surest way to conserve oil is to let the price of oil products rise. The only sure way to induce more "good" is to raise the reward for doing "good." The price system is the more efficient way of changing behavior. This does not mean that the price system does not work through laws and fines. The point is that voluntary behavior, except in special circumstances, does not work well in the long run.

In the case of competitive firms voluntary behavior cannot work. In fact, laws that raise the costs of some firms but do not raise the costs of their competitors will simply drive the affected firms out of business.*

---

* We might note here that in certain types of industrial organizations (called oligopoly) under certain conditions, voluntary restraint, such as pollution reduction, may come about. We will discuss this in Chapter 9.

TECHNICAL PROBLEMS

1. Use the output-cost data computed from problem 1 in Chapter 6.
    a. Suppose the price of the commodity is $1.75 per unit.
        i. What would net profit be at each of the following outputs?
            1,314
            1,384
            1,444
            1,494
            1,534

    ii.   What is the output that yields the greatest profit?

    iii. Is there any output that will yield a greater profit at any price?

    iv. How much more revenue is obtained by selling this number of units than by selling one fewer? What is the relation between marginal revenue and selling price?

    v.   If you are given selling price, how can you determine the optimum output by reference to marginal cost?

b. Suppose price is $0.70.

    i.   What would net profit be at each of the following outputs?

       410

       560

       700

       830

       945

       1,234

       1,444

    ii.   Is there any output that will earn a net profit at this price?

    iii. When price is $0.70, what is the crucial relation between price and average variable cost?

    iv. Consider any price for which the corresponding marginal cost is equal to or less than $0.70. At such a price, what is the relation between marginal cost and average variable cost?

    v.   When the relation in (iv) exists, what is the relation between average and marginal product?

    vi. What will the producer do if faced with a permanent price of $0.70?

    vii. Why is it not socially desirable to have a producer operating when price is $0.70?

c. Suppose price is $0.80.

    i.   What will the optimum output be?

    ii.   Can a profit be made at this price?

    iii. Will the producer operate at all at this price?

    iv. For how long?

d. Determine the supply schedule of this individual producer.

Price	Quantity supplied
$0.60	
0.70	
0.80	
0.90	
1.00	
1.10	
1.20	
1.30	

Price	Quantity supplied
1.40	
1.50	
1.60	
1.70	
1.80	
1.90	
2.00	

2. Use Figure E.7.1 to answer these questions.

   a. If price is $7 the firm should produce _____ units.

   b. Since average total cost at this profit-maximizing output is $_____, total cost is $_____.

   c. Therefore the firm makes a total profit of $_____.

   d. Price then falls to $3. The firm will produce approximately _____ units.

   e. Since average total cost at this output is $_____, total revenue less total cost is $_____.

   f. Total variable cost is $_____; thus, the firm's total revenue covers all of variable cost, leaving approximately $_____ to apply to fixed costs.

   g. If price falls to $2 the firm will produce _____ units. Why?

FIGURE E.7.1

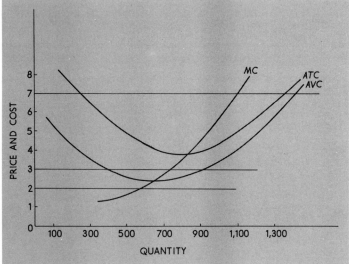

3. Draw precisely and label the following curves:
       Long-run average cost.

Long-run marginal cost.

Short-run average cost.

Short-run marginal cost.

Let the relevant short-run be for optimal production at an output greater than that of minimum long-run average cost.

The firm is a perfect competitor making short-run profits. It could, however, increase profits (maximize profits) by decreasing plant size.

a. Show the current output price and profit.

b. Show the profit that could have been earned and the optimal output if at the same price the firm was in long-run equilibrium.

c. Show price and output of this firm after the industry goes into long-run equilibrium.

d. Explain how this long-run competitive equilibrium situation is attained.

4. The supply of labor to all firms in a perfectly competitive industry is reduced. Explain the effects on the wage rate, the quantity of labor employed, total industry supply of the commodity produced, and the price of the product.

5. Is the long-run supply curve of a competitive industry more or less elastic if the industry as a whole has some effect on the prices of some inputs than if it has none? Consider the short run and the long run and explain why.

6. Explain how a perfectly competitive industry can have a horizontal (perfectly elastic) supply curve for its product when each firm in the industry is subject to increasing costs.

7. If price falls below average total cost in the short run, the firm in the long run will do one of two things. What are these and under what circumstances will each be done?

8. Figure E.7.2 shows a graph of a perfectly competitive firm's short-run cost structure.

a. Label the three curves.

FIGURE E.7.2

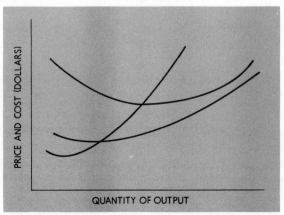

PRICE AND COST (DOLLARS)

QUANTITY OF OUTPUT

b. Show a price at which the firm would make a pure profit. Show the quantity it would produce at this price and the amount of pure profit earned.

c. Show a price at which the firm would continue to produce in the short run but would suffer losses. Show the output and losses at this price.

d. Show the price below which the firm would not produce in the short run.

9. The marginal revenue of a firm operating under perfect competition is $5.00. The elasticity of marginal cost (supply) in the neighborhood of equilibrium is .25. What is selling price?

10. Show that a perfectly competitive firm would never produce an output at which marginal cost is falling. Hint: Begin where $P = MC$ and examine what happens when one more unit of output is produced.

ANALYTICAL PROBLEMS

1. Insurance agents receive a commission on the policies they sell. The recent state hearings on insurance rates in Texas were attended by agents from all over the state. Would higher or lower rates raise the income of agents? Distinguish between the short-run and the long-run effects.

2. You are an executive in a rather large firm that manufactures farm machinery. Your firm is a large user of tires. If there are economies of scale in tire production would you recommend your firm to buy tires from outside sources or to make its own? Explain.

3. There is a drought now in California. What businesses would you expect to suffer? What businesses might prosper?

4. You are advising a prospective entrepreneur who has $100,000 to invest. It could be invested in a manufacturing plant in which the going rate of return is 20 percent. The person's highest alternative salary is $8,000 per year. The individual could earn a return of $5,500 a year from investing the $100,000 in another company. What would this person's yearly *pure profit* be if the choice was to invest the $100,000 in the manufacturing plant and run it himself?

5. Some cities license taxi cabs. The cities also fix the rate that taxis may charge. If after several years no new licenses are issued, an "unofficial" market for licenses generally arises.

a. Discuss the factors that determine the price of a license.

b. Would a change in the allowed fare raise or lower the price of a license?

c. Who would benefit and who would lose from an expansion in the number of licenses issued by the city?

6. Assume that the peanut industry is a constant-cost industry. Let society's demand for peanuts increase. Explain precisely the steps that must be taken for society to have more peanuts at the same price. Suppose that government becomes alarmed at the first sign of rising peanut prices and imposes a ceiling price on peanuts at the original level. What will occur now? Explain. What will happen if the peanut industry is an increasing cost industry?

7. I recently served on a citizen's planning commission for the city in which I live. This ad hoc committee was set up to advise the city council on possible projects for the city in the next five years. One of the suggestions made was to encourage businesses to locate in the northwest side of the city. This is incidentally one of the less wealthy sections of the city.

   a. Why are businesses not now locating on the northwest side of the city?

   b. Aside from actions by the city council, what would encourage businesses to locate there?

   c. How could the city council encourage businesses to locate on the northwest side of the city? What businesses might object?

8. The downtown portion of the city is also deteriorating as the base of the population moves away from downtown. A professor at our university—not an economist, incidentally—was quoted as saying that downtown businesses should voluntarily remodel and they should voluntarily stop moving to the suburbs in order to stop the downtown deterioration for the good of the city.

   a. How would you answer this professor?

   b. Why are downtown businesses moving to the suburbs?

   c. When will the movement of businesses from downtown to the suburbs cease?

   d. Is the movement optimal? Can you even answer this final part of the question?

9. "Economists are silly to say that profits are competed away in the long run. No firm would operate unless it made profits." Explain.

8

Theory of price
under pure monopoly

8.1 INTRODUCTION

"Perfect competition" provides the economist with a very useful analytical model, even though the exacting conditions of the model never hold entirely in the real world. The same statement in large measure applies to the model of pure monopoly, to which we now turn. The conditions of the model are exacting; and it is difficult, if not impossible, to pinpoint a pure monopolist in real-world markets. On the other hand, many markets closely approximate monopoly organization, and monopoly analysis often explains observed business behavior quite well.

A pure monopoly exists if there is only *one firm* that produces and sells a particular commodity or service. Since the monopoly is the only seller in the market, it has neither rivals nor direct competitors. Furthermore, no other sellers can enter the market, or else a monopoly would not exist. Yet, as we shall see, monopoly does not necessarily guarantee success; it only guarantees that the monopolist can make the best of whatever demand and cost conditions exist without fear of new firms entering the market and competing away any profits.

While pure monopolists have no *direct competitors* who sell the same product, they do have *indirect competition*. In the first place, all commodities compete for a place in the consumer's budget. Thus, to a certain extent, the monopolist's product competes with all other goods and services in the general struggle for the consumer's dollar. Some goods, however, are closer substitutes for the monopolist's product than others. While there are no perfect or nearly perfect substitutes for a monopoly product (otherwise a monopoly would not exist), a second source of indirect competition lies in the existence of imperfect substitutes.

For example, American Telephone and Telegraph almost has a monopoly in providing long-distance telephone service in the United States. However, there are various substitutes that can be used: mail, messengers, personal visits, smoke signals. When the Aluminum Company of America (Alcoa) was the only manufacturer of aluminum (prior to World War II), it had no direct competitors, but it did have competition from producers of other metals that were imperfect substitutes. Until recently, International Nickel has been in a similar situation. Gas is a fairly good substitute for electricity (usually a regional monopoly) in many cases. Any real-world monopolist, therefore, has competition to a greater or lesser degree, which in some measure tends to weaken the monopolist's position. There are, however, no other producers of the monopolist's specific product in the market.

To summarize:

Definition. A pure monopoly exists when there is only one producer in a market. There are no direct competitors or rivals in either the popular or technical sense. However, the policies of a monopolist may be constrained by the indirect competition of all commodities for the consumer's dollar and by reasonably adequate substitute goods.

8.1.a Monopoly and profit maximization

The theory of monopoly is relatively simple; it follows directly from the theory set forth in the introduction to Chapter 7. As was the case for the competitive firm, we assume that the monopolist wishes to maximize profit under the given cost and demand conditions. As you know from the preceding analysis, any firm can increase profit by expanding output so long as marginal revenue from the expansion exceeds marginal cost. The firm would not expand if marginal revenue is less than marginal cost. The basic principle that profit is maximized by producing and selling the output at which marginal cost equals marginal revenue is the same for the monopoly as for the competitive firm.

The fundamental difference is that for the monopolist the marginal revenue for additional units sold is less than the price at which these units sell. Unlike the competitor, the monopoly cannot sell all it desires to sell at the going market price. Since a monopolist is the only firm selling in the market, the market demand *is* the demand curve facing the monopolist. While additional sales by a competitive firm do not lower the market price, a monopoly firm can sell more only by lowering price. Therefore, the marginal revenue from additional units sold is the price of those units less the *reduction* in the price of those units that could have been sold at the higher price. We will analyze this point in more detail in the next section. But let us reemphasize, the basic principle of profit maximization is the same for the monopoly as for the competitive firm: *profit is maximized at the output at which marginal revenue equals marginal cost.*

8.1.b Important points developed

The basic concepts to be learned in this chapter are

1. How equilibrium price and output are determined for a monopoly in the short run and the long run.
2. Why a monopolist has no supply curve.
3. How to determine the social cost of monopoly.
4. The conditions under which a monopolist would charge different prices for the same commodity.
5. Principles of monopoly regulation.

8.2 DEMAND AND MARGINAL REVENUE UNDER MONOPOLY

As we noted in the introduction the fundamental difference between a monopolist and a competitor is the demand and marginal revenue curves that they face. Let us use a numerical example to show the relation between demand and marginal revenue for a monopoly. Suppose a firm has the demand schedule shown in columns 1 and 2 of Table 8.2.1. Price times quantity gives the total revenue obtainable from each level of sales. Marginal revenue in column 4 shows the change in total revenue from an additional unit of sales. The only time marginal revenue equals price is for the first unit sold. That is, at zero sales total revenue is zero; for the first unit sold total revenue is the demand price for one unit. Thus, the change in total revenue is the same as price. Since the monopolist must reduce price to sell additional units, at every other level of output, marginal revenue is less than price.

As you will recall from Chapter 6, when average cost decreases, marginal cost is less than average cost. Similarly, since average revenue (price) decreases over the entire range of outputs, marginal revenue is less than average revenue over this range.

Since marginal revenue is the addition to total revenue attributable to an additional unit of sales, total revenue at any level of sales is the summation of all marginal revenues up to that level. This relation is illustrated in column 5 of Table 8.2.1. Also, Table 8.2.1 shows that marginal revenue can be positive or negative, or even zero if output is sufficiently divisible.

Relations. Marginal revenue is the addition to total revenue attributable to the addition of one unit of output to sales per period of time. After the first unit sold, marginal revenue is less than price.

Figure 8.2.1 illustrates the relations between demand, marginal revenue, and total revenue for a monopolist with a linear demand curve. In panels A and B the scales of the vertical axes differ but the horizontal axes have the same scale. Total revenue (panel A) first increases when price is reduced and sales expand; it reaches a maximum at Ox_0 and declines thereafter. Panel B indicates the relations between marginal revenue (MR) and demand. As mentioned above, MR is below price at every output level except the first (since we have assumed continuous data, the two are equal infinitesimally close to the vertical axis). Also, since demand is negatively sloped, MR is, as well. Finally, when TR reaches its maximum, MR is zero (at output Ox_0, price Op_0). At greater rates of output MR is negative. These relations are clearly indicated

TABLE 8.2.1

MONOPOLY DEMAND AND MARGINAL REVENUE

(1) Units of sales	(2) Price	(3) Total revenue	(4) Marginal revenue	(5) Sum of MR entries
1........	$2.00	$2.00	$2.00	$2.00
2........	1.80	3.60	1.60	3.60
3........	1.40	4.20	0.60	4.20
4........	1.20	4.80	0.40	4.80
5........	1.00	5.00	0.20	5.00
6........	0.70	4.20	−0.80	4.20

FIGURE 8.2.1

TOTAL REVENUE, MARGINAL REVENUE, DEMAND

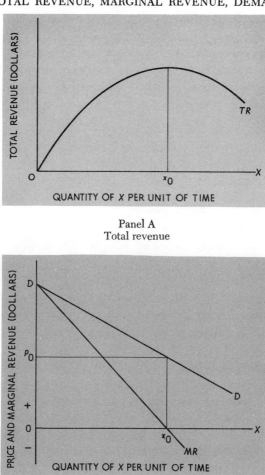

Panel A
Total revenue

Panel B
Demand and marginal revenue

when we consider the characteristics of marginal revenue: if TR increases, an additional unit of sales per period adds a positive amount to revenue; hence MR is positive. The opposite holds for a decrease in TR.

We can be more specific about the relations between marginal revenue and demand. We will set forth these relations without proof.[1]

---

[1] Geometric proofs of all the relations are available in C. E. Ferguson and J. P. Gould, *Microeconomic Theory*, 4th ed. (Homewood, Ill.: Richard D. Irwin, 1975), chap. 4.

First, when demand is linear, the relation to marginal revenue is shown in Figure 8.2.2. If DD' is demand, marginal revenue, shown as DM, is a straight line lying exactly half the distance between the vertical axis and the demand curve. Thus the distance PE equals the distance ER. Furthermore, at any quantity, say, OQ, the amount by which price exceeds marginal revenue, RN, is exactly the distance between price and the vertical intercept, D. Thus $DP = RN$. Finally the absolute value of the slope of MR is exactly double the absolute value of the slope of demand.

FIGURE 8.2.2

DERIVATION OF MARGINAL REVENUE
WHEN DEMAND IS LINEAR

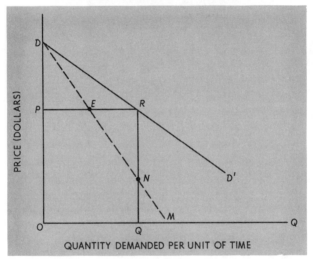

QUANTITY DEMANDED PER UNIT OF TIME

When demand is concave from above, as in Figure 8.2.3, panel A, the marginal revenue curve is concave from above also and lies less than halfway from the vertical axis to demand. When demand is concave from below, as in panel B, marginal revenue is concave from below also and lies more than halfway from the vertical axis to demand.

Finally, the relation between marginal revenue and price at any quantity can be expressed more precisely as

$$MR = P\left(1 - \frac{1}{E}\right),$$

where E is the absolute value of demand elasticity at this quantity. From this equation it is apparent that when marginal revenue is negative, de-

FIGURE 8.2.3

RELATION OF MARGINAL REVENUE
TO NONLINEAR DEMAND

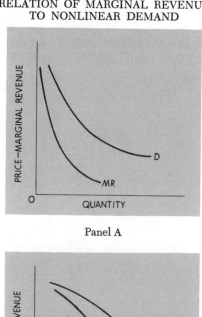

Panel A

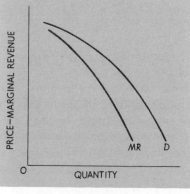

Panel B

mand is inelastic $(E < 1)$. When marginal revenue is positive, demand is elastic $(E > 1)$. Finally, when marginal revenue is zero, demand has unitary elasticity $(E = 1)$.

The relation between positive or negative marginal revenue and the elasticity of the demand curve is intuitively apparent. As you will recall from Chapter 2, changes in total expenditure are related to demand elasticity. When demand is elastic, an increase in quantity (decrease in price) causes an increase in total expenditure. Over an inelastic segment of demand, an increase in quantity occasions a decrease in total expenditure, while in the unitary portion, total expenditure remains unchanged. Since total consumer expenditure on a commodity is the same as the

TABLE 8.2.2

RELATIONS AMONG MARGINAL REVENUE, ELASTICITY,
AND CHANGES IN TOTAL REVENUE

	1	2	3
Marginal revenue	Positive	Negative	Zero
Demand elasticity	Elastic	Inelastic	Unitary
Change in total revenue for an increase in quantity	Increase	Decrease	No change

monopolist's total revenue, the relation of elasticity to marginal revenue follows directly from the above relations. If marginal revenue is positive (negative), a unit increase in sales leads to an increase (decrease) in total revenue. If marginal revenue is zero, a unit change in sales does not change total revenue. Therefore, a positive (negative) marginal revenue indicates that demand is elastic (inelastic) at that quantity. Zero marginal revenue means unitary elasticity. These relations are summarized in Table 8.2.2. They can be seen also in Figure 8.2.4, which shows a straight-line demand curve.

Relations. When demand is negatively sloped, marginal revenue is negatively sloped and is less than price at all relevant quantities. The difference between marginal revenue and price depends upon the price elasticity of demand as shown by the formula $MR = p(1 - 1/E)$. Total revenue increases at first, reaches a maximum, and declines thereafter. The maximum point on the total revenue curve is

FIGURE 8.2.4

RELATIONS AMONG MARGINAL REVENUE,
ELASTICITY, AND DEMAND

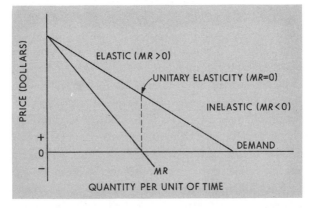

attained at precisely that rate of output and sales for which marginal revenue is zero and elasticity is unitary.

EXERCISE

A computation

Show that $MR = P\left(1 - \dfrac{1}{E}\right)$ for the following demand schedule:

Price	Output
$10..........	1,000
8..........	1,500

For P use the average price of $9. Use the averaging formula for elasticity.

$$E = \frac{\Delta Q/Q}{\Delta P/P} = \left[\frac{\dfrac{Q_1 - Q_2}{(Q_1 + Q_2)/2}}{\dfrac{P_1 - P_2}{(P_1 + P_2)/2}}\right]$$

8.3 SHORT-RUN EQUILIBRIUM UNDER MONOPOLY

Monopoly analysis is based upon two of the important assumptions discussed in the theory of perfect competition: (1) the firm attempts to maximize profit, and (2) the firm operates in an environment free from outside control. Though certain other assumptions differ to some extent, as we have noted, the profit-maximizing conditions are similar. We have already examined demand and marginal revenue conditions under monopoly. We will now analyze short-run cost conditions under monopoly, then discuss in more detail short-run equilibrium.

8.3.a Cost under monopoly

Short-run cost conditions confronting a monopolist are essentially similar to those faced by a perfectly competitive firm. The theory of cost follows directly from the theory developed in Chapter 6. Cost depends upon the production function and input prices. The chief difference for a monopolist lies in the potential impact of output changes on factor prices.

In the theory of perfect competition we assume that each firm is very small relative to the total factor market and can therefore change *its own* rate of output without affecting factor prices, just as any one consumer can change the amount of a good purchased without affecting its price.

But recall that if *all firms* in the industry change output and therefore the use of all inputs, the prices of some of those inputs may change, unless of course the industry is a constant-cost industry. The output of the monopolist, the sole firm in the industry, is accordingly the output of the industry. Certainly a monopolist, just as a competitive industry, may be so small relative to the demand for all inputs that its input use will have no effect on the price of any input. To be sure, even a very large monopolist will purchase some inputs (such as unskilled labor) the prices of which are not affected by the monopolist's rate of use.

On the other hand, there is a good probability that a monopoly will purchase certain inputs for which the firm's rate of purchase will have a definite effect on the prices of these factors of production. One would think that in many cases factor prices will vary with the monopolist's rate of use.

Notwithstanding the monopolist's possible effect upon factor prices, the cost curves are assumed to have the same general shape as those described in Chapter 6. The primary implication of rising supply prices of variable inputs is that the average and marginal cost curves rise more rapidly or fall less rapidly than if the input supply prices were constant. Thus, for example, marginal cost may rise not only because of diminishing marginal productivity but also because input prices rise with increased use.

8.3.b Short-run equilibrium

A monopolist, just as a perfect competitor, attains maximum profit (or minimum loss) by producing and selling at that rate of output for which the positive (negative) difference between total revenue and total cost is greatest (least). This condition occurs when marginal revenue equals marginal cost (even though for the monopolist MR does not equal price).

Figure 8.3.1 depicts the marginal cost and marginal revenue curves of a monopolist. Maximum profit or minimum loss occurs at output Ox_0, where MC equals MR. At any lower output, for example Ox_1, the monopolist can gain additional profit or can reduce losses by producing and selling an additional unit per period of time. Since MR exceeds MC at Ox_1, the added revenue from the sale of another unit per period is greater than the additional cost of producing it. The firm therefore pro-

FIGURE 8.3.1

MC = MR FOR PROFIT MAXIMIZATION

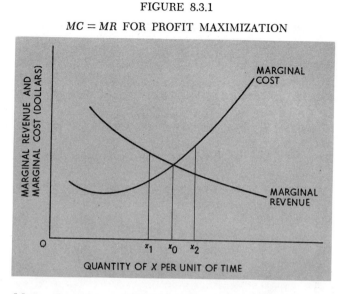

duces additional units until *MR* equals *MC*. Likewise, it would not produce more than Ox_0, for example Ox_2, since at larger outputs the marginal cost of producing another unit per period is greater than the marginal revenue gained from selling it. Thus producing more or less than Ox_0 causes profit (loss) to diminish (increase).

Using the proposition just established, the position of short-run equilibrium is easily described. Figure 8.3.2 shows the relevant cost and revenue curves for a monopolist. Since *AVC* and *AFC* are not necessary for exposition, they are omitted. The profit maximizer produces at *E* where *MC* = *MR*. Output is *Ox*, and from the demand curve we see that price must be *Op* per unit in order to ration the *Ox* units among those who wish to buy the commodity. Total revenue is *Op* × *Ox*, or the area of the rectangle *OpBx*. The unit cost of producing this amount is *Oc*. Total cost is *Oc* × *Ox*, or the area *OcDx*. Profit is *TR* − *TC*, or the shaded area *cpBD*.

In the example of Figure 8.3.2, the monopolist earns a pure profit in the short run. This need not be the case, however; a monopolistic position does not assure profit. If demand is sufficiently low, a monopolist may incur a loss in the short run, just as a pure competitor may. For example, Figure 8.3.3 shows a loss situation. Marginal cost equals marginal revenue at output *Ox*, which can be sold at price *Op*. Average cost is *Oc*. Total cost, *OcDx* exceeds total revenue *OpBx*; hence the firm makes a loss of *pcDB*.

FIGURE 8.3.2

SHORT-RUN EQUILIBRIUM UNDER MONOPOLY

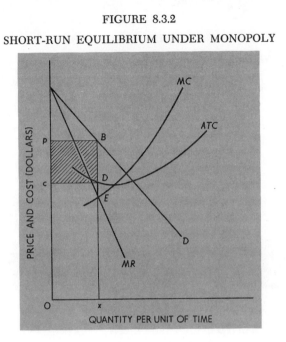

Note that the monopolist would produce rather than shut down in the short run, since revenue exceeds variable cost ($OvNx$); there is still some revenue ($vpBN$) left to apply to fixed cost. If demand decreases so that the monopolist cannot cover all of variable cost at any price, the firm would shut down and lose only fixed cost. This situation is analogous to that of the perfect competitor.

To understand why a monopolist does not have a supply curve, recall the definition of supply: a list of prices and the quantities that would be supplied at each price in the list per period of time. But, for a monopolist any number of prices may be associated with a given level of output, depending upon the position of demand at that output level. In other words the price of a given output depends on the position of demand at that output; an infinite number of prices can be associated with one level of output.

To illustrate this point, assume first that demand and the associated marginal revenue are $\overline{D}$ and $\overline{MR}$ in Figure 8.3.4. (Recall that, for a straight-line demand curve such as this, marginal revenue lies exactly halfway between the vertical axis and demand.) In this case $\overline{MR}$ equals MC at output Q and price is $\bar{p}$. Next, let marginal revenue and demand be $\widehat{MR}$ and $\hat{D}$. While marginal revenue again equals marginal cost at Q,

FIGURE 8.3.3

SHORT-RUN LOSSES UNDER MONOPOLY

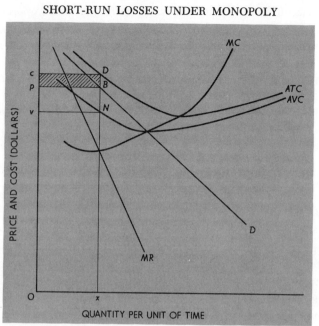

QUANTITY PER UNIT OF TIME

in this situation commodity price is $\hat{p}$. By changing the slope of the demand and therefore MR curves, the same output, Q, can be sold at an infinite number of prices. Thus the monopolist has no supply curve.

In the short run the primary difference between monopoly and a per-

FIGURE 8.3.4

WHY A MONOPOLY HAS NO SUPPLY CURVE

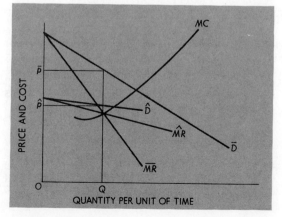

QUANTITY PER UNIT OF TIME

fect competitor lies in the slope of the demand curve. Either may earn a pure profit; either may incur a loss. Of course, another important differerence is that the monopolist who earns pure profit need not worry about new firms entering the industry and competing away profits.

Principles. If a monopoly produces a positive output, it maximizes profit or minimizes losses by producing the quantity for which $MC = MR$. Since the monopolist's demand is above MR at every positive output, equilibrium price exceeds MC.

8.3.c Numerical illustration

A numerical example can illustrate the principal points of this section. In Table 8.3.1 the demand schedule in columns 1 and 2 yields the total revenue schedule in column 3. We can simply subtract the total cost of producing each relevant level of sales from total revenue to obtain the profit from that output. Examination of the profit column shows that maximum profit ($4.50) occurs at 50 units of output. Marginal revenue and marginal cost, given in columns 5 and 6 give the same result. The monopolist can increase profit by increasing sales so long as marginal revenue exceeds marginal cost. If marginal cost exceeds marginal revenue, profit falls with increased sales. Hence, the monopolist produces and sells 50 units, the level at which marginal cost and marginal revenue are equal.

TABLE 8.3.1

MARGINAL REVENUE-MARGINAL COST APPROACH TO
PROFIT MAXIMIZATION

(1) Output and sales	(2) Price	(3) Total revenue	(4) Total cost	(5) Marginal revenue	(6) Marginal cost	(7) Profit
5.....	$2.00	$10.00	$12.25	—	$0.45	$—2.25
13.....	1.10	14.30	15.00	$0.54	.34	—0.70
23.....	0.85	19.55	18.25	.52	.33	+1.30
38.....	.69	25.92	22.00	.42	.25	+3.92
50.....	.615	30.75	26.25	.35	.35	+4.50
60.....	.55	33.00	31.00	.23	.48	+2.00
68.....	.50	34.00	36.25	.13	.66	—2.25
75.....	.45	33.75	42.00	—.03	.82	—8.25
81.....	.40	32.40	48.25	—.23	1.04	—15.85
86.....	.35	30.10	55.00	—.46	1.35	—25.10

ASIDE

Some evidence concerning changes in monopoly power in the United States

One hears a considerable amount of talk concerning the increasing monopolization of industry in the United States. We frequently read that industry, particularly manufacturing, is becoming more and more monopolistic. The available evidence, however, shows that this simply is not so.

If we use the strict theoretical definition of monopoly—the single seller of a greatly differentiated product—monopoly is practically nonexistent. This definition is never used in statistical estimation. Most empirical studies have used the four-firm concentration ratio as a proxy for monopoly. The four-firm concentration ratio is the percentage of the output of a well-defined industry produced by the four largest firms in the industry.

We should note that those types of industries in which the output is produced by a few firms are called oligopolies, not monopolies. Oligopoly is part of the subject matter of the next chapter, thus the evidence about four-firm concentration ratios possibly belongs in that chapter rather than in this chapter on monopoly. However, since empirical studies on the subject traditionally stress the "monopolization" of industry rather than "oligopolization," we include the evidence in this chapter.

One widely cited study analyzed the change in industrial concentration from the turn of the century to 1937.* This study defined as monopolistic those industries in which the largest four firms had 50 percent or more of the total sales. In 1899, 17.4 percent of national income originated in monopolistic industries. Using one definition, by 1937 this percentage declined to 15 percent. Another definition showed a small increase, but the average of the two showed a decline in the percent of national income originating in monopolistic industries.

Using only data for manufacturing it was found that under one definition monopoly increased slightly while under another it decreased a little. In any case there was no substantial increase over this period.

Neither has there been much hard evidence that the extent of monopoly has increased more recently. In a *Fortune* article appearing in 1969 the results of four studies were shown. These four studies

---

* G. Warren Nutter, *The Extent of Enterprise Monopoly in the United States, 1899–1939* (University of Chicago Press, 1951).

FOUR CONCENTRATION STUDIES
(average 4-firm concentration ratio*)

Study	1947	1954	1958	1963	1966
1........	43	46	46	46	
2........	41	41	40	41	
3........	36	37	36	37	
4........	41.2	40.6	40.2	41.4	41.9

* Differences attributable to sampling difference and weighting procedure.

showed little or no increase in the average four-firm concentration ratio from 1947 through 1963.†

A more recent study shows a slight but probably insignificant increase in average industrial concentration in manufacturing in the United States from 1947 to 1972.‡ In that paper the change in concentration from the year in which three of the *Fortune* studies ended (1963) to 1972 was a slight 0.6 percent.

We should note that this insignificant change in the average does not mean that monopolization cannot be a problem. The 1947—72 study showed that while the average changed scarcely at all, concentration increased significantly in some industries while it declined substantially in others. Thus some industries could present a problem. On the other hand we should note also that mere numbers and size alone do not always indicate monopoly power. Over this century we have seen a decline in the number of banks. But, consumers have access to many more banks. If you were a borrower in a small town around 1900 you probably had available to you only one bank in the town. Now, that small town may not have a bank at all. But consumers are probably within easy driving distance of many large banks. There are other such examples as well.

---

† Sanford Rose, "Bigness Is a Numbers Game," *Fortune,* November 1969.

‡ See Bruce T. Allen, "Average Concentration in Manufacturing 1947–1972," *Journal of Economic Issues,* September 1976, pp. 664–73.

8.4 LONG-RUN EQUILIBRIUM UNDER MONOPOLY

A monopoly exists if there is only one firm in the market. Among other things this statement implies that "entrance" into the market is closed. Thus whether or not a monopolist earns a pure profit in the short run, no other producer can enter the market in the hope of sharing whatever pure profit potential exists. Therefore, pure economic profit is not eliminated in the long run, as in the case of perfect competition. The monopolist will, however, make adjustments in plant size as demand conditions warrant them, even though entry is prohibited.

A monopolist faced with the cost and revenue conditions depicted in Figure 8.4.1 would build a plant to produce the quantity at which long-run marginal cost equals marginal revenue. In each period Ox units are produced, costing Oc per unit and selling at a price of Op per unit. Long-run profit is $cpBE$. By the now familiar argument, this is the maximum profit possible under the given revenue and cost conditions. The monopoly operates in the short run with plant size indicated by SAC_1 and SMC_1. New entrants cannot come into the industry and compete away profits.

But demand or cost conditions can change for reasons other than the entry of new firms; and such changes cause the monopolist to make adjustments. Assume that demand and marginal revenue change. At first the firm will adjust without changing plant size. It will produce the quantity at which the new MR equals SMC_1, or it will close down in the short run if it cannot cover variable costs. In the long run the monopolist can change plant size.

Long-run equilibrium adjustment under monopoly must take one of two possible courses. First, if the monopolist incurs a short-run loss, and if there is no plant size that will result in pure profit (or at least, no loss), the monopoly goes out of business. Second, if it suffers a short-run loss

FIGURE 8.4.1

LONG-RUN EQUILIBRIUM UNDER MONOPOLY

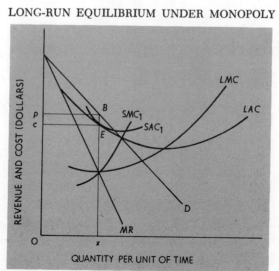

or earns a short-run profit with the original plant, the entrepreneur must determine whether a plant of different size (and thus a different price and output) will enable him to earn a larger profit.

The first situation requires no comment. The second is illustrated by Figure 8.4.2. DD' and MR show the market demand and marginal revenue confronting a monopolist. LAC is the long-run average cost curve, and LMC is the associated long-run marginal cost curve. Suppose in the initial period the monopolist built the plant exemplified by SAC_1 and SMC_1. Equality of short-run marginal cost and marginal revenue leads to the sale of $O\bar{x}_{SR}$ units per period at the price OA. At this rate of output unit cost is OD; short-run monopoly profit is represented by the area of the shaded rectangle $ABCD$.

Since a pure economic profit can be reaped, the monopolist would not consider discontinuing production. But now the long-run marginal cost becomes the relevant consideration. The long-run profit-maximum is attained when long-run marginal cost equals marginal revenue. The associated rate of output is $O\bar{x}_{LR}$, and price is OE.

By reference to LAC, the plant capable of producing $O\bar{x}_{LR}$ units per period at the least unit cost is the one represented by SAC_2 and SMC_2. Unit cost is accordingly OH, and long-run maximum monopoly profit is

FIGURE 8.4.2

CHANGE IN LONG-RUN EQUILIBRIUM FOR A MONOPOLIST

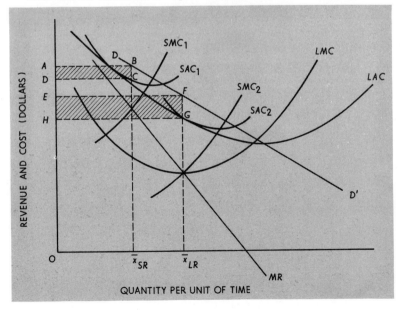

given by the area of the shaded rectangle *EFGH*. This profit is obviously (visually) greater than the profit obtainable from the original plant.

Generalizing, we have the following:

Proposition. A monopolist maximizes profit in the long run by producing and marketing that rate of output for which long-run marginal cost equals marginal revenue. The optimal plant is the one whose short-run average cost curve is tangent to the long-run average cost curve at the point corresponding to long-run equilibrium output. At this point short-run marginal cost equals marginal revenue.

The organization described by the proposition above is the best the monopolist can attain; and it *can* be attained because in the long run plant size is variable and the market is effectively closed to entry.

APPLICATION

Analysis of effects of divestiture

An important question now being hotly debated is the issue of divestiture of some of the major oil companies. Some people (for example, certain congressmen), allege that one of the problems of the oil industry is that some of the major oil companies have a large share of the market at more than one phase of the production process. Exxon, for example, owns refineries and also owns or leases service stations. Moreover, these critics suggest that certain firms with a large share of the refinery market are in the drilling phase also and are attempting to obtain a larger share of the pumping phase.

Proponents of divestiture argue that if a company with a large share of the market in one phase of the production process has a large share of the market in another, price will be higher, output lower, and profits greater. In the extreme, they argue that if a company has a monopoly in one phase, say refining, and then monopolizes another phase, say pumping, which had previously been competitive, this vertical integration will increase the price of the final product, decrease the output, and increase the profit of the firm that previously had the monopoly in the refining phase. Let us use some of the tools we have developed in this and the preceding chapter to analyze the situation. What would be the effect of forcing a company with a large share of the market in one phase of the production process to divest itself of its holdings in another phase?

For analytical simplicity, let us make the following assumptions.

First assume that there are only two phases of production, refining and final sales or pumping. Assume that if either phase is operated competitively the industry would be a constant-cost industry and the long-run industry supply would be a horizontal line (recall the discussion of constant-cost industries in Chapter 7). Finally assume that if either phase of the process is monopolized—taken over by one company—this horizontal line would be the monopoly's long-run average cost curve. Since long-run average cost is constant (a horizontal line), average cost equals marginal cost in the long run.

Figure 8.4.3 shows the situation graphically. The long-run average cost of the pumping industry, excluding the cost of gasoline from the refinery, is shown as AC_p. This would be long-run supply less the cost of gasoline, if the pumping industry is competitive. If the pumping industry is a monopoly, the average cost of pumping, OG, is constant and OG equals marginal cost as well; in other words $AC_p = MC_p$ is a horizontal line at OG.

Moreover, refining is a constant-cost competitive industry, and long-run industry supply is AC_R. If the refining industry is monopolized, OR is the constant long-run average cost, which equals marginal cost; that is $AC_R = MC_R$. Let DD_g be the final demand for gasoline and let a gallon of gasoline from the refinery equal a gallon sold at the pump. Thus there is fixed-proportions production.

Assume first that each phase of production is organized competitively and transportation costs are zero. Thus, in the long-run

FIGURE 8.4.3

MONOPOLY IN THE GASOLINE MARKET

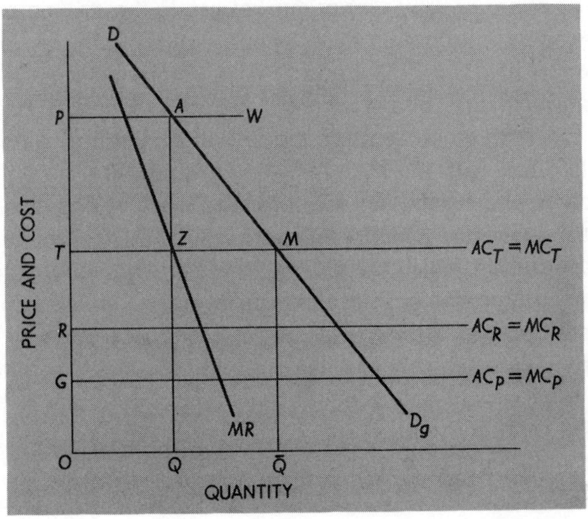

the supply at the retail or pumping phase will be $OG + OR = OT$. Demand equals supply, AC_T, at point M; price is OT (average total cost) and output is $O\overline{Q}$.

Next, let both phases of production be taken over by a monopolist. If there are no economies of integration, that is, no reduction in cost from having one firm control both phases of production, the monopolist's marginal cost is the line $AC_T = MC_T$. Marginal revenue equals marginal cost at Z. Price rises to OP, and output falls to OQ, the output at which profits are maximized. These maximum profits are shown as the area $TPAZ$.

Next, let the refining phase be competitive while the pumping phase remains under control of the monopolist. Cost conditions remain the same. Since the refining industry is competitive, the price of gasoline to the monopolist in pumping is OR. Marginal cost is, therefore, the same as before, $OG + OR = OT = MR_T$. Since marginal revenue and marginal cost are unchanged, equilibrium price and output remain at OP and OQ, and profit is unchanged ($TPAZ$).

Finally, consider the case in which the monopolist controls the refining phase of production, but the pumping phase is competitive. Now, if gasoline were free from the refining phase to the pumping phase, long-run gasoline supply would be AC_p and final price would be OG. But the refining monopoly can cause the long-run supply in the final, or pumping, phase to be any horizontal straight line desired, simply by setting the price of gasoline from the refineries to the stations.

Clearly, it would charge a price above OR, or the total refining costs would not be covered. What would be the price that maximizes the profits of the refining monopoly? We know that the maximum profit possible when one firm controls both phases of production is represented by the area $TPAZ$. If the refinery monopolist imposes on the pumping industry a price that equals $(OP - OG) = GP$, the long-run supply price of the pumping industry will be $OG + GP$, or the horizontal line PW. In this case the demand for gasoline equals long-run supply at A. Price is OP and output is OQ. The refinery profit is $(OP - OG - OR)$ times OQ; or the area (TP times OQ) equals $TPAZ$. Thus in this case, final price, final output, and monopoly profit are the same as when the monopolist controls both phases of production. Any price charged by the refinery to the pumping industry greater or less than PG would result in a final price greater or less than OP. In either case profit is less than the maximum profit $TPAZ$.

Thus, under these assumptions, a monopoly at either phase of production, when the other phase is competitive, leads to the same equilibrium price, output, and profit that would result if the monopoly owned or controled both phases. In other words, nothing changes if the monopoly is forced to give up one phase or the other in the production process, and that phase then becomes competitive. Moreover, if there are more than two phases, a monopoly at any one phase can extract all of the profit it could gain if it controlled all phases, if all other phases are competitive.

This analysis is not to imply that if both phases are competitive, price might not be lower. This may or may not be the case, depending upon the cost structure of the industry. The analysis simply shows that divestiture would not lower gasoline prices under the above assumptions. Furthermore, we have analyzed the situations under the assumption of fixed proportions, a gallon of gasoline at the refinery becomes a gallon at the service station, and under the assumption that both phases are constant-cost industries. The assumption of increasing cost in either or both phases does not change the results at all. The assumption of variable proportions does change the solution a little bit but does not change the welfare result much at all.*

The situation would change somewhat if there are possible economies of integration when one firm owns both phases of production. These economies of integration could result because of decreased transaction costs or possibly decreased management costs, causing a higher price after divestiture than would result when both phases are controlled by the same firm. Thus, it may well be that an action designed to lower gasoline prices could raise prices.

---

* For an early analytical treatment of the subject see J. J. Spengler, "Vertical Integration and Antitrust Policy," *Journal of Political Economy,* August 1950, pp. 347–52. For a discussion of the difference made by assuming variable-proportions production and a review of some of the literature, see J. S. McGee and L. R. Basset, "Vertical Integration Revisited," *Journal of Law and Economics,* April 1976, pp. 17–38.

8.5 COST OF MONOPOLY TO SOCIETY

Economists have done extensive research, both theoretical and empirical, into the welfare effect of monopoly with, as yet, no clear, generally accepted results. On the one hand, we frequently hear of the overwhelming power of monopoly in the economy. Others present an opposing point of view that monopoly poses only a very minor social problem. Let us first attempt to compare theoretically the monopoly equilibrium situation with that of perfect competition. We will then present some empirical evidence concerning the welfare cost of monopoly in the United States.

8.5.a Comparison with perfect competition

Most comparisons between the equilibria of monopoly and perfect competition are tenuous. For example, one sometimes hears that price is lower and output greater under perfect competition than under monopoly. This statement is based upon the following analysis. The monopolist depicted in Figure 8.5.1 produces Ox_M per period of time and sells at a price of Op_M. If we can also assume that MC represents competitive supply, supply equals demand at E. The perfectly competitive industry would sell Ox_C (greater than Ox_M) at a price of Op_E (less than Op_M). There is reason to doubt, however, that MC can represent the supply curve of a perfectly competitive industry. As we have seen, competitive supply is not always the sum of the marginal cost curves. Even if this were so, the sum of a large number of firms' marginal cost curves would not necessarily be the marginal cost curve of a single, much larger firm. One can only say that a monopoly is more likely to earn a pure profit because it can effectively exercise some market control.

FIGURE 8.5.1

PRICE AND OUTPUT COMPARISONS

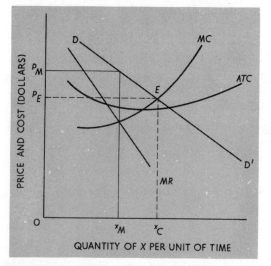

We can also say that in long-run industry equilibrium under perfect competition, production occur at the point of minimum long- and short-run average cost. The monopolist utilizes the plant capable of producing long-run equilibrium output at the least unit cost. Only under the extremely rare circumstances in which marginal revenue intersects marginal cost at minimum long-run average cost would this plant be the one associated with the absolute minimum unit cost. In any case the slightest change in demand would upset this equilibrium.

We should also note that while the perfect competitor produces at the point where marginal cost and price are equal, the monopolist's price *exceeds* marginal cost. Under certain conditions, demand represents the social valuation of the commodity. Similarly, long-run marginal cost, with some exceptions, represents the marginal social cost of production. Under monopoly the marginal value of a commodity to a society exceeds the marginal social cost of its production. Society as a whole would, therefore, benefit by having more of its resources used in producing the commodity in question. The profit-maximizing monopolist will not do this, however, for producing at the point where price equals marginal cost would decrease profit. Alternatively, the perfect competitor in long-run equilibrium produces the quantity at which the marginal social cost of production equals the marginal social valuation, but does so, however, not because of any innate social consciousness but because the market forces this situation.

We should strongly emphasize the very tenuous nature of the comparison of the output-price decisions of a monopolist to the results under perfect competition. These comparisons are based upon extremely rigid assumptions. The most rigid assumption is that the cost structure is such that under competitive conditions the industry supply would be the monopolist's marginal cost. Economies of scale may be such that a large enough number of firms to assure competition would force these firms to operate at a much higher cost than that at which the monopolist produces. This assumption must be recognized when making actual policy recommendations.

8.5.b Consumer surplus and the welfare loss from monopoly

One tool frequently used by economists to measure the cost of monopoly is the concept of consumer surplus. This concept enables economists to establish a value of the consumer losses resulting from having an industry monopolized rather than operated under competitive conditions. Be cautioned again, however, that these comparisons are made under the very rigid assumptions about cost discussed above.

To illustrate the concept of consumer surplus, assume that you would be willing to pay up to $1,000 for a weekend vacation in Bermuda. If the market price for this vacation is $700, the $300 difference between what you must pay and what you are willing to pay is called consumer's surplus. Or, consider the following demand schedule for units of X:

Quantity	Price
400............	$7
600............	5
900............	3
1,500............	1

Now, if a firm is selling a good and if it is able to discriminate, that is segregate the market, to those willing to pay $7 each, it would sell 400 units at $7; to those willing to pay $5, it would sell 200 more units at $5 each, 300 more at $3 each, and so forth, as long as it could make a profit. Alternatively, assume the competitive price is $3. Assume also that the downward-sloping demand is caused by new consumers entering the market. Those willing to pay up to $7 (400 units) save $4 each, and those willing to pay up to $5 rather than do without, save $2 each. The consumer's surplus is $(400 \times \$4 = \$1,600) + (200 \times \$2 = \$400) = \$2,000$.

For a continuous demand curve the consumer's surplus can be represented by Figure 8.5.2. DD' is the demand for the good, Op is the price, Ox is the quantity sold at Op, and the rectangle $Opcx$ is total revenue. The striped area pDc represents consumer's surplus. This is the amount that consumers would pay rather than do without the good, if the sellers could discriminate and sell to each consumer at the *maximum price* each would pay rather than do without.

Definition. Consumer's surplus is the area below a demand curve and above the market price. It is frequently used to measure the welfare gain or loss of a decrease or increase in market price.

Now let us use the concept of consumer's surplus to indicate the loss from monopoly. Assume that DD' in Figure 8.5.3 represents the demand for a particular commodity. The industry is at first a competitive, constant-cost industry. Long-run industry supply is at OR. Thus OR equals marginal cost equals average cost.

Prior to the monopolization of the industry when price was OR, total consumer surplus was the area RDC. After a monopoly is formed and price rises to OP, consumer surplus is shown as PDB. This represents a reduction in consumer surplus shown by the area $RPBC$.

But this reduction in consumer surplus does not entirely represent a

FIGURE 8.5.2

CONSUMER'S SURPLUS

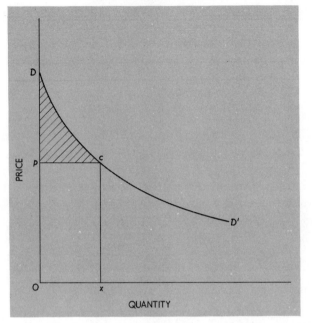

FIGURE 8.5.3

WELFARE LOSS FROM MONOPOLY

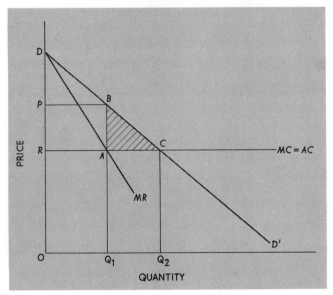

loss to society. The total profit of the monopolist is $RPBA$ (price minus average cost times output). Therefore, this portion of the former consumer surplus is simply a transfer from the consumer to the monopolist, in the form of lost consumer surplus transferred to monopoly profit. The transfer is analogous to the economics of theft. If a thief steals $100 from you, we cannot say that society is worse off. You are $100 worse off; the thief is $100 better off. Unless one is willing to compare utilities, society as a whole is neither better off nor worse off. The theft is simply a transfer of wealth. Thus the reduction of consumer surplus by the area $RPBA$ and the increase in monopoly profit by the same area represent a similar type of transfer. Similarly the area Q_1ACQ_2 represents a transfer of resources from this industry into other segments of the economy.

The welfare loss to society from the monopolization is the lost consumer surplus that is not transferred. This loss is the area of the shaded triangle ABC. If society wishes to retain its consumer surplus by increasing output to OQ_2 and decreasing price to OR, it must transfer resources valued at CAQ_1Q_2 from other industries into this industry. Many economists have asserted that the true welfare cost of monopoly in the economy can be measured by the total welfare loss triangles for all monopolized industries.

APPLICATION

Welfare loss from monopoly in the United States

In 1954 Arnold C. Harberger attempted to measure both the total welfare loss (lost consumer surplus) from all monopoly in the United States, along with the value of the resources that society would have to transfer from monopolized industries to competitive industries in order to make the economy fully competitive—that is, to eliminate all monopoly in the economy.* As in the model presented in this chapter, he assumed constant marginal and average costs, and that those industries with higher than average returns on capital have too few resources, and those yielding lower than average returns have too many. Because of the relative tranquility of the period and the availability of good data, Harberger used the years 1924–28 for his estimation.

Harberger found from his data that $550 million in resources

---

* See Arnold C. Harberger, "The Welfare Loss from Monopoly," *American Economic Review,* May 1954, pp. 77–87. For some additional insights into this question, see F. M. Scherer, *Industrial Market Structure and Economic Performance* (Chicago: Rand McNally, 1971), chap. 17.

would have to have been transferred from low-return to high-return industries to eliminate excess profit during this period. Since only 45 percent of all companies were included in the sample, the estimate was raised to 1.2 billion. This transfer would have involved about 4 percent of all resources in manufacturing, or 1½ percent of total resources.

He then estimated how much better off society would have been had the transfer of resources taken place by reducing monopoly price to average cost and increasing output. This figure would equal the sum of all increases in consumer surplus due to changing monopolies to competition. This is the sum of the areas of all of the welfare loss triangles. The total welfare gain estimated from the resource transfer was $59 million, less than one tenth of 1 percent of national income. In terms of 1954 income this averaged less than $1.50 per person in the United States. When Harberger included certain intangibles in the data, the necessary transfer rose from 1½ percent to 1¾ percent of national income, and the welfare loss rose to $81 million. (We might note that the welfare change does not consider the reallocation of income from the rest of society to the monopoly.)

In all the estimates the total welfare loss came to less than one tenth of one percent of national income, and in most instances, Harberger used assumptions that biased the estimates upward. This extremely low estimate was startling at the time. Aside from the transfer of resources from consumers to monopoly, it appeared that the total welfare cost was quite small.

The estimates did not go unchallenged by other economists. Several economists made similar types of estimates of the welfare cost of monopoly for different industry classifications and for different time periods. Again these estimates of loss were very small. Does this result indicate that if we ignore pure transfers, monopoly has little effect on welfare?

Gordon Tullock added a new insight to the discussion, comparing the welfare loss from monopoly to the economics of theft.[†] While it may be argued that if one person steals $100 from another the theft simply involves transfer of resources, the very *existence* of theft does have a large cost to society even though theft only involves interpersonal wealth transfers. In the first place, potential thieves would invest in resources—time, burglar tools, getaway cars, lookouts—until any additional resources would cost more than the marginal return in stolen assets from using these resources. (Even thieves can use a

---

† See Gordon Tullock, "The Welfare Costs of Monopolies and Theft," *Western Economic Journal*, June 1967, pp. 224–32.

knowledge of economic theory.) Similarly potential victims wish to protect their wealth. A potential victim would invest in preventive resources—watchdogs, locks, guns, etc.—as long as the expected marginal saving from such resources is expected to exceed their marginal cost. Furthermore, the return to resources used in theft depends upon the number of resources used in theft prevention, and vice versa.

In time, society would attain an equilibrium amount of theft, which would probably be positive, since the prevention of all theft would cost too much. But, even though the equilibrium amount of theft involves only transfers, the *existence* of theft costs society considerably. Those resources used to steal and to prevent stealing cost the individuals involved, and they cost society the use of those resources that could be used to produce other products. They are *completely wasted* from society's point of view. They are used only to cause or to prevent transfers of wealth, not to produce wealth.

Society generally attempts to prevent theft collectively. People find that enforcement of laws by courts and police are sometimes technologically more efficient in preventing theft than individual expenditures on resources. To the extent that collective expenditures are more efficient than private, the returns to theft are reduced, which in turn reduces theft. To be sure, public expenditure does not replace all private preventive expenditure. People still buy locks, hire watchmen, and keep dogs. Both the public and the private preventive expenditure costs society those resources used in prevention. The important point is not how societies allocate between public and private prevention but that the existence of theft costs society resources that could be used to produce wealth.

Monopoly involves only a transfer of resources from the public to the monopolists plus an empirically insignificant welfare loss. According to Tullock's analysis, the welfare losses estimated using Harberger's technique underestimate the true welfare loss from monopoly. Because the return from establishing a *successful* monopoly is so great, one would expect potential monopolists to expend considerable resources in attempting to form monopolies. In fact, entrepreneurs should be willing to invest resources in attempts to form monopolies until the marginal cost equals the expected discounted return. After a monopoly is formed, others will invest resources toward trying to break the monopoly, which in turn means that the monopolist must use additional resources trying to prevent the break. Just as successful theft encourages additional theft, successful monopoly encourages additional attempts to monopolize.

As Tullock noted, identifying and measuring the resources used to gain, break, and hold monopoly are quite difficult. But, it appears that a large amount of the very scarce resource, skilled management, is used toward this end. In any case, the welfare triangle measurement ignores this cost and underestimates the social cost of monopoly. The monopoly question is still far from being settled.

EXERCISE

Optimal antitrust activity

Suppose government had rather complete knowledge of the costs and results of governmental antitrust activities. How much antitrust activity would you recommend?

The answer is certainly clear by now. Government would optimally carry out antitrust litigation as long as the marginal cost of additional activity—lawyers, etc.—exceeds the marginal benefit to society from such activity. Government would not wish to spend more to break up a monopoly than the total benefit.

While the suggestion of complete information on the part of antitrust authorities is a bit farfetched, attempts have been and are being made to implement this idea of obtaining better information. In an article that appeared in *Business Week*,‡ there was a discussion of attempts by the FTC to build computer models that could use existing governmental data to locate illegal actvities and to aid the FTC lawyers in setting priorities for prosecution. The data being used are, among other things, concentration ratios, industry growth trends, profit margins, price trends, welfare loss, and many other factors. What other data do you think might be important indicators that an industry is becoming more monopolized?

---

‡ "The FTC Builds a Model Informer," *Business Week*, March 11, 1972, p. 94.

8.6 PRICE DISCRIMINATION UNDER MONOPOLY

Earlier in this chapter we stated that a pure monopoly exists if a commodity has only one seller in a well-defined market. Price discrimination can exist under monopoly if the monopolist is the only seller of a commodity in two or more well-defined, separable markets. Price discrimination means that a monopolist charges different prices for the same commodity in different markets. Price discrimination can occur when a monopolist charges different prices domestically and abroad or perhaps when a doctor charges one fee for an operation to low-income patients and another fee for the same operation to high-income patients.

8.6.a Price discrimination in theory

Certain conditions are necessary for the monopolist to be able to discriminate. First, the markets must be *separable*. If purchasers in the lower-price market are able themselves to sell the commodity to buyers in the higher-price market, discrimination will not exist for long. For example, a lower-price patient cannot resell his operation to a higher-price patient, but a lower-price buyer of some raw material could perhaps resell it to someone in the higher-price market. Discrimination would not be practiced in the latter case. Second, demand elasticities must be different in the different markets.

The analysis of discriminatory pricing is a straightforward application of the $MC = MR$ rule. As a first step in that analysis, let us assume that a monopoly has two separate markets for its product. Demand conditions in each market are such that the marginal revenues from selling specified quantities are as given in Table 8.6.1. Assume also that for some reason the monopoly decides to produce 12 units. How should it allocate sales between the two markets?

Consider the first unit; the firm can gain $45 by selling it in the first market or $34 by selling in the second market. Obviously, if it sells only one unit per period, it will sell it in market I. The second unit per period is

TABLE 8.6.1

ALLOCATION OF SALES BETWEEN
TWO MARKETS

Quantity	Marginal revenue market I		Marginal revenue market II	
1...........	$45	(1)	$34	(3)
2...........	36	(2)	28	(5)
3...........	30	(4)	22	(7)
4...........	22	(6)	13	(10)
5...........	17	(8)	[10]	(12)
6...........	15	(9)	8	
7...........	[10]	(11)	7	
8...........	7		4	
9...........	4		2	
10...........	0		1	

also sold in the first market since its sale there increases revenue by $36, whereas it would only bring $34 in market II. Since $34 can be gained in II but only $30 in I, unit three per period is sold in market II. Similar analysis shows that the fourth unit goes to I and the fifth to II. Since unit six adds $22 to revenue in either market, it makes no difference where it is sold; six and seven go to each market. Eight and nine are sold in I because they yield higher marginal revenue there; ten goes to II for the same reason. Unit 11 can go to either market, since the additional revenues are the same, and unit 12 goes to the other. Thus we see that the 12 units should be divided so that the marginal revenues are the same for the last unit sold in each market; the monopolist sells seven units in market I and five in market II.

Exercise. Establish that any further reallocation of the 12 units diminishes total revenue; also establish that 17 units should be divided 8 in market II and 9 in market I.

Principle. The discriminating monopolist allocates a given output in such a way that the marginal revenues in each market are equal. The firm sells any additional unit in the market with the higher marginal revenue.

Intuitively, one would predict that if there are two separate markets and the firm price discriminates, the higher price would be charged in the market with the more inelastic demand at the point of price, and the lower price would be in the more elastic. Consumers in the more elastic market would have better substitutes; thus price could be raised only at the expense of a large decrease in sales. In the inelastic market there are poorer substitutes; thus higher prices bring less reduction in sales. The conclusion that the higher price is charged in the more inelastic market and the lower price in the more elastic can be proved using the following method:

ASIDE

An algebraic proof

Let there be two distinct markets for one monopolistically produced good; call these markets A and B. P_A and P_B are respectively the prices in markets A and B. MR_A and MR_B are the marginal revenues; E_A and E_B are the absolute values of demand elasticity. Recall from above the relation

$$MR = P\left(1 - \frac{1}{E}\right). \text{ Use this relation to}$$

prove that if $P_A > P_B$, $E_A < E_B$.

A discriminating monopolist divides output between the two markets so that the marginal revenues are equal in equilibrium. Thus

$$P_A\left(1 - \frac{1}{E_A}\right) = P_B\left(1 - \frac{1}{E_B}\right);$$

If $P_A > P_B$, then

$$\frac{\left(1 - \dfrac{1}{E_B}\right)}{\left(1 - \dfrac{1}{E_A}\right)} > 1.$$

Since the monopolist would never choose a point at which MR is negative

$$\left(1 - \frac{1}{E_B}\right) > \left(1 - \frac{1}{E_A}\right).$$

Manipulation of this inequality yields

$$E_B > E_A.$$

In order to analyze the situation graphically, assume that a monopoly can separate its market into two distinct markets. The demands and marginal revenues of each are shown in panel A, Figure 8.6.1. $D_1D'_1$ and MR_1 are demand and marginal revenue in the first market; $D_2D'_2$ and MR_2 are demand and marginal revenue in the second. Panel B shows the horizontal summation of the two demand and marginal revenue curves. For example, at a price of $O\bar{p}$ consumers in market I would take Ox_0 and consumers in market II would take Ox_1. The total quantity demanded at $O\bar{p}$ is accordingly $Ox_0 + Ox_1 = OX_0$, shown in panel B. All other points on $D_mD'_m$ are derived similarly. $MR_1 = O\bar{p}$ at output Ox_2; $MR_2 = O\bar{p}$ at output Ox_3. Therefore, in panel B, $MR_m = O\bar{p}$ at a quantity of $Ox_2 + Ox_3 = OX_1$. Other points on MR_m, the total market MR curve, are derived similarly.

The demand and marginal revenue conditions depicted in panel A, Figure 8.6.1, are reproduced in Figure 8.6.2, along with average and marginal costs of production. The profit-maximizing output is $O\bar{X}$, the quantity at which the total market marginal revenue equals marginal

FIGURE 8.6.1

SUBMARKET AND TOTAL MARKET DEMANDS AND
MARGINAL REVENUES

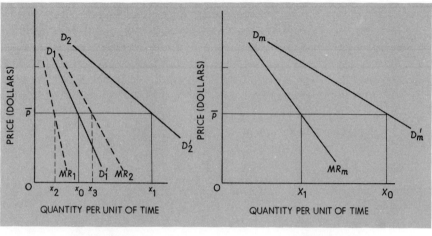

Panel A	Panel B
Demand and marginal	Monopoly demand and
revenue in submarkets	marginal revenue

FIGURE 8.6.2

PROFIT MAXIMIZATION UNDER
PRICE DISCRIMINATION

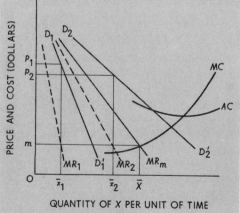

cost. The marginal revenue (equals marginal cost) associated with this output is Om.

The market allocation rule, previously determined, requires that marginal revenue be the same in each submarket. Since the total market marginal revenue is the added revenue from selling the last unit in either submarket, $MR_1 = MR_2 = Om$. At a marginal revenue of Om, the quantity sold in submarket one is $O\bar{x}_1$; in submarket two, $O\bar{x}_2$. Since MR_m is the horizontal summation of MR_1 and MR_2, $O\bar{x}_1 + O\bar{x}_2 = O\bar{X}$, the total output. Furthermore, from the relevant demand curves the price associated with output $O\bar{x}_1$ in market one is Op_1, the price associated with $O\bar{x}_2$ in market two is Op_2. Because these prices clearly differ and the costs of production are the same, discrimination exists.

Summarizing these results:

Proposition. If the aggregate market for a monopolist's product can be divided into submarkets with different price elasticities, the monopolist can profitably practice price discrimination. Total output is determined by equating marginal cost with aggregate monopoly marginal revenue. The output is allocated among the submarkets so as to equate marginal revenue in each submarket with aggregate marginal revenue at the $MC = MR$ point. Finally, price in each submarket is determined directly from the submarket demand curve, given the submarket allocation of sales.

APPLICATION

Some examples and analyses of price discrimination

The theory of price discrimination has many applications in business decision making, and we can use the theoretical structure to analyze the pricing policy in certain sectors of the economy. Recall the basic theoretical conditions necessary for discrimination: (1) little possibility of exchange of goods between markets and (2) different demand elasticities in the market; the higher elasticity is associated with the lower price. Finally, in the real world there is the added condition that the price differential is not competed away. In our theory we assumed monopoly; thus there could be no close competition. In the real world pure monopoly seldom exists. Many firms that actually practice price discrimination are faced with a certain amount of competition. Other things determine whether or not discrimination can last for very long. Let us analyze a few examples to gain some insight into how and why firms price discriminate.

The typical textbook example of price discrimination is the medical profession. Doctors frequently scale fees according to income. Economists say that this is done in order to increase income. The medical profession argues that doctors price discriminate in order to act as a collection agency for a medical charity. They charge high-income patients a high fee to finance the low fees charged to low-income patients.

In a classic article on the subject Reuben A. Kessel tested the hypothesis that doctors price discriminate because of charitable motives*. He asked why we do not observe parallel behavior in nursing and dentistry, or even by grocery stores since food is as "necessary" as medical care. The argument presented is that the state supplies food and shelter to the poor but not medical care; therefore, this type of charity is up to the medical profession.

According to Kessel, if the charity hypothesis is in fact correct, there should be no price discrimination between those who have medical insurance and those who do not. If maximization is the reason for discrimination, those who have insurance should pay, on average, higher fees than the uninsured. Insurance affects the *demand* for doctors but does not change the income of an individual. Those with insurance would, other things equal, have a more inelastic demand than those without, and would pay higher fees. The evidence cited by Kessel does show that medical fees are higher for the insured than for the uninsured. This evidence comes from unions and from the insurance industry. Kessel pointed out that the effect of insurance upon fees, abstracting out variations in income, suggests that fees are determined by "what the traffic will bear."

A second bit of evidence that profit rather than charity motivates price discrimination in medicine is the stand of the American Medical Association (AMA) on different types of insurance. The first type of insurance, cash indemnity plans, has not been opposed at all by the AMA or by local medical societies. Cash indemnity plans such as Blue Cross and Blue Shield allow doctors and patients to determine fees just as though there were no insurance. Doctors are, therefore, able to discriminate, and under such plans the demand for medical care is increased.

In contrast, the AMA and local medical societies have strongly opposed prepaid plans that supply medical services directly to patients. Costs of such cooperative plans are independent of income, and as such, represent a threat to doctors' ability to discriminate.

---

* Reuben A. Kessel, "Price Discrimination in Medicine," *Journal of Law and Economics,* October 1958, pp. 20–53.

These plans provide the means for extensive price cutting to high-income patients. The opposition of organized medicine to these types of plans is in strong support of the profit-maximizing discriminating monopolist hypothesis.

The two conditions necessary for firms to be able to price discriminate are met: Differences in income would probably cause different price elasticities, and patients cannot easily sell medical services among themselves. That is, low-price patients cannot resell their operations to high-price patients. But doctors do not have a monopoly. Since there are many, many doctors, why do not some doctors break the agreement, causing the price for high-income patients to fall?

According to Kessel, the reasons doctors do not attempt to cut prices individually is the extensive control of the AMA over medical education. Every doctor must undergo an internship administered by hospitals and only hospitals approved by the AMA are sanctioned for internship and residency. Hospitals value intern and residency training, because they can provide medical care more cheaply with interns and residents than without them. Thus, the AMA controls an important resource for hospitals, and its "advice" that hospitals use only doctors who are members of their local medical society is almost always adhered to. Doctors who are "price cutters" can be removed from the local medical societies, and thus are denied access to hospitals. It would be supposed that any doctor who is denied hospital services finds the demand for his services substantially weakened. It, therefore, pays doctors not to lower prices.

What other kind of businesses can and do practice price discrimination? Many drug stores that offer discounts on drugs to persons 65 and over are one example. Thus the drug stores discriminate in price. One would suppose that retired persons have a more elastic demand for drugs, because the market value of their time is lower. Thus retired persons would tend to shop around more for lower prices, and differences in price among different age groups can be explained by different price elasticities, resulting from different evaluations of time.

But the other conditions are absent in the case of drugs. There are many drug stores that would be willing to reduce prices, and if the price differential becomes sufficiently large, older people would buy drugs and sell to younger persons. There may be some prevention of reselling because of prescription laws (not applicable in cases like toothpaste, aspirin, etc. How important these are is an empirical question.)

Movies, plays, concerts, and similar forms of entertainment practice price discrimination according to age. Generally younger people pay lower prices. Supposedly in this case younger people have more elastic demands for such tickets, possibly because of the availability of more substitute forms of entertainment. (It is not correct to say that different ticket prices for afternoon and evening performances or for Tuesday and Saturday are evidence of price discrimination. These are different products in the eye of the consumer.)

Airlines have in the past discriminated by student versus nonstudent distinctions and now by vacation versus business travel. The regulatory agency allowed these prices to be maintained. One would believe that students or vacation travelers would have a more elastic demand than business travelers, probably because the value of time in business travel is greater.

Other examples of price discrimination are electric companies that charge lower rates to industrial users than to households (although this may be due to differences in costs), and university book stores that charge lower prices to faculty than to students. Citizens of the United States vacationing in Mexico pay higher prices in restaurants than Mexican nationals. Trucking companies frequently charge different rates for different goods when the distance and size of the goods are the same.

Try to explain in terms of elasticity in these four cases why the differences in price exist. Are all conditions met so that discrimination will last over time? Why or why not?

8.7 MULTI-PLANT MONOPOLY

A situation quite similar analytically to the case of monopoly price discrimination is the situation of the monopolist that produces output in one or more plants, possibly with different cost structures. As in the case of price discrimination this situation has many interesting implications.

Consider first how a firm would allocate a given level of output among several plants. For simplicity we use only the case of two plants. After our analysis of the discriminating monopolist, you have probably already deduced that the firm allocates a given output between two plants so that the total marginal costs in both plants are equal.

Assume there are two plants, A and B. Suppose at the desired level of output, the following situation holds

$$MC_A < MC_B.$$

Clearly the firm should transfer output out of the higher cost B into the lower cost A. If the last unit produced in B costs $10, but one more unit produced in A adds only $7 to A's cost, that unit should be transferred from B to A. In fact, output should be transferred from B to A until

$$MC_A = MC_B.$$

We would suspect eventual equalization because of increasing marginal cost. As output is transferred out of B into A, the marginal cost in A rises, and the marginal cost in B falls. It is simple to see that exactly the opposite occurs in the case of

$$MC_A > MC_B.$$

Output is taken out of A and produced in B until

$$MC_A = MC_B.$$

The total situation is pictured graphically in Figure 8.7.1. Demand for the product is D, and total marginal revenue for the firm is MR. Total marginal cost for the firm, $MC_A + MC_B$, equals marginal revenue at output OQ. The product price is OP and marginal cost in each plant is OM. Plant A produces OQ_A units; plant B produces OQ_B units. Because of the way in which the curves were derived $OQ_A + OQ_B = OQ$. Thus the firm is in equilibrium. Exactly the same principles apply for firms producing in more than two plants.

FIGURE 8.7.1

MULTI-PLANT MONOPOLY

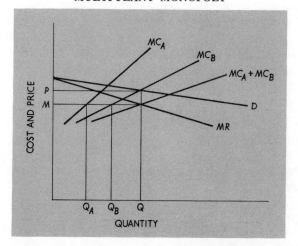

APPLICATION

Use of the theory in decision making

The theories of multi-plant monopoly and monopoly price dis-crimination are quite applicable to many decision-making problems not related to monopoly firms. We can apply certain parts of the theories to governmental decision making and to the decisions of nonprofit institutions as well as to firms that are not monopolies. The basic principles are that when allocating resources, returns and costs are equalized at the margin.

Someone running for political office generally has two resources that are reasonably fixed, campaign funds and time. The politician would not in general spend all of these resources in only one part of the district, or state, or nation, depending upon which office is be-ing sought. Neither would the funds and the time be spread equally over the total area. Money and time would be allocated so that the probable return in votes per dollar spent and per unit of time spent in each area is equalized. This maximizes the *total* number of votes for the total amount of money and time spent in the campaign.

A similar type of analysis can be used by city officials in allo-cating funds for the police force. Generally a city government has a reasonably fixed amount to spend on police. There are many ways to divide the budget among the various branches or types of law en-forcement. We frequently hear complaints that police should not be spending time and money giving parking tickets, arresting drunks, making pot raids, and so on when they could be catching murderers, thieves, and rapists.

How should the money and time be allocated? Ideally the budget should be spent so that the marginal value of crime deterrent to the community per dollar spent is equal in all areas of activity. The prob-lem is, as you well know, that this marginal value is difficult to esti-mate and impossible to measure precisely. How do we compare the social value of capturing a rapist with the value of arresting six gam-blers, or giving 22 parking tickets. A rough approximation is really all that can be hoped for. But the economic principles still hold and are good guidelines. Difficult as values are to measure, city officials must make these decisions, and economics can help them in making the choices.

Use your theory to try to solve the following problem. Suppose you are asked to lead a campaign to raise funds for a particular civic project—perhaps the United Fund. You have at your disposal vol-unteer workers and a certain amount of funds; calling on businesses, door-to-door visits, phone calls, mailing letters, and possibly other methods can be used to raise money. How would you allocate your money and volunteers in order to raise the most money?

8.8 MONOPOLY REGULATION

Since some of the social effects of monopoly behavior are thought to be "undesirable," governments from time to time attempt to regulate their behavior by imposing price ceilings and by enacting certain forms of taxation. Without considering social desirability, we can analyze some effects of such regulation upon the price-output behavior of monopolists.

8.8.a Price regulation

If government believes a monopolist is making "too much" profit, is charging "too high" a price, or is "restricting" output, it can set a price ceiling on the commodity. As you will recall from Chapter 2, a ceiling price under perfect competition causes a shortage, and some form of non-price allocation of the good will evolve. This may or may not be the case under monopoly.

Consider first the situation in Figure 8.8.1. Under the cost and revenue conditions depicted, the nonregulated monopoly sells Ox_e at a price of Op_e; it obviously makes a substantial pure profit. Now let us assume that the government imposes a price ceiling (that is, a price less than Op_e). Suppose Op_c is the maximum price allowed. The segment p_cC becomes the new demand and marginal revenue up to the output Ox_c. The monopoly can sell any quantity up to Ox_c at a price of Op_c because over this range actual demand lies above p_cC; it would certainly charge no lower price. Thus over the segment p_cC, the monopolist's effective demand is a horizontal line and $P = MR$. After Ox_c the old demand and marginal revenue curves become effective. The entire new demand is, therefore, the line p_cCD'. With the new demand curve, marginal revenue now equals marginal cost at C; the monopolist sells Ox_c units per period at a price of Op_c. Since C lies on DD', quantity supplied equals quantity demanded and the market is cleared. Price falls, quantity increases, and marginal cost now equals price. Profit clearly diminishes. Since Ox_e and Op_e gave *maximum* profit, any other combination, including Op_c and Ox_c, must give less than maximum profit.

But in this case price would be equal to marginal cost. If price represents the social marginal valuation of the commodity and marginal cost represents the social cost of the commodity, the two are equal. One of the results of perfect competition is obtained even though in the long run production need not take place at minimum average cost.

Other ceiling prices would not give this result. For example, at any ceiling price set between Op_e and Op_c, price would equal MC at an output greater than the quantity the market would demand at that price. Therefore the monopolist sells the quantity given by the demand curve (DD') at the ceiling price. Again price falls from Op_e and quantity increases from Ox_e, but in contrast to Op_c, price exceeds the marginal cost of the last unit sold.

FIGURE 8.8.1

EFFECTS OF PRICE CEILINGS
UNDER MONOPOLY

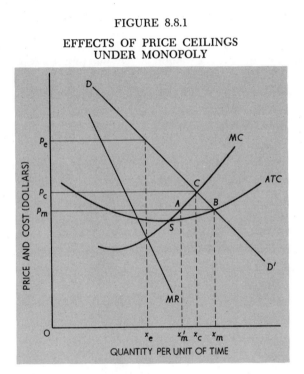

You may think, "If Op_c causes price to fall, quantity to rise, and profit to diminish, why not lower price even farther, possibly to Op_m?" True enough, at Op_m the monopolist could sell Ox_m and still cover costs, since $ATC = Op_m$ at Ox_m. Note, however, that the new demand and marginal revenue curve is p_mBD'; therefore, $MR = MC$ at A and the firm would produce Ox'_m, which is *less* than Ox_m. Since quantity demanded at Op_m is Ox_m, a shortage of $x'_m x_m$ results. In this case the monopolist must allocate by means other than price. In fact, any price below Op_c causes a decrease in quantity sold from Ox_c and hence a shortage, inasmuch as quantity demanded exceeds quantity supplied. The monopolist will produce along the MC curve over the portion SC; but the market demands a greater quantity at each of these prices. If price is set below minimum ATC (point S), the monopolist will go out of business.

Under the conditions assumed in Figure 8.8.1 the greatest quantity is attained by setting the ceiling price so that the monopolist produces where MC intersects actual demand. This result, however, may not always be obtainable by a ceiling price. Figure 8.8.2 depicts such a case. The nonregulated profit-maximizing monopolist in Figure 8.8.2 sells Ox_1 units per period at price Op_1. If the government sets a ceiling price of Op_3, the price at which MC crosses demand, the monopoly in the long run would go out of business; at this price it could not cover total costs. In fact, the ceiling could be no lower than Op_2 without forcing the firm to cease production. At Op_2 the firm would sell Ox_2 units per period and make no pure profit. The monopolist would have to reduce price to sell a greater output and would hence make a loss. Therefore, at any ceiling price between Op_1 and Op_2, the firm sells the quantity given by the actual demand curve at that price; at any ceiling price below Op_2 the

FIGURE 8.8.2

EFFECTS OF PRICE CEILINGS UNDER MONOPOLY

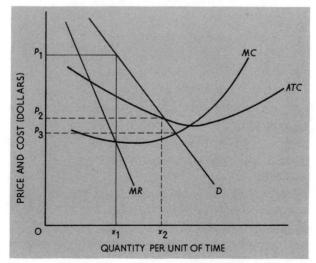

firm eventually shuts down. Clearly, the conditions conducive to governmental price setting depend upon economies and diseconomies of scale.

8.8.b Taxation

An alternative method of monopoly regulation is some type of special taxation. We examine here the effects of three common types: the excise or per unit tax, the lump-sum tax, and the percentage-of-profits tax.

An excise or per unit tax means that for every unit sold, regardless of price, the monopolist must pay a specified amount of money to the government. Assume that the monopolist, whose cost curves ATC_0 and MC_0 are shown in Figure 8.8.3, is charged a tax of k dollars for every unit sold. Total cost after the tax is the total cost of *production* (presumably the same as before) plus k times output; thus average or unit cost must rise by exactly the amount of the tax, k dollars. The after-tax ATC in Figure 8.8.3 rises from ATC_0 to ATC_1, or by the vertical distance k. MC also rises by k dollars. If it costs MC_0 to produce and sell an additional unit of output before the tax, after the tax it costs $MC_0 + k = MC_1$ to produce and sell that unit. This also is shown in Figure 8.8.3.

FIGURE 8.8.3

EFFECTS OF AN EXCISE TAX UNDER MONOPOLY

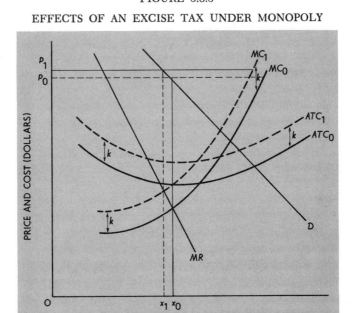

Before the tax is imposed the monopolist produces Ox_0 and charges a price of Op_0. After the imposition of the tax, the cost curves shift vertically by the amount k to ATC_1 and MC_1. MC_1 now equals MR at the output Ox_1, so price rises to Op_1. This effect, of course, differs completely from the effect of the ceiling price that causes price to fall and quantity to rise.

Note that the firm absorbs some of the tax and shifts some to the consumers in the form of higher prices. The proportion shifted depends upon the slope of marginal cost and the slope of demand. We can extend the horizontal lines from p_1 and p_0 to the MC curves to see the proportion of k that is shifted. This shows the difference between Op_0 and Op_1, the amount of the tax shifted, as a fraction of the tax k.

A lump-sum tax has a somewhat different effect upon price and quantity. Assume that instead of imposing an excise tax on the monopolist, the government charges a license fee that remains the same regardless of quantity sold. The license fee is, therefore, a fixed cost to the monopolist. ATC rises after the fee is imposed; at very small outputs ATC rises more than at larger outputs because the larger the output the more units the fee is "spread over." Once the fee is paid, however, no additional tax is charged for an additional unit of production per period. MC, therefore, remains unchanged. Since MC and MR do not change after the lump-sum tax, their point of intersection does not change, and thus price and quantity remain the same after the tax is imposed. The lump-sum tax, which does reduce profits, must not, of course, be so large as to drive ATC above demand, consequently causing a loss and driving the monopolist out of business.

A percentage-of-profits tax, just as the lump-sum tax, does not affect quantity or price. Assume that a monopolist must pay π percent of profit (regardless of the profit) as a tax. Since π is presumably between 0 and 100, the monopolist retains $(100 - \pi)$ percent of profits after paying the tax. Revenue and cost curves remain the same. Before the tax is imposed the monopoly chooses price and quantity so as to maximize profit. After the tax it still chooses the same price and quantity so as to maximize before-tax profit, since $(100 - \pi)$ percent of the maximum profit is clearly preferable to $(100 - \pi)$ percent of some smaller amount.

Tax regulation, therefore, differs from price regulation in several ways even though profits are reduced in all cases. In particular, taxation, in contrast to some price ceilings, cannot force the monopolist to set price equal to marginal cost.

APPLICATION

Taxation of natural resources

Taxation of natural resources is now receiving a great deal of attention. There is currently a certain amount of public opinion in the United States and Canada holding that government can tax away all of the profits of the owners of a natural resource without having any effect upon production. For example, suppose a firm owns a deposit of coal, or the right to extract the resource, and is in fact extracting the coal. Assume that the firm is making a substantial profit above its opportunity cost. It is frequently asserted that the government can tax away all of the profit above opportunity cost in each year without having any effect upon output. Since the firm covers all costs including opportunity costs and possibly is left with a little profit after taxes, the firm owners are doing as well as would be possible in an alternative use of the resources. Clearly the tax could not be so large that the firm could not cover variable cost; in this case it would not extract any coal. But if all costs can be covered, the firm will continue producing at the optimal rate. No marginal conditions are changed. Thus the government benefits at the expense of the firm, and society loses no resources or output.

Suppose you are a member of Congress, who is deciding on such a tax. What would you think would be the effect of such a tax? Would such a tax affect society's output?

The answer is that the tax, if it is expected to continue, would probably not affect the output of the taxed firm that is mining coal from the given deposit. The firm would presumably make the best out of the conditions it is faced with. But such a tax would very likely decrease the future output of coal and of other resources faced with such a tax.

Exploration and other forms of investment are undertaken in the hope of a future stream of profits. Firms would carry out exploration, for example, as long as the marginal cost of exploration exceeds the expected marginal return. Any tax that reduces the *expected return* consequently reduces exploration, and anything that reduces exploration reduces future resource extraction—in the case of coal, the output of coal would fall in the future. The situation is similar in the case of other forms of investment, which are carried out in the expectation of a stream of returns in the future. A tax that is expected to lower the stream of returns in the future lowers investment. Reduced investment causes a reduction in future output. Therefore, while the tax profit would possibly not affect current output, such a tax would affect future output, possibly quite significantly.

We used coal as a hypothetical example. We can extend the analysis to oil or gas, a much more current topic of debate. As of now the price of oil from old wells is regulated below the equilibrium price, whereas the price of oil from new wells is not regulated. It appears that the effect of such a distinction depends upon the expectation of companies undertaking exploration that the regulators will not some day declare "new oil" to be "old oil" and expropriate the expected revenues. Even though "new" oil is not now regulated, to the extent that companies fear that its price will be regulated in the future, exploration and investment will decline.

Remember that all investment is undertaken in the hope of *future* gains. When there is the fear that future gains from a particular business will be expropriated, investment will fall, even though such gains are not expropriated now. If the government suddenly passes a law taxing all the pure profits of businesses in New York, it may not affect the short-run decisions of firms in New York, but potential investors in Pennsylvania may think a little harder about future investments there, realizing that Pennsylvania firms may be next. Likewise, regulations in one industry affect not only future investment in that industry but investment in other industries as well.

8.9 MONOPOLY PRICE CUTTING

Under some circumstances a monopoly might charge a price below that at which profit is maximized and therefore produce and sell an output greater than that at which marginal revenue equals marginal cost. One such circumstance would be the case of a monopolist, facing *potential* competition, who lowers price to block the entry of these potential competitors. For this tactic to be economically sound, the monopolist must enjoy a certain cost advantage over competitors.

Figure 8.9.1 illustrates an example in which a monopolist might lower price to prevent entry. A monopolist's long-run average and marginal costs are AC_M and MC_M. Market demand and marginal revenue are D and MR. The profit-maximizing price and quantity are Op_1 and Oq_1. Assume that for technological reasons the most advantaged potential rival would have the long-run average cost curve, AC_C. Even though the competitor does suffer a cost disadvantage, entry into the industry could be made at a price lower than Op_1 but above AC_C; thus some of the monopolist's business

FIGURE 8.9.1

PRICE CUTTING AS A BARRIER TO ENTRY

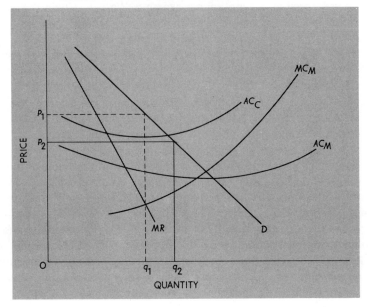

would be taken away. The monopolist would then be forced to lower price.

The monopoly, however, can set a price slightly below the minimum point of the potential competitor's long-run average cost curve. For the competitor to make any profit its price must be above AC_C. If the monopoly sets the price Op_2 and sells Oq_2, the competitor will not be able to make profit and hence will not be induced into competition. The monopoly's profit, of course, will be lower than maximum, but its rival's entry could lower profit even more. If it takes a very long time for a new firm to become established, the monopolist may not wish to sacrifice the stream of higher earnings. But if entry is easy, the monopoly firm may well be satisfied with lower profit and the retention of its monopoly situation. An analysis of this situation requires the use of a method of approach set forth in the following exercise.

EXERCISES

The value of a monopoly and price cutting as a barrier to entry

What is the value of a monopoly? If you could buy a profitable monoply, will you continue to make a profit? Perhaps not. Consider the following case. A certain piece of property has an expected life span of ten years. It is expected to return a pure profit of $1,000 a year, received at the end of the year, for the next ten years. In the tenth year the salvage value of the property is expected to be $500.

How much would you be willing to pay for this piece of property? The total expected yield is $10,000 profit plus $500 salvage value. You certainly would not be willing to pay $10,500 now. A dollar sometime in the future is worth less than a dollar today. Why? Because you can invest less than $1 now at the existing interest rate and have $1 in the future.

Suppose the interest rate is 8 percent and is expected to remain constant. If you invest $925.93 today at an 8-percent rate of interest, you would have $1,000 in one year because

$$925.93 + (.08 \times 925.93) = 1.08\,(925.93) = \$1,000.$$

Thus the value today of $1,000 in one year is $925.93 which is

$$\frac{\$1,000}{1.08}.$$

Similarly the value today of $1,000 in two years at an interest rate of 8 percent is $857.34 because

$$(\$857.34) \times (1.08) \times (1.08) = \$1,000.$$

In other words the value today of $1,000 in two years is

$$\frac{\$1,000}{(1.08)^2}.$$

It follows that the value today of $1,000 in three years is

$$\frac{\$1,000}{(1.08)^3} = \$793.83$$

and so on up to ten years:

$$\frac{\$1,000}{(1.08)^{10}} = \$463.19$$

Therefore, the value of the property described here at the present time is:

$$\text{Value} = \frac{\$1,000}{1.08} + \frac{\$1,000}{(1.08)^2} + \frac{\$1,000}{(1.08)^3} + \cdots + \frac{\$1,000}{(1.08)^{10}} + \frac{\$500}{(1.08)^{10}}$$

$$= \sum_{t=1}^{10} \frac{\$1,000}{(1.08)^t} + \frac{\$500}{(1.08)^{10}} = \$6,941.70.$$

An investor would not be willing to pay more than this amount at the present time under the circumstances described for this property. But, if there are competitive potential investors, they will bid up the price of the property until the price approaches $6,941.70. The former owner capitalizes the profits by selling out. The new owner must pay a price, because of competition, high enough to eliminate pure profits. That is, there are no returns over the normal return, which in this case is the market rate of interest, 8 percent.

This concept of discounting is a powerful tool in decision making and in economic analysis. It is used in determining the value of a license to do business. For example, in some cities taxis must be licensed. These licenses are issued by the city, but they can be sold by the owners.

Suppose you choose to put yourself through college for 4 years by driving a cab. You estimate that you can make $5,000 a year for the four years of school in your spare time. You could buy a license for $100,000 and, at the end of four years, you are assured that you can sell your license back to the owner at the present market rate for licenses, $100,000. Would you pay $100,000 for the license if the rate of interest is 10 percent? The answer is no, because the present value of the license is

$$\frac{\$5,000}{1.1} + \frac{\$5,000}{(1.1)^2} + \frac{\$5,000}{(1.1)^3} + \frac{\$5,000}{(1.1)^4} + \frac{\$100,000}{(1.1)^4} = \$84,151.19$$

This is, of course, an approximation because of errors in rounding and the entire $5,000 is not received at the end of each year. If the interest rate is only 5 percent, the license would be about a break-even investment because,

$$\frac{\$5,000}{1.05} + \frac{\$5,000}{(1.05)^2} + \frac{\$5,000}{(1.05)^3} + \frac{\$5,000}{(1.05)^4} + \frac{\$100,000}{(1.05)^4} = \$100,000.46$$

In each case we have assumed the $5,000 is profit over and above the value of your time and any capital owned.

Recall our discussion of monopoly price cutting as a barrier to entry. As you can see, the discounting process is crucial to this decision. The present values under the two situations, price cutting now with lower profit over the total time horizon or maximum profit now but reduced profit later, must be compared when making the decision.

For an additional insight, consider a firm that has a 5-year time horizon. It could set a lower price at which entry would be discouraged and the firm could obtain a pure profit of $50,000 a year for five years; or the firm could set the profit-maximizing monopoly price for the first two years and earn $80,000 a year. The higher price is expected to encourage entry, which will drive profits to $30,000 a year for the following three years. Which is the better policy if the interest rate is 8 percent?

Under the first situation the present value is

$$\sum_{t=1}^{5} \frac{\$50,000}{(1.08)^t} = \$199,636.$$

Under the second situation the present value is

$$\sum_{t=1}^{2} \frac{\$80,000}{(1.08)^t} + \sum_{t=3}^{5} \frac{\$30,000}{(1.08)^t} = \$208,945.$$

Thus the second strategy is more profitable.

Clearly, a real business situation is not so simple as these, but the basic approach is the same. Future returns must be discounted and are therefore not so valuable as present returns. This concept must be taken account of in most business decision making.

Finally, recall that while developing the theory of cost we analyzed a firm's decision-making process when determining whether to sell a sterile asset or hold on to that asset, expecting that price will increase at a rate in excess of the rate of interest. A monopolist may well face a similar type of decision. Of course the monopoly sets its own price, and therefore would not consider changes in market price. It would consider withholding the sale or extraction of some asset if it expects demand for the asset to increase sufficiently. Thus it would compare the expected increase in the *profit-maximizing* price to the expected rate of interest. The analysis is more complicated but quite similar in method.

8.10 SUMMARY

The pure monopolist chooses the output at which $MC = MR$. In contrast to perfect competition, the market does not force the monopolist in the long run to produce the quantity at which long-run ATC is at its minimum and to charge a price equal to minimum long-run ATC and MC. This does not necessarily indicate that price must be higher and quantity lower under monopoly than under perfect competition. Cost conditions may differ between the two forms of organization. We can only say that price under monopoly will not, in the absence of regulation, equal marginal cost and that the entry of competitors will not reduce pure profit to zero. Demand conditions certainly can change so as to eliminate profit, however, since a monopoly position does not guarantee pure profit.

In particular we wish to stress the following definition:

Definition. Marginal revenue is the addition to total revenue obtained from selling an additional unit of output. For a perfect competitor marginal revenue is price. Since a monopolist must lower price to sell more output, marginal revenue is less than price. In particular the relation is given by $MR = P\left(1 - \dfrac{1}{E}\right)$, where E is demand elasticity. If demand is elastic (inelastic), marginal revenue is positive (negative).

For a discriminating monopolist we have the following relations:

Relations. A discriminating monopolist maximizes profit by selling the output at which the market marginal revenue (the horizontal summation of all submarket marginal revenues) equals marginal cost. The firm allocates the output so that the marginal revenues in each submarket are equal. It charges the associated price in each submarket; the more inelastic the demand, the higher the price. For discrimination to continue there cannot be reselling among submarkets. Governments can regulate monopoly by taxation or price fixing. Only in certain cases of price fixing can price be made equal to marginal cost.

APPLICATION

A study of the effect of environmental regulations

The concept of discounting revenues had important implications in a recent study of environmental controls in the Canadian mining industry. This study, done for the Ontario Ministry of Natural Resources, estimated the impact of environmental regulations, imposed during the early 1970s, on investment in Canadian mining.

The environmental laws regulated the amount of impurities a mine or smelter could emit into the atmosphere or into lakes and streams. Compliance with these regulations generally required a certain amount of capital investment before mining and smelting operations could be resumed. This was investment over and above the investment that would have been carried out by the firm in the absence of the regulations.

Proponents of the stricter regulations asserted that such regulations would have very little, if any, impact upon productive investment and future output in the mining industry because the pollution-reducing investment required would make up such a very slight proportion of the total profits over the life of a mine or smelter. They estimated that the total additional required investment would make up only about 2 to 4 percent of the total profit stream. Thus it was stated that such a small percentage reduction should have little impact on future output; that is, the effect would be negligible because the required increase in capital cost would be slight relative to total profit.

The above-mentioned study analyzed this position by first pointing out that the required capital expenditures had to be made very early under the law. Thus most of these capital expenditures required to comply with the regulations would come in the first two or three years. Profits from ordinary investments would be delayed and would be spread over a very long period of time, sometimes 20 years or longer. Thus the early expenditure would be discounted slightly, whereas the later profits would be discounted greatly because they are so far in the future. It was shown that the estimate that required investment would be only 2 to 4 percent of the total profits changed to an estimate of nearly 10 percent when the streams of expenditures and streams of receipts were discounted. This represented a considerable impact on mineral investment.

TECHNICAL PROBLEMS

1. Assume a monopoly with the demand and cost curves shown in Figure E.8.1. It is in the short run with the plant designed to produce 400 units optimally.
    a. What output should be produced?
    b. What will be the price?
    c. How much profit is made?
    d. If the firm can change plant size and move into the long run, what will be output and price?
    e. Will profit increase? How do you know?

FIGURE E.8.1

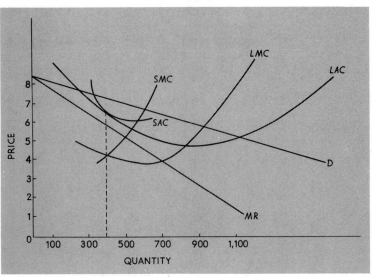

f.   Draw the new short-run average and marginal cost curves for the new
     output.

2.   Explain why a percent-of-profits tax on a monopolist will change neither
     price nor output. Do the same for a lump-sum tax. Explain why either tax
     may affect future investment.

3.   When will a discriminating monopolist with two separate markets do the
     following:
     a.   Charge the same price in both markets?
     b.   Sell the same output in both markets?

4.   Explain why a profit-maximizing monopolist always (in theory) produces
     and sells on the elastic portion of the demand curve. If costs were zero,
     where would the monopolist produce?

5.   Compare the perfectly competitive firm and the monopolist as to how it
     makes the following decisions:
     a.   How much to produce.
     b.   What to charge.
     c.   Whether or not to shut down in the short run.
     d.   What happens in the long run if losses persist.

6.   Assume that a monopolist can divide output into two submarkets, the de-
     mands and marginal revenues of which are shown in Figure E.8.2, along
     with marginal cost. ΣMR is the horizontal sum of the two marginal rev-
     enue curves.
     a.   Find equilibrium output and price in each market.
     b.   Which market has the more elastic demand?

FIGURE E.8.2

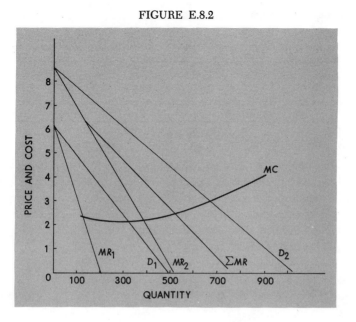

c. What would be price and output if the monopolist could not discriminate?

7. A monopolist's revenue and long-run cost curves are shown in Figure E.8.3.

FIGURE E.8.3

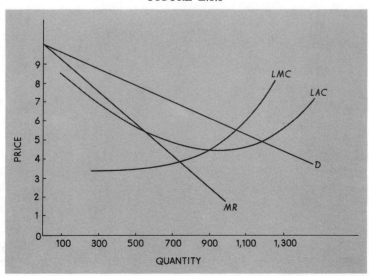

    a. Output and price are _____ and \$_____.
    b. A ceiling price of \$_____ would eliminate profit.
    c. Output and price would change to _____ and \$_____.
    d. An excise tax of \$2 per unit would change price to \$_____ and output to _____.

8. Draw demand, marginal revenue, marginal cost, average variable cost, and average total cost for a monopolist making short-run losses but continuing to produce. Label all curves and show output price and the amount of loss. What two options will the monopolist have in the long run?

9. If a monopolist is not making enough profit, it can simply raise price until it does. Comment critically.

10. A monopolist takes over a perfectly competitive industry composed of many plants. There can be no entry now. How would the monopoly allocate output among the various firms? What happens to output? Does supply elasticity increase or decrease? (This last is tricky.)

11. There are two industries; one is composed of one firm, the other of 1,000 firms. At the point of equilibrium the demand elasticity is 1.75 for one industry and .86 for the other. Which industry has which elasticity? Why?

ANALYTICAL PROBLEMS

1. Some people say that a per-unit excise tax has no effect on a monopolist, because the monopolist simply passes the tax along to the consumer, whereas the competitive firm cannot shift the tax. Show graphically that with a given marginal cost and a given excise tax, the elasticity of demand determines the percent of tax that can be shifted to the consumer and the percent that is absorbed by the monopolist.

2. You are adviser to a local government agency. The agency will grant a monopoly license to a firm to operate a profitable business. You are asked to set a price at which the government will grant the license. How would you advise setting the price?
    a. Assume you wish to maximize the government's revenue.
    b. Assume government will not set a monetary price. How would you make the decision as to who gets the license?

3. Some bars charge women half price for drinks. Is this consistent with profit maximization? Are all conditions of price discrimination met in this case? Is there an alternative explanation?

    Speaking of bars, many establishments have a "happy hour," meaning that in a certain time, say, 4 to 6 P.M., drinks are served at a reduced price. Is this consistent with price discrimination?

4. The patent system conveys monopoly rights to some good or process. It is often claimed to be beneficial to economic growth because it encourages

research. But in general it is asserted that monopolies result in inefficient resource allocation. Discuss.

5. Suppose a monopolist made a certain product, say a tire, in two styles. The two styles of tire are *exactly* alike in every way except one. One tire lasts *precisely* twice as long as the other and costs exactly twice as much to produce. Will the longer-lived tire sell for *exactly* twice the price of the shorter-lived? Explain your answer. (Ignore shopping time.)

6. Why do faculty get discounts from the university bookstore while students do not? Don't just say price discrimination. Why can price discrimination exist? Are *all* conditions necessary for price discrimination met? Discuss.

7. Consider a monopolist with the labeled curves shown in Figure E.8.4. Where would the monopolist produce and what output will be sold? Note they need not be the same. Does the solution tell us anything about why economists do not even consider the case of decreasing total cost as production increases?

FIGURE E.8.4

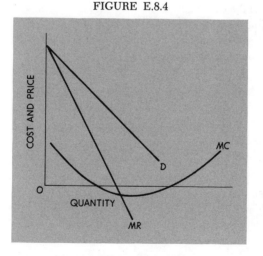

8. Large food chains like McDonald's sell their product through independently owned franchises.
   a. Why don't these chains retail their own product?
   b. Under what circumstances might they do so?
   c. What would determine the price of each franchise to the franchise owner?
   d. What would determine the number of franchises permitted?

9. Many universities either own, issue a franchise to, or license one bookstore on the campus. Textbook orders are placed by instructors in courses. But other bookstores frequently spring up around the campus.

     a.   In what sense is the university bookstore a monopoly?

     b.   In what sense is it not?

     c.   Do students benefit by having alternative bookstores available?

10.   In what sense is the only bank in a small town a monopoly? In what sense is it not? In what sense is GM or Exxon a monopoly? In what sense is it not? How about the U.S. Postal Service or your local electric company? If you were adviser to a Supreme Court Justice, how would you decide what does or does not constitute a monopoly? How could cross elasticity of demand help you decide? How about percent of the market?

11.   Suppose you were a governor of a state in which the legislature suddenly makes gambling legal. It has thus far been illegal, but obviously there has been some illegal gambling. You have two choices: you can either grant a statewide monopoly to one firm for all gambling or force the gambling industry in your state to be competitive. That is, you can enforce antitrust laws. Discuss the implications of each form of organization as to:

     a.   Amount of gambling.

     b.   Price to the consumer.

     c.   Amount the state can collect in taxes.

     d.   Effect on tourism.

     e.   Effect on your being reelected.

9

Imperfect competition

9.1 INTRODUCTION

Between the extremes of perfect competition and monopoly come a large number of theoretical market structures, none of which lends itself to the rigorous analysis of Chapters 7 and 8. For convenience, we classify all these "intermediate" market structures into two categories: monopolistic competition and oligopoly. Many of the theories of markets in these classifications were developed during the late 1920s and early 1930s because of the reaction to the theories of perfect competition and monopoly. Several economists, after pointing out that the two "extremes" are not accurate pictures of the real world, turned their attention to the "middle ground" between monopoly and perfect competition.

Monopolistic competition was developed to analyze the cases in which a large number of firms produce and sell commodities that are rather similar, but the various commodities have some distinguishing characteristics. Competition exists in the sense that the firms compete with one another to sell closely related products. Monopoly exists in the sense that each firm produces a product that is *slightly* distinguishable from the product of every other firm.

Oligopoly is the term used for the market structure in which a *few* firms compete in the sale of a commodity. Fewness, as we shall see, is defined as the case in which each firm recognizes that its actions will have a discernible impact upon the other firms. In other words, the firms are interdependent in many of their activities. In an oligopoly situation the firms can all produce an almost homogeneous product, as is the case for the few firms that produce aluminum, or they can produce a somewhat more differentiated product, as is the case for the few firms that produce automobiles.

During the 1920s and 1930s economists predicted great analytical results from the theories developed then to cover these "intermediate" market structures. This analytical usefulness has not really come about. Although, as we shall see, there is some economic analysis possible using the models of monopolistic competition and the various theories of oligopoly, they are far from being as useful in prediction and decision making as the theories of competition and monopoly. Although we do not dwell on the matter, it should become reasonably clear that most real-world problems can be analyzed within the context of competition or monopoly.

We present these intermediate structures because well-trained economists should be familiar with them and should be able to recognize both the usefulness and short-comings of these models. We first deal with monopolistic competition and then analyze some of the models of oligopoly.

The basic concepts to be learned in this chapter are

1. How equilibrium is attained when there are a large number of firms producing closely related but slightly differentiated products.
2. Why we have no *general* theory when there are a few firms producing a reasonably closely related product (oligopoly).
3. How the oligopoly problem is frequently "solved."
4. Why collusion among firms takes place and why it generally breaks up.
5. How some aspects of imperfect competition can be used in analysis.

9.2 FUNDAMENTALS OF MONOPOLISTIC COMPETITION

One of the most notable achievements of economists who examined the middle ground between competition and monopoly was that of an

American economist, Edward H. Chamberlin. Our attention is directed first to his theory of monopolistic competition.[1]

Chamberlin based his theory of monopolistic competition on a solid empirical fact: there are very few monopolies because there are very few commodities for which close substitutes do not exist; similarly, there are very few commodities that are entirely homogeneous. Instead, there is a wide range of commodities, some of which have relatively few good substitutes and some of which have many good, but not perfect, substitutes.

In a multitude of cases, the products are *heterogeneous* rather than homogeneous; hence perfect, and impersonal, competition cannot exist. On the other hand, although heterogeneous, the products are only slightly differentiated. Each is a rather close substitute for the other; hence competition exists, but it is a personal competition among rivals who are to a greater or lesser extent aware of each other.

When products are closely related but heterogeneous, one cannot speak of an industry, which is defined as a collection of firms producing a homogeneous good. Nonetheless, it is useful to lump together firms producing very closely related commodities and refer to them as a *product group*. Each producer in the product group has some degree of monopoly power; but not much, because other producers market a differentiated but closely related commodity. It is generally assumed that there are a rather large number of firms in the product group.

9.2.a Two demand curves

In the analysis of perfect competition two demand curves are used— the negatively sloped industry demand curve and the horizontal demand curves confronting each seller. Similarly, in the theory of monopolistic competition two demand curves are used also, but in this case both are negatively sloped.

The two curves are shown in Figure 9.2.1. Suppose that one of the firms in the product group is producing output Ox per period and selling at price Op (point E). If the firm changes price while all other firms in the product group hold prices constant, the firm would expect a substantial increase in sales following a price reduction. Sales to its existing clientele will increase, but more important, if other firms do not reduce price, the firm in question will capture a large part of their market also.

---

[1] E. H. Chamberlin, *The Theory of Monopolistic Competition* (Cambridge: Harvard University Press, 1933).

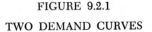

FIGURE 9.2.1

TWO DEMAND CURVES

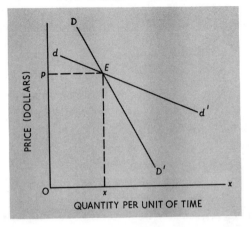

On the other hand, the firm will expect to experience a substantial loss in sales from a price increase if the other closely related firms do not increase price also. Not only will sales to existing customers decline, but some, perhaps many, customers will switch to other producers who have not raised prices. Consequently, assuming such a large number of sellers in the market that each firm expects its actions to go unnoticed by its rivals, every entrepreneur will perceive the demand curve to be very elastic. The entrepreneur's expected demand curve is shown by the relatively elastic curve *dd'* in Figure 9.2.1.

Under the assumption of a highly elastic demand, each entrepreneur may have an incentive to reduce price; and thus *all* entrepreneurs have this incentive. But if all prices are reduced simultaneously, each entrepreneur will gain only that increment in sales attributable to the general price reduction. No firm will capture large portions of its rivals' markets. Thus, if the actions of one entrepreneur are matched by all other entrepreneurs in the product group, demand will in fact be far less elastic, such as the curve *DD'* in Figure 9.2.1. In other words, *DD'* is the curve showing the actual quantity demanded from any one firm at various prices under the assumption that competitors' prices are always identical with its own price.

Relations. The curve *dd'* shows the increased sales any entrepreneur can expect to enjoy by lowering price, providing all other entrepreneurs maintain their original prices. *DD'*, on the other hand, shows the actual sales to be gained as a general downward movement of prices takes place. The situation is similar for a price increase.

9.2.b Short-run equilibrium

The theory of monopolistic competition is essentially a long-run theory. In the short run there is virtually no difference between the analysis of monopoly and of monopolistic competition. Each producer of a differentiated product behaves so as to maximize profit. Each producer thinks that its demand is like the expected demand curve dd' in Figure 9.2.1 and each attempts to maximize profit subject to the expected demand. With the expected demand and marginal revenue curves the firm maximizes profit or minimizes loss by equating marignal cost with marginal revenue.

So far as the short run is concerned there appears to be very little *competition* in monopolistic competition. But when a longer view is taken one essential element of monopoly is missing. In particular, a monopoly cannot be maintained if there is free entry. If pure profit is present in the short run, other firms will enter and produce the product; and they will continue to enter until all pure profits are eliminated.

In the present case the product is differentiated, not homogeneous, so there is no industry to enter. But other firms are free to produce a closely related product, since entry into the product group is not closed. If one or a few firms are obviously enjoying a highly prosperous situation, other firms will begin to produce a closely related product. They will "enter" the product group, and their entry will have market repercussions not greatly different from the entry of perfectly competitive firms into an industry.

9.2.c Long-run equilibrium

Using all of the above assumptions and analytical tools we can proceed immediately to the analysis of long-run equilibrium in the monopolistically competitive product group. Because of easy entry, all pure profit must be competed away in the long run. Only two types of situations are consistent with zero profit. These are shown as points A and B in Figure 9.2.2. At point A the expected demand (the demand assuming no other firm changes price) is tangent to LAC; at B the firm's actual demand (the demand when all firms change price together) is tangent to LAC.

FIGURE 9.2.2

LONG-RUN EQUILIBRIA WITH ENTRY OF FIRMS

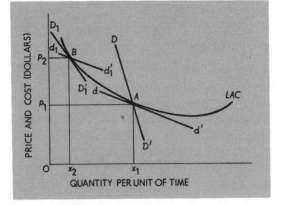

Firms reach a point such as A in the following way. Let firms in the product group be in short-run equilibrium, making pure profit. Since entry into the product group is open, new firms, selling slightly differentiated products, are attracted into the group. The greater variety and number of available products cause the actual demand for each seller's product to contract. In the process, DD' shifts to the left. Simultaneously, if entrepreneurs, noting a decline in sales, attempt to increase profit by reducing price, the firms decrease price, expecting the demand to be very elastic. That is, they expect substantial increases in sales from decreases in price. However, if all firms cut price, the quantity demanded will follow DD'; and in essence the individual demands, dd', slide down along DD'. At the same time, the individual demand curves become more elastic due to a wider range of substitutes. These firms decrease price until there is no more incentive to do so. With an output of Ox_1 and a price of Op_1, any change in price would result in losses for the firms. Thus each firm reaches a point of zero-profit long-run equilibrium, but the point of tangency is on the downward sloping portion of average-cost rather than at the minimum point, as is the case in perfect competition.

Equilibrium characterized by the tangency of dd' to LAC comes about because of active price competition among the various firms. The only way that a point such as B could be a point of long-run equilibrium is for the market *not* to be characterized by active price competition. A "live and let live" outlook on the part of sellers, tacit agreements, open price associations, price maintenance, customary prices, and professional ethics are a few causes of nonaggressive price policies. If price competition is, in fact, lacking, individual entrepreneurs will have little regard for the existence of curves such as $d_1d'_1$. They will be concerned only with the effects of a general price rise or decline, or with the DD' curve. Pure profit is eliminated when enough firms have entered to push demand to $D_1D'_1$; the individual firm produces Ox_2 and sells at Op_2, which is a higher price and lower quantity than those forthcoming under active price competition.

If all firms in this situation do attempt to reduce price and expand along $d_1d'_1$, the movement takes place along $D_1D'_1$. Each firm incurs a pure loss. If price cutting continues and exit occurs because of the losses being suffered, a new equilibrium such as that at A is attained. Each firm, while having a monopoly of its own product, is forced to a zero-profit position by the competition of rivals producing readily substitutable goods.

One might also question whether businessmen are so incredibly stupid that they continue to think their price changes will go unnoticed. Time after time they change price, believing the movement will take place along dd'. Each time, however, others do the same and DD' is relevant. Obviously businessmen are not dumb. But when there are large numbers of firms in the groups, each firm changes its price to its own advantage, hoping to get to a more optimal point first, or at least soon enough to capture some of the frictional gains before everyone changes. This hope of being first and capturing frictional gains seems to be a more realistic explanation of the way businessmen act. When we discuss cartels—organized groups of firms that are engaged in price fixing—we shall show that this motivation to cut prices in order to capture frictional gains is an important reason that cartels are rather unstable.

Proposition. Large group, long-run equilibrium under price competition and free entry in a monopolistically competitive product group is attained when the expected demand is tangent to the long-run unit cost curve. If there is no price competition (collusion) but free entry, equilibrium occurs where actual demand is tangent to *LAC*.

APPLICATION

Zero profit without price competition

It is sometimes the case that a point of zero-profit equilibrium such as point *B* in Figure 9.2.2, in which the actual demand, D_1D_1', is tangent to long-run average cost, may occur even though there is no price collusion in the industry or product group. This solution can at times occur when some branch of government regulates an industry. (We will continue to use the more familiar term "industry" rather than "product group.") As is frequently the case, regulation results in above-normal profits for firms in the industry. Obviously, if the regulatory board allows "reasonably free" entry into the industry, this entry will continue until profits are competed to the normal rate of return.

For example, suppose insurance rates are regulated so that insurance salesmen are earning a substantial pure profit. More and more people will enter the insurance business and the average rate of return will be driven down. To be sure, some insurance salesmen are better than others and will earn more profit, but because they are better their opportunity cost may be higher and their return may only cover opportunity cost. Less successful salesmen may make lower returns, but again their opportunity cost is lower. The point is, an increase in a regulated price will at first benefit those already in the industry; but in the long run, with reasonably free entry, the average yearly rate of return will be driven to the normal rate, or the opportunity cost.

Indeed, a zero-profit point such as *B* can come about even under restricted entry in an industry in which price is regulated above that which would result in the absence of competition. In this case, firms frequently compete in other ways, such as additional services, more advertising and other promotional schemes, additional conveniences to customers, and so on. All of these extra activities, designed to attract customers, increase costs. These firms do not want to add the extra activities, but they know that in the absence of collusion they must do this or their rivals will, and they will lose business.

While the airline industry may not fit all of the assumptions of monopolistic competition (it may be closer to oligopoly, which we discuss next), it does fit the model of an industry with a regulated price and restricted entry. With price above that which would occur in absence of regulation, the airlines compete for passengers in other ways, such as better in-flight service and, possibly more important, more frequent flights so as to reduce consumers' waiting time. These extra services and added flights add to costs, and the airlines would find their profits being competed away. Obviously they could all agree to drop the extra services and to limit the number of flights; but this would be collusion, and thus illegal. Even if such collusion was not illegal, there would be, as we shall see below, the incentive for airlines, particularly in hard times, to break the agreements. Only if government enforces the collusion will the agreement be certain of being maintained. Thus, as costs rise from competition, the airlines ask for higher and higher regulated fares.

EXERCISES

Application to the petroleum situation

At the beginning of the oil crisis when the price of oil was dramatically increased, the major airlines said that if they would be exempted from antitrust action, they would get together and reach an agreement to reduce the number of flights in an effort to reduce the nation's gasoline consumption. Sheer patriotism may have been one motivation for such voluntary action. What might have been another motivation?

Suppose in order to reduce gasoline consumption, the government drastically increased the price of gasoline and made it illegal to sell at a price below the floor price. Discuss all of the implications in the service station industry in the typical city under the assumption that entry and exit are not restricted. What would happen to profits, the number of stations, consumer services, and so on? Assume no black market.

9.2.d Comparison of long-run equilibria

A comparison of long-run equilibria is rather difficult inasmuch as it must rest essentially upon statements pertaining to cost curves. Conditions giving rise to monopoly probably lead to noncomparable differences between competitive and monopolistic costs; for similar reasons, noncomparability is also likely between either of these two structures and monopolistic competition. However, a few generalizations are possible if one bears in mind that the statements are relative, not absolute.

A monopolistically competitive firm is like a monopolist in that it faces a downward sloping demand. At the same time it is like a perfectly competitive firm in that it faces impersonal market competition, and in the long run pure profit is competed away.

In long-run competitive equilibrium, total industry output is produced in a group of plants each of which operates at (long-run) minimum average cost. The product is sold at a price equal to minimum average cost and, it is significant to note, long-run marginal cost equals both price and average cost at this point. Each firm operates a plant to produce the quantity associated with minimum long-run average cost, and that size plant and output is called by some "ideal" plant size and "ideal" output. When production of the quantity associated with minimum long-run average cost occurs, the industry's output is sometimes referred to as "ideal." Excess capacity, defined as the difference between actual output and the output associated with minimum long-run average cost, does not exist in long-run equilibrium under perfect competition.

Monopolistic competition is somewhat more difficult to analyze in these terms. In large-group equilibrium with active price competition, price is above marginal cost, although price equals average cost. Since demand is negatively sloped, tangency must occur where average cost is negatively sloped. Therefore, price equals average cost at a point above minimum average cost and at a lower rate of output than that associated with minimum long-run average cost. The difference in levels of output is called excess capacity. In long-run equilibrium under monopolistic competition, each firm has excess capacity.

Some economists, however, argue that the difference is the "cost" society pays for product differentiation and that it is a valid social cost. They then argue that although actual average cost exceeds minimum average cost, when *all* relevant social costs (including the cost of heterogeneity) are included, the firm produces at minimum attainable average cost. Each firm, and the product group as a whole, produces the "sort of ideal" output, and excess capacity does not appear in long-run equilibrium. This argument, however, is *not* universally accepted.

In short, the social welfare aspects of monopolistic competition are ambiguous. From a very microscopic standpoint, each firm produces less than the socially optimal output. On the other hand, if each firm were somehow forced to produce this seemingly desirable level of output at a price that equals marginal cost, private enterprise would no longer represent a viable economic system. Thus the abolition of private enterprise would violate a social welfare criterion (existence of private property rights) that transcends microeconomic considerations, at least in the United States and in most industrially advanced Western nations. While the theoretical analysis of monopolistic competition is quite clear, the welfare implications of this analysis are not. Micro- and macroeconomic welfare criteria are not consistent or reconcilable. The economist can only indicate the dilemma; establishing definitive social goals and welfare standards is beyond the economist's professional capacity.

During the early stages of its development, the theory of monopolistic competition excited the imaginations of economists, largely because they regarded it as a more *realistic* abstraction from the real world. The expected usefulness of the model, however, far exceeded its actual usefulness as an analytical tool or as a framework for developing economic policy.

9.3 OLIGOPOLY

Oligopoly is a market situation intermediate between the cases previously studied. In monopoly only one seller is in the market; competition, in either the technical or the popular sense, does not exist. Perfect competition and large-group monopolistic competition represent the opposite. So many firms are in the market that the actions of each are thought to be imperceptible to the others. Oligopoly is said to exist when more than one seller is in the market, but when the number is not so large as to render negligible the contribution of each. A market has few enough sellers to be considered oligopolistic if the firms recognize their *mutual interdependence*. In monopoly and competition, firms make decisions and take action without considering how these actions will affect other firms and how, in turn, other firms' reactions will affect them. Oligopolists must take these reactions into account in their decision-making process.

When contemplating a price change, a design innovation, a new advertising campaign, and so on, Ford Motor Company must anticipate how GM and the Chrysler Corporation will react because, without doubt, Ford's actions will affect the demand for Chevrolets and Plymouths.

This, in short, is the oligopoly problem and the central problem in oligopoly analysis. The oligopolistic firm is large enough to recognize (*a*) the mutual interdependence of the firms in the oligopoly and (*b*) the fact that its decisions will affect the other firms, which in turn will react in a way that affects the initial firm. The great uncertainty is *how one's competitors will react*.

Since so many industries meet the general description of oligopoly, it would at first glance seem that a general theory of oligopoly would have been developed. The problem in developing an oligopoly theory, however, is the same as the oligopoly problem itself. Mutual interdependence and the resulting uncertainty about reaction patterns make it necessary for the economist to make specific assumptions about behavioral patterns; that is, specific assumptions about how oligopolists *believe* their competitors will react and about how their competitors actually react.

Therefore, as we shall see, the solution to the oligopoly model (that is, equilibrium price and output) depends critically upon the assumptions

the economist makes in regard to the behavioral reaction of rival entrepreneurs. Since many different assumptions can and have been made,
many different solutions can and have been reached. Thus there is no
"theory of oligopoly" in the sense that there is a theory of perfect competition or of monopoly. There is no unique, general solution but merely
many different behavioral models, each of which reaches a different solution. Further, none of these models gives a reasonably realistic account
of any *one* oligopolistic industry, so no general result can be expected.
And to complicate the problem even more is the fact noted in the introduction to this chapter, that oligopolists can produce a homogeneous
product, quite differentiated products, or something in between.

ASIDE

Suppression of inventions and forcing of undesired "extras" by oligopolists

We frequently hear stories that the large oligopolistic firms, the
giants in the economy, frequently suppress inventions that would
make their presently profitable products obsolete or that would
change technology. There is very little evidence that this suppression
actually takes place, but the stories persist.

In the past there was suspicion that the battery producers were
withholding a battery that would outlast an automobile; tire manufacturers were supposed to have a tire that would triple the life of
the best tires available, but these were suppressed. As it turns
out these inventions have in fact come onto the market; at the time
of the rumors of suppression these products were in the development
stage but were too costly to be in great demand.

Unless there is out-and-out collusion, this suppression would be
unlikely under oligopoly; and, even with collusion, there is always the
possibility that a company will break the agreement. Under oligopoly
the management of each company realizes that if they have this
product or have made this invention, their rivals either have already
done it or are on the verge of doing so. If they do suppress the product, there exists the uncertainty that other firms will not do so, even
if it decreases the demand for the products currently being produced.
This uncertainty about rival behavior makes it unlikely that an oligopolist can withhold an invention for very long. Certainly this could
occur for a short period of time, but if entry into the market or im-
ports are not prohibited, suppression cannot go on for very long, if

demand is sufficient for the invention or the new product to be profitable.

There are similar stories of companies forcing aspects of their product on the public that the public does not really want. This was supposedly the case for automobile firms and manufacturers of certain household appliances. Certainly the firms would like to force these "unwanted" extras on the public, clearly at a higher cost; but there is always the possibility that rival firms will make available close substitutes that the public desires at a lower price. Even if the firms all agree to add these extras, the uncertainty of rival behavior will eventually cause some firm to break the agreement; or some other firm may produce the product that the public demands.

There is a way, of course, to "force" the "extras" onto the public and add to the cost of the product. If a lobbying group representing the firms or consumer interest groups can get laws passed making these extras mandatory, then there is governmentally enforced collusion. Right now the pressure is on the automobile manufacturers to make air bag safety devices mandatory on all cars in a few years. These will, of course, add to the price of the car and prevent any firm's breaking the agreement. One or two manufacturers recently introduced these as options, but hardly anyone bought them. If they were to become mandatory, every car buyer would have to purchase these extras. The same thing happened with seat belts, with safety shields on lawn mowers, and with other safety devices on certain household appliances, all of which added to price.

One might argue that even though these extras add to the price of the product and to the profit of the oligopolies, such laws are necessary to ensure public safety. This may be the case in some instances, but as we shall show below, if the public demands these extra features, oligopolistic firms have the incentive to produce them.

Of course, oligopolies can and frequently have colluded among themselves without the aid of government, even in the face of laws forbidding such collusion. However, before continuing our study of oligopoly by analyzing oligopolistic behavior under collusion, let us first examine briefly why some industries are oligopolistic or even approach monopoly while others are much closer to perfect competition or monopolistic competition.

A major question that must be addressed is: Why in some industries do the few largest firms produce a large percentage of total output while in other industries no firm has a substantial share of the total market?

Part of the answer to this question lies in the barriers to entry of new firms. If oligopoly or monopoly is to exist for long, something must prevent new firms from entering the industry or prevent those that do enter from growing. Another part of the answer lies in the reasons why some firms are able to attain an oligopoly or monopoly position in the first place. These factors are called the bases of oligopoly or monopoly.

One of the most important bases of monopoly or oligopoly is the control of raw material supplies. If one firm (or perhaps a few firms) controls all of the known supply of a necessary ingredient of a particular product, the firm or firms can refuse to sell that ingredient to other firms at a price low enough for them to compete. Since no others can produce the product, a monopoly or oligopoly results. For example, for many years the Aluminum Company of America (Alcoa) owned almost every source of bauxite, a necessary ingredient in the production of aluminum. The control of resource supply, coupled with certain patent rights, provided Alcoa with an absolute monopoly in aluminum production. Indeed, it was only after World War II that the federal courts effectively broke Alcoa's monopoly of the aluminum market. The International Nickel Company enjoyed much the same position over a relatively long period.

Nonetheless, a firm's control of the source of raw material supply does not guarantee that it will choose to exploit its opportunity to be a monopolist. If diseconomies of scale set in at a low level of output, relative to demand, the firm may find it more profitable to sell the raw material to other firms. The number of firms that may enter the industry depends in large part on economies of scale. If economies of scale are only attainable at a relatively large level of output (but not the entire market output), few firms will enter and oligopoly will result. If all economies of scale are attainable at low levels of output, more firms will enter. However, the sole owner of the raw material remains a monopolist in the raw material market. Only if it is more profitable will the firm choose to be a monopolist of the product as well.

Another barrier to competition lies in the patent laws of the United States. These laws make it possible for a person to apply for and obtain the exclusive right to produce a certain commodity or to produce a commodity by means of a specified process that gives it an absolute cost advantage. Obviously, such exclusive rights can easily lead to monopoly or, if a few firms hold the patents, to oligopoly. Alcoa is an example of a monopoly based upon both resource control and patent rights. E. I. Du Pont de Nemours & Co. enjoyed patent monopolies over many commodities, cellophane being perhaps the most notable. At one time the Eastman Kodak Company enjoyed a similar position.

Despite many notable examples, holding a patent on a product or on a production process may not be quite what it seems in many instances. In the first place, like the exclusive owner of some necessary raw material, the holder of a product patent may not choose to exploit the monopoly position in the production of the product. If diseconomies of scale set in at a low level of production, the patent holder may find it more profitable to sell production rights to a few firms (in which case oligopoly results) or to many. Second, a firm that owns a patented lower-cost production process may have a cost advantage over competitors but may sell only a small part of the industry's total output at the equilibrium position. The new technique will lead to patent monopoly only if the firm can supply the market and still undersell competition. Third, a patent gives one the exclusive right to produce a particular, meticulously specified commodity or to use a particular, meticulously specified process to produce a commodity others can produce. But a patent does not preclude the development of closely related substitute goods or closely allied production processes. International Business Machines has the exclusive right to produce IBM computers, but many other computers are available and there is competition in the computer market. The above-mentioned Du Pont patent on cellophane gave Du Pont a monopoly in that product. According to the U.S. Supreme Court, however, the relevant market is not the cellophane market but the market for flexible packaging material, in which Du Pont had an 18-percent share—obviously not a monopoly position. The same is true of production processes. Thus, while patents may sometimes establish pure monopolies or oligopolies, at other times they are merely permits to enter highly—but not perfectly—competitive markets.

A third source of oligopoly or monopoly, clearly related to the two sources just discussed, lies in the cost of establishing an efficient production plant, especially in relation to the size of the market. The situation we are now discussing is frequently called "natural" monopoly or "natural" oligopoly. It comes into existence when the minimum average cost of production occurs at a rate of output so large that one or a few firms can supply the entire market at a price covering full cost. If minimum average cost occurs at a rate of output sufficient, or more than sufficient, for just one firm to supply the entire market and cover full cost, a natural monopoly results.

Suppose there exists a situation in which a few firms supply the entire market, and each enjoys a pure profit. Because of the advantages of large size, cost at smaller rates of output is so high that entry is not profitable for small-scale firms. On the other hand, the entry of another large-scale producer is also discouraged because the added production of this firm would increase supply and drive price below the pure-profit level for all firms. Therefore, entry is discouraged.

Suppose a similar situation exists, but now only two firms are in the market. Suppose also that the long-run average cost curve of each is such that splitting the market between the two requires each firm necessarily to produce at a relatively high average cost. Each has an incentive to lower price and increase output because average cost will also decline. But if both act in this fashion, price will surely fall more rapidly than average cost. The ultimate result is likely to be the emergence of only one firm in a monopoly position. The term natural monopoly simply designates that the natural result of market forces is the development of a monopoly organization. One may carry the analysis further and describe similar circumstances in which the relations between average cost and market demand can cause an industry to become oligopolistic.

Examples of natural monopoly are not hard to come by. Virtually all public utilities are natural monopolies, and vice versa. Municipal waterworks, electrical power companies, sewage disposal systems, telephone companies, and many transportation services are examples of natural monopolies on both local and national levels.

Another frequently cited barrier to competition is the advantage that established firms sometimes have over new firms. On the cost side the established firms, perhaps because of a history of good earnings, may be able to secure financing at a more favorable rate than new firms. On the demand side, older firms may have built up over the years the allegiance of a group of buyers. New firms might find these advantages difficult to overcome. Buyer allegiance for durable goods can be built by establishing a reputation for service. No one knows what the service or repair policy of a new firm may be. Or, the preference of buyers can be built by a long successful advertising campaign; this type of allegiance is also probably more prevalent for durable goods. Although technical economies or diseconomies of scale may be insignificant, new firms might have considerable difficulties establishing a market organization and overcoming buyer preference for older firms.

The role of advertising in fostering oligopoly has, however, been a source of controversy. Some argue that advertising acts as a barrier to entry by strengthening buyer preferences for the products of established firms. On the other hand, consider the great difficulty of entering an established industry without access to advertising. A good way for entrenched oligopolists to discourage entry would be, in fact, to get the government to prohibit advertising. The reputation of the old firms would enable them to continue their dominance. A new firm would have difficulty informing the public about the availability of a new product unless it was able to advertise. Thus advertising may be a way for a new firm to overcome the advantages of older firms from being established. The effect of advertising on oligopoly remains a point of disagreement among economists.

The final source of monopoly and oligopoly to be discussed here is government. Although the United States does enforce antitrust laws with varying degrees of severity, governments at all levels frequently act to further monopoly and erect barriers to competition. One method is the granting of a market franchise. Use of a market franchise is frequently associated with natural monopolies and public utilities, but it need not be. A market franchise is actually a contract entered into by some governmental body (for instance, a city government) and a business concern. The governmental unit gives a business firm the exclusive right to market a good or service within its jurisdiction. The business firm, in turn, agrees to permit the governmental unit to control certain aspects of its market conduct. For example, the governmental unit may limit, or attempt to limit, the firm to a "fair return on fair market value of assets." In other cases the governmental unit may establish the price and permit the firm to earn whatever it can at that price. There are many other ways in which the governmental unit can exercise control over the firm. The essential feature, however, is that a governmental unit establishes the firm as a monopoly in return for various types of control over the price and output policies of the business.

Another way in which the government inhibits competition, some assert, is by purchasing from the larger firms rather than the smaller firms in many industries. Those who hold this position maintain that government contracts give the larger firms an advantage not only over other firms in the industry but also over prospective entrants. Others posit that tariffs hinder entry into oligopolistic industries. While tariffs do not necessarily prevent competition, they do make it easier for firms in an industry to collude. Another governmentally fostered base of oligopoly and monopoly is the federal tax structure. When this tax structure encourages reinvestment in established corporations at the expense of investment in new entrants, even though the new firms would be more efficient, competition is inhibited.

EXERCISE

Regulated oil prices and the effect on drilling

This exercise concerns the effect of governmental price regulations on oil drilling. Some say oil drilling is basically oligopolistic in nature; others say that drilling is competitive. In either case, the exercise shows how pronouncements by governmental agencies can affect the actions of firms.

In a news story appearing in the Houston Post, March 3, 1977, it was announced that the Federal Energy Administration is reducing the ceiling price for domestic crude oil by 45 cents a barrel for the next five months to make up for previously "excessively high" ceilings (whatever that means) the previous year. The story indicated that American oil producers say that domestic prices are not adequate to encourage exploration. The lower price would, they argued, discourage production even more. But the FEA reported that they were charged with keeping the average price of oil moving upward at "just the right slow pace" (whatever that is, again). Their estimate for the previous year had been slightly off, permitting the average price to rise "too high," and an assistant general counsel of the FEA said that the ceiling would be raised gradually over the next five months in small steps.

A reporter asked one FEA official whether the new rollback might reduce domestic production. This official replied, "We're hoping it won't have a significant impact because hopefully producers can see light at [the] end of [the] tunnel, with things returning to normal after July."

Who seems to know more about economics, the reporter or the FEA official? Well, first, "light at the end of the tunnel" must mean that producers know price will rise from March to August. Because they know price will be higher in the future, the official must mean that production would not fall immediately. To go a step further, the official must feel if there were no light—i.e., if prices were expected to stay low—producers would produce the same amount between March and August as they would if they knew the price would be higher in August. Surely, knowing prices will be higher in the future would to some extent discourage present production. Thus the light at the end of the tunnel will discourage present production.

Provide a criticism of the preceding analysis of the official's remarks about expected future price increases not affecting the present production. What variable has been left out that may well distort
both the official's and my analysis? Would the expected rate of interest have any effect? (This may not really have an obvious answer.
The rate of interest would have affected the rate of extraction anyway.) What do you think?

9.4 OLIGOPOLY AND COLLUSION

Thus far we have excluded to some extent a formal analysis of one possible form of oligopolistic behavior. The firms in an oligopoly may decide
that competive behavior is unprofitable and decide to collude or fix price,
either implicitly or explicitly. Explicit collusive behavior is illegal in the
United States under the Sherman Act, and other legislation. But antitrust litigations still flourish. Thus, there is probably some such behavior
still going on.

9.4.a Cartels and profit maximization

A cartel is a combination of firms whose objective is to limit the competitive forces within a market. It may take the form of open collusion,
the member firms entering into contracts about price and other market
variables. On the other hand the cartel may involve secret collusion among
members. Or it can operate like a trade association or a professional organization. At this time the most famous cartel is OPEC, a cartel of major oil
producing nations. Cartels may have an enforceable contract or they
may not. We will speak of all such cases of organized collusion as cartels.

Let us consider an "ideal" case. Suppose a group of firms producing a
homogeneous commodity forms a cartel. A central management body is
appointed, its function being to determine the uniform cartel price. The
task, in theory, is relatively simple, as illustrated in Figure 9.4.1. Market
demand for the homogeneous commodity is given by DD', so marginal
revenue is given by the dashed line MR. The cartel marginal cost curve
must be determined by the management body. If all firms in the cartel
purchase all inputs in perfectly competitive markets, the cartel marginal
cost curve (MC_c) is simply the horizontal sum of the marginal cost
curves of the member firms. Otherwise, allowance must be made for the
increase in input price accompanying an increase in input usage; MC_c

will stand further to the left than it would if all input markets were perfectly competitive.

In either case the management group determines cartel marginal cost MC_c. The problem is the simple one of determining the price that maximizes cartel profit—the monopoly price. From Figure 9.4.1, marginal cost and marginal revenue intersect at the level OA; thus the market price Op is the one the cartel management will establish. Given the demand curve DD', buyers will purchase Ox units from the members of the cartel. The second important problem confronting the cartel management is *how* to distribute the total sales of Ox units among the member firms.

9.4.b Cartel and market sharing

Fundamentally, there are two methods of sales allocation: nonprice competition and quotas. The former is usually associated with "loose" cartels. A uniform price is fixed and each firm is allowed to sell all it can at that price. Firms cannot reduce price but can compete by other means. For instance, in most localities both medical doctors and lawyers have associations whose code of ethics is frequently the basis of a price agreement. Each person selects a doctor or lawyer on the basis of considerations other than price. Similarly, the generally uniform prices of haircuts and major brands of gasoline result from tacit and sometimes even open

FIGURE 9.4.1

CARTEL PROFIT MAXIMIZATION

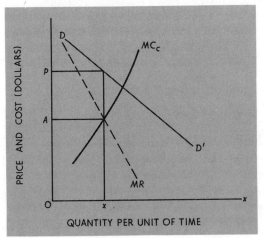

agreement on price. Even in the case of illegal activities such as prostitution there is generally a rather uniform price charged for the same commodity in the same general area.

APPLICATION

Price competition and advertising in the legal profession

Until recently most legal codes of ethics prohibited lawyers from doing any advertising other than listing in the telephone directory. There was absolutely no price advertising permitted. Recently the courts have made legal the advertising of services by lawyers. There is some debate concerning the legality of price advertising.

Suppose you are a student in law school or perhaps a beginning lawyer. Would you be for or against the restriction on advertising, particularly price advertising? How would the new court ruling affect you? What if you were an older established lawyer?

It seems likely that a beginning lawyer would oppose the restriction on advertising or price cutting. By and large, other things—such as the legal fee—remaining constant, people requiring legal help would prefer experienced lawyers rather than beginning lawyers *at the same price.* If the beginning lawyer is not connected with an established firm, competing with established lawyers is difficult under the restrictions. The best way for a young lawyer to secure clients is to offer services at a lower price and let people know about the lower price through advertising. If the beginning lawyer can survive and establish a reputation, then he or she should favor the restriction that limits the competition from inexperienced lawyers. Once lawyers become well known and established in the profession, then they would welcome restrictions on the advertising of reduced prices by the newer lawyers.

The problem of a young lawyer becoming established is closely related to search costs, a topic we covered earlier in the text. When people demand legal services and do not already have a lawyer in mind, they must search for a lawyer. Older established lawyers would be the ones recommended by word of mouth or merely be known by reputation. It takes valuable time to seek out information about qualities of other lawyers. These lesser known lawyers can become better known and can overcome to some extent the problem of search costs by advertising, particularly by price advertising. Therefore, because of these search costs, one would expect established lawyers to sup-

port restrictions on advertising, particularly price advertising and
new lawyers to oppose such restrictions, at least until they become
established themselves.

Incidentally, immediately after the court ruling making advertising
by lawyers legal, the local paper in the small city in which I live ran
an article reporting the results of a series of interviews with local lawyers about this ruling. Many lawyers were interviewed. The lawyers
interviewed split about half and half. *Each and every lawyer,* who in
the interview was opposed to advertising by the legal profession, I
knew either personally or by reputation; and in a good many cases I
had served on civic committees with them. *Each and every lawyer*
who was in favor of advertising by the legal profession, including
price advertising, was unknown to me, to any member of my family,
or to the few people I talked to about the news story. While econometricians would not consider this the best way to test an economic
theory, there is some evidence here. Evidence: neither well-known,
established lawyers nor little-known, unestablished lawyers are economically illiterate.

The second method of market sharing is the quota system, of which
there are several variants. Indeed, there is no uniform principle by which
quotas can be determined. In practice, the bargaining ability of a firm's
representative and the importance of the firm to the cartel are likely to be
among the more important elements in determining a quota. Beyond this
there are two popular methods. First, either the relative sales of the firms
in some pre-cartel base period or the productive capacities of the firms
are used. As a practical matter, the choice of base period or the measure
of capacity is a matter of bargaining among members. The second basis
is a geographical division of the market. Many of the more famous examples involve international markets.

While quota agreement is difficult in practice, in theory some simple
guidelines can be laid down. Consider the cartel solution that was shown
in Figure 9.4.1. MC_c is the horizontal summation of all firms' marginal cost
curves. The cartel produces and sells the output level Ox at a price Op.
The minimum cartel cost of producing Ox, or any other level of output, is
achieved when each firm produces the output such that every firm's
marginal cost is the same and equals the common cartel marginal cost
and marginal revenue. Thus each firm in the cartel shown in Figure
9.4.1 produces the output at which its marginal cost is OA. Note that this

solution is precisely that set forth in the case of the multiplant monopolist, discussed in Chapter 8 above.

To reinforce the analysis, suppose that two firms in the cartel are producing at different marginal costs; that is, assume

$$MC_1 > MC_2$$

for firms one and two. In this case the cartel manager could transfer output from the higher cost Firm 1 to the lower cost Firm 2. So long as the marginal cost of producing in Firm 2 is lower, total cartel cost can be lowered by transferring production. Thus in equilibrium the marginal costs will be equal for all firms.

There still exists the problem of allocating the profit among firms. If the cost structure for all firms were alike, the firms could of course simply share profits equally. But if cost differences exist, the voluntary profit sharing would probably collapse. That, as we shall see, is what is most likely to happen to cartels.

9.4.c Short and turbulent life of cartels

Unless backed by strong legal provisions, cartels in the United States are very likely to collapse from internal pressure (before being found out by the Antitrust Division of the Justice Department). A few large, geographically concentrated firms producing a homogeneous commodity may form a very successful cartel and maintain it, at least during periods of prosperity. But the greater the number of firms, the greater the scope of product differentiation, and the greater the geographical dispersion of firms, the easier it is to "cheat" on the cartel's policy. In times of marked prosperity profit may be so great that there is little incentive to cheat. But when profits are low or negative, there is a marked incentive; and when the incentive exists, enterprising entrepreneurs will discover what they believe to be ingenious methods of cheating.

The typical cartel is characterized by high (perhaps monopoly) price, relatively low output, and a distribution of sales among firms such that each firm operates at less than minimum unit cost. In this situation any one firm can profit greatly from secret price concessions. Indeed, with a homogeneous product, a firm offering price concessions can capture as much of the market as desired, providing the other members adhere to the cartel's price policy. Thus secret price concessions do not have to be extensive before the obedient members experience a marked decline in sales. Recognizing that one or more members are cheating, the formerly obedient members must themselves reduce price in order to remain viable. The cartel accordingly collapses. Without effective *legal* sanctions, the life of a cartel is likely to be brief, ending whenever a business recession occurs.

If entry is relatively simple and there are no great economies of scale, the probability of collapse increases. If firms can produce relatively similar products and sell at lower prices, these entrants must be absorbed into the cartel or the price-fixing agreement will break up. But entry will compete away all profits even with price fixing. Recall the situation mentioned in our discussion of monopolistic competition and shown again in Figure 9.4.2. Price fixing and entry lead to an equilibrium for each firm at point A, with no pure profits. The demand *DD′* is the typical firm's demand under the assumption that all firms change price together. If a firm changes price while all other firms maintain the old price, its demand is *dd′*.

FIGURE 9.4.2

WHY CARTELS COLLAPSE

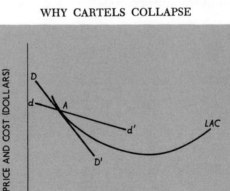

An unrecognized decrease in price by any one firm would increase profit substantially. Furthermore, each firm knows that every other firm is strongly motivated to decrease price also. Thus every firm is induced for two reasons to lower price and attempt to capture the frictional gains before the other firms do likewise. In this way the cartel breaks up because everyone has the incentive to cheat on the agreement before the other firms do so. As an aside, this is somewhat like the situation when everyone expects a huge price increase for a product or even zero availability of the product in the very near future (for example, Cuban cigars immediately after the United States broke off trade relations with Cuba). Everyone goes out and buys up huge amounts of the product before the "dirty hoarders" get it all.

Of course, the fewer the number of firms in a price-fixing agreement, the easier it is to detect firms that break the agreement and reduce price. Thus in the case of very few firms, the detection cost is low and the cartel is more likely to survive. The situation shown in Figure 9.4.2 is not so likely in the case of few firms in the agreement. Economies of scale may make it impossible to enter on a small scale, and the oligopoly is maintained even with free entry.

9.4.d Price leadership in oligopoly

Another type of solution to the oligopoly problem is price leadership. This solution does not require open collusion, but the firms must tacitly agree to the solution. Price leadership has in fact been quite common in certain industries. It was characteristic of the steel industry quite some time ago. At times it has characterized the tire, oil, and cigarette industries. At the present time, the most famous cartel characterized by price leadership is OPEC.

Any firm in an oligopoly can be the price leader; while it is frequently the dominant firm in the oligopoly, it may be the most efficient firm or simply one with a past reputation for good judgment. The price leader sets a price that will maximize industry profits, and all firms in the industry compete for sales through advertising and other types of marketing. The price remains constant until the price leader changes the price, or one or more other firms break away.

Another form of price leadership occurs when there is one firm that has the capability of becoming a monopoly. The dominant firm sets a price at which the smaller firms behave as competitors and sell all that they wish at that existing price. The dominant firm will supply the rest of the quantity demanded at the market price. The dominant firm, therefore, sets a price that maximizes its own profit subject to the constraint that the fringe firms will supply the remaining portion of the market at that price. This form of price setting is still prevalent in a large number of industries.

APPLICATIONS

Some problems concerning cartels

As noted, the OPEC countries formed a cartel to fix the price of oil. At recent (1977) OPEC meetings most OPEC countries argued for substantial increases in the price of oil. Saudi Arabia has, until now at these meetings, consistently held out for no price increase or at least for very small price increases. The other countries have largely gone along, but they have been unhappy with the small price increases. Editorial writers have "explained" the situation in two ways. First, Saudi Arabia is a good friend of the United States and Western Europe and because of past good relations does not wish to "gouge" the West. The second explanation is that Saudi Arabia is so poor that it cannot absorb all of the income into the economy; therefore, it does not need any more profit. Can you think of an alternative explanation?

A logical explanation, based upon economic analysis as well as some evidence, is that Saudi Arabia is the dominant firm in OPEC. Its production and reserves are by far the largest. When the price of oil increases substantially, sales fall to some extent. Some country or countries must be willing to absorb the decline in sales; otherwise, price cheating will be encouraged and the cartel will break up. Until now the dominant firm, Saudi Arabia, has largely absorbed the decrease, at times along with Iran. Thus, the Saudi government realizes that the burden of decreased sales from increased price would fall on them. The other countries can only benefit from the increased prices if Saudi Arabia, and possibly Iran, absorb all or most of the decrease in sales. This may explain why in price negotiations Saudi Arabia "likes the West while the others do not."

The college you are attending may very well belong to a rather powerful cartel that differs to some extent from those about which we have spoken. It certainly belongs if your school competes in major college football or basketball. This cartel is the National Collegiate Athletic Association (NCAA). Many years ago, as college football increased in popularity, schools paid prospective athletes to play for them. Colleges did not like to pay for resources that they previously got free. They formed the NCAA, which established recruiting rules making it illegal to pay athletes. In other words, they fixed wages rather than commodity prices. There are substantial penalties for schools that violate the recruiting rules—loss of TV revenue, bans from appearing in Bowls, and so on.

Certain highly successful coaches such as a former UCLA basketball coach and a former football coach at the University of Texas, during the later years of their coaching careers, frequently deplored the recruiting practices of universities and called for increased restriction in recruiting and harsher punishment for those schools that violate the restrictions. Sports writers explained this by pointing out that these coaches were very moral men, men of great integrity. Admittedly these successful coaches are men of great morality and integrity; but can you offer an alternative explanation for why the most successful coaches, those with the best records, are almost always the ones calling for increased restrictions on the recruiting of high school athletes?

The solution to this question is similar to the problem of advertising in the legal profession. Those athletic programs that have been highly successful during the recent past have a significant initial advantage over other, less successful schools in recruiting high school players. The less successful schools and coaches can overcome their initial disadvantage by strong recruiting, possibly by recruiting methods that may be illegal—not illegal by law but illegal by the rules of the price-fixing cartel.

Thus, the stricter the rules about recruiting high school players, the more difficult it is for the less successful or less well-established schools to recruit and compete successfully with the more established programs. For economic reasons the schools with the most successful athletic programs are in favor of severe recruiting regulations. Integrity and morality have very little to do with it, even though forbidding payments to young athletes is always explained as being "for the good of the athlete." (By the way, the NCAA differs slightly from the other price-fixing cartels we have discussed, since it operates on the buying side of the market. It is called a *monopsony*—a term meaning a "single buyer"; this concept is discussed in the next chapter.)

9.5 COMPETITION IN OLIGOPOLY MARKETS

There is a certain amount of debate among economists as to the amount of price competition in industries characterized by oligopoly. Certainly prices do fluctuate under oligopoly, but this is frequently because of price leadership. It is still questionable just how rigid or how flexible prices are under oligopoly. In any case, oligopoly is characterized by much more non-price competition than are other market structures. We shall first examine the question of price rigidity, then discuss non-price competition.

9.5.a Oligopoly and price rigidity

A traditional feature of oligopoly stressed by many economists since the 1930s is the prevalence of rigid or "sticky" prices in industries characterized by oligopoly. It was assumed that competitive industries and monopolistic firms adapted to changes in the environment by changing prices and output. Oligopoly supposedly was not so adaptable, since prices were administered and kept rigid. Certainly this hypothesis would have significant microeconomic implications for resource allocation if prices did not react to changes in costs in the case of oligopoly. Implications were even carried over into macroeconomics in order to explain disequilibrium in the economy as a whole. For example, if prices were not flexible downward in many large industries during a downturn in the business cycle, unemployment could result.

Many theories have been set forth to explain why prices are inflexible in an oligopoly market structure. The most frequently cited hypothesis took the following form: If one oligopolist increases its price, competing oligopolists will hold their prices constant. Thus the oligopolistic firm that raises price will lose considerable sales to rivals. On the other hand, if one oligopolist lowers price, the rival firms, fearing substantial losses in sales, will lower their prices also. Thus, the oligopolist that lowers price will experience only an insignificant increase in sales, because of the price competition. For these reasons the oligopolist would have little motivation to change prices. This theory was supposed to explain why oligopoly is characterized by sticky prices, but of course it could not explain why price is what it is in the first place. The thesis must therefore be regarded as an ex-post rationalization of market behavior rather than an ex-ante explanation of market equilibrium.

ASIDE

Some evidence about oligopolistic price rigidity

It may be the case that the above-stated hypothesis rationalizes a phenomenon that noes not occur as frequently as was formerly thought. In 1947 George J. Stigler, using industrial data from the 1930s, carried out some tests of the hypothesis.* Recall that the

---

* George J. Stigler, "The Kinky Oligopoly Demand Curve and Rigid Prices," *Journal of Political Economy*, October 1947, pp. 432–49. Reprinted in George J. Stigler, *The Organization of Industry* (Homewood, Ill.: Richard D. Irwin, 1968).

theory states that when an industry is characterized by oligopoly, price reductions will be followed but price increases will not. As a first piece of evidence Stigler found that in seven highly oligopolistic industries (cigarettes, automobiles, anthracite coal, dynamite, oil, potash, and steel) both price decreases and increases by firms in the industry were rapidly followed by other firms. In none of the seven industries was there any evidence consistent with the theory of very sticky prices. In fact, based on experience, firms would expect both increases and decreases to be matched rather quickly.

Stigler then compared the stickiness of oligopoly price in many industries with that of prices in industries characterized by monopoly. Even though their outputs varied significantly more than that of most of the oligopolistic industries tested, two monopolies (aluminum and nickel) were characterized during the period by significantly more price rigidity than was the case for the oligopolies. Further-more, the oligopolists, who had periods of known explicit collusion, experienced extreme price rigidity during collusion. The hypothesis would predict that collusion would eliminate the stickiness and lead to greater flexibility. There was much more flexibility during periods of non-collusion.

The hypothesis would also predict that the fewer the number of firms in the oligopoly, the more flexible the price. Stigler's data showed the opposite effect; the average number of price changes in the industry during the period of observation varied *directly* with the number of dominant firms in the oligopoly. In summary, Stigler's sample, while small, showed little evidence of extreme price rigidity in oligopolies.

Much later, Julian L. Simon tested the oligopolistic sticky price hypothesis, using changes in advertising rates in business magazines for the period 1955–64.† His data indicated that monopolistic maga-zines, that is, magazines with no competitors in the same category, do not change rates any more frequently than do magazines with a few close competitors within their classification. In fact, Simon found that with one exception, magazines in one-magazine groups change price less frequently than do magazines in multiple-magazine groups. Also, there was progressively more frequent price change in going from single-magazine to ten-magazine groups. The main results of the test show no evidence that oligopoly changes price less fre-quently than does monopoly.

---

† Julian L. Simon, "A Further Test of the Kinky Oligopoly Demand Curve," *The American Economic Review,* December 1969, pp. 971–75.

9.5.b Non-price competition

Notwithstanding the above evidence, oligopoly is also characterized by considerable non-price competition. The alternative forms of non-price competition are as diverse as the minds of inventive entrepreneurs can make them. Yet there is one central feature: an oligopoly frequently attempts to attract customers to its own product (and, therefore, away from that of rivals) by some means other than a price differential. Non-price competition accordingly involves the differentiation of a product that is fundamentally homogeneous. The ways of differentiating are diverse, but three principal methods deserve mention.

Perhaps the most important technique of non-price competition is advertising. In the United States and in many European countries advertising is the uniformly most accepted method of attracting customers, accepted at least by businessmen if not by economists. The "pros and cons" of advertising expenditure have been argued at length; the argument is likely to continue because there are many aspects to the question. But for good or not, advertising is an established practice that is presumably considered worthwhile, for businessmen otherwise would not continue to spend billions of dollars annually on this type of non-price competition.

There is considerable argument about the effect of advertising on industrial concentration—the market share of the largest few firms. Some say that large-scale advertising is a barrier to the entry of new firms into the industry. That is, the largest firms do so much advertising that new firms would have to advertise their products on a very large scale. Some say that because of economies of scale in advertising, a new firm could not compete initially at a small scale of operation. Thus the largest firms are protected somewhat against the entry of new rivals. Others argue that the effects of advertising are cumulative and favor established firms.

Some counter by arguing that the only way new firms can successfully compete with established firms is through advertising. If advertising were banned, the established firms would still be able to maintain sales because of their past reputation; consumer recognition would continue. New firms would have no way to gain consumer recognition without advertising. In this way the established firms would be protected from new entries, and concentration would continue. There is as yet no clear statistical evidence supporting either side, and the impact of advertising on concentration is still undetermined.

APPLICATION

An effect of the ban on broadcast advertising on cigarette consumption

The model of oligopoly and advertising along with some statistical evidence were used in a recent paper by James L. Hamilton to estimate the degree to which cigarette smoking in the United States was affected by the congressional ban on TV and radio advertising of cigarettes.* He first estimated statistically the demand for cigarettes. He estimated the effect on cigarette consumption of (1) per capita income, (2) a cigarette price index, (3) advertising expenditures, and (4) several variables representing the cigarette health scare.

It was shown that cigarette advertising expenditure—both per capita and aggregate—had very little if any effect on total cigarette consumption. Why would cigarette manufacturers advertise at all if advertising does not affect sales significantly, unless they are dumb? Economists generally think that cigarette advertising is used competitively by the different firms to expand (or hold on to) their share of the market. Any firm that stopped advertising would soon experience a substantial loss in sales to the other firms. On the other hand, all firms together could increase or decrease total advertising without much change in total sales. It appears that while total smoking may not be connected with total advertising, the sales of any one manufacturer are related to its own advertising. Quite possibly the ban on some cigarette advertising increased profits for most of the established firms. The firms' expenses fell while *total sales* dropped very little.

On the other hand, the variables for the health scare were very significant. Further statistical tests indicated that the health scare was several times more powerful as a deterrent to smoking than advertising was as a sales stimulant. When Congress, to reduce cigarette smoking, banned broadcast advertising of cigarettes, it also ended the free broadcast time for antismoking advertising required by the FCC under its fairness doctrine for controversial issues. Antismoking groups now had to pay for advertising and, of course, did not or could not continue to advertise close to the level attained before the ban. In 1970 the free antismoking advertising was about one third of total cigarette advertising, a subsidy of about $75 million.

---

* James L. Hamilton, "The Demand for Cigarettes: Advertising, the Health Scare, and the Cigarette Advertising Ban," *The Review of Economics and Statistics,* November 1972, pp. 401–11.

Antismoking advertising after the ban on cigarette advertising dropped to a small fraction of what it had been before.

Although no substantive results are in as yet, Hamilton points out that cigarette advertising fell 20 to 30 percent in 1971 while per capita consumption increased noticeably after being sluggish for several years. The statistics seem to suggest that the ban increased consumption above what it would have been with both broadcast cigarette advertising and subsidized health-scare advertising. Furthermore, the ban seems to strengthen the present manufacturers, since the easiest way for a new company to enter the market had been through large-scale broadcast advertising.

Whatever the case, these results point to the value of careful theoretical and empirical analysis of policy changes prior to those changes. They also show an important use of demand analysis and estimation.

Another important type of non-price competition consists of creating bona fide (but sometimes spurious) quality differentials among products. The general effect of quality differentiation is to divide a broad market into a group of submarkets among which there is usually a relatively large price differential. The automobile market offers a good example. There are definite, physically specifiable differences between a Ford Pinto and the Ford Motor Company's Continental. There is also a substantial price difference; no one buyer is likely to be a potential customer in both markets, except perhaps for automobiles to perform two fundamentally different services (family car and business runabout).

Ford is not alone in creating quality differentials, however. General Motors and Chrysler do the same; and they engage in active non-price competition within each of the submarkets. Further, the automobile market example brings to light a social criticism of quality competition. Quality differentials may be created so that items supposedly in one class overlap with items in another, as do, for example, Pontiac, Oldsmobile, and Buick. Thus within the broad market not only is there competition to create new quality classes and gain the competitive edge of being the first in the market; there is also competition within quality classes.

Finally, a third major technique of non-price competition is design differences. This type could also be illustrated by the automobile market; but the market for golf clubs serves just as well. MacGregor, Wilson,

Spalding, and other producers now change models annually, just as do automobile manufacturers. They also create (possibly spurious) quality differentials as between sporting-goods stores and pro shops. But within, say, the pro-shop market, the competition among companies is strictly a matter of club design. These three types of non-price competition far from exhaust the possible methods, but they do illustrate the ways in which entrepreneurs can spend resources in an effort to attract customers to their particular "brands."

9.5.c Government and oligopolistic non-price competition

As noted above, cartels, which are established to fix prices, break up under intense competitive conditions. Frequently, government—local, state, or national—is induced to regulate an industry, ostensibly in the public interest. The regulation usually takes the form of forbidding or hampering entry into the industry and of regulating price. Most studies of this area have indicated that price regulation establishes a price above that which would exist in the absence of regulation.

With a higher price and with entry prohibited one might suppose that the government regulation would be quite profitable for the firms in the protected industry. As we have mentioned, this is often the case, but regulated industries are not always profitable. Sometimes the regulated firms compete away the pure profit through non-price competition.

As noted, airlines are a case in point. All evidence shows that the regulated fares are considerably above the fares that would be established in the absence of regulation. For example, airlines operating only intra-state flights, and therefore not subject to interstate federal regulation, charge much lower prices for the same distance traveled than the inter-state, regulated airlines. Again, as we noted, the airlines have not been particularly profitable because the non-price competition for passengers has competed away the pure profit even though price was kept high. Thus price regulation does not always guarantee profit.

9.6 SUMMARY

Because of interdependence, there is no real theory of oligopoly, and it is difficult to be very precise about the welfare effect of oligopoly. Certainly there is no reason to believe that oligopolists will produce at minimum long-run average cost. Thus, oligopoly requires more units of resources per unit of output than absolutely necessary. Price is frequently higher than both average and marginal cost.

Furthermore, many resources are devoted to non-price competition under oligopoly. If, as some say, many of these resources are "wasted," then too many resources are devoted to oligopoly. On the other hand, much advertising and quality and design differentials may be socially desirable. There is no clear evidence on either side. But, the welfare criteria imposed are static. Dynamic considerations are also important.

Industrial research and development has been essential in the development of our modern industrial economy and is essential to its continued viability and growth. Many argue, with considerable persuasiveness, that R&D usually thrives only in oligopolistic markets. Neither perfect competitors nor pure monopolists have the incentive; and perfect competitors are usually not large enough to support research departments. Oligopolistic firms, on the other hand, always have the incentive: improve the product or reduce its cost so as to increase profit. Furthermore, such firms are typically large enough to absorb the short-run cost of R&D in order to reap its long-run payoff. In short, all sorts of static welfare criteria may be violated more or less with impunity if the dynamic rate of growth is sufficiently rapid. Some economists, and all oligopolists, hold that oligopolistic market organization is essential for the dynamic growth of the economy.

APPLICATIONS

Some market incentives for oligopolists to reduce pollution and install safety devices

It is not altogether correct to say that the theories of oligopoly are totally useless for economic analysis. For example, a colleague of ours, W. P. Gramm, used some theoretical characteristics of oligopoly to make some points and predictions (that later proved reliable) about the capacity of the market system to abate pollution.*

As Gramm noted, pollution generally is analyzed as a social cost imposed upon society by the market system with no possibility for self-correction. Supposedly, only government through direct controls, fines, or subsidies can act against pollution. In the absence of governmental intervention no firm is motivated to act alone to de-

---

* W. P. Gramm, "A Theoretical Note on the Capacity of the Market System to Abate Pollution," *Land Economics*, August 1969, pp. 336–38.

crease its own polluting because of the cost involved. Gramm, however, showed that the standard analysis is relevant only to competition and monopoly; under oligopoly there can exist both the means and motivation to decrease pollution.

As noted, oligopolists do not particularly like price competition; they do attempt to compete among themselves by product differentials. Any oligopoly likes to differentiate its product, in the minds of consumers, from those of its close competitors. Therefore, Gramm suggested that if consumers can be marginally motivated to purchase on the basis of pollution and non-pollution, firms will be motivated to some extent to correct pollution. Non-pollution is a form of product differentiation. Firms gain advantages by advertising and identifying with non-pollution, but the consumers must be aware of pollution and care enough about correction.

Competitors would have no reason for pollution abatement. They produce a homogeneous product, indistinguishable from that of any other competitor. A monopoly may have the resources to act against pollution, but, because of its strong market position, it would have little motivation to do so. A monopolistic competitor would have the motivation to differentiate products but would quite possibly lack resources. Thus, oligopoly appears to be, at least theoretically, the most responsive to consumer pressure to cease polluting, particularly when the oligopolists have large financial resources and a research department. While pollution abatement is a cost to the firm, it does not necessarily follow that product price must rise if oligopolists voluntarily undertake abatement for product differentiation. If the public is motivated to buy on the basis of non-pollution, the oligopolists may substitute some abatement for advertising. In any case, if consumers are motivated sufficiently to purchase from non-polluting firms, they may be willing to bear some of the costs of abatement in the form of higher prices.

We might note that Gramm's paper admittedly was concerned solely with the theoretical existence of motivation and not with the empirical relevance of that motivation. He did, however, question why oligopolistic firms had not been motivated in the past to seek product differentiation through non-pollution. He answered that this may indicate that the consuming public was uninformed of the problem or was unconcerned; that is, unwilling to pay the price. If either is the case, pollution is not solely attributable to the market system. If people will pay the price, many firms will differentiate by non-pollution. When there is a demand, there is usually someone to fill it, if it can be done at a profit. If a polluter could not sell its products, it would soon stop polluting or go out of business.

In passing, we might note that Gramm actually predicted a coming trend. Since the paper appeared, we have noted an increasing tendency for firms, most of which are oligopolies, to do considerable advertising telling the public that they do not pollute. The oil companies in particular seem to be turning in that direction. It will be interesting to see how successful consumer pressure—if any is forthcoming—will be. In any case, this is one example in which oligopoly theory was used to analyze a problem and make a prediction.

There are other examples of firms remedying social problems if there is sufficient consumer demand to do so. As we noted above, frequently government agencies force manufacturers to add extras onto products in order to make these products safer to the users, even though the demanders are not willing to pay, if given the choice, for the extra safety features.

If, however, the public demands the added safety features, oligopoly firms will not only add these features but will actually compete by advertising this added safety as a means of product differentiation, even without governmental intervention. For this to occur there must be noticeable product identification and consumer demand for the extras.

Chain saws are a good case in point. For quite some time they were used only by professionals, who did not desire additional safety. These safety features decrease the efficiency of the saw. But, as individual households became a growing market for chain saws, the old style saws were too dangerous for nonprofessionals. Companies began, through advertising, to compete in telling the public about the safety of their chain saws. More and more safety features have been added voluntarily, because of consumer demand. There are other examples of power tools that improved in safety as they began to be used more and more by nonprofessionals.

TECHNICAL PROBLEMS

1. The smaller the seller's share in a cartel, the greater would be the temptation to cut prices in slack times. Why?

2. Describe the major features of monopolistic competition:
   a. How is it similar to monopoly?
   b. How is it similar to competition?
   c. What characterizes short-run equilibrium?
   d. Differentiate between the two possible long-run equilibria, discussing how each is attained.
   e. What is excess capacity under monopolistic competition?

3. Why is there no general theory of oligopoly?

4. What type of barriers might permit a profitable oligopoly to last a long time?

5. A monopolistic competitor has the cost and revenue curves in Figure E.9.1.

FIGURE E.9.1

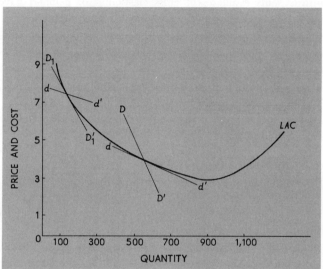

The demands *DD'* and *dd'* are those described in the text.

a. If the market is characterized by intense price cutting and some entry, long-run equilibrium is at _____ units of output and a price of $_____.

b. Excess capacity is _____ units.

c. If there is no price competition but free entry, long-run equilibrium is established at _____ units and a price of $_____.

d. Excess capacity is now _____ units.

e. What would be the long-run price if the firm were a perfect competitor?

6. Assume that the bituminous coal industry is a competitive industry in long-run equilibrium. Now assume that the firms in the industry form a cartel.

a. What will happen to the equilibrium output and price of coal and why?

b. How should the output be distributed among the individual firms?

c. After the cartel is operating, are there incentives for the individual firm to cheat? Why or why not?

ANALYTICAL PROBLEMS

1. Explain in the terms of the two demand curves why cartels tend to break up.

2. "One sure test that an industry is competitive is the absence of any pure profit." Comment critically.

3. In antitrust suits estimates of cross elasticities of demand have been of major importance. Why would such estimates be of importance?

4. Oil companies advertise that they are very pollution-conscious. Beer companies do also. Why do not cotton farmers advertise that they use pollution-free insecticide?

5. If you were attempting to establish a price-fixing cartel in an industry,
    a. Would you prefer many or few firms? Why?
    b. How could you prevent cheating (price cutting) by cartel members? Why would members have an incentive to cheat?
    c. Would you keep substantial or very few records? What are the advantages and disadvantages of each?
    d. How could you prevent entry into the industry?
    e. How could government help you prevent entry and even cheating?
    f. How would you try to talk government into helping? Under what conditions might this work?

6. In 1969 an informal price survey was conducted of the prostitutes in a particular four-block area in San Francisco. From the 30 to 40 prostitutes sampled (that is, questioned about prices) it was found that the price of each was identical to the price of every other for equivalent services even though they differed somewhat in certain characteristics.
    a. Give two possible explanations for the uniformity of prices. (Note: prostitution was illegal at the time.)
    b. If one of your explanations was a cartel, how would price cutting or cheating have been discouraged?
    c. Since there was no price competition, how do you suspect the firms competed? We noted above that young lawyers would benefit by price cutting. Would young or old prostitutes benefit by making prostitution legal, therefore legalizing price cutting?

10

Theory of distribution

10.1 INTRODUCTION

We have now developed the modern or neoclassical theory of value— a theory explaining the origin of demand, supply, and market price. A central part of this theory of value is the marginal cost of production and its possible reflection in the supply curve. Costs and supply, in turn, depend upon the technological conditions of production and the cost of productive services. So far we have generally assumed that both are given. We will continue to assume that the physical conditions of production are technologically given and do not change over the time period relevant to our analysis; but now we must determine the prices of productive services, the distribution half of "value and distribution," or modern microeconomic theory.

Broadly speaking, the theory of input pricing does not differ from the theory of pricing goods. Both are fundamentally based upon the interaction of demand and supply. In the present case, demand arises from business firms (rather than consumers) and supply, at least the supply of labor services, arises from individuals who are not only sellers of labor time but are also consumers. Furthermore, for the more interesting cases of capital and labor, one determines the price of using the resource for a stipulated period of time, not the price of purchasing the resource. In

other respects, however, the theory of distribution is the theory of value
of productive services.

10.1.a Fundamentals of the theory

As you no doubt already suspect, the entire theory of distribution is
based upon marginal analysis. The theory is quite simple. Suppose you
own a business and a worker applies for a job. Would you hire this
worker? If the worker is expected to add more to revenue than you must
pay in wages, the answer is obviously, "Yes." If the worker is expected
to add less in revenue than you must pay in wages, the answer is obviously, "No." The same is true for any factor of production. A firm
would increase its use of a particular input of any type if the additional
unit of the input is expected to add more to revenue than it adds to cost.
If the additional unit increases cost more than it increases revenue, no
more of the input would be added. As noted, the basic theory is simple;
but it is simple probably because you have already learned a great deal
about marginal analysis—the economic way of thinking.

The amount that an additional unit of the input adds to total revenue
is called *marginal revenue product* (*MRP*). That is,

$$MRP = \frac{\triangle \text{ Revenue}}{\triangle \text{ Input usage}}.$$

The amount that an additional unit of the input adds to total cost is called
marginal factor cost (*MFC*).[1] Thus

$$MFC = \frac{\triangle \text{ Cost}}{\triangle \text{ Input usage}}.$$

The basic rule then is, if for a particular input

$$MRP > MFC,$$

the firm would add more of the input. If

$$MRP < MFC,$$

the firm would add no more of the input; it would, in fact, decrease its use.
Thus, equilibrium input use requires

$$MRP = MFC.$$

---

[1] Marginal factor cost is sometimes referred to as marginal expenditure on input
(*MEI*). This term was used in the first two editions of this text. From the comments
of users it appears that marginal factor cost is preferred.

While the fundamentals are the same for a competitor or a monopolist, marginal revenue product for a monopolist differs from that for a competitive firm. Similarly, marginal factor cost can differ somewhat among different firms. We will analyze the various aspects of the theory in this chapter.

10.1.b Basic points developed

In this chapter you will learn the following concepts:

1. The fundamental determinants of the demand for factors of production in the cases of a monopolist, a competitive firm, and a competitive industry.
2. How firms decide how much of an input to use.
3. What differences occur when a firm's input use has some effect on the price of that input.
4. How unions can affect wages and employment.
5. How the firm's investment decision is made.
6. What determines an input's price and amount of use in the market.

10.2 DEMAND FOR A PRODUCTIVE SERVICE: PERFECT COMPETITION IN INPUT MARKETS, ONE VARIABLE INPUT

This section begins the theory of distribution with the very simplest case. We assume that only one resource or input is variable to the firm (we will relax this assumption later). The theory developed here is applicable to any productive service, although the most natural application refers to the demand for labor. Thus, when we speak of the demand for labor, the demand for any productive service is implied.

10.2.a Demand of a perfectly competitive firm

As we stressed above, it is intuitively obvious that a firm would increase the amount of labor used if the additional labor contributes more to the firm's income than to its cost; that is, if the marginal revenue product exceeds marginal factor cost. Consider the following example. A perfectly competitive firm sells its product at a market price of $1. It can hire one unit of the variable input, labor, at $10 per day. If increasing its labor force by one more worker adds more than 10 units of output per day, the firm would hire the additional worker.

Since each additional worker adds $10 to cost, the marginal factor cost in this case is the wage rate, $10. Marginal revenue product is the amount each additional worker adds to revenue. Each additional worker adds its marginal product times the price at which the marginal product can be sold. In other words marginal revenue product is marginal product times marginal revenue, which is for the competitive firm the commodity price, $1. In the case of a competitive firm, for which marginal revenue equals commodity price, marginal revenue product has a specific name, *the value of the marginal product*. We shall use this latter term throughout the discussion of the competitive firm.

> **Definition.** The value of the marginal product *(VMP)* of a factor of production for a competitive firm is the addition to total revenue attributable to the addition of one more unit of the factor. Thus the value of the marginal product is equal to the marginal product multiplied by commodity price.

Let us consider a numerical example. A perfectly competitive firm sells a product for $5 and employs labor at a wage rate of $20 a day. Table 10.2.1 lists the daily total product, marginal product, and value of marginal product (price of the product times marginal product) for zero through nine workers. Under these conditions the firm hires six workers. It would not hire fewer than six, since hiring the sixth adds $25 to revenue but costs only $20. The firm increases net revenue by $5. It would not hire seven workers because revenue would increase by $15 while cost would increase by $20, thereby causing a decrease in net revenue of $5. If, however, the wage rate dropped below $15 (say to $14) the work

TABLE 10.2.1

VALUE OF THE MARGINAL PRODUCT AND
INDIVIDUAL DEMAND FOR LABOR

Units of variable input	Total product	Marginal product	Value of marginal product
0............	0	—	—
1............	10	10	$ 50
2............	30	20	100
3............	50	20	100
4............	65	15	75
5............	75	10	50
6............	80	5	25
7............	83	3	15
8............	84	1	5
9............	81	−3	−15

force would increase to seven (an additional $15 revenue can be gained
at a cost of $14). If wages rose above $25 but remained below $50, the
firm would reduce the labor force to five.

> **Exercise.** In order to ascertain that hiring six workers is profit
> maximizing at a wage of $20, assume a fixed cost of $100 and com-
> pute the profit rates for all units in stage II (recall from Chapter 5 that
> stage II is the range from maximum average product to zero marginal
> product).

To get more directly to the proposition, consider Figure 10.2.1. Suppose the value of the marginal product is given by the curve labeled
VMP. The market wage rate is $O\bar{w}$, so the supply of labor to the firm is
the horizontal line S_L. First, suppose the firm employed only OL_1 units of
labor. At that rate of employment, the value of the marginal product is
$L_1C = Ow_1 > O\bar{w}$, the wage rate. At this point of operation an additional
unit of labor adds more to total revenue than to total cost (inasmuch as
it adds the value of its marginal product to total revenue and its unit
wage rate to cost). Hence a profit-maximizing entrepreneur would add
additional units of labor and indeed would continue to add units so
long as the value of the marginal product exceeds the wage rate.

Next, suppose OL_2 units of labor were employed. At this point the
value of the marginal product $L_2F = Ow_2$ is less than the wage rate.

FIGURE 10.2.1

PROOF OF $VMP = \bar{w}$ THEOREM

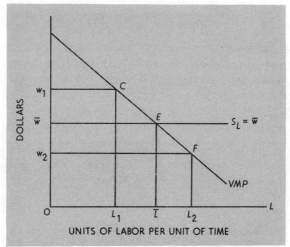

Each unit of labor adds more to total cost than to total revenue. Hence a profit-maximizing entrepreneur would not employ OL_2 units, or any number for which the wage rate exceeds the value of the marginal product. These arguments show that neither more nor fewer than $O\overline{L}$ units of labor would be employed and that employing $O\overline{L}$ units leads to profit maximization. The statements are summarized as follows:

Proposition. A profit-maximizing competitive firm will employ units of a variable productive service until the point is reached at which the value of the marginal product of the input is exactly equal to the input price.

In other words, given the market wage rate or the supply of labor curve to the firm, a perfectly competitive producer determines the quantity of labor to hire by equating the value of the marginal product to the wage rate. If the wage rate were Ow_1 (Fig. 10.2.1), the firm would employ OL_1 units of labor to equate the value of the marginal product to the given wage rate. Similarly, if the wage rate were Ow_2, the firm would employ OL_2 units of labor. By definition of a demand curve, therefore, the value of the marginal product curve is established as the competitive firm's demand curve for labor, when only labor is variable.

Definition. The competitive firm's demand curve for a *single* variable productive service is given by the value of the marginal product curve of the productive service in question. This is, of course, limited to production in stage II.

10.2.b Monopoly in the commodity market

The analytical principles underlying the demand for a single variable input are the same for perfectly and imperfectly competitive commodity markets. However, since commodity price and marginal revenue are different in imperfectly competitive markets, the marginal revenue product does not equal the value of marginal product—price times marginal product.

When a perfectly competitive seller employs an additional unit of labor, output is augmented by the marginal product of that unit. In like manner, total revenue is augmented by the value of its marginal product inasmuch as commodity price remains unchanged. When a monopoly employs additional labor (we restrict our attention to monopoly since the principles are the same for all noncompetitive firms), output also increases by the marginal product of the additional workers. However, to sell the larger output, commodity price must be reduced; hence total revenue is not augmented by the price times the marginal product of the additional workers.

A numerical example might clarify this point. In Table 10.2.2 columns (1) and (2) give the production function when labor is the only variable input. Columns (2) and (3) show the demand for the commodity that is produced by labor. Column (4) is the total revenue (price times quantity) associated with each level of labor use, and column (6) is the marginal product of labor. The crucial amounts in the demand for labor are shown in columns (5) and (7). Column (5) shows the addition to total revenue (from column [4]) from increasing labor by one unit. This figure is called the *marginal revenue product* (*MRP*) of labor. *MRP* can also be computed by multiplying marginal product times marginal revenue, in this case the average or per-unit-of-output marginal revenue. For example, the average marginal revenue associated with changing from three to four units of labor is $350 (the additional revenue) divided by the change in total product, 15; or MR $= \triangle R/\triangle Q$.

> **Definition.** Marginal revenue product for a monopolist is the additional revenue attributable to the addition of one unit of the variable input. It is per-unit marginal revenue times marginal product.

Note that in this case marginal revenue product is less than the value of marginal product, since marginal revenue is less than price. Marginal revenue product is the *net* addition to total revenue. For example, the gross addition to revenue from increasing the variable input from three to four units is 15 (the additional units of production) times $30 (the selling price) or 15 $\times$ $30 = $450. But to sell 15 additional units, price must fall by $20. Thus, the "lost" revenue from the price reduction is 5 $\times$ $20 = $100, since five units could have been sold for $50. This "loss" must be subtracted from the gross gain; or, $450 $-$ $100 = $350 = *MRP*.

Columns (5) and (7) of Table 10.2.2 show the monopolist's demand for a single variable input. For example, if the daily wage is $25, the monopolist would hire eight workers. Each worker up to the ninth adds more than $25 (the additional daily cost per worker) to revenue. The ninth adds $13, and thus would cost the firm $25 $-$ $13 = $12. If wages rise to $50 a day, the firm would reduce labor to six units. Both the seventh and the eighth add less than $50 to total revenue.

To illustrate graphically, consider the marginal revenue product curve in Figure 10.2.2. It must quite obviously slope downward to the right because two forces work to cause marginal revenue product to diminish as the level of employment increases: (a) the marginal physical product declines (over the relevant range of production) as additional units of the variable service are added, and (b) marginal revenue declines as output expands and commodity price falls.

FIGURE 10.2.2

MONOPOLY DEMAND FOR A SINGLE
VARIABLE SERVICE

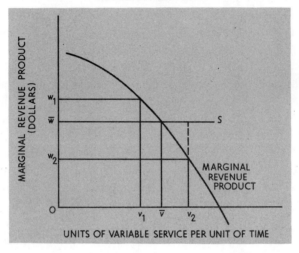

By assumption, the monopoly purchases the variable service in a perfectly competitive input market. Hence it views its supply-of-input curve as a horizontal line at the level of the prevailing market price, $O\bar{w}$.

Given the market price $O\bar{w}$, we wish to prove that equilibrium employment is $O\bar{v}$. Suppose the contrary, in particular that Ov_1 units of the variable service are used. At the Ov_1 level of utilization the last unit adds Ow_1 to total revenue but only $O\bar{w}$ to total cost. Since $Ow_1 > O\bar{w}$, profit is augmented by employing that unit. Furthermore, profit increases when additional units are employed so long as marginal revenue product exceeds the market equilibrium price of the input. Thus a profit-maximizing monopolist would never employ fewer than $O\bar{v}$ units of the variable service. The opposite argument holds when more than $O\bar{v}$ units are employed, for then an additional unit of the variable service adds more to total cost than to total revenue. Therefore, a profit-maximizing monopolist will adjust employment so that marginal revenue product equals input price. If only one variable productive service is used, the marginal revenue product curve is, therefore, the monopolist's demand curve for the variable service in question.

Proposition. An imperfectly competitive producer who purchases a variable productive resource in a perfectly competitive input market will employ that amount of the service for which marginal revenue product equals market price. Consequently, the marginal revenue product curve is the monopolist's demand curve for the variable service when only one variable input is used. Marginal revenue product declines with output for two reasons: (1) marginal product declines as more units of the variable input are added, and (2) to sell the additional output, the monopolist must lower commodity price.

10.2.c Determinants of demand

We should mention the variables that are assumed to be held constant when deriving the competitor's or the monopolist's demand for a single variable input. Obviously we hold the use of all other inputs constant; otherwise it would not be the demand for a *single* variable input. Recall from Chapter 5 that when the rate of use of another input changes, the marginal product curve of the other input shifts. Thus if the use of another input changes, the *VMP* curve for a competitor or the *MRP* curve for a monopoly would shift also, and neither would be the demand for the input. In the second place, technology is held constant, since technological change shifts the marginal product curves.

In the case of a competitive firm the commodity price is held constant if the *VMP* curve is the demand. Similarly, commodity demand remains fixed if the *MRP* curve is the monopolist's demand for a single variable input. Finally, until now, we have assumed that the wage bill is the *total* payment to the input; there are no additional or fringe payments such as contributions to social security or to group insurance plans.

All of the conditions held constant except the last are quite apparent. The last point requires some discussion. If you are an employer, you would use the theory described above, but you might look at the wage rate or the price of an input in a slightly different way. In the real world workers cost an employer more than simply the money wage rate. There are certain *additional* payments to workers required by law or perhaps paid by tradition. The most familiar legal requirement is the employer's contribution to social security. Firms also frequently make contributions

TABLE 10.2.2

(1) Units of labor	(2) Total product	(3) Commodity price	(4) Total revenue	(5) Additional total revenue per unit additional labor	(6) Marginal product	(7) Marginal revenue product MR × MP
3..........	5	$50.00	$250			
4..........	20	30.00	600	$350	15	$350
5..........	30	25.00	750	150	10	150
6..........	38	22.00	836	86	8	86
7..........	44	20.00	880	44	6	44
8..........	48	19.00	912	32	4	32
9..........	50	18.50	925	13	2	13
10..........	51	18.00	918	-7	1	-7

to the employees' insurance policies or their retirement plans. There are other fringe benefits such as improvements in working conditions, noise controls, lounge facilities, and so on.

All of these additional payments are not costless to the firm. Firms simply view the *total wage bill* as the market-determined wage plus the cost of the fringe benefits, such as the social security payment. Thus at any market-determined wage, fewer workers are hired if additional payments are required than would be hired in the absence of such payments. This is not to say, however, that the employer absorbs *all* of the cost of the benefits that are required. As we shall see, this is far from the case.

EXERCISE

Who pays for fringe benefits?

We will deal with the subject of who pays for fringe benefits in greater detail below. See now, however, if you can analyze or make a prediction concerning the following circumstances. At the present time, all state university faculty in our state pay half the social security payments and the university pays the other half. The state legislature recently passed a bill that requires each state university next year to begin paying the entire amount of social security. Many faculty members are quite pleased, saying that this represents a substantial increase in pay over the salary they would have received if the law had not been changed. How would you answer them? How do you think faculty raises will compare next year with what they would have been had the legislature not voted to pay all of the social security payments? Only the first $16,500 of salary is subject to social security. How will this bill change the distribution of income for university faculty? Consider the short run, then the long run.

10.3 DEMAND FOR A PRODUCTIVE SERVICE: PERFECT COMPETITION IN INPUT MARKETS, SEVERAL VARIABLE INPUTS

When a production process involves more than one variable productive service, the derivation of input demand curves is more complicated. The value of the marginal product curve and the marginal revenue product curve are no longer the perfect competitor's and the monopolist's demand curves for an input. The reason lies in the fact that the various inputs are interdependent in the production process, so a change in the price of one input leads to changes in the rates of utilization of the others. As we noted previously, a factor's marginal product curve is derived under the assumption that the amount of other inputs remains constant. Therefore, changes in the rates of utilization of other inputs shift the marginal product curve of the input whose price initially changes. We now examine input demand when the use of more than one input is allowed to vary.

10.3.a Perfect competition in the commodity market

Consider Figure 10.3.1. Suppose that equilibrium for a perfectly competitive firm initially exists at point A. The market wage rate is Ow_1, the value of the marginal product curve for labor is VMP_1 when labor is the only input varied, and OL_1 units of labor are employed. Now let the wage rate fall to Ow_2, so that the perfectly elastic supply curve of labor to the firm is S_{L2}.

When the wage rate falls from Ow_1 to Ow_2, the use of labor expands. However, the expansion does not take place along VMP_1. When the quantity of labor used and the level of output change, the use of other variable inputs changes as well. Under these conditions labor's marginal product curve shifts.

FIGURE 10.3.1

INDIVIDUAL INPUT DEMAND WHEN SEVERAL
VARIABLE INPUTS ARE USED

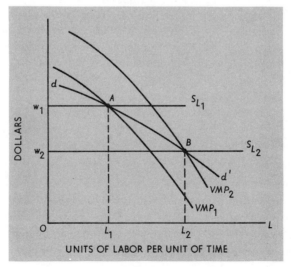

UNITS OF LABOR PER UNIT OF TIME

Since the value of the marginal product is equal to marginal product multiplied by the constant market price of the commodity, the value of the marginal product of labor curve must shift as well. Suppose it shifts to VMP_2. The new equilibrium is reached at point B. Other points similar to A and B can be generated in the same manner. Thus the demand curve dd' can be determined from successive changes in the market wage rate and the value of the marginal product curve. The input demand curve, while more difficult to derive, is just as determinate in the multiple-input case as in the single-input situation.

10.3.b Monopoly in the commodity market

Analogous to the case of perfect competition, when more than one variable input is used in the production process of a monopolist, the marginal revenue product curve is not the demand curve (for the reasons already discussed in this section). After a change in the wage rate the marginal revenue product curve shifts as all variable inputs are adjusted. The input demand curve is generated exactly as in Figure 10.3.1; the only change is that marginal revenue product is not price times marginal product (VMP) as in the competitive case.

The results can be summarized in the following important proposition:

Proposition. An entrepreneur's demand curve for a variable productive agent can be derived when more than one variable input is used. This demand curve must be negatively sloped. Even though the demand, when more than one input is variable, is no longer the marginal revenue product curve (which is the value of marginal product in the competitive case), we should stress that at every point on the demand curve the wage rate still is equal to marginal revenue product (VMP for the competitive firm).

10.3.c Monopolistic exploitation

The important difference between monopoly and perfect competition is that the monopolist's demand is based upon marginal revenue times marginal product rather than price times marginal product. This gives rise to what is sometimes called monopolistic exploitation.

According to a frequently used definition, a productive service is "exploited" if it is employed at a price that is less than the value of its marginal product. As we have seen, it is to the advantage of any individual producer (whether monopolist or competitor) to hire a variable service until the point is reached at which an additional unit adds precisely the same amount to total cost and total revenue. This is simply the input market implication of profit maximization.

When a perfectly competitive producer follows this rule, a variable service receives the value of its marginal product because price and marginal revenue are the same. This is not true, however, when the commodity market is imperfect. Marginal revenue is less than price and marginal revenue product in this case is correspondingly less than the value of the marginal product. Profit-maximizing behavior of imperfectly competitive producers causes the value of an input's marginal product to exceed its market price.

If the market price of the commodity reflects its social value, the productive service receives less than its contribution to social value. Raising the input price is not a remedy, however, because producers would merely reduce the level of employment until marginal revenue product equals the higher input price. The trouble initially lies in the fact that imperfectly competitive producers do not use as much of the resource as is socially desirable and do not attain the correspondingly desirable level of output. The fundamental difficulty rests in the difference between price (marginal social valuation) and marginal (social) cost at the profit-maximizing output. Thus, so long as imperfectly competitive producers exist, there must be some "monopolistic exploitation" of productive agents.

The significance of this exploitation can easily be exaggerated. Furthermore, the alternatives to exploitation are not attractive. Either there must be state ownership and operation of all nonperfectly competitive industries or else there must be rigid controls by the state. For a variety of reasons, either alternative is likely to create more problems than it solves.

EXERCISE

Why are workers exploited?

Why would people work for a monopolist and be exploited when they could work for a competitor and escape exploitation?

By and large, workers are not interested in whether or not they are being exploited, but in their total wage income and their fringe benefits. Wages are determined in the market place—as we shall see—by supply and demand. One would think that with equal working conditions and wages a worker would be indifferent as to the type of firm doing the employing and, therefore, would be indifferent as to the amount of exploitation involved. The fact that *MRP* for a monopolist is less than *VMP* for a competitor does not mean that a monopolist pays lower wages. Market-determined wages are the same. This relation only means that a monopolist ceases hiring labor before the wage rate equals the value of marginal product.

10.4 MARKET DEMAND FOR AN INPUT

The industry demand for a variable productive service, in contrast to the market demand for a commodity, is not necessarily the horizontal summation of the constituent individual demands. In general, the process of addition for productive services is considerably more complicated, because when all firms in an industry expand or contract simultaneously the market price of the commodity changes. Nonetheless, the market demand curve can be obtained.

The situation is analogous to the derivation of a perfectly competitive industry's supply curve from the firms' supply curves. Recall that any firm can change its level of output without affecting input prices. But when all firms attempt to vary output together, input prices change and each firm's supply curve shifts. Therefore, industry supply is the horizontal summation of these "shifted" supplies. In the case of input demand any perfectly competitive firm can vary its inputs, and thus its output, without affecting commodity price. When all firms respond to a change in the price of an input, commodity price does change. Since each firm's demand for the input is derived holding commodity price constant, all input demands shift when all firms change simultaneously.

To illustrate the process, assume that a typical employing firm is depicted in Figure 10.4.1, panel A. For the going market price of the commodity proceduced, $d_1 d'_1$ is the firm's demand curve for the variable productive service, as derived in Figure 10.3.1. If the market price of the resource is Ow_1, the firm uses Ov_1 units. Aggregating over all employing firms in the industry, OV_1 units of the service are used. Thus point A in panel B is one point on the industry demand curve for the variable productive service.

Next, suppose the price of the service declines to Ow_2 (because, for example, the supply curve of the variable service shifts to the right). Other things being equal, the firm would move along $d_1 d'_1$ to point b', employing Ov'_2 units of the service. But other things are not equal. When

FIGURE 10.4.1

DERIVATION OF THE MARKET DEMAND FOR A
VARIABLE PRODUCTIVE SERVICE

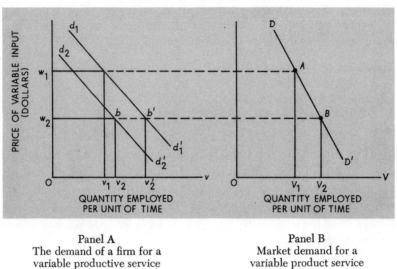

Panel A
The demand of a firm for a
variable productive service

Panel B
Market demand for a
variable product service

all firms expand their use of the input, total output expands. Or stated differently, the market supply curve for the commodity shifts to the right because of the decline in the input's price. For a given commodity demand, commodity price must fall; and when it does, the individual demand curves for the variable productive service also fall.

In panel A, the decline in individual input demand attributable to the decline in commodity price is represented by the shift leftward from $d_1d'_1$ to $d_2d'_2$. At input price Ow_2, b is the equilibrium point, with Ov_2 units employed. Aggregating for all employers, OV_2 units of the productive service are used and point B is obtained in panel B. Any number of points such as A and B can be generated by varying the market price of the productive service. Connecting these points by a line, one obtains DD', the industry demand for the variable productive service.

If an industry is monopolized by a single firm, the monopoly demand for an input is the same as the industry demand. If several industries demand an input, the total market demand is the horizontal summation of every industry's demand, assuming, of course, that we ignore the effect of changes in commodity price in one industry upon commodity prices in other industries that demand the input. There is some minor qualification in case of oligopoly and monopolistic competition. In these cases it must be considered that, like perfect competition, when all firms attempt to expand output, market price falls.

10.5 SUPPLY OF A VARIABLE PRODUCTIVE SERVICE

All variable productive services may be broadly classified into three groups: natural resources, intermediate goods, and labor. Intermediate goods are those produced by one entrepreneur and sold to another, who in turn utilizes them in the productive process. For example, cotton is produced by a farmer and (after middlemen) sold as an intermediate good to a manufacturer of damask; the damask, in turn, becomes an intermediate good in the manufacture of upholstered furniture. The short-run supply curves of intermediate goods are positively sloped because they are the *commodity outputs* of manufacturers, even if they are variable inputs to others; and, as shown in Chapter 7, short-run commodity supply curves are positively sloped.

Natural resources may be regarded as the commodity outputs (usually of mining operations). As such, they also have positively sloped short-run supply curves. Thus our attention can be restricted to the final category: labor.

There are several types of labor supply. We discussed one type in Chapter 4 when we showed how an individual's supply of labor is derived from indifference curves between leisure and income. In that chapter we showed that given a wage increase, an individual might choose to work more (sacrifice leisure) or to work less (take more leisure), depending upon the shape of his or her indifference map. Therefore, an individual's supply-of-labor curve may be positively sloped over some range and negatively sloped over other ranges of the wage rate. The crucial question, however, is how the sum behaves—what is the shape of the market supply curve of any specified type of labor.

A firm, monopolist or competitor, can face two types of supply for a specific kind of labor. In the cases discussed thus far in this chapter, the supply of labor is a horizontal line at the market-determined wage rate, indicating that the firm can hire all of that type of labor it wishes at the going market wage rate. In certain cases firms have some effect upon the wage rate. In these instances, the firm faces an upward sloping supply of labor, indicating that in order to hire more of a specified kind of labor the firm must pay higher wages. Under this set of circumstances the firm is called a monopsonist, a situation to be analyzed theoretically below.

Next there is the situation in which one industry uses a specialized type of labor, specialized in the sense that the industry's use of the input affects that input's price. In the long run the supply to the industry must be positively sloped because of labor mobility; an industry must bid away people from other occupations in order to get more of the specific type of labor or to induce people to enter that occupation. If there are a given number of people in a specific occupation and the firms in a particular industry desire more of that type, they must lure them away by paying higher wages.[2] The situation is similar when more than one industry uses a particular type of labor. If output is to be expanded in one or more of these industries, the employment of workers must increase.

EXERCISES

Some problems in labor supply theory

Consider the following rather old, but rather famous, joke. It is told that the great Irish humorist George Bernard Shaw was seated next to an attractive lady at a dinner party. After making small talk with the lady for some time, Shaw asked her if she would consider sleeping with him that night for the payment of one million pounds. The lady thought for some time then said that, yes, she probably would. Shaw then asked her if she would spend the night with him for one pound. The lady answered, indignantly, "Sir, what do you think I am?" Shaw replied, "Madame, we have already settled upon what you are; now we are merely haggling over price." Analyze the economic content of the story.

Shaw may have been quite clever in his retort, but he was exhibiting an utter lack of economic understanding. As an analogy I might ask one of my students if he would haul away my garbage for $100 a week. Probably most students would, although most would not do it for ten cents a week. This would, by no means, classify those students as garbage collectors. Neither would the lady be classified as whatever Shaw classified her.

---

[2] There are two possible exceptions, each of which leads to a horizontal industry supply-of-labor curve. First, if the industry is exceedingly small or if it uses only very small quantities of labor, its effect upon the market may be negligible. That is, the industry may stand to the market as a perfectly competitive firm does to the industry. Second, if there is unemployment of the particular type of labor under consideration, the supply of labor to all industries may be perfectly elastic up to the point of full employment. Thereafter the supply curve would rise. The latter is a disequilibrium situation not encompassed in the analysis here.

Economic theory recognizes that people get different levels of utility from working in different occupations. Economists also observe that people are willing to make a trade-off between less desired occupations and increased incomes. Just as in the case of commodities, supply and demand determine relative wages and the relative numbers of employees among different occupations.

Analyze the following news story that appeared in the *Houston Post* on March 3, 1977. In this story the shortage of registered nurses was termed "serious" to "very crucial" in at least 11 major Houston hospitals. One of the hospitals could not open 100 beds because of the problem. Officials said that all of the hospitals need a minimum of 500 more RNs.

The story went on to list the various hospitals with the number of beds and nurses needed. The shortage of nurses was also said to be responsible for the delay in opening some new medical facilities. Hospital officials who were interviewed agreed unanimously that the worst problems in staffing were the 11.00 p.m. to 7:00 a.m. shifts, and several officials said that evening and weekend duty often is objected to by nurses who know they are in demand and can go elsewhere to get to work a day shift.

Most administrators interviewed in the story emphasized, "Salaries and fringe benefits aren't the 'answer'." One administrator was quoted as saying, "Starting RN salaries have gone from $600 to more than $925 on the average in just the last seven years . . . Most major hospitals . . . have stayed competitive and kept pace with salary increases."

Do you agree with the administrators? Are salaries and fringe benefits the answer? Have salaries stayed competitive and kept pace?

In the first place it is nonsense to assert that salary and fringe benefits are not the answer. If the hospital wants more nurses, or if employers of people in any occupation want more employees, the only way to get them is to bid them away from other locations. Or in the long run they must bid them away from other occupations. The higher bids can only be in the form of higher salaries and/or increased benefits. What else would attract more nurses? Of course, it may be that the hospital administrators do not want to pay higher salaries or to increase fringe benefits. In this sense higher salaries and benefits may not be the answer for them.

In the story it appears that nurses do not wish to work weekends and nights. They can work weekdays elsewhere. What is the problem? Clearly hospitals are not paying a sufficient differential to attract nurses to the less desirable hours. If there are jobs with more desirable hours at the same rate of pay, nurses obviously would choose these. With all forms of labor, as with commodities, a shortage will continue in the long run if the wage is below equilibrium. To increase the number of people in a particular occupation or in a particular location, the total wages, salary, and/or benefits must be increased.

There is an interesting point to make about the administrator's using as evidence that "salaries are not the answer" the fact that starting RN salaries have risen from $600 to more than $925 over the past seven years. This represents slightly more than a 50-percent increase. During the same seven-year period the consumer price index increased slightly more than 50 percent also. Thus the cost of living rose about as much as beginning nurses' salaries, and *real* salaries remained about the same. This probably explains in large part why Houston hospitals are experiencing a great shortage of nurses.*

In a recent "Dear Ann Landers" column someone signed "A Conscientious Taxpayer," cited all of the advantages for "Aid to Dependent Children (ADC) Mothers" in obtaining employment training or in working. The "conscientious taxpayer," incidentally employed by the Public Welfare Division, said there were few ADC mothers who want to acquire the needed skills to get off welfare. The writer said, "Those who use the excuse of 'being worse off when working' don't have their facts straight—or they are using this as an excuse for not being self-supporting."

Ann Landers answered, simply, that she checked the facts and they are correct. Use your economic knowledge to give Ann Landers a better explanation of why the ADC mothers do not choose to acquire the needed skills. Are they merely making excuses, or is there another explanation? Do you think the ADC mothers have their facts straight?

You may want to refer back to the section in Chapter 4 in which we analyze the labor-leisure decision resulting from a guaranteed minimum income. Could some ADC mothers really be "worse off" when working? Of course they could, even when they have their "facts

---

* As an aside, in order to do research on the nurse shortage I became ill the day after writing this segment. During the 12 days I was in the hospital, I questioned most of the attending nurses about the critical nurse shortage. They agreed unanimously that there was a nurse shortage. They also agreed unanimously that higher wages are the answer, citing many retirements of married nurses, who no longer found it "worthwhile" to work at the going wages. They also mentioned many examples of nurses leaving for other higher-wage areas. It appears that nurses may be better economists than the administrators whom I quoted above.

straight." As economists (but perhaps not as advice columnists) we must look on the decision more analytically and less ideologically.

Compare the marginal decision-making process. An ADC mother can be trained and can work. But the cost is the state payment given up, the leisure given up, and the time spent with her children given up. Clearly, there is a marginal decision. Some mothers may make one decision, some the other, depending on the relative utility functions. Is society better or worse off if the ADC mother stays home rather than works? No one can say. We can only say that the state sets up a set of constraints and people maxamize subject to these constraints. People cannot be condemned or accused of ignorance simply because they maximize in one way rather than in the way someone else wishes them to behave. Who is to say what way benefits society? Certainly as economists we cannot say.

Let us return to the analysis of the determinants of the various supply curves of labor. As population increases and its age composition changes, as people migrate from one area to another, and as education and re-education enable people to shift occupations, rather dramatic changes can occur in the supply of various types of labor at various locations throughout the nation. These changes represent *shifts* in supply curves and are quite independent of their slopes. To get at the supply curve for a well-defined market, assume that the following are held constant: the size of the population, the labor force participation rate, and the occupational and geographic distribution of the labor force.

As was the case in the supply of products, the time period of adjustment is one of the most important factors influencing the elasticity of supply of a particular type of labor. If the salary in a particular occupation rises, people may choose to enter that occupation, but acquiring the needed skills takes time. However, given the necessary period of adjustment, an increase in the relative wages in a particular occupation will induce additional people into that occupation.

Thus we can say almost unequivocally that except for the case of an individual worker, the supply of labor to a specific occupation is upward sloping. This reflects the fact that, at least in the long run, higher wages or benefits must be paid in order to induce more persons into the occupation. The longer the time period of adjustment, the more people are induced to enter. The same thing applies to the supply of a particular type of labor in a specific area—city, state, region. When you hear people complaining that a city can't get enough teachers, or a county can't get enough doctors, or a college can't get enough professors, or a community can't get enough garbage collectors—and these are things we hear every day—you should be able to suggest a solution. This is not to say the solution will be acceptable to those paying the bill. What people who make such statements generally mean is they cannot get enough of a particular type of worker at a price low enough to suit themselves.

APPLICATION

Price rationing and peak loads at airports

By now it probably is obvious to you that price is a rather effective rationing device. But as is apparent in the above statements, the suggestion that higher prices can solve the problems of shortages of inputs is not always well received. Furthermore, recall from Chapter 9 that oligopolists, particularly regulated oligopolists, do not like commodity price competition. Neither do they like price competition for scarce inputs. Let me illustrate with a true story.

My graduate assistant, Paul Pautler, spent a summer internship a few years ago working with the Department of Transportation in Washington. One of his training assignments was attending meetings concerning the problem of the extremely long waiting times for international passengers entering the United States at Kennedy Airport. It seems that almost all of the international flights landed at Kennedy during a period of about two to three hours each day.

During this short period of time the waiting lines at the customs area were extremely long. The checkers, the inspectors, the baggage handlers, and the other workers at customs were terribly overworked during this period, and the passengers were frequently irritated. But during the rest of the day the international flights landed so seldom that the customs section was seldom crowded and no employee really had much to do during this long period of inactivity. At times the international section was practically deserted.

For several years representatives of the major international airlines had been meeting with representatives of the Department of Transportation. Almost everything had been suggested. Some wanted to double or even triple the facilities for international passengers—at a cost of many millions. Others suggested adding many additional personnel, particularly during the peak period, again at a huge cost. Others brought up governmental allocation of permits to land at the peak hours. No one could agree on a "fair" formula for allocation. There were many other suggestions, each at a great cost to society.

After a few meetings, Paul, at that time a beginning graduate student, made a suggestion to the meeting. What would you have suggested?

Paul suggested charging a landing fee for international flights, the fee being much higher at the peak landing hours but practically zero during the unpopular arrival periods. In this way the price structure would spread the landings more evenly over the day. Those who were willing to pay the high fee could still land at the peak demand hours. But others would wish to save money and land at other times. Thus the huge peak congestion would be eliminated.

Paul reports being very satisfied that he, a young student, had solved the problem. He was wrong. A chill fell over the entire meeting. No one said a word, except the chairman, who simply said, "It won't work." When Paul asked why not, the answer was "It just won't, and that's it." Absolutely no one wanted a price allocation of the problem. As far as we know, they are still arguing about the problem.

All we want to show is that even though you know that changes in relative prices will solve problems of shortages of resources or problems of allocation, this solution is frequently met with great disfavor by those concerned. When you make similar suggestions that price is an efficient allocator of scarce resources, as you probably will after completing this course, be prepared for the brilliant rebuttal, "It just won't work in this case." Why not? "It just won't."

10.6 MARKET EQUILIBRIUM AND RETURNS TO INPUTS

The demand for and supply of a variable productive service jointly determine its market equilibrium price; this is precisely marginal productivity theory. In Figure 10.6.1, DD' and SS' are the demand and supply curves. Their intersection at point E determines the equilibrium price $O\bar{w}$ and quantity demanded and supplied $O\bar{v}$ in a particular market.

If the price of the variable input (say, labor) exceeds $O\bar{w}$, more people wish to work in this occupation than employers are willing to hire at that wage. Since there is a surplus of workers, wages are bid down by the workers until the surplus is eliminated (in the absence, of course, of minimum wages). If the wage rate is below $O\bar{w}$, producers want to employ more workers than are willing to work at that wage. Employers, faced with a "shortage" of labor, bid the wage rate up to $O\bar{w}$. The analysis is similar to that in Chapter 2. The only features unique to this analysis are the methods of determining the demand for variable productive

FIGURE 10.6.1

MARKET EQUILIBRIUM DETERMINATION OF THE
PRICE OF A VARIABLE PRODUCTIVE SERVICE

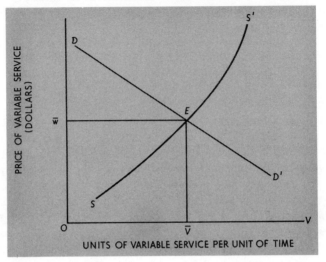

services and the supply of labor services. The fact that input demand is based upon the marginal revenue product or the value of the marginal product of the input gives rise to the label "marginal productivity theory."

Since all resources are variable in the long run, marginal productivity theory covers all resources in the long run. However, in the short run certain inputs are fixed; they cannot be varied and hence a "marginal product" cannot readily be generated. The return to short-run fixed factors is called "quasi rent." Quasi rent is the difference between total revenue and total variable cost. It must always be non-negative since, you will recall, the firm will shut down in the short run if it cannot cover all of variable costs. Sometimes, when a pure profit is being enjoyed in the short run, quasi rent exceeds fixed costs. Sometimes, when the firm operates at a loss in the short run, quasi rent is less than total fixed cost, and some of the fixed cost must be paid by the entrepreneur, who suffers the loss.

It should be emphasized that in general quasi rent is a short-run phenomenon. In the long run when all factors are variable, quasi rent is eliminated. We might note, however, that contrived or sometimes natural barriers may lead to continued quasi rent over a long period of time. There might be a natural barrier to entry—possibly the ownership of some specialized, highly productive resource that allows these rents to continue.

Or the barriers may be artificially set by governmental licensing regulations. For example, in some cities taxis are issued licenses, which are given free or at a very low charge. But these licenses are limited in number. Therefore, entry is prohibited and quasi rents can persist over a long period. Other businesses are licensed, leading to the effect of preventing or hindering entry. Some land has tobacco allotments, giving the owner the right to grow a certain amount of tobacco on that land. The holders of these licenses or permits can continue to receive quasi rent so long as large numbers of additional licenses or permits are not issued.

EXERCISE

Setting the price of a license

Suppose that in your city one must have a city permit to operate a mortuary. There are only 20 mortuaries in operation, and in all likelihood the city will issue no more licenses in the near future. Each of the mortuaries is doing a thriving business because of the prevention of entry as the city grows.

Now suppose you are a young mortician and one of the licensed mortuaries comes up for sale. The license goes with the business. If you purchase the mortuary, will you make positive quasi rents over a reasonable period of time, because you hold a license to do business in a thriving industry in which entry is prevented?

Probably not. Why? Well in the first place other morticians will also be bidding for the licensed business. How high will the bidding go? Probably the business will sell for the value of the equipment *plus* the amount of rent due to the ownership of the license. For example, if the license enables the mortuary to make $100,000 a year *additional* or pure profit because of protected entry, the discounted value of this stream of profit will be added to the selling price. In other words when you buy *a business and a license,* you pay the value of the business *plus* the value of the license. Thus you as a new owner will probably earn no quasi rent because this rent would have to be paid to the original owner. Licenses only benefit those who receive them first from government, and only when there is a limit on the number of licenses.

Earlier in this chapter we spoke of the effect of fringe benefits; either externally imposed benefits such as social security payments by employers, or voluntary benefits such as improved working conditions or low-cost group insurance plans. You will recall that employers simply considered the added cost of the benefits as an addition to wages, and they adjusted their use of labor accordingly. In that analysis we may have given you the impression that employers absorb the entire cost of such benefits—that the only effect on employees is that fewer workers are hired but those hired receive higher *total* wage rates (that is, wages plus the value of the benefits). That is only one part of the story. We neglected the supply side of the market in that analysis.

Remember that demand and supply determine the wage rates in markets. If working conditions in a particular market improve or if there are additional fringe benefits paid to workers in this market, jobs in that market become more desirable relative to jobs in markets in which conditions do not change. This increased desirability of jobs in that market will, at least in the long run, increase the supply of labor to that market. As we know, the increase in supply will drive down wages in that market relative to what they would have been in the absence of the increased desirability of the occupation. Thus at least some of the cost of improved conditions is passed on to the workers involved. The proportion depends upon demand and supply elasticities and how the curves shift. A somewhat factual, analytical example, using the tools we have developed in this section may give a more complete insight into the process.

APPLICATION

Effect of improved working conditions in mining industries

Let us consider the case of the Northern Canadian mining and smelting industry. This industry mines and processes, among other things, zinc, nickel, gold, and lead. The mines and smelters are in rather desolate parts of the country, and the working conditions have historically been quite harsh. Thus wages have had to be rather high to lure workers away from other more desirable areas.

Recently, laws have been passed to make working conditions more amenable. Such laws are pollution controls, dust and safety regulations in mines and smelters, and other types of regulations. Moreover, mining companies voluntarily, in order to attract labor, have improved working conditions in other ways. These changes in working conditions took the form of improved housing, civic improvements, and so on. Now, as you know, these fringe benefits are added to the total wage income for each worker. But, the question is what was the overall effect of the additional benefits? Who really paid for fringe additions to the wages?

We can use Figure 10.6.2 to analyze the effect. Let *DD* be the total demand for labor in the Northern Canadian mining industry. This demand reflects the relation between *money wages only* and the quantity of labor hired. That is, the wage rate on the vertical axis is the money wage rate and does not include the value of amenities. As we noted above, employers simply add the cost of fringe benefits to the market-determined wage rate in choosing the amount of labor hired.

Let S_1S_1 be the supply of labor to the industry prior to the imposition of additional benefits. Again this supply is the relation between money wages and labor supplied; it is obviously upward sloping. Equilibrium wages and labor hired are, respectively, OW_1 and OL_1. Next let fringe benefits be imposed. These would be improved environmental conditions, possibly added insurance benefits, improved housing, and so on. Suppose, to take the most farfetched example possible, that government absorbs all of the costs of such benefits. In this case, analysis would not be complicated by a downward shift in input demand.

But, because of improved working conditions, one would suppose that the supply would increase. That is, at each wage rate more workers than before would be willing to work in the industry because of improved working conditions. Thus, even though government pays for all of the fringe benefits—absurd though it may be—the wage rate

FIGURE 10.6.2

EFFECT OF FRINGE BENEFITS

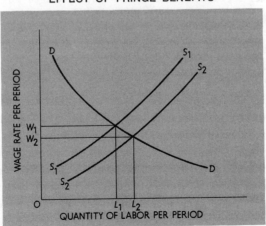

falls to OW_2. Of course, the amount of labor increases to OL_2. Thus workers themselves absorb some of the cost of the benefits.

To be more realistic, if the companies themselves are forced to pay for most of the added benefits, they would be willing to hire fewer workers at each wage rate. That is, each worker costs more because of the added benefits. In this case the demand for labor, *DD*, would shift downward and to the left, resulting in even lower wages than OW_2 and in fewer than OL_2 workers being hired.

Therefore, we can see that it is not necessarily the employer who absorbs the cost of any compulsory or voluntary fringe benefits. If the market works at all, the employees bear some part of the cost in the form of wages below the rate that would exist in the absence of regulations. The extent to which wages are reduced because of fringe benefits depends on several factors: (1) the valuation by workers of the fringe benefits, reflected in the extent to which supply increases; (2) the elasticity of supply for a given shift; (3) the extent to which demand decreases; (4) the elasticity of demand. To see this last point, draw a much steeper demand through the original equilibrium point A. Note that with the given supply shift, wages fall much more with this more inelastic demand.

This analysis should emphasize a previously made point. There is always a trade-off between wages and fringe benefits. Now you may wish to return to the exercise set forth in subsection 10.2.c concerning university faculty and payment by the state of all social security. Do you arrive at the same answer as before?

To some extent the above analytical exercise might explain why, in the absence of regulations and labor unions, wages might differ from industry to industry. Other things being equal, if the wage rate for equal skill is higher in one industry than in another, workers would leave the low-wage industry and increase the supply of labor to the high-wage industry. In this way, wages would rise in the previously low-wage industry and fall in the previously high-wage industry, until wage rates were the same in both. Therefore, in the absence of external interferences, the wages should be approximately equal in the two industries for equal skills. If over the long run one industry continues to pay higher wages than another, and there are no external interferences, then the working conditions for some reason or other—location, risk of danger, amenities, and so on—must differ between industries. Thus the attractiveness of an industry relative to another affects relative wage rates for equal levels of skill.

10.7 EFFECTS OF LABOR UNIONS AND MINIMUM WAGES

The theoretical discussion thus far may seem far removed from the dramatic world of General Motors versus the United Automobile Workers. Indeed it is, in a certain sense. Yet the theoretical results obtained do set limits within which collective bargaining agreements are likely to occur.

Our analysis sets broad limits within which the solution lies. To push further requires one or more *courses*, not chapters. For example, there is a substantial body of theory concerning the collective bargaining process, but an understanding of labor markets also requires an extensive knowledge of the institutional framework within which labor unions and businesses operate. This type of knowledge must be acquired in "applied" courses or contexts, just as other applied courses supplement other portions of microeconomic theory.

This is not to say that we cannot gain considerable insight into the effect of unions on wages and employment by using our simple marginal productivity theory. The basic fundamentals of what unions can and cannot do are easily developed within our basic framework. Furthermore we can use our fundamental theory to analyze the effect of external interferences in the labor market, such as the imposition of minimum wages. Much of the simple framework set forth here is used by professional economists to predict the impact of external interferences such as these on the market.

10.7.a Labor unions

Consider any typical labor market with some type of positively sloped supply of labor. If the workers in this market are unionized, the union bargaining representative has two powers to exert. First, the representative can set a wage rate above equilibrium and guarantee the availability of workers at this price (up to a limit) but also guarantee no workers at any lower price. Second, the union can limit membership in some way below the equilibrium number that would be hired in the absence of a union. This limitation in effect allows the market to raise wages above equilibrium.

Let us consider the first strategy. Suppose the labor market in question is perfectly competitive (large number of purchasers of this type of labor) and unorganized. The situation is depicted in panel A, Figure 10.7.1,

FIGURE 10.7.1

EFFECTS OF A LABOR UNION IN A PERFECTLY
COMPETITIVE LABOR MARKET

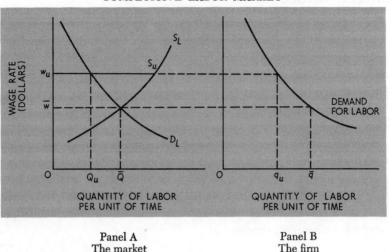

Panel A
The market

Panel B
The firm

where D_L and S_L are the demand for and supply of labor, respectively.
The market equilibrium wage rate is $O\bar{w}$ and $O\bar{Q}$ units of labor are employed. Each individual firm (panel B) accordingly employs $O\bar{q}$ units.
Next, suppose the labor market is unionized. If the union does not attempt
to raise wages, the situation might remain as it is. However, scoring wage
increases or other benefits is the raison d'être of unions. Thus, suppose the
bargaining agency sets Ow_u as the wage rate. Firms can now hire all of
the labor they want at the rate Ow_u, as long as the industry does not hire
beyond the point S_u on the labor supply curve. Thus a total of OQ_u
(where Ow_u equals demand) units of labor are employed, each firm taking Oq_u units. The result is an increase in wages and a decline in employment. The fact that the imposed increase in wages causes a reduction in
the amount of labor hired does not necessarily mean a union cannot
benefit its members. If the demand for labor is inelastic, an increase in the
wage rate will result in an increase in total wages paid to the workers,
even though the number of workers employed declines. If the union can
somehow equitably divide the proceeds of OQ_u employed workers among
the $O\bar{Q}$ potential workers, all will benefit. Such a division is easy to
achieve. Suppose $OQ_u = \frac{1}{2} O\bar{Q}$ and that a 40-hour week characterizes the
market. Then OQ_u units of labor can be furnished by having $O\bar{Q}$ units
work a 20-hour week.

The other side of the coin is worth examining, however. If the demand for labor is elastic, total wage receipts will decline and the union cannot compensate the $Q_u\bar{Q}$ workers who are unemployed because of the increase in wage rates.

The second option available for a union to raise wages is simply to limit the number of persons in an occupation. In terms of Figure 10.7.1, if the union could limit the number of union workers to OQ_u and somehow prevent nonunion workers from working in the industry, pure market forces would cause the wage rate to be bid up to Ow_u. Thus limiting entry is an alternative way of raising wages. The problem here of course is that nonunion members can offer to work at lower wages and break the union. For this reason the union must obtain, through threat of strike, boycott, or some other method, a contract with the firms preventing the hiring of nonunion labor. Or, the union can get government to issue a limited number of licenses, thereby restricting entry. The more difficult and time-consuming it is to get a license, the more entry is restricted and the higher are wage rates. But in either case, under reasonably competitive conditions wage gains can be obtained only at the expense of reduced employment.

This analysis does not mean that unions deliberately set out to cause unemployment. Certainly they do considerable lobbying in Congress to restore full employment by expansionary monetary and fiscal policy. They continually support full employment as an economic policy. But the fact is that wage gains in a specific industry are frequently obtained at the expense of employment in that industry.

The point is that the presence of unions in some industries but not in others can cause differences in wage rates between unionized and nonunionized industries. Those workers who wish to be employed in the higher-wage unionized industry, but are not employed, add to the supply of workers in nonunionized industries, thus driving down wages there. This does not necessarily mean decreased employment in the economy as a whole.

Again we should emphasize that this has been a rather simplified account of the effect of unions. There are some who argue that unions have had no impact on the average wage rate, but only on the distribution. Others argue the opposite. Some say that wages have risen no faster in unionized than in nonunionized industries. Again others argue otherwise. The whole question is an empirical one, with which you will deal if you take a course in labor economics. Furthermore, the question of unemployment versus full employment is the subject of a course in macroeconomics. Thus we have only touched the surface here.

10.7.b Minimum wages

The effect of a minimum wage rate placed above equilibrium is similar to the effect of a union. Those who retain their jobs in industries covered by the minimum wages are better off with the higher wage. Those who lose their jobs (that is, the "surplus" labor) are worse off. They must find work in industries not covered by minimum wages. The supply of labor increases in these uncovered industries, and the wage rate there is bid down. Therefore, a minimum wage makes some better off and some worse off. The question is, who benefits and who gains?

If all workers were homogeneous, as in our theory, the impact would be randomly distributed. If, as in the real world, workers differ in productivity and in employers' feelings toward them, the least productive workers and those most disadvantaged in their "reputation" with employers are released. While theory can say no more, we can examine a little empirical evidence for further insight into the problem.

APPLICATION

Effect of minimum wages: Some evidence

As noted above, an increase in the minimum wage causes some unemployment or shifting to industries not covered. In addition, there may be some shifting by employers from unskilled to skilled labor in the industries covered. The burden largely falls on those who are least skilled, least productive, or least desirable in the eyes of employers. Economists largely agree on this point. Any major disagreement concerns the magnitude of the unemployment effect. As was emphasized in the case of labor unions, the unemployment effect of an externally imposed wage increase can vary from negligible to substantial, depending upon the elasticity of the demand for labor.

A recent study by Thomas Gale Moore examined the impact of the minimum wage on disadvantaged classes of workers.* Moore notes, as we emphasized, that theoretically an increase in the minimum

---

* Thomas Gale Moore, "The Effect of Minimum Wages on Teenage Unemployment Rates," *Journal of Political Economy,* July/August 1971, pp. 897–902. The remainder of this application is based upon that paper.

wage rate increases the wages of unskilled (those affected by the minimum wage) relative to the wages of the skilled. Recall from Chapter 5 that changes in *relative* input prices cause substitution away from the relatively more expensive input. Since it takes time for employers to substitute capital and skilled labor for unskilled labor, the impact upon the unskilled increases over time. Thereafter, the impact gradually lessens as the *general* level of wages rises. Therefore, the unemployment effect of a specific increase in the minimum wage rate at first increases then decreases over time. Furthermore, the total unemployment effect should be greater the more extensive is the coverage. For example, if all industries were covered, anyone whose productivity was less than the minimum wage would be unemployed. If only a few industries were under the regulation, those unemployed in these industries would seek jobs in the uncovered industries, driving down wages there. But they would not be unemployed. The more extensive the coverage, the more difficult it is for the disadvantaged to find a job.

For the period 1954–68 Moore obtained the following results. The minimum wage rate as a proportion of hourly earnings was highly significant in explaining unemployment in all categories of teenagers. This variable was not significant in explaining unemployment for males between 20 and 25. The general unemployment level (that is, the unemployment rate for males 25 and older) was highly significant in explaining unemployment for all categories. The percentage of workers covered by minimum wages was highly significant in explaining unemployment for males and females 16–19, and for males, 20–24. It was somewhat less significant for other categories. It appears that the burden of minimum wages is much less by the time a worker becomes 20. By then the workers would have gained experience or undergone training and would no longer be disadvantaged. Moore points out that his results may understate the impact of the minimum wage. High unemployment can cause potential workers to drop out of the labor force. There is evidence that this has happened in the teenage labor force.

In 1969, the United States secretary of labor recommended making the minimum wage universal. Using the model, Moore estimated this would raise non-white teenage unemployment an additional 9.7 percent. He also showed that the Secretary's proposal to increase the minimum wage rate would increase unemployment in all teen-age categories.

This analysis by no means is meant to imply that administration officials and particularly secretaries of labor are ignorant of economics or are totally unfeeling about teen-age unemployment. On July 29, 1977, the secretary of labor, Dr. Ray Marshall, a widely known labor economist, was quoted by the UPI as saying that a proposed increase in the minimum wage to $2.65 an hour could cost the economy 90,000 jobs. Therefore, he certainly recognized the effect of an increased minimum wage on unemployment. But he also was quoted as saying that public service employment would create more jobs than those lost. Presumably this means that goverment would create jobs at the minimum wage or above for those workers who could not find jobs, because their value to privately owned firms is less than the minimum wage.

As an economist, one cannot say whether this is a good or bad policy; we cannot say whether or not society benefits by having more public service employees and fewer in the private sector. We only cite Secretary Marshall's statement to show that if an increase in the minimum wage is not to cause unemployment, something else must be done to counteract an increase in the minimum wage; and we wish to indicate also that this topic will continue to be an important policy matter in the future. Thus, you should understand all the implications.

EXERCISE

Why unions support increases in the minimum wage

Why would the major labor unions, in which all members make much more than the minimum wages, be the major supporters of increases in the minimum wage and increases in the coverage of the minimum wage? Surely these union leaders are not unfeeling men who want to see teen-agers, particularly non-white teenagers, unemployed.

But, consider the fact that nonunion members can compete with union members for jobs. Furthermore, firms that have union contracts compete for business with firms that hire nonunion labor. Suppose, for example, New England textile mills hire all union labor. Southern textile mills use lower cost nonunion workers. Other things equal, the Southern mills could undersell the Northern mills, resulting either in some New England mills going out of business or moving to the South. In any case the Northern union workers would be out of work at least temporarily. In either situation nonunion workers are competition to union workers. Do not forget that, in general, substitution is possible. If the minimum wage makes some nonunion labor less cheap, then there is marginally less competition for union members. Of course, this may not always be the only motive, but the higher the minimum wage the less competition for union workers. This is not to deny that union leaders may have additional philanthropic motives. We only say there exist economic motives also.

10.8 MONOPSONY: MONOPOLY IN THE INPUT MARKET

Thus far we have assumed that the price of an input is determined by supply and demand in the resource market. Entrepreneurs, whether perfect competitors or monopolists, believe they can acquire as many units of the input as they want at the going market price. In other words no firm, acting alone, has a perceptible effect upon the price of the input. This obviously is not the case in all situations. There are sometimes only a few, and in the limit one, purchasers of a productive service. Clearly when only a few firms purchase an input, each will affect input price by changing input use. We therefore need new tools to analyze the behavior of such firms.

For analytical simplicity we consider only a single buyer of an input, called a monopsonist. However, the analytical principles are the same when there are a few buyers of an input, called oligopsonists.

10.8.a Marginal factor cost under monopsony

The supply curve for most productive services or productive agents is positively sloped. Since a monopsonist is the sole buyer of a productive service, the supply curve of the input is upward sloping. In order to hire more of an input the monopsonist must raise the price of that input. Each unit of the input hired receives the same price. Therefore, in order to increase the use of an input, the monopsonist must pay *all* units an increased price. Thus marginal factor cost is not, as above, simply the price of an additional unit of input but the *marginal expense* of purchasing additional units.

Table 10.8.1 might clarify this point. Columns (1) and (2) indicate the labor supply to the monopsonist. Column (3) is the *additional* expense of increasing labor by one unit. The firm can hire 5 workers at $10 an hour. To hire an additional worker the wage rate must rise to $12 an hour. With five workers the hourly wage bill is $50 an hour; with six, it is $72. Hiring the additional unit costs an additional $22 an hour, even though the wage rate rises by only $2. Hiring the additional unit costs

TABLE 10.8.1

INPUT SUPPLY AND MARGINAL FACTOR COST

(1)	(2)	(3)	(4)
		Marginal	Marginal
	Quantity	factor	revenue
Price	supplied	cost	product
$10..........	5		
12..........	6..........	$22..........	$70
14..........	7..........	26..........	50
16..........	8..........	30..........	40
18..........	9..........	34..........	36
20..........	10..........	38..........	34
22..........	11..........	42..........	31

$12; but, increasing the wage of the previous five workers from $10 to $12 increases expenses an additional $(5 \times \$2) = \$10$. We can use the same analysis to derive each entry in column (3). When we consider the addition of one unit of an input, the addition to total cost is the *marginal factor cost*. It includes the price paid to the additional unit *plus* the increase that must be paid to the units already employed. Therefore, for every unit except the first, the marginal factor cost exceeds price.

The supply curve of a variable input and the marginal factor cost curve are shown graphically in Figure 10.8.1. Since the price per unit rises as employment increases, the marginal factor cost exceeds supply price at all employment levels; and the marginal factor cost curve is positively

FIGURE 10.8.1

MARGINAL FACTOR COST

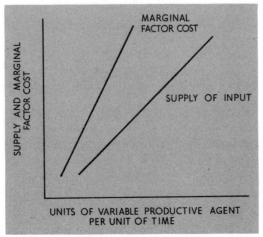

sloped, lies to the left of the supply curve, and typically rises more rapidly than the latter.

Definition. The marginal factor cost of an input to a monopsonist is the increase in total cost (and in total variable cost and in total cost of input) attributable to the addition of one more unit of the variable productive agent.

10.8.b Price and employment under monopsony

The relevant curves for price determination under monopsony are the *MFC* and the value of the marginal product curve (if the firm is a perfect competitor in the commodity market) or the marginal revenue product curve (if it is a monopolist), assuming one variable input. Assume that the firm is a monopolist. The firm is confronted with a positively sloped supply of input curve and the higher marginal factor cost curve. The situation is illustrated in Table 10.8.1 and in Figure 10.8.2. Using this table and graph we will prove the following:

Proposition. A profit-maximizing monopsonist will employ a variable productive service until the point is reached at which the marginal factor cost equals its marginal revenue product. The price of the input is determined by the corresponding point on its supply curve.

The proof of this proposition follows immediately from the definitions of marginal revenue product and marginal factor cost. Marginal revenue product is the addition to total revenue attributable to the addition of one unit of the variable input; the marginal factor cost is the addition to total cost resulting from the employment of an additional unit. Therefore, so long as marginal revenue product exceeds the marginal factor cost, profit can be augmented by expanding input use. On the other hand, if the marginal factor cost of an input exceeds its marginal revenue product, profit is less or loss greater than if fewer units of the input were employed. Consequently, profit is maximized by employing that quantity of the variable service for which the marginal factor cost equals marginal revenue product.

For example, assume only one variable input in Table 10.8.1. The marginal revenue product schedule for 6 through 11 workers is given in column (4). Each worker up through the ninth adds more to hourly revenue (*MRP*) than is added to hourly cost (*MFC*). Thereafter, the tenth and eleventh add more to cost than to revenue. The firm hires nine units.

In the continuous case the equality of *MRP* and *MFC* occurs at point *E* in Figure 10.8.2, and $O\bar{v}$ units of the service are accordingly employed. At this point the supply-of-input curve becomes particularly relevant. $O\bar{v}$ units of the variable productive agent are associated with point *E'* on the supply-of-input curve. Thus $O\bar{v}$ units will be offered at $O\bar{w}$ per unit. Hence $O\bar{w}$ is the equilibrium input price corresponding to market equilibrium employment $O\bar{v}$. If the monopsonist is a perfect competitor in the commodity market the situation is similar, except that the relevant curve is the value of marginal product curve. It employs the variable input until the value of marginal product equals the marginal factor cost of the input.

FIGURE 10.8.2

PRICE AND EMPLOYMENT UNDER MONOPSONY

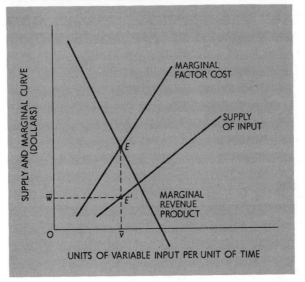

Recall that in Section 10.3 it was shown that monopoly in the commodity market leads to monopolistic exploitation in the input market. Each productive service is paid its marginal revenue product, which is less than the value of its marginal product. In addition there could exist "monopsonistic exploitation," as illustrated in Figure 10.8.3. The monopsonist-monopolist depicted here hires *Ov* units of the variable input, because at this level *MFC* = *MRP*, with a price of *Ow*. Some monopolistic

FIGURE 10.8.3

MONOPSONISTIC EXPLOITATION

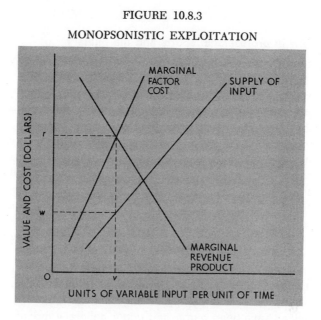

exploitation is involved because in this case marginal revenue product is less than the value of the marginal product of Ov units. Some additional (monopsonistic) exploitation develops also because the variable input receives even less than its marginal revenue product. It receives Ow, and its marginal revenue product is Or, which in turn is less than the value of its marginal product.

Thus the workers are doubly "exploited" because of the presence of both monopoly and monopsony. Again let us emphasize that this does not mean the workers receive less than they could earn elsewhere. Obviously if higher wages could be earned elsewhere, workers would leave for the higher-paid occupation. Thus the term "exploitation" does not in economics indicate that workers are paid less than they "deserve." Such would be a value judgment not used in economics. Such a definition of "exploitation" is used only in the popular sense; it has no meaning in economics.

We should note in passing one peculiarity of monopsony. In some cases, when a previously nonunionized monopsony is unionized, it is possible for the union to score wage gains without causing the firm to decrease employment, and in some cases to increase employment. Economists generally regard this simply as a technical curiosity. We will treat this case in Technical Problem 5 at the end of this chapter.

APPLICATION

Monopsony in professional sports and the military

The typical textbook example of monopsony is the professional athletic leagues, particularly baseball. This situation has changed to some extent because of the possibility of a player's playing out his option and signing with another team. But, there are still vestiges of monopsony remaining.

Take baseball a few years ago. The two major leagues were the sole employers of professional players. Obviously a prospective player had the option of some other occupation, but this alternative job would generally be at a considerably lower salary. The monopsony—the major leagues—developed a plan so that the various teams in the league would not have to bid against one another for talented young baseball players. Every year a draft was held. The player could then negotiate only with the team that drafted him. Furthermore, the player was bound to the original team until he retired, or until that team either traded or released him entirely. Therefore, even though baseball players must generally be regarded as highly paid labor, their services have been purchased under generally monoposonistic conditions. Other professional sports leagues that have a monopsony situation have generally resorted to a draft. Until recent legal rulings, the players were bound to the drafting team, and even now strong vestiges of this situation remain in sports.

Another employer that had significant monopsonistic characteristics and until very recently resorted to a draft in order to hire labor is the military services. While at this time the military draft is no longer used, there are strong advocates for its reinstatement. For example, on December 29, 1976, United Press International quoted Senator John C. Stennis of Mississippi as advocating a return to the draft system for the U.S. armed forces. He said that the voluntary military force is a "bothersome" idea, causing the military now to spend 58 percent of its money on personnel, leaving not much money left over to spend on "all of those expensive weapons," which the Senator said maintain military superiority for the United States. "We are going to have to have the Selective Service Act put on the books in a few years to assure we have enough talent to go around," Stennis said.

Let us use our employment theory to compare the social cost of a volunteer army versus the social cost of an army conscripted in large part by drafting. Since the military meets many of the characteristics of a monopsonist, we would suppose that it faces an upward sloping supply of personnel classified as "suitable" by the military. Assume that *SS* in Figure 10.8.4 represents this supply, showing the number of suitable personnel that would volunteer for military service at each wage rate in the list.

Now if the military were a profit-maximizing monopsonist, it would equate its marginal revenue product curve to the marginal factor cost curve associated with *SS* in order to choose the optimal number of personnel. It would pay the wage given by the corresponding point on the supply curve. But the military does not attempt to maximize profits and therefore operates under somewhat different principles.

First, assume the military resorts to a draft, as it did for so many years. Suppose the general staff decided it "needed" OL_1 people in the services per year. If the military did not have the right to draft, it would have to pay a wage rate of OW_1 in order to hire OL_1 suitable personnel. This would cost society a total of OW_1RL_1 (excluding any fringe benefits) in money payments.

FIGURE 10.8.4

ECONOMICS OF THE DRAFT

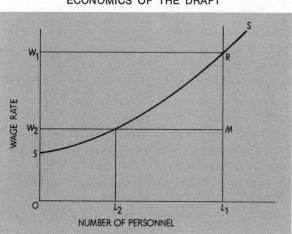

Suppose now that the military sets a lower wage of OW_2. Clearly in this model only OL_2 people would volunteer under the circumstances. If the military still "needed" OL_1, it would have to draft the difference or the shortage of personnel. Now society pays a money cost of OW_2ML_1, clearly a lower cost than before.

But as you probably realize already, this money cost does not represent the total cost to society. Suppose the yearly wage rate in the military for draftees is $5,000. Suppose also that a young man or young woman is drafted for two years. If that person could be making

$10,000 a year in the best alternative, perhaps in business, the opportunity cost to that person drafted is, therefore, $5,000 a year for two years. In fact, any young man or woman drafted, whose supply price for volunteering for military service exceeds $5,000, pays an implicit tax of the difference between the asking price and $5,000. It is not just a matter of the draft costing society less than the volunteer army, it is also simply that the tax burden under the draft is shifted from the older taxpayers to the young people who are drafted.

Thus Senator Stennis is probably correct in pointing out that the voluntary army is costing the *government more money,* but he is neglecting the *implicit costs* borne by the people who are drafted under a draft system. We might also note in passing that if the military is forced to pay higher wages under a volunteer system, it would probably use its personnel more efficiently; and it would probably also find that over time less personnel was "needed" than under the low-wage system. It should be rather obvious why the young people were the leaders in the battle to abolish the draft. After all they were the ones paying the implicit taxes.

EXERCISE

Economics of the draft

Use the model developed here to solve the following problem. Assume the army wishes to hire X number of people. Assume that more than X meet the army's standards. The army has three choices. (1) It can let supply and demand determine the wage that will attract X people (assume an upward sloping supply); (2) it can set wages below equilibrium and draft the number needed; or (3) it can set the wage below equilibrium, draft the number needed, but let people who are drafted pay others to serve for them if they wish and are qualified. Analyze the costs to society, to those drafted, and to the army. Compare the makeup of those who serve under the three choices.

Let us analyze the problem with the aid of Figure 10.8.5. Assume that from the total number of the population who meet the military's criteria for duty (ON_T), the military desires ON_R. SS' is the supply curve of the ON_T for military duty. The upward slope reflects the difference in taste for military duty and the differences in other opportunities. A free market wage of OW_e would induce the required number ON_R to volunteer. The total cost to society would be OW_eCN_R. If wages are set below OW_e, say at OW_D, ON_D would volunteer and N_DN_R would be drafted. The wage cost to society would be OW_DBN_R. However, those who were drafted from the N_DN_T who did not vol-

FIGURE 10.8.5

MORE ECONOMICS OF THE DRAFT

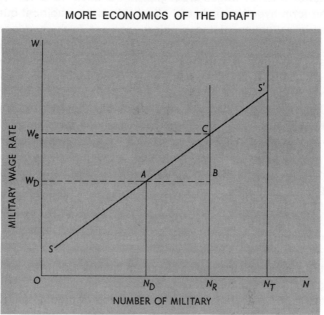

unteer would pay (in foregone earnings) the difference between their wage rate and their supply price. The drafted persons would be scattered randomly among $N_D N_T$ if people could not pay others to serve. If draft notices were negotiable, the same people would serve as would be induced to enter by the equilibrium wage, OW_e. Anyone who was drafted and had a supply price above OW_e would be induced to pay anyone who was not drafted and had a supply price below OW_e the difference between that supply price and OW_D. Society would still pay $OW_D BN_R$. Those who were drafted would pay ACB (recall consumer's surplus). Society as a whole thus shifts some of the military costs to those who are chosen by the draft.

ASIDE

Some evidence about the effect of monopsony

Our theory has told us nothing about the effect of monopsony upon wages in specific industries. Certainly workers receive less than the value of their marginal product, but that is not what concerns workers. Their primary interest is the amount of salary they can spend, not whether or not they are "exploited." In theory we cannot answer whether wages are higher in the absence of monopsony. We can form hypotheses, but in effect this is an empirical question.

One investigation of the problem was set forth in a paper by John H. Landon and Robert N. Baird.* That paper attempted to demonstrate the effect of monopsony in the market for public school teachers. Their hypothesis was that competition in the market for teachers should result in higher salary levels. They examined the question of whether the salaries of first-year teachers were higher where many small districts competed or where there was only one large consolidated district in the region. In their analysis the single large consolidated district constituted a monopsony in hiring new teachers. A large number of competing districts gives more options to beginning teachers.

Landon and Baird used data from 1966–67 from 136 school districts. They used the number of school districts in the county of the district to reflect monopsony power. In a heavily populated area with a single system, for example, the district is in essence a monopsonist. Teachers must move to change assignments. If formerly competing districts collude, they form a monopsony.

When all 136 districts were included, the degree of monopsony power was shown to be negatively related to the salaries of beginning teachers, and the relation was statistically highly significant. The authors concluded that the more districts in a county, the less monopsony power possessed by the district and the higher the salaries of beginning teachers.

From the results of the investigation it appears that monopsony in the local market for teachers does affect teachers' salaries significantly. As the authors point out, the recent popular proposals for school district decentralization should result in pressures for higher teachers' salaries. Any movement toward consolidation would increase the bargaining position of administrators.

ASIDE

Bilateral monopoly

We have neglected one aspect of monopsony analysis that has probably occurred to you during the above discussion. This situation occurs when a single buyer of a resource—some form of labor perhaps—confronts a single seller of that resource, say, a union of that type of labor. This situation, when a monopsonist hires a resource from a monopolist, is called "bilateral monopoly." A situation that

---

* John H. Landon and Robert N. Baird, "Monopsony in the Market for Public School Teachers," *American Economic Review*, December 1971, pp. 966–71. This aside is based upon that paper.

approximates this would be when the United Automobile Workers bargains with General Motors or the "big three" auto makers. It could occur on a smaller scale when the only textile mill or coal mine in a small town bargains with a union of the workers.

These and other similar situations you can think of approach true bilateral monopoly but do not meet all of the exacting requirements. About all we can say is that there is no unique theoretical equilibrium solution. The final results depend in large part on the bargaining power of the concerned parties. We can use our theory to set forth boundaries within which the agreement will fall, but we cannot predict the point. For this reason we will not go any further into bilateral monopoly. Much of the literature on union-management bargaining and agreements takes the form of a case-by-case discussion. This is part of the material you will study if you take a course in labor economics. You will use your basic economic theory but apply it to specific cases.

10.9 THEORY OF INVESTMENT

Thus far in our theory of distribution we have simply assumed that a firm rents a piece of capital equipment each time period in the same way that it hires labor, land, and other inputs for each period. This is a powerful body of analysis and much insight can be gained from it. But there is another body of distribution theory that is also quite useful but can be, and generally is, extremely complex. This is the theory of capital investment. It is probably, more realistically, the proper subject matter for more advanced courses. Investment theory is, however, an extremely important concept in economic decision making, both in business and in one's personal affairs. Businesses purchase buildings and machinery that are expected to yield a stream of income over a long period of time. Individuals purchase cars, houses, furniture, and other durables that are expected to yield a stream of utility over a long period of time.

Because of its usefulness, we need to cover some parts of investment theory. Due to the complexity of this concept we shall cover only the bare essentials of the theory and use a very simplified version to analyze a few problems.

The problem of an individual firm's decision to invest in a capital asset such as a piece of machinery is quite simple. So long as the asset is expected to yield a higher rate of return than its cost, the asset is purchased; if not, it is not purchased. The return to a capital asset is the *discounted* after-tax stream of returns the asset is expected to yield over its lifetime. Do not forget that future returns have to be discounted, because income *now* can be invested at the market rate of interest; therefore, one dollar ten years from now is not worth a dollar now. In any case, a capital asset is expected to yield a yearly rate of return over its lifetime, the rate of return depending upon the price of the asset and the expected stream of income after tax.

The cost of a capital asset is the relevant rate of interest. A firm can borrow the price of the asset but must pay back the cost at the relevant rate of interest. Thus if an asset is expected to yield a rate of return of 15 percent and the interest rate is 9 percent, the asset would be purchased. If the expected yield is only 8 percent, no firm would purchase it. Do not forget, the interest rate is the opportunity cost of capital.

For large segments of society the situation can be depicted in Figure 10.9.1. Let us assume that the prevailing interest rate in the economy is *OR*. Since the way in which the economy's interest rate is determined is a subject in macroeconomics, not microeconomics, we will not discuss how society's rate, *OR*, is determined. Let us assume that for this industry or group of industries there are a large number of potential investments for the period under consideration. These potential investments can be ranked according to their potential rates of return, from the highest rate to the lowest. *DD* shows these rates of return on potential investments for the industry. Obviously those investments on the highest portion of *DD* are expected to yield the highest rate of return, and vice versa. Recall these must be rates of return after taxation, since before-tax returns are irrelevant in the decision-making process.

FIGURE 10.9.1

DETERMINATION OF INVESTMENT

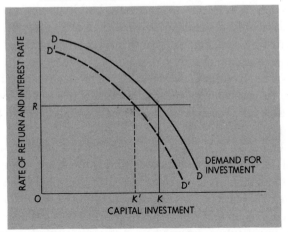

All investments expected to yield a rate of return in excess of the going rate of interest, *OR*, will be undertaken. No investment expected to yield a return lower than *OR* will be carried out. Therefore, in this industry or group of industries, with an interest rate of *OR*, the amount of investment in the relevant period will be *OK*. In this situation *DD* is the demand for investment for the relevant period.

Suppose now that the government imposes an additional tax on the return from capital in this industry. The after-tax rate of return on every potential investment must consequently fall. To illustrate, suppose the added tax causes the demand for investment to fall from *DD* to *D'D'*. With the same interest rate, investment in the industry falls to *OK'*. Some investments that previously would have been undertaken now do not yield a rate of return sufficient to exceed, after all taxes, the rate of interest. These are not carried out. In order to be undertaken, the before-tax return on the investment good must be higher after the tax increase.

On the other hand, a reduction in taxation, possibly in the form of tax credits or a faster rate of depreciation for tax purposes, would increase the demand for investment, represented by an outward shift from *DD*. Some previously unprofitable investments would then be undertaken. At a constant interest rate of *OR*, investment would exceed *OK*. Therefore, the degree of taxation plays an important role in determining the amount of investment undertaken. Of course, so does the rate of interest, the physical availability of potential investments, and the demand for the products produced by the capital in which investment is made.

Let us mention again that we have covered investment theory much more sketchily than we have treated most other major topics thus far in the text. In many economics departments capital and investment theory is one of the *graduate,* not undergraduate courses, although finance courses do develop the topic further. In any case the subject matter is quite complicated.

All we want to emphasize here are the very important role played by the rate of interest and that capital is purchased in order to yield a discounted stream of income. Anything that alters the rate of interest or the discounted stream of income from potential investments changes the amount of investment.

While we have not stressed it thus far, it should be clear from the preceding discussion that expectations by persons in business, admittedly difficult, perhaps impossible, to quantify, play a crucial role in determining the position of the demand for investment. If entrepreneurs forecast a gloomy future—gloomy in the sense of expectations of higher taxes, lower sales, higher wages, and so on—the expected flow of income from investment is reduced and the demand for investment declines. Investment is undertaken to yield returns far into the future. Since the future is so uncertain, the feelings of potential investors must play an important role in determining investment. The investor's confidence in the government and in other relevant institutions may play the most important role of all. For example, in countries with unstable governments—ones that change governments every few years, confiscate the assets of those out of power, and continually inflate then revalue the currency—investors would acquire assets that are quite mobile, such as Swiss bank accounts, gold, or precious jewelry. Productive capital is too risky an asset in a country in which confiscation or other types of capital loss is so probable. In order to induce investment in productive capital in that situation the expected rate of return must be astronomically high. On the other hand, a stable environment and government encourage investment, other things remaining the same.

APPLICATION

Effect of different tax treatments in different industries

There is a tendency in the long run for after-tax average rates of return on capital to equalize among industries. This tendency is offset to some extent by differences in risk in various industries. But, when capital is free to move in the long run from industry to industry, the trend is for investment capital to leave low-return industries and to enter high-return industries. As investment is reduced in the low-return industry, the average rate of return is driven up in that industry. As investment enters the high-return industry, investments yielding lower returns in that industry are undertaken, thereby lowering the average rate of return in that industry. We must emphasize that this tendency toward equalization is only a tendency and is a long-run phenomenon. Thus at any one time some industries will be making high returns and some much lower; but these differentials will *tend* to disappear.

We must emphasize also that this tendency toward equalization pertains only to after-tax rates of return. Before-tax rates reflect, among other things, differences in tax treatment and will persist over long periods of time.

A good example is the petroleum industry from 1950 through 1972, a period during which that industry enjoyed a certain tax advantage because of the depletion allowance in the case of returns from oil. (Recall our discussion of this allowance above.) During this period, the average *after-tax* return on capital in this industry was not significantly different from the after-tax return in manufacturing as a whole in the entire United States. But the tax break allowed by the depletion, as would be expected, caused over-investment in petroleum. Therefore, the average yearly before-tax rate of return on capital was significantly lower than the before-tax rate of return on capital in manufacturing in the United States as a whole. It appears that the tax advantage in petroleum lured investment capital into that industry until the after-tax returns were driven to the going rate in the economy as a whole.

A numerical example should clarify things somewhat. Suppose that there is a society with no taxation. The existing rate of return in all industries is 20 percent. Now let a tax be imposed upon two of the industries, call them A and B. Let a 25-percent tax be levied on A and a 50-percent tax on B. Now, if the before-tax returns in both remain the same, 20 percent, the after-tax return in both will be below the going rate in the economy as a whole, and the after-tax return in A will be significantly higher than the after-tax return in B; 10 percent in B and 15 percent in A.

Investment capital will be withdrawn from both industries because of the higher taxes. But a larger number of lower-yield investments in B will be dropped than will be dropped in A, because of the *relative* tax advantage in A. In the long run the after-tax returns in both will equal the going return in the economy, but the before-tax returns in B, the more heavily taxed industry, will exceed the before-tax returns in A, and the before-tax returns in both will exceed the average return in the economy.

A similar thing happened recently in the Canadian mining industry. Until the early 1970s after-tax returns in Canadian mining were not significantly different from after-tax returns in Canadian manufacturing as a whole. In the early 1970s much heavier taxes were imposed on mining. The after-tax returns to capital in mining and manufacturing as a whole continued to be not significantly different. But the before-tax returns to capital in mining almost immediately became significantly higher than before the change. This change reflected that the higher mining taxes caused lower-yield capital investments to be abandoned.

Even though we have only touched upon the fundamentals of capital investment theory, we still have enough of the basic tools to solve many of the day-to-day investment decisions you will be making in your business and personal life. In attempting the following exercises do not forget the very crucial role played by the interest rate.

EXERCISES

Discounting and its effect on investment

First let us take a personal investment, the purchase of a central air conditioning system. As are many people today, prospective purchasers are worried about energy prices. Suppose that there are two choices open, (1) a gas air conditioner, which carries a higher purchase price but costs less to run in yearly gas expenditures, and (2) an electric air conditioner, which has a lower initial purchase price but has higher yearly operating costs. How would you make the decision?

Well, consider the following hypothetical investment example. Both the gas and the electric air conditioner are expected to last 15 years. We will ignore maintenance costs, assuming that they are the same. The gas air conditioner has an initial purchase price of $6,000; it will cost $300 a year to operate for the 15 years. Thus the total expenditure will be $6,000 + (15 × $300) = $10,500. The electric air conditioner initially costs $5,000, but it will cost $400 a year to operate. The total cost is $5,000 + (15 × $400) = $11,000. Thus the gas air conditioner is clearly $500 cheaper; but is it really?

Recall the effect of discounting. Ten dollars one year from now is worth now only $9.26, if the interest rate is 8 percent. You can invest $9.26 now at 8 percent and have $10 in one year. You can invest $8.57 now at 8 percent and have $10 in two years; thus the *present value* of $10 in two years in $8.57. Remember the present-value formula. If the interest rate is r, the present value of X dollars in t years is

$$PV = \frac{X}{(1 + r)^t}.$$

Let us compare the present value of the costs of the two air conditioners if the interest rate is 8 percent. The gas air conditioner costs

$$\$6,000 + \frac{\$300}{1.08} + \frac{\$300}{(1.08)^2} + \frac{\$300}{(1.08)^3} + \ldots + \frac{\$300}{(\$1.08)^{15}} = \$8,566.50.$$

The electric air conditioner has a total cost of

$$\$5,000 + \frac{\$400}{1.08} + \frac{\$400}{(1.08)^2} + \frac{\$400}{(1.08)^3} + \ldots + \frac{\$400}{(1.08)^{15}} = \$8,422.00.$$

Thus when the *true costs* of the two units are considered, the electric unit costs less in this hypothetical example, even though the total undiscounted cost of the electric unit is higher.

Try the following example. You can buy a piece of machinery for your office now for $5,000. It will last five years. The rate of interest is 10 percent. You can rent the same piece of machinery for your office for $1,200 a year for five years. Which plan is cheaper?

10.10 SUMMARY

We have covered many topics and developed many theories in this chapter. The more important points are in the following propositions:

Proposition. When only one input is variable for the firm, the demand for that resource is its *marginal revenue product.* For the perfectly competitive firm this is commodity price times marginal product, called the *value of marginal product.* For the monopolist, marginal revenue product is marginal revenue times marginal product. These curves represent the value of additional units of the resource to the firm. Since price exceeds marginal revenue for a monopolist, the value of marginal product exceeds the monopolist's marginal revenue product. When several resources are variable, these curves shift when the use of one input changes, but the resource still receives its *MRP* in equilibrium.

Proposition. The demand for an input by a perfectly competitive industry is not the horizontal summation of each firm's demand. While any firm can change its level of output without changing commodity price, the industry as a whole cannot. Thus, in deriving industry demand, one must take account of the effect upon commodity price. The demand of a monopolist is the industry's demand, since the monopolist is the industry.

Proposition. Input prices are determined in input markets by the interaction of supply and demand. The supply of an input is generally, though not always, upward sloping to an industry.

Proposition. A monopolist is a firm that faces an upward sloping supply curve for one or more inputs. It hires the quantity at which *MRP* equals the marginal factor cost. The input receives a lower price than its *MRP.*

Proposition. An input is said to be exploited if it receives less than the value of its marginal product. This does not mean that the input receives less than it could receive elsewhere, or less than it "deserves."

Proposition. An investment is undertaken if the expected rate of return exceeds the interest rate. In the case of an industry, investment in a period will continue until the rate of return on the *marginal* investment equals the rate of interest.

We should end the summary of this chapter with a warning. Do not attach too much normative content (value judgment) to the marginal productivity theory of wages and distribution. That is, do not simply draw the conclusion that marginal productivity theory says that all workers get what they "deserve" or what they "ought ot get." The theory says no such thing. It is a positive predictive or explanatory theory. It enables us to predict the effect of a change in the minimum wage or the unionization of an industry. It enables us to explain differences in wage rates among occupations. It does not allow us to say whether such differences are desirable from a social point of view. It does not allow us to state that a distribution of income based upon marginal productivity is somehow more "just" than any other distribution.

Many decades ago economists got something of a bad name because of making such moral judgments. People begin with a specific amount of resources that they own—capital, labor skill, social position, and so on. Who is to say that the original distribution of resources is somehow more just than any other?

On the other hand, neither can we say that some other method of allocation or distribution may be more just, or may give people more closely what they deserve. We merely want to emphasize that our marginal productivity theory does not say anything about deservedness. It simply explains to a great extent why people receive what they receive. We can only say that society or some part of it believes that the resources owned by individuals are worth a certain amount.

We frequently hear or read someone bemoaning that Mohammed Ali does not deserve $5 million a fight; that O. J. Simpson, Dr. J (Julius Erving), and Tom Seaver, and other athletes do not deserve their huge salaries; that Robert Redford or Barbra Streisand should not get $3 million a movie; or that Professor X at the University of Y does not deserve his large salary because he teaches only a few students a year. We also hear and read that someone or some group deserves more income.

Whether we feel this way or not, our theory, and we as economists, can say nothing about deservedness. Mohammed Ali, Barbra Streisand, and others receive their income because someone thinks that the return from hiring them will be greater than the amount paid out. That is all we, as economists, can say.

APPLICATION

Wage theory and career counseling

You can use some of the material in this chapter for career counseling. When returns in a particular occupation seem high, do not forget that others are entering this occupation in which salaries seem out of equilibrium. Remember that it takes time to train to enter an occupation; while you are training, enough people may have entered to drive the salary below that in alternative occupations. Holders of Ph.D.'s in some fields in great demand a few years ago are now driving taxis or pumping gas.

Do not neglect the opportunity cost of training for an occupation. Even though the returns in this occupation are higher than the amount you could be earning in what you could do now, these are future returns and must be discounted at some finite rate of interest. In the cost of your training you must consider the present returns you are giving up.

It may certainly be the case that a change in the interest rate can affect the decision to go to college or to continue on in graduate school. Quite possibly an extra three or four years in graduate school can increase someone's stream of earning after completion of the degree. But with a sufficiently high rate of interest the present value of the *increase* in the stream after four years more education may be less than the present value of the monetary cost and the cost in lost income from continuing in school. This is not to say that economic considerations are all that count. Certainly the increased utility from the different job may outweigh the loss in discounted total income. We only say that the interest rate is an important economic variable in making such a decision.

The length of the time horizon is an important variable also. We know that the cliché "you're never too old to learn" is probably correct in most cases, but the current trend toward "you're never too old to get retrained for a new occupation" may be true, but frequently uneconomical. In fact, a candidate for the U.S. Senate from Texas recently stated that the reeducation of older persons for new, better-paying occupations would be one of his major objectives if elected.

Now we cannot analyze the difference in utility from retraining but we can analyze the economics of the situation. As one becomes older, one also becomes more and more "locked in" economically, to an occupation. We know that the retraining has monetary and opportunity costs. But, the increase in the *discounted* stream of income after retraining may well exceed the total cost of retraining, including opportunity cost. As one becomes older the time horizon over which the increase in income is spread becomes shorter. Thus the increase in the discounted stream of income becomes less.

Carried to the extreme, it takes a very large future salary indeed to make it worthwhile for someone 58 years old and making $20,000 a year to give up four years of income to go to medical school then practice medicine for three years until age 65. The point is that when considering retraining for a different job or deciding on additional education, the important economic decision-making variables are (1) the difference in the present value of the stream of future income, (2) the cost of training, (3) the time horizon, and (4) the rate of interest. These, of course, are only economic variables; subjective factors may offset them.

Furthermore, keep aware of economic events in the economy. Many fortunes are made by those who recognize a coming trend and get in on the ground floor, both those entering an occupation and those starting a business. Remember also that much money is lost by those entering and getting in on the ground floor when the ground floor is made of quicksand.

Try to use your knowledge of theory to predict the economic consequences of governmental activities. This, of course, takes experience. Recall that above all it is the frictional gains that count. Above-normal returns are generally competed away in the long run. Finally, remember that there are factors other than economic forces that should influence your career or business decision. These may be most important. But since this is an economics text and that is our field of expertise, we have chosen to stress these economic forces. Remember also, however, that no matter what field you choose, your knowledge of economics will enable you to be better decision makers in that field.

TECHNICAL PROBLEMS

1. Analyze some effects of a Federal minimum wage. How do these effects differ from a state or local minimum wage?

FIGURE E.10.1

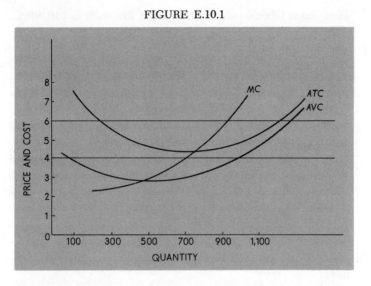

2. Recall the definition of quasi rent. Figure E.10.1 shows the short-run cost curves of a competitive firm.
   a. If price is $6, what is output?
   b. What is the amount of quasi rent?
   c. How much of quasi rent is attributable to the opportunity cost of the fixed inputs and how much is pure profit?
   d. Answer questions a, b, and c in the case of a $4 price.

3. Consider the firm using one variable factor of production. The following table gives information concerning the production function (columns 2 and 3), demand for output (columns 1 and 2), and supply of labor (columns 3 and 4) for the firm. Not all information will be used in each section of the problem. Add to the table any columns you wish.

(1) P ($ per unit)	(2) Q (units)	(3) L (units)	(4) w ($ per unit)
10.50	5	5	4.00
5.36	10	6	4.25
5.00	14	7	4.50
4.00	17	8	4.75
3.00	19	9	5.00
2.60	20	10	5.25

   a. Suppose the firm is a perfect competitor in the output market and also a perfect competitor in the labor market. Draw a graph showing the demand for labor if the price of output is $3.50 per unit.

How much labor would the firm use if the wage is $10.50? _____ units.

b.   Suppose instead that the firm is a monopsonist in the factor market facing a supply curve for labor given in columns 3 and 4. This firm is a perfect competitor in the output market and the price of the output is $3.50 per unit. How much labor would be used? _____ What would be the wage _____?

Explain your answers and graph your solution, showing on the graph how you got your answers.

c.   Now suppose the firm is a monopolist in the output market and a monopsonist in the input market where the demand for the output is given in columns 1 and 2 and the supply of labor is given in columns 3 and 4. What would be the profit-maximizing amount of labor used by this firm _____ and what would be the market wage? _____.

Explain your answer and graph your solution.

4.   Suppose you can get the following information on a firm that makes electric forks:

Production function

Quantity of forks	Amount of labor used
Q_1	L_1
Q_2	L_2
Q_3	L_3
Q_4	L_4

Market demand for electric forks

Price of forks	Quantity demanded
P_1	Q_1
P_2	Q_2
P_3	Q_3
P_4	Q_4

Market supply of labor

Price of labor	Quantity of labor supplied
W_1	L_1
W_2	L_2
W_3	L_3
W_4	L_4

Current price for forks is P_3. Curent wage rate is W_3.

a.   Draw this firm's demand for labor if the firm is a perfect competitor in the output market and the labor market. What would happen to this demand for labor if the price of the forks rose (due to, say, a change in consumer tastes)?

b.   How much labor would the firm use if it were a perfect competitor in the labor market but a monopolist in the output market?

    c. How much labor would the firm use if it were a perfect competitor in the output market but a monopsonist in the labor market?

    d. How much labor would the firm use if it were a monopolist in the output market and a monopsonist in the labor market?

    What would happen to the amount of labor used if the supply of labor shifted left? Show on your graph.

5. Consider the monopolist-monopsonist shown graphically in Figure E.10.2. Labor is the only variable input.

    a. Show the equilibrium quantity of labor hired and the wage rate.

    b. We emphasized in the text that in the typically assumed case a union that comes in and forces a wage increase will cause some unemployment. Suppose you represent such a union of this firm's employees. You can set any wage that you wish. In effect you can simply set a wage and say to the firm, "You can hire all the labor you wish at this wage rate, but below this wage you get none." Thus the wage is parametrically given to the firm by you.

       i. Show on the graph the *highest* wage that you can set and cause no *less* labor to be hired than was hired in part *a* of the question.

      ii. Show how much labor would want to work for the firm at this wage but would not be hired.

     iii. Show the wage that maximizes the amount of labor hired. (At this wage everyone who wants to work for this firm at the wage you set will be hired.)

  Note: This problem shows a minor exception to the point made in the text. The same thing could result from a minimum-wage law. But the analysis in the text generally holds.

FIGURE E.10.2

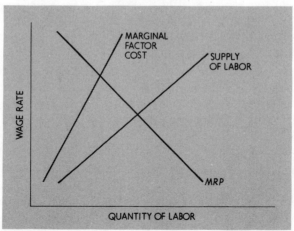

6. Explain why the demand of a competitive industry for an input is less elastic than the sum of the demands of all the firms in the industry.

7. Monopolization of an industry will reduce the demand for an input but will not change wages unless the monopoly has monopsony power. Comment.

8. What would be the marginal product of an input that is free to a firm; that is, the input costs the firm nothing?

9. After the first unit of an input hired, why is the marginal factor cost of that input to a monopsonist greater than the supply price of the input?

10. The demand for a factor of production depends to some extent on the demand for the products produced by the input. Explain the connection.

11. "Unskilled workers have low wages because their productivity is low." Is this precise? Give a more complete explanation.

12. The wage rate is solely determined by the marginal productivity of labor. In any case, the marginal productivity theory says that all workers get what they deserve. Comment critically.

ANALYTICAL PROBLEMS

1. You are attempting to get a labor union started. What conditions would make your job easier? What would make your job harder? Analyze the case of an individual firm, an industry, and an entire trade or profession.

2. "Some female laundry workers, who are not covered by the minimum wage law, have standards of living that are too low because they are paid only $1.75 per hour. In order to improve their lot, a law should be passed making it unlawful to pay them less than $3.00 an hour."
   a. If you were a female laundry worker would you support such a law? Under what conditions? Answer, assuming competition.
   b. Would you be surprised to learn that the most active supporters of such legislation were male laundry workers whose wives are not laundry workers? Why or why not?

3. Suppose that a particular firm in a competitive industry had a bigoted manager who refused to hire workers of a particular race even though these workers are as productive as those of other races.
   a. Under what conditions could the firm so discriminate?
   b. Under what conditions could it not?
   c. Would a monopolist be more likely to discriminate? Why or why not?

4. There is a proposal that government should provide an incentive payment to firms that hire unskilled handicapped workers. There would be a fixed amount per unskilled handicapped-hour used. How would this affect the wage and number of unskilled handicapped hired? If the payment is a lump sum regardless of the number hired, how would this affect your answer?

5. The fact that industries must pay a higher wage to get workers to work more means that none of these workers can have a negatively sloped supply of labor. Analyze.

6. Theft is an occupation. How would each of the following circumstances affect the number of thieves and their remuneration. Think in terms of *VMP*.
   a. Higher minimum wages and broader coverage.
   b. Technological advances in the burglar-alarm industry.
   c. Longer sentences for theft.
   d. Economic prosperity.
   e. Recession.
   f. Laws restricting hours of work.

7. A congressman was quoted as saying that an increase in the minimum wage will not cause unemployment, since it will raise labor productivity. Comment critically.

8. There is a "shock theory" of minimum wage laws. They supposedly "shock" inefficient firms into becoming more efficient. The evidence is that after increases in minimum wages firms purchase new capital equipment to use with labor. Comment. (Hint: recall our theory of production.)

9. In many cities the wages of school teachers are the same in any school for teachers with similar experience. Why do schools in the wealthier areas of the city generally get the best teachers?

10. A state government has recently spent $3 million of state funds to send units of the national guard to a riot-torn city. What is the relevant economic cost? What other items should be included? Could you measure them all?

11. Go back to the exercise and solution about the draft associated with Figure 10.8.4. Analyze the possible differences in situations 2 and 3 as to their impact on the total output in the economy.

11

Welfare and competition

11.1 INTRODUCTION

In the introduction to this text we emphasized that economics is the study of choice. Because of scarcity, individuals must make decisions, and this involves choice. Economics is concerned with the way people make these choices and the results of such choices. We can make predictions and explain economic phenomena using our theories about the way people make their choices.

Until now we have been concerned with the decision making or choice processes of *individuals*. Demand theory is based upon the theory of individual consumer behavior. To be sure, we combine these individuals into groups in order to obtain market demands, but these market demands result from the behavior or preferences of groups of separate individuals, not from explicit group behavior or the decisions of a group as a whole.

Supply theory is likewise based upon the decision-making process of individual firms. Again we can combine individual firms into groups called industries or product groups, but industry behavior results from the decision making of the individual firms, not the group as a whole. We discussed briefly the fact that individual firms sometimes combine voluntarily into groups called cartels, and the group as a whole makes decisions, or someone makes the decision for the group, such as how to distribute profit and production. But, for the most part, under these circumstances, we simply threw up our hands and said that the results of such combinations usually depend upon the bargaining power of the individual firms and that there is usually the incentive for cartels to break up.

Distribution theory is likewise based upon individual decision making. The supply of factors of production results from the choices of separate individuals as does the demand for inputs by firms and industries. We did mention the choice behavior of a group called a union, but as in the case of cartels we only mentioned these in passing, with little analytical content in the analysis. Thus we have stressed that microeconomic theory is basically concerned with the choices of individuals and the economic consequences of these choices.

There is, however, a branch of economics that is concerned with group choice or the decision-making processes of groups of individuals acting together. This branch of economics is frequently called welfare economics. In this chapter we will concern ourselves with group choice, and what economists can say about group choice.

Certainly the first groups that come to mind when discussing group decision making are various branches of government—city, county, state, and federal governments make decisions ostensibly in behalf of groups of individuals. But there are other groups that are set up voluntarily—clubs, fraternities, sororities, etc. Workers combine into unions, and decisions are made for the union as a whole. In these cases and particularly in the case of government, the decision-making process or the analysis of choice is not simple and straightforward.

We must emphasize that a thorough study of welfare economics usually involves one or more courses, frequently at the graduate level. This branch of study is based upon the concept of general equilibrium, which requires for rigorous treatment rather complex mathematical analysis. For this reason this chapter is not at all analytical in nature; but rather is meant to allow the student to get a feel for the more complex general equilibrium analysis and welfare theory. It is only meant as an introduction to the area. It is also designed to introduce the student to the role of government in economic decision making.

We begin with the concept of social welfare, then discuss what economists have to say on the subject. We analyze the effect of competition on welfare and some forces that disrupt the market process. Finally we introduce, and we should emphasize that we only introduce, the role of government in the process.

11.2 SOCIAL WELFARE

Groups of people—society as a whole—do make choices, or people make choices for these groups. It follows, therefore, that we frequently (constantly?) hear statements that would lead one to believe that a group of people can have a single utility function or preference pattern, or even statements implying that a non-human institution can have a preference ordering.

We read and hear statements such as "The 55 mile-per-hour speed limit is good for the nation," or "Selling grain or arms or computers to other countries hurts the nation," or "The new energy policy will be good for the country." My newspaper recently had an editorial asserting that the recent crackdown on pornography will be good for Houston. I recently served on a civic committee that recommended that governmental rejuvenation of the downtown core area is "essential" for the good of the city. Sports writers for months have been bemoaning that the repeal of the reserve clause will be bad for baseball or for sports in general. Academic writers have been asserting that alleged grade inflation would be harmful to the university; the basketball coach has recently said that a new colosseum will be good for the university.

None of these statements, and I am sure you have heard or seen a multitude similar to these, really makes any sense, outside of a very narrow definition to be discussed below. The problem actually boils down to the fact that the nation, Houston, baseball, the university, and so forth simply do not have utility functions or preference ordering. Individuals have preference orderings; groups generally do not. Let us analyze why this is the case.

11.2.a The difficult concept of social welfare

The concept of social welfare is difficult either to define or to describe. This is largely because it encompasses so many conflicting interests. In any group from a nation to a state to a city to a club, a policy or action that benefits one set of people may very well, and frequently does, harm another set within the same group. One group in a society may wish to use resources to fight a war while another group wants more spent on highways and schools. Others may want more spent on welfare and less on defense. The point is that we cannot say that a particular policy benefits an entire group if some in the group are made better off while some are made worse off. Therefore, we cannot make statements such as those mentioned in the introduction to this chapter. Maybe I prefer a 55 mile-per-hour speed limit because it lowers the price of gasoline, while you oppose it because you place a higher value on your time. One person may feel that all pornography must be banned, whereas for other people reading pornography is their only leisure activity. Consider the even more farfetched example of a university being better off or worse off. What do people making this assertion mean by this statement? Many faculty members want more books and journals in the library, at the expense of student study space. Students may want much more study space in the library. Who is the university? The faculty, the students, former students, the administration? In fact, could the entire student body speak as a unit? Some students may want a new colosseum, while others want more classroom space or study space or a greater recreation area.

Moreover, the problem is not merely that actions taken by groups, or choices made by leaders of those groups, may harm some in the group and help others, and, therefore we cannot say whether the group is better off or worse off. There is the further complication that we cannot compare changes in utility of different people. If I gain ten hamburgers and you lose five six-packs of beer, we cannot compare my added utility with your loss in utility because utility is neither measurable nor comparable. Even in the case of a social decision that takes $1,000 from you and gives it to me when you are much richer than I am, one cannot say that society's utility increases. No one has ever proven that the marginal utility of income diminishes with increased income. Thus, in economics we do not recognize the concept of a social utility function or a group preference ordering.

Any decision, whether the action of private producers or governmental decision makers, that benefits one group at the expense of another cannot be said to benefit or harm society, since we cannot compare changes in utility.[1] For the reasons given, it is virtually impossible to define social welfare accurately, and in particular, it is impossible to define *maximum* social welfare. Yet almost daily a society must make decisions that affect its welfare: *Should* we give foreign aid to underdeveloped countries? *Should* we tax the consumption of tobacco, alcohol, gasoline, jewelry, and so on? *Should* we give income to those households that cannot earn a spe-

---

[1] This statement is not quite accurate but is very close to being so. Say a social action harms one person and benefits another. If the one who is benefited is willing to bribe the one who is harmed sufficiently to compensate for the harm, both can be better off. This entire process is part of the subject matter in more advanced courses.

cified level of income? There are many such qusetions that confront a society.

To specify maximum welfare or increases in welfare, we would have to specify a welfare function for society as a whole. Certainly, you might say, a society could vote upon all possible organizations and distributions, but even this leads to complications. Consider the following simple hypothetical case. There are three individuals in the society who will vote on three possible events, A, B, and C. The preference orderings of individuals 1, 2, and 3 are as follows:

1. (ApB)(BpC)(ApC)
2. (BpC)(CpA)(BpA)
3. (CpA)(ApB)(CpB)

In the listing (ApB) denotes that the situation A is preferred to situation B. Note that each individual is rational in the sense that if A is preferred to B and B to C, then A is preferred to C. If this three-person society voted upon events A and B, A would get a majority as would B if they chose between B and C. But note that society would vote for C over A. This is inconsistent. If for society (ApB) and (BpC), then consistency would surely imply (ApC). But we see that this is not the case; this society might be said to be irrational. In any case this simplified example shows that there can be inconsistency in determining social welfare by voting. Moreover, even with consistency in voting we cannot say that majority rule must specify maximum social welfare. This method would involve interpersonal utility comparisons, and as you know, economists cannot make such value judgments.

11.2.b Pareto optimality

Many, if not most, welfare problems, such as those discussed, involve economic considerations; so surely economists must be able to say *something* about them. Actually they can say very little. Economists cannot establish the goals of a society nor can they say what is "good" for one person or for a collection of people. In general, economists can only determine the most efficient way by which to achieve a stipulated goal. Nonetheless, economists can make one prescriptive statement: If a change can be made such that one or more people are made better off and *none* worse off, the society's welfare will be increased if the change is made. We must first define "better off":

Definition. A person is said to be better off in organization *A* than in organization *B* if he gets as much of every good and service and more of at least one good or service in *A* than he gets in *B*.

Recall our earlier definition of Pareto optimality.

Definition. A social organization is said to be Pareto optimal if there is no change that will benefit some people without making some others worse off.

This is admittedly a very weak concept of social welfare. To illustrate this, suppose a new transcontinental highway is to be constructed. This will benefit millions of travelers. But it also forces the government to condemn (under the right of eminent domain) the homesteads of a few families. These families, of course, are paid a "fair market price" for their property. However, some of the families may be unwilling to sell for a fair market price; yet they must by law, and they are made worse off. Millions may benefit and one be harmed. Economists as economists cannot say that the new highway increases or decreases social welfare. For this reason economists are primarily interested in Pareto optimality because it expresses efficiency and not because the concept is a social goal. The technical efficiency aspect of welfare economics is a major aspect of the subject to economists.

To summarize, the implications of the concept of Pareto optimally:

Principles. *(a)* If there is a change that will benefit one or more people without making *anyone* worse off, the change is socially desirable, *(b)* if a change helps some and hurts others—the *numbers* are immaterial—no conclusion can be reached by an economist.

11.3 PERFECT COMPETITION AND PARETO OPTIMALITY

While the concept of Pareto optimality is a weak one, it does establish some useful boundaries for the role of economists in making welfare recommendations. We should emphasize that Pareto optimality is an efficiency condition, that a move toward Pareto optimality is simply a move to a more efficient allocation. An action that moves a group toward a Pareto optimal situation is the only condition in which we can say that a group is made better off. We must emphasize, however, that an infinite number of resource allocations can be said to be Pareto optimal, in the sense that no one can be made better off without making someone else worse off. None of these infinite number of allocations can be said to maximize social utility or to be socially preferable.

Before turning to the relation between Pareto optimality and perfect competition, the purpose of this section, it is necessary to say a few words about general equilibrium. Since, as noted above, a complete analysis of general equilibrium involves rather complex mathematical concepts, we shall be quite brief and limit ourselves only to a few basic points.

11.3.a General equilibrium

As was implied in the introduction to this chapter, we have thus far been concerned with conditions of partial equilibrium. These are equilibrium conditions for individual consumers, firms, industries, and markets. These conditions provide our basic decision-making tools in economics.

General equilibrium is concerned with the conditions under which all markets are in equilibrium. Given a set of commodity prices, consumers determine their demands by equating marginal rates of substitution with the corresponding commodity price ratios. Given a set of input prices, producers determine supply by equating the marginal rates of technical substitution with the corresponding input price ratios. Finally, workers determine the supply of labor by equating the marginal rate of substitution of income for leisure with the wage rate. *The problem* of general equilibrium is as follows: can we find a set of prices at which the demands of consumers are voluntarily fulfilled by the supplies of producers who use all productive resources that are voluntarily supplied at the going set of prices? If so, a general equilibrium may exist.

Clearly we could provide a fanciful example in which an auctioneer assembles all participants in the economy and "zeros in" on a set of prices in which all markets are in equilibrium. But this process is not even approximately descriptive of any real world markets. However, competitive bids and counterbids in all markets do tend to push the economy *toward* a general equilibrium. Needless to say, such an equilibrium is never in fact even approximately attained. But there is a *tendency* toward it; and at times we can profitably analyze the situation that would exist if the general equilibrium existed. This is true for many problems; but it is perhaps most important in analyzing the social welfare results of various forms of market and economic organization.

Therefore we can discuss briefly the conditions that would obtain under general equilibrium. The first condition is the equilibrium of exchange, which we discussed previously in Chapter 3, with the use of the Edgeworth box diagram. The general equilibrium of exchange occurs at a point where the marginal rate of substitution (MRS) between every pair of goods is the same for all persons consuming both goods. The exchange equilibrium is not unique; it may occur at any combination at which the MRS for each consumer equals the MRS for any other consumer. Every organization that leads to such a point is a Pareto-optimal organization, because any change that makes some people better off will make others worse off.

The analysis of the general equilibrium of production is quite similar to that of the general equilibrium of exchange. The general equilibrium of production occurs at a point at which the marginal rate of technical substitution between every pair of inputs is the same for all producers who use both inputs. The production equilibrium is also not unique; it can occur at an infinite number of combinations. But each point represents a Pareto-optimal equilibrium organization in the sense that at such a point no producer can increase production without some other producer having to decrease production. All that this requirement means is that all resources are being used and the society is producing on its production possibilities frontier. As you will recall, the production possibilities frontier shows the opportunity cost of producing more of some good; that is, the rate at which some goods must be given up in order for society to have more of some other goods. Again society can choose any point on the frontier, each of which is Pareto optimal.

11.3.b Effect of perfect competition

Assume that there is perfect competition in every market. We shall show that the set of input and output prices that establishes a general economic equilibrium will also in general establish a Pareto-optimal organization of society.

Let us first consider consumers. If there is perfect competition, all consumers face the same set of commodity prices. Since each consuming unit sets MRS equal to the price ratio, the MRS of any one consumer is equal to the MRS of *any other* consuming unit. Since all consumers are just willing to exchange commodities in the same ratio, it is impossible to make one better off without making another worse off. (That is, suppose the *common* MRS of X for Y is 3:1. If someone is allowed to trade 2:1, others must be *forced* to trade at a ratio at which they would not voluntarily trade.) Thus, a Pareto optimum is established.

Next consider producers. In maximizing profit, entrepreneurs necessarily arrange the combination of inputs so as to minimize the unit cost of production. Under perfect competition, the factor-price ratios are the same to all producers. Since each producer equates $MRTS$ to the common factor-price ratio, the $MRTS$ is the same for all. Consequently, there is no reallocation of inputs that would increase one producer's output without reducing another's. Again we have a Pareto-optimal organization.

Finally, in this competitive general equilibrium, the number of hours of work voluntarily offered is exactly equal to the number of hours voluntarily demanded. An increase in wages would help some, but some others would be unemployed. That is, an increase in wages would make some better off, some worse off. A decrease in wages would cause an excess demand. Thus a change in wages from the general equilibrium level will upset both Pareto optimality and general equilibrium.

Let us reemphasize that Pareto optimality does not necessarily indicate maximum attainable welfare or the maximum attainable level of utility for society as a whole. As we stressed above in this chapter, to specify maximum welfare we would have to specify a welfare function for society as a whole. This we cannot do. Thus perfect competition does lead to *some* final Pareto-optimal equilibrium point, but this is an arbitrary point in the sense that any other point on the production possibility frontier can also be Pareto optimal in the sense of being efficient.

The final point that is attained depends upon, among other things, the initial "starting point," or the initial distribution of income. Government may well become involved, and generally does become involved, in deciding what the initial distribution of income will be. But while representatives may decide that the existing income distribution is preferable to any other, or that some other distribution is more preferred, the role of an economist is not to decide what distribution is best, even under perfect competition. An economist's role does include pointing out the economic consequences of changing the distribution. All an economist can say is that if one or more people can be made better off by an action without anyone else being made worse off, the action makes the group better off.

11.4. PERFECT COMPETITION AND SOCIAL WELFARE

So far we have said that perfect competition will lead to a Pareto optimum, and this is the best economists can do. In certain cases, even this is not true. Either perfect competition may break down or the results

of perfect competition are not socially desirable in the sense of being
Pareto optimal. In concluding this book we shall treat these cases briefly,
with one *tremendous caveat*. What we have to say is only an introductory
statement. It requires one or more courses to treat adequately this problem called market failure.

There are several possibilities for market failure—failure in the sense
that the existence of perfect competition does not lead to a Pareto-optimal
situation. We will briefly discuss some of these in this section, then in the
next section turn to what is in our opinion (though not all economists
would agree) the most significant factor in market failure—the question of
property rights and externalities.

The first case to be discussed is that of public goods. A *public good* is
a good for which consumption by individual A does not preclude its
consumption by individuals B, C, D, and so on. An apple is a private good.
If I consume an apple, you cannot consume the same one. While there is
perhaps no "pure" public good, many goods exhibit some characteristic
of public goods. Some examples may be open-air concerts or fireworks
displays. Up to a point, as many people as desire can "consume" these
goods. Up to a very limited point, the same applies to public schools,
libraries, roads, and so on. But after a point, a certain "crowding" effect
sets in, and they are no longer public goods.

If there is such a thing as a "pure" public good, a competitive organization of society provides too little of the good. If the good is privately
produced, some consumers will choose to consume none of the good since
the price is "too high." It costs society nothing for these "additional" consumers to consume the good. Thus if these customers could consume the
good at zero price, they would be better off and no one would be worse
off, in the sense that none of society's resources would have to be used to
add an additional consumer.

To summarize, regardless of the total consumption of the public good,
the same amount of society's resources must be used to produce it. Now it
is reasonable to assume that for some consumers who elect not to purchase
the public good, the marginal utility of the good is not zero. That is, even
though for some consumers in the case of good A

$$\frac{MU_a}{p_a} < \frac{MU_b}{p_b} = \frac{MU_c}{p_c}, \text{ etc.,}$$

$MU_a \neq 0$. Thus if a zero price were charged these consumers, some would
consume good A. If A is a public good, they would be better off, and no
one would be worse off because no more of society's resources are used
when they consume it.

Principle. If the production of a public good is in the hands of private enterprise, social welfare is less than it would otherwise be because some consumers are excluded from the market when price is greater than zero. Since their consumption of the good is "free" to society in the sense that it entails no further resource sacrifice, society as a whole would be better off if these people were allowed to consume the good at zero price; but under free enterprise, they are not allowed to.

This is not an indictment of the free enterprise system. It is merely a recognition of the fact that there may be some goods that are not optimally consumed when price is set by the competitive market mechanism.

Of course, the problem is, who should pay the initial cost of the public good? This is a question still open to debate and the subject of classes in public finance. There is also the problem concerning whether or not there really exists such a thing as a pure public good.

A very closely related problem is that for some goods, exclusion from consumption is not technically feasible. Some examples are lighthouses, national defense, and dams. Suppose, for example, that 1,000 families live along a river that floods every few years and causes these people damage. An enterprising person could come along and offer to build a dam, charging each household an amount per year less than the expected value of the damage from flooding in the absence of the dam. Suppose you lived on the river; what would you say when asked to pay your share of the price? Probably, "Forget it." There would be no incentive to pay. How could a dam be built to protect everyone else's property but not protect yours? If one person had no incentive to pay, neither would anyone else. Thus a dam that would benefit everyone more than it costs everyone, would not be constructed because of the inability to exclude those who do not pay.

Or, how could the nation defend itself from attack without defending St. Louis, Houston, or any other individual cities, in which the citizens did not choose to pay for defense. While it may be technically possible to exclude nonpaying ships from the use of a lighthouse, it might be economically unfeasible to do so. Frequently in such cases people allow government the role of providing such services, for which there is this "free rider" problem.

Another way in which the competitive market mechanism may break down is by a breakdown in competition itself. Let us suppose there exists a commodity for which the production function exhibits continuously increasing returns to scale. Further suppose that factor prices are constant or that they do not rise fast enough to offset increasing returns to scale. In this situation, the long-run average cost curve is not U-shaped—it is a continuously declining curve over the relevant range.

Suppose such a market is initially organized competitively. Each firm has an incentive to expand output because: (a) average cost declines as output expands, and (b) each perfect competitor expects its actions to go unnoticed by rivals. Thus *each* competitor expects to reduce average cost and expand output tremendously (believing all other producers will continue their previous price-output policies).

But what one producer has an incentive to do, all have an incentive to do, and as industry output expands, the industry "slides down" the negatively sloped market demand curve. As this sliding down continues, a point will be reached at which price is less than average cost. Then all firms make losses, and some firms will leave the industry. But so long as the firm believes its demand curve is a horizontal line, it has an incentive to expand output so as to reduce average cost; and of course the firm believes that if it expands enough, it will eliminate losses.

Again, however, *all* entrepreneurs have the same incentive; and as industry output expands, losses increase. More firms leave the industry. This must continue until the number of firms is so small that each recognizes that its actions *do affect* market price.

The ultimate organization of the market is uncertain. Perhaps "economic warfare" may result, with all but one firm finally eliminated from the market. In this case, monopoly emerges. On the other hand, the last few entrepreneurs left in the market may decide upon the quiet life of collusive oligopoly. They decide to "live and let live" and divide the monopoly profit among themselves. In either case, perfect competition breaks down. Marginal cost is set equal to marginal revenue, which is below price.

This is the result that always comes about under monopoly or oligopoly. There is "underproduction" of the commodity in the sense that society is *willing* to give up more resources than are necessary to expand output. But output is restricted to preserve the monopoly profit.

Principle. If there are constantly increasing returns to scale, competition will break down; and the market price mechanism will not allocate resources optimally (that is, the price mechanism will not allocate enough resources to the monopolized sectors).

There is not uniform agreement among economists concerning the role of government in such cases. Some say, "Let it go; conditions are not perfect but government would make it worse." Others say the government should take over and run the industry. Still others take an intermediate position, saying that a private firm should produce the good, but government should carry out some form of regulation. There is not universal agreement, and the opinions are generally based on past observations and value judgments.

Another opinion, not unanimous among economists, is that market failure may occur because of the absence of perfect knowledge, and in some of the more extreme cases government has a role to play because of this absence. Perfect knowledge includes knowledge on the part of consumers of all benefits or hazards associated with a product. These products may be as diverse as old-age insurance, automobile brakes, education, health care, and so on. In some cases consumers may agree to allow specific governmental bodies (FDA, for example) or governmental representatives in general to interefere from time to time with their consumer sovereignty. Consumers may agree to let government force them to spend their own income, instead of a general revenue subsidy, for these required products, such as certain safety devices required on cars—not for the protection of others but for the protection of the people in the cars. (Recall, however, the voting problem discussed above.) While these devices are mandatory, they are not paid for by government. *Maybe* required motorcycle helmets fit this category, or mandatory education up to age 16, or social security. Whether these regulations are imposed because of market failure is certainly a debatable question, and which products fit this category is even more debatable, but many economists and many governmental officials would maintain that this type of market interference is a legitimate function of government.

11.5 OWNERSHIP EXTERNALITIES

We have covered very briefly some circumstances in which perfect competition may not necessarily mean a Pareto-optimal situation, or conditions even remotely resembling perfect competition may not be possible. In these cases many arguments have been made for some type of governmental intervention. The empirical importance or relevance of such situations has, however, not been thoroughly established.

Quite possibly a much more important problem of the competitive market concerns the question of externalities, where the marginal private cost or benefit of some activity does not equal the marginal social cost or benefit of that activity. A very large part of the problem of externalities is closely related to the incomplete assignment of property rights.

For the most part in this text, though certainly not always, we have simply assumed away the problem of externalities and incomplete assignment of property rights. In this section we will examine some aspects of these problems. While these are complex and far-reaching problems, we will be able here merely to touch upon the major issues involved. You will get some idea about a very important area in which much interesting research is now being carried out.

An external economy is said to exist when marginal social cost is less than marginal private cost. Thus when marginal private cost equals marginal social benefit, marginal social cost is less than marginal social benefit. More resources *should* be allocated to producing the commodity in question, but they are not. On the other hand, an *external diseconomy* exists when marginal social cost exceeds marginal private cost. At such a point, marginal social benefit is less than marginal social cost. An undesirably large amount of resources is allocated to producing the commodity in question.

Definition. An external economy (diseconomy) exists when marginal social cost is less than (greater than) marginal private cost.

At this stage it is quite reasonable to ask *how* marginal private cost and marginal social cost can diverge. One of the chief answers is "by the existence of ownership externalities." Briefly, this means that there is some scarce resource owned by a person, but for some reason the owner cannot charge a price for the use of this resource. And when prices cannot be charged, misallocation of resources results.

Our discussion up to this point may seem to be a bit murky. Perhaps we can simplify somewhat with a few analytical examples. We turn first to a problem concerning urban renewal.

APPLICATION

Externalities and urban renewal*

Based on our economic theory we would expect that an individual who owns a piece of property would keep the property developed and repaired so long as the marginal benefits exceed the individual mar-

---

* This section is based upon a paper by Otto A. Davis and Andrew B. Winston, The Economics of Urban Renewal," originally appearing in *Law and Contemporary Problems,* vol. 26, no. 1 (Winter 1961), published by Duke University School of Law, Durham, N.C.

ginal costs of such repairs. There should be no reason for more than the optimal amount of "urban blight" under these circumstances. But with certain ownership externalities, completely rational people may well allow their property to deteriorate under these conditions.

Note first that the value of a piece of urban property, houses, apartments, and so on, depends to some extent on the condition of other property in the neighborhood. Suppose there are only two properties, one owned by owner A, the other by owner B. Each is attempting to decide whether or not to make an added investment in repair. Both are reaping some return from the property. Each owner has made an initial investment and has an additional sum invested in bonds. Each is making an average return of 4 percent from the property and the bonds, and this return is expected to continue even if no money is taken out of bonds and put into property repair.

If both owners take their money out of bonds and invest in property repair, each will make a return of 7 percent. Clearly each will be better off. There is a problem, however. Suppose one owner invests the bond money in repairs while the other does not. One property is improved and the other remains run down. The owner who improves the property gives up the return from the bonds, but the property return does not increase much because it remains next to a deteriorated property. In this case the improving owner's total return falls to 3 percent. The loss of bond income more than offsets the increase in income from improving the property.

On the other hand, the owner who did not improve the property retains the bond income and in addition finds that the return on the unimproved property increases because of being next to an improved piece of property. Perhaps the total return from property and bonds increases to 10 percent. These changes in return result no matter who does the repair and who does not. The owner who does not repair the property keeps the bond return and benefits from the better neighborhood.

Suppose both owners know the expected return but do not know what the other will do. If owner A decides to invest it will be to owner B's advantage not to invest—a 10-percent compared to a 7-percent return. Owner A knows this and therefore knows that the investment will cause a decrease in total return from 4 to 3 percent. Owner B knows the same conditions apply to his own investment decision also. Therefore, neither invests. However, if both invest, each would be better off.†

---

† Such analysis is based upon a concept called the Prisoner's Dilemma. The district attorney has two prisoners, who have been kept separated. He is sure they are both guilty of a specific crime but does not have sufficient

As the authors of the paper that set forth this example noted, the "neighborhood" effect must be strong enough to get the results set forth. They also noted—and you probably have already deduced it—that there is a solution to the problem. One owner can simply buy out the other owner and improve both properties. Each would be made better off.

But if there were many such properties in the area the transactions cost or the cost of "putting the deal together" might very well outweigh the benefits from one individual buying up all of the property. In any case one owner of a small piece of property might hold out for so large an amount as to thwart the deal.

Many argue that this type of situation demands governmental intervention in order to prevent such urban blight or decay in many neighborhoods. Others offer the counter-argument that historically governmental urban renewal has meant merely destroying subpar housing of the poor and building office buildings, shopping centers, and high-rise apartments for the wealthy. The evicted poor are then, it is alleged, simply crowded into other blighted areas that have not yet been torn down. We do not, however, in this brief summary have sufficient space to discuss the problem fully. (In other words, we do not know the "answer.")

---

evidence for conviction. Neither prisoner knows the amount of evidence available. The district attorney tells each prisoner separately that he can confess or not confess, and makes the following threat or proposition. If neither confesses, each will receive a small punishment for a minor crime. If one confesses while the other does not, the one who confesses will receive a minor punishment while the one who does not will receive severe punishment. Finally, if both confess, each will receive less than the most severe punishment. The dilemma is that in the absence of collusion the rational action of each is to confess.

The above problem involved ownership externalities. In that case, if one person could acquire the property rights to the entire area, all could be made better off. But the more owners are involved, the more difficult it becomes to internalize the externalities. Other similar cases involve ownership externalities in production and property rights.

APPLICATION

A comon property problem

Petroleum technology is such that for a given pool of oil there is a particular rate of extraction that maximizes the total amount of oil

that can be extracted.‡ This rate, to be sure, is the *technically* optimal rate and not necessarily the *economically* optimal rate. But suppose for a given pool that the technically optimal rate is the same as
the economically optimal rate. Suppose that the pool of oil is so large
that many people own pieces of land over the pool, and therefore,
many people can pump oil from the pool. Suppose also that the
amount pumped from this particular pool does not affect the world
price of crude oil.

If one person owned all of the land over the pool, oil would be
pumped at the profit-maximizing optimal rate. But if many people
can pump from the pool, there is no incentive to pump at the optimal
rate. Any single extractor would have no incentive to cut back. In
fact, each landowner would have the incentive to pump as rapidly as
possible in order to get as much as possible before the other landowners get it all. If one person cuts back on extraction, it simply
means others get more. Thus oil is pumped at a rate that is greater
than is economically optimal.

Again one person or group could buy up all the pumping rights
and make everyone better off, but, with a very large number of owners the transactions cost may be too high. Some argue that this is a
case for state interference; others argue that the state should simply operate the field as a cartel. We will not go into the problem
here, beyond stating that this is an example of ownership externalities.

Note that these are not the same as the situation in which a group
of formerly competitive firms collude to fix prices. Competition still
exists in both this and the above example. But even in the case of
competition Pareto optimality does not exist.

---

‡ For a complete discussion of the economics of petroleum extraction,
see Paul Davidson, "Policy Problems of the Crude Oil Industry," *American
Economic Review*, March 1963, pp. 85–108.

We can think of other cases in which ownership externalities give rise
to problems even under competitive situations and well-defined property
rights. There is the danger of carrying such analysis too far, in attributing
too many problems to such ownership externalities and saying simply
that the competitive marketplace does not allocate efficiently. One may or
may not be happy with the results of competition, but market failures as a
result of these externalities when property rights are well defined are not
all that easily come by. Moreover, the "solution" of governmental intervention may be no more satisfactory than the market solution.

We could, and many do, carry the externality problem to the extreme. Certainly if a large group of people drive big fast cars, the price of gasoline rises. Some benefit; some lose. Selling wheat to Russia may increase the price of bread; again, some benefit, some lose. If I burn coal, the world has less coal. These externalities are not what we mean by market failure or the problems of competition. In these cases governmental intervention makes some better off and some worse off. The decision simply involves interpersonal utility comparisons, a domain in which the economist does not belong. What we have stressed thus far are cases in which competition may not be Pareto optimal. To intervene or not to intervene is a decision for government. Economists can only point out the potential results, theoretical and historical, of such intervention.

11.6 PROPERTY RIGHTS

Up to now in the discussion of externalities the property rights of resource owners were fairly well defined. Problems would arise only because the production or investment or even consumption decisions of some affected the incomes or utilities of others. The problem of externalities becomes more serious when property rights are not well defined or when no one has property rights in the case of some scarce resources. We first discuss the different types of property rights, and then show some problems when no one owns a scarce resource. We finally discuss problems that evolve when property rights are not well defined.

11.6.a Types of property rights[2]

The most complete concept of property rights, and that which we have used throughout the text, is that of ownership of one's property. One can use the property in any way, subject to laws concerning injury to other parties. A less complete right is the right to use the property of someone else and to gain benefits from its use, but not to sell it or alter its form. Most rental properties and community-owned properties fall into this category, as do your classroom, my office, and some government properties such as national parks. Finally there is the right to hold a good but not to use it, change it, or sell it.

There are many shades between the various forms of property rights,

---

[2] This section is in large part based on a discussion with Steve Pejovich and on chapter 2 of his book *Fundamentals of Economics*, to be published by Wadsworth Publishing Company.

but these are the principal categories. Furthermore, even the right of ownership is not unrestricted. I may own a good but not be able to sell it above a governmentally fixed price. I may own land but not be permitted to build a swimming pool on it unless I build a fence. I may own a cigar but not be allowed to smoke it in an elevator.

As it turns out, most of the problems of externalities result from two situations. The first is incomplete or communal assignment of property rights or even no assignment of property rights. The second problem results when certain uses of one's fully owned property have harmful effects on someone else's property.

11.6.b Non-owned or community-owned property

A scarce resource that is not owned is both over-used and under-produced. No early settlers in the United States had the incentive to postpone chopping down trees or to plant forests. If one group did not do it, others would. Forests were destroyed. Buffalo, which were not owned, were practically wiped out, while cattle, which were owned, were not. Rivers, which were not owned were polluted. No one owned the valuable whales, and they practically disappeared when whale oil was the major source of light and lubrication. Neither perfect competition nor human greed was the problem. The problem was that no one had the incentive to kill fewer whales so that the whales could reproduce at a rate sufficient to maintain the population. Similarly, no one has the incentive to produce goods that they cannot own and hence realize returns from them. There is no point in individuals planting trees on publicly owned land. No one can reap the economic benefits from keeping publically owned beaches clean. This is not to say that some people will not refrain from littering out of civic-mindedness; there is no economic incentive to do so, however, if there is no cost. People do not normally throw beer cans in their own yards, but many do so along the roadside.

As we have implied, publically owned property gives rise to similar problems as non-owned property. A government- or community-owned property may not be used efficiently. Suppose a community owned a large piece of property that is better suited for growing vegetables than for cattle grazing. If anyone can use the property, it will probably be used for cattle grazing, because if anyone can harvest the vegetables, growers would have to expend added resources to protect their crops. Cattle owners can drive their cows home at night from the community property.

The point is that publically owned property may not be put to its most efficient use. This may not be bad for the society. The society may wish to have free beaches and parks rather than have private ownership of these scarce resources. People may prefer overcrowding to paying for the use of the facilities. We only wish to stress that publically owned resources will be put to uses different from those that would result from private ownership.

11.6.c Private ownership and externalities

One of the fundamental problems of economics is the legal assignment of property rights when the marginal social cost of some activity exceeds the private social cost. A factory or group of factories pollutes a publicly owned river. The owners of property along the river downstream are damaged by this externality; possibly these are fishermen. Or we could have the same problem with air pollution.

Now, as we have mentioned previously, the polluting factories do not pay the full cost of pollution. The social cost is the total private cost plus the cost of the pollution to the property owners downstream. Or, the full cost of production of a factory that is polluting the air is the total private cost of production plus the lowered values of the other people's property that is damaged by the smoke. We can think of many other cases; for example, noise pollution from a factory, oil spills from offshore drilling, even the pollution caused by people smoking in a crowded room. There are such externalities all around us; externalities caused by the production of firms and externalities caused by the consumption patterns of individual households.

In all the examples, the marginal private cost of polluting—dumping waste into rivers, belching smoke into the air, and so on—is quite small. The marginal social cost is greater because of the resources required to eliminate or reduce such pollution. No one owns the rivers or the air, only the land adjacent to the rivers or under the air. Thus no one sets a price on this scarce resource. In the absence of well-defined property rights, there is no automatic corrective device built into the competitive market mechanism.

What is the solution? In the last edition of this text at the end of the discussion of pollution externalities we simply threw up our hands and ended the discussion by saying, "Some type of external control is necessary if the externality problem is to be solved." We were admonished, correctly I feel, by some users of the text for giving students the impression that this is all that economists can say about the subject. Certainly many volumes could be written about solutions. We will touch on only a few in the next subsection.

11.6.d Some solutions

The "solution" that says some sort of external control is necessary gives the impression that the only solution is for government to forbid the polluting firms from discharging waste into the river, smoke into the air, or noise into the ears. You know by now that this type of control may not be socially optimal.

In the first place, the market may well have already "solved the problem." You will recall that we discussed above that some property owners choose to purchase property they know is being polluted because they could purchase that property more cheaply than equivalent unpolluted property. Those who suffer windfall losses are owners who acquire property *prior to its being polluted* and therefore prior to its being made relatively less valuable. The market adjusts the value of the property after it is subject to pollution.

Or, government could redefine property rights in the case of rivers. The river owner (owners) might charge the factories for polluting if the downstream landowners own the river, and in this way make up the loss in property value. Alternatively, if the factory is given property rights in the river, the downstream owners could bribe the factories to reduce the amount of pollution. Clearly in either case there would not be zero pollution. In the case of bribery, if the factory owners owned the river, the downstream landowners would bribe the factories until the marginal cost of an additional bribe equals the marginal reduction in pollution to the downstream landowners. If property rights were assigned downstream and a charge set to the factories per unit of pollution, the factory would pollute until the marginal cost of polluting one more unit equals the marginal return from polluting.[3]

As you have perhaps already recognized, the efficiency of such a solution depends upon the number of parties involved. If 1,000 factories are damaging 10,000 fishermen downstream, it would be very difficult and expensive to work out a transaction. Even if an *outside party* owns the

---

[3] In a very famous article by Ronald Coase, "The Problem of Social Cost," *Journal of Law and Economics*, October 1960, pp. 1–44, it was shown that if one party is damaging another through its productive activity, the optimal amount of damage is the same regardless of the party to whom property rights are assigned, given zero transactions costs.

river, the policing costs may outweigh the potential returns. Or if 9,999 downstream property owners agree to bribe the factories not to pollute and one party does not agree, how could the non-payer be excluded from the benefits? In the case of one damager versus one damagee, the solution would be simple if property rights are assigned. But the more parties involved, the greater the cost of making the transaction.

Another solution is, of course, for government to force a "solution" by charging the damagers and compensating damagees. Again there is the question (moral or economic?) of compensating those who acquired property at a lower cost because of the damage. A further question in the case of government control is how much pollution to permit. Surely a goal of zero air and water pollution is ridiculous. If there is diminishing marginal utility from pollution and increasing marginal costs in terms of resources used in reducing pollution, surely the solution is to have pollution at some optimal, but non-zero, rate. It is frequently the task of economists and engineers to determine that rate. Marginal costs are not easily measured, and, in the absence of a social utility function, marginal benefits are generally impossible to measure.

We have merely touched upon the problem of external ownership effects. Many more examples and solutions could be discussed. The economics profession is certainly not in agreement about the problem and the solution. Neither is the legal profession. The sole purpose of this discussion is to make you aware of the problem and some possible solutions. We want you to think about the problem of externalities in economic terms rather than in the emotional way in which problems of this type are frequently considered.

11.7 SUMMARY

In most cases competition by means of the price mechanism leads to a Pareto-optimal allocation of resources. This allocation is optimal in the sense that it is efficient. It is not optimal in the sense that society's welfare or utility is maximized, because economists cannot define a social utility function. When government makes choices about allocation in order "to make society better off" it is generally making (implicitly) interpersonal utility comparisons. Economists as economists cannot do this.

In some cases of the type mentioned in this chapter competition does not lead to an efficient allocation. It is impossible to determine empirically just how important these are. Certainly most economists would agree that in any economic society there is some role for government control or regulation in such cases. There is disagreement over how great a role government should play. Again probably the majority of economists would agree that governmental control should not extend to arbitrary controls over markets where demand and supply are an efficient allocative device. This may seem to be a weak conclusion, but in fact it is not. A function of microeconomic theory is to determine the relative efficiency of various types of market organization. The major conclusion is that competition is, in general, efficient. The purpose of these last few sections is simply to show that there are some situations, the importance of which cannot be determined, when this conclusion may not hold. Generally, however, competitively determined prices in competitive markets allocate resources in something like a Pareto-optimal way.

11.8 EPILOGUE

In the introduction to each chapter we included a subsection setting forth what you will learn in that chapter. After coming this far you have learned, we hope, a great deal. Certainly you have learned the basic tools of microeconomic theory—marginal revenue, marginal cost, opportunity cost, supply and demand, marginal product, equilibrium, and so forth. You have also learned the fundamental determinants of many equilibrium situations—consumer equilibrium, the equilibrium of competitive firms and industries, wage equilibrium, the equilibrium of individual markets for goods, and some equilibrium conditions for a society (although the last situation was much less thoroughly covered). You are familiar with the determinants of demand and supply in both commodity markets and markets for factors of production, as well as with the importance of the interest rate in discounting streams of income over time.

We have also tried to make you well aware of some things that economists cannot do, for example, define a social welfare function for a group of people. Economists frequently cannot say that one set of circumstances is better than another, since they cannot make interpersonal utility comparisons. They can, of course, show the costs of various decisions or alternative solutions. They can compare the results of solutions that would occur under free market determination with the results of governmentally determined solutions. They usually cannot say which is better; they can only say who benefits and who loses under each solution.

Economists have had little success in developing a general theory of market situations between competition and monopoly, particularly in the case of oligopoly, when there are a few closely interdependent firms in the industry. They have had a certain amount of success in using competitive or monopoly theory in predicting and explaining some results in these "intermediate" market structures.

Perhaps the most important thing you have learned, and one of our basic points of emphasis in this text, is how to use economic theory to solve real-world problems. By now you are probably thinking like an economist. That is, in analyzing problems you immediately think in terms of marginal analysis, comparing marginal benefits with marginal costs. Fixed costs are generally irrelevant and there are generally no "all or nothing" situations. Most decisions are made at the margin.

You should now be able to question and to comment critically on most of the economic analysis you hear on TV, read in newspapers or magazines, and hear from politicians. You are now able to predict the economic consequences of governmental decisions or activities at all levels of government. Possibly most important, we feel, you can use your economic expertise to aid in your own professional, business, and personal decision making.

Many of you are economics or agricultural economics majors. We hope and we believe that the tools and methods you learned here will be useful in your future courses and your careers as economists. Others of you who are not economics majors may wish to take additional economics courses. Those interested in the effects of government policies, control of the money supply, inflation, or taxation, may wish to take a course in macroeconomics or public finance. These are useful for people planning a career in government service. A course in industrial organization, or an equivalent course, will give you a slightly different and interesting insight into market structures. This course and a course in law and economics or government and business will be useful for those planning a business career or career in law, as would a course in managerial economics. Labor economics would be useful in many careers, businesses, government services, unions, or work with nonprofit organizations.

For many of you, perhaps the majority, this will be your last economics course. Do not let it be the last time you use economic analysis in decision making. You will find such analysis useful no matter what career you choose.

TECHNICAL PROBLEMS

1. Explain why equality of marginal rates of substitution between any two goods for any pair of consumers implies that no consumer can be made bet-

ter off without making some other consumer worse off. Why does perfect competition guarantee this result?

2. Assume two firms, each using capital and labor to produce two goods. The marginal rates of technical substitution between capital and labor are the same for each firm. *Total* capital and labor are fixed in amount. Explain why one firm cannot increase output without causing the other to decrease output.

3. Explain why there can generally be no social welfare function or social preference ordering.

4. Why would a commonly owned forest be depleted more rapidly than a privately owned forest?

5. Explain in what sense a national park is a public good and in what sense it is not.

6. Is your school library a public good? Could the time of the year affect your answer?

ANALYTICAL PROBLEMS

1. Suppose the social return to education is 8 percent and the return to other investment is 10 percent. This shows too many resources are being used in education. Comment.

2. Suppose from time to time a certain theater has long lines for a particular movie and sometimes has to turn away customers. Is this evidence of market failure? Why or why not?

3. Suppose your professor sets forth the following class policies. Identify those which would make the *class* unequivocally better off, those which would make the class worse off, and those for which the conclusion is indeterminate. Explain.
   a. There will be no final exam. Everyone receives as a final grade his or her present average.
   b. The final is optional. You may take your present average or take the final.
   c. The final is mandatory but it only counts if it improves your average.
   d. There will be a final, but points will be taken from the high-grade students and given to the low-grade students until everyone has the same grade.
   e. The professor gives everyone an A, regardless of average.
   f. The final is mandatory, but there will be a make-up final if a student is not satisfied with his or her final grade.

4. Suppose there are two classes made up of very similar students. In one class each student receives the grade made on each test. In the other class each student receives the class average on each test. These policies are known by

all. In which class would you expect the higher average grade? Explain in
terms of externalities, or the free-rider problem.

5. In the state of Texas the state owns all the beaches. Analyze the following
    statements and determine if they are true or false.
    a. If private individuals owned the beaches, poor and middle-income
        people would be denied access.
    b. Since the state can afford to clean the beaches, there is less litter than
        if they were privately owned.
    c. Since the state can regulate the beaches, it can keep off sleazy mer-
        chants, and the people using the beaches are better off.
    d. Since the state owns the beaches, more people use them and the people
        are better off because a beach is a public good.

Index

This book has been set in 10 and 9 point Caledonia, leaded 3 points. Chapter numbers are 36 point Craw Modern; chapter titles are 18 point Craw Modern. The size of the type page is 27 by 45½ picas.